Associations, Synagogues, and Congregations

Associations, Synagogues, and Congregations

Claiming a Place in Ancient Mediterranean Society

PHILIP A. HARLAND

Fortress Press
Minneapolis

To Teresa
and to little Nathaniel Thomas,
with love

Contents

Maps   vii–ix
Illustrations   xi
Preface   xiii

Introduction   1

PART 1
ASSOCIATIONS IN ROMAN ASIA

1. Associations and Guilds: Varieties and Social Makeup   25
2. Internal Activities and Purposes:
   Honoring the Gods, Feasting with Friends   55
3. Associations in Civic Context:
   Symptoms of Decline or Participants in Vitality?   89

PART 2
IMPERIAL CULTS AND CONNECTIONS
AMONG ASSOCIATIONS

4. Imperial Gods within Religious Life: Cultic Honors   115
5. Positive Interaction:
   Imperial Connections and Monumental Honors   137
6. Tensions in Perspective:
   Civic Disturbances and Official Intervention   161

PART 3
SYNAGOGUES AND CONGREGATIONS
WITHIN SOCIETY

7. Comparing Socioreligious Groups in Antiquity   177
8. Positive Interaction:
   Jews, Christians, and Imperial Honors in the Greek City   213
9. Tensions in Perspective:
   Imperial Cults, Persecution, and the Apocalypse of John   239

Conclusion   265

Appendix: Some Dionysiac Associations   *271*
Abbreviations   *277*
Notes   *283*
Bibliographies   *313*
   1. Epigraphic and Papyrological Collections   *313*
   2. Ancient Literary Sources   *321*
   3. Other Sources   *324*
Index of Ancient Sources   *379*
Index of Subjects   *393*

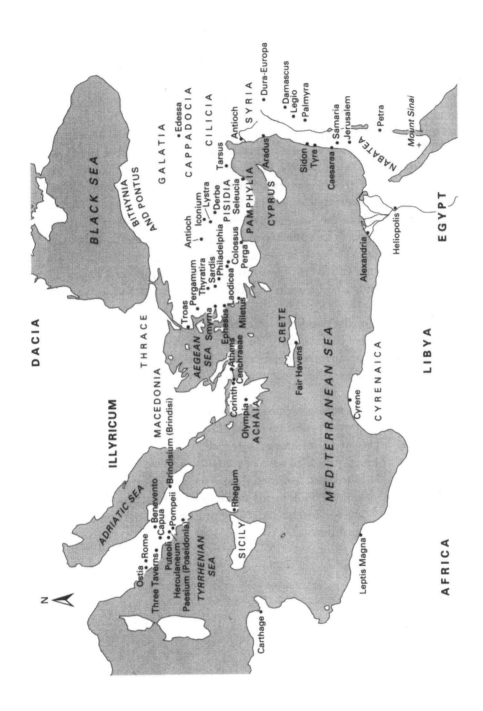

Ekkehard W. Stegemann and Wolfgang Stegemann, *The Jesus Movement: A Social History of Its First Century* (Minneapolis: Fortress Press, 1999).

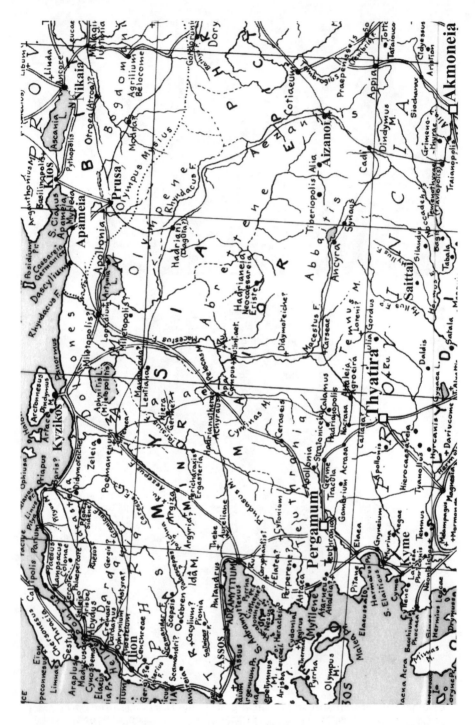

WESTERN ASIA MINOR (ROMAN ASIA). From W. M. Calder and George E. Bean, *A Classical Map of Asia Minor* (London: British Institute of Archaeology at Ankara, 1958), partially reproduced and modified by Philip A. Harland with permission from the British Institute of Archaeology at Ankara.

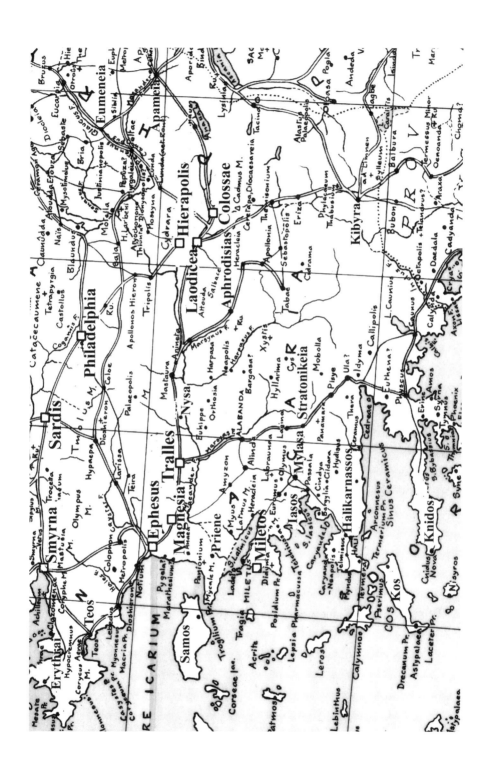

Illustrations

1.	Harbor street at Ephesus	4
2.	Monument from the fishery toll office at Ephesus	5
3.	Theater at Ephesus	6
4.	Statue of Artemis the huntress, now in the Louvre	7
5.	Some occupational associations in Roman Asia	39–40
6.	Statue of Silenos and the baby Dionysos, now in the Louvre	47
7.	Monument dedicated to Zeus Hypsistos with a relief of the association's gathering	56
8.	Monument dedicated in honor of Stratonike, priestess of Cybele and Apollo, with a relief of the association's gathering	58
9.	Main hall of the guild of grain measurers at Ostia	64
10.	Building plan of the grain measurers' meeting-place	64
11.	Mosaic floor depicting grain measurer	65
12.	Plan of the builders' meeting-place at Ostia	66
13.	Dining room in the builder's meeting-place	67
14.	Plan of the meeting-place of the merchants from Berytos on the island of Delos	67
15.	Statue of Aphodite and Pan from the merchants' meeting place at Delos	68
16.	Hall of Benches at Pergamum, meeting-place of the cowherds of Dionysos	79
17.	Altar dedicated to Dionysos Kathegemon found in the Hall of Benches	80

18.   Plan of the meeting-place of the Iobacchoi at Athens   81
19.   Sketch of the inscribed column of the Iobacchoi   82
20.   Stadium at Aphrodisias   109
21a.   Reserved seating for the "Jews and God-fearers"   110
       in the theater at Miletos
21b.   Reserved seating for the "friends of the Augusti"   110
       in the theater at Miletos
22.   Temple for Trajan and Zeus Philios at Pergamum   122
23.   Family tree of a Julian family of Asia Minor   141
24.   Diagram of some connections of the guild of dyers   144
       at Thyatira
25.   Family tree of Claudia Ammion   146
26.   Diagram of associations' connections with elites   149
27.   Wall-painting from Pompeii depicting the riot   167
       in the amphitheater
28.   Main hall of the synagogue within the bath-gymnasium   204
       at Sardis
29.   Imperial cult hall within the bath-gymnasium at Sardis   204
30.   Blocked doorway between the synagogue   205
       and the imperial cult hall.

Acknowledgments for Illustrations

Figures 1, 3, 4, 6, 7, 9, 13, 20, 21, 22, 28, 29: Philip A. Harland (© 2003).

Figure 2: Courtesy of the Österreichischen Archäologischen Institut. Used by permission.

Figure 8: Courtesy of the Deutsches Archäologisches Institut, Athens. Used by permission.

Figures 10 and 12: Courtesy of the University of Alberta Press. Used by permission.

Figure 11 by Teresa Harland (© 2003). Used by permission.

Figures 14 and 15: Courtesy of l'École francaise d'Athènes (EFA). Used by permission.

Figures 16 and 17: Courtesy of the Deutsches Archäologisches Institut, Istanbul. Used by permission.

Figure 27: Erich Lessing/Art Resource © 2003. Used by permission.

Preface

This book could not have been completed without the help and support of many people. John S. Kloppenborg's (University of Toronto) guidance has been indispensable as this project made its way from a faint idea for a doctoral dissertation to its present form. One could not hope for a more thorough, wise, and engaging advisor. Special thanks also go to Peter Richardson (University of Toronto) who was a source of encouragement along the way and who read earlier versions of the manuscript. Roger Beck's (University of Toronto) expertise in Greco-Roman religions has been invaluable; his course on the mysteries sparked my initial interest in associations specifically. Both Michel Desjardins (Wilfrid Laurier University) and Philip Sellew (University of Minnesota) read the work as a dissertation and provided helpful suggestions for improvement.

Dave Graham (M.A., Wilfrid Laurier University) thoroughly read the entire manuscript and made innumerable suggestions for stylistic and other improvements. I am very grateful for his help. Harold Remus (Wilfrid Laurier University) and Leif E. Vaage (University of Toronto) read and commented upon earlier papers which informed chapters three, four, and five. Members of the Canadian Society of Biblical Studies, especially those involved in the Religious Rivalries Seminar, interacted with and contributed to the ideas that ended up in this book. As did the members of the Hellenistic Texts Seminar at the University of Toronto. Patricia Saxton and Mayjee Philip (doctoral students at Concordia University) made their contributions by preparing the indices and assisting in final proofreading respectively. I would also like to thank those at Fortress Press for their help, including K. C. Hanson, Ann Delgehausen, and Larry Willard.

My family has been a consistent source of support. I cannot overstate my gratitude to my mother, Freda, and my father, Tom. Were he still with us, my dad would have taken great joy in the completion of this work. This book is dedicated to Teresa, whose support and patience were shown throughout my research, and to little Nathaniel Thomas, who, I'm sure, will be glad that this was largely completed before his arrival (he did "help" with the final proofreading, however). Teresa read the work at several stages and made important contributions. My brother's and sister's families–Stephen, Rachel, Luke, and Victoria, and Pauline, David, Emma, Lyam and Abigail–have also been a welcomed break from my research.

Friends and colleagues, too many to name, have assisted in a variety of ways. Gatherings with Jeff and Michelle McPherson and Dave and Beth Kraulis have been a constant source of laughter and escape, and I could not imagine completion of this project without the support of friends like these. Jeff in particular has been an encouragement as we both made our ways from being unruly teenagers to being (perhaps equally unruly) "doctors." Likewise, the members of our small-group at Kitchener Mennonite-Brethren have helped along the way. As have our good friends Peter, Brent, and Angela and Justin. Many fellow-students at the University of Toronto were a support in some way, including Keir Hammer, Dana Sawchuk, Laurence Broadhurst, and Michelle Murray. I have also appreciated the support of colleagues at Concordia University in Montreal, including Norm Ravvin, Leslie Orr, Munit Merid, Tina Montandon, and others.

For financial assistance I am grateful to the Social Sciences and Humanities Research Council of Canada (for doctoral fellowships) and to Concordia University for research funds that helped to bring this book through its final stages. I would also like to thank the following institutions or publishers who granted permission to include photographic or other materials (see the acknowledgments following the list of illustrations for full copyright details): Deutsches Archäologisches Institut, Athens and Istanbul (figs. 8, 16–17); Österreichisches Archäologisches Institut (fig. 2); L'École francaise d'Athènes (figs. 14–15); University of Alberta Press (figs. 10, 12). Photos in figures 4, 6, 9, 11, and 13 were taken by the author at the Louvre and at Ostia in 1999 (© Philip A. Harland). Photos in figures 1, 3, 20, 21, 22, 28–29 were taken while on a tour of Roman sites in Turkey in 1991 (© Philip A. Harland); I would like to thank Peter Richardson, leader of the tour, who gave me the opportunity to visit the ancient world I was studying.

I am grateful to the Continuum International Publishing Group for permission to include material (in chapters 7, 8, and 9) which overlaps with an article that appeared as "Honouring the Emperor or Assailing the Beast: Participation in Civic Life among Associations (Jewish, Christian and Other) in Asia Minor and the Apocalypse of John," *Journal for the Study of the New Testament* 77 (2000), 99–121. Portions of chapter 4 overlap with an article that appears as "Imperial Cults within Local Cultural Life: Associations in Roman Asia," *Ancient History Bulletin/Zeitschrift für Alte Geschichte* 16.3-4 (2003) (© Philip A. Harland). Portions of chapters 1 and 5 overlap with "Connections with Elites in the World of the Early Christians," in *Handbook of Early Christianity: Social Science Approaches,* ed. by Anthony J. Blasi, Jean Duhaime, and Paul André Turcotte (Alta Mira Press, 2002), 385–408 (© Philip A. Harland).

For further interactive discussion of associations, synagogues, and congregations, as well as photos from the cities of Asia Minor, also see my website: www.philipharland.com.

Introduction

Western Asia Minor:
Key Center of Early Christianity and Diaspora Judaism

Western Asia Minor (modern Turkey) was a hub of early Christian social and literary activity (see map on p. vii). Paul himself spent considerable time in the region (esp. at Ephesus), perhaps several years, and a circle of his followers actively wrote from there to "congregations" or "assemblies" (*ekklēsiai*; commonly translated "churches") in the same vicinity, producing the writings we know as the Pastoral Epistles (1–2 Timothy, Titus), Ephesians, and Colossians. Stories of Paul's adventures in this part of the Mediterranean were told and retold well after his death, as the Acts of the Apostles and the apocryphal *Acts of Paul* show. Writings attributed to Peter likewise find their home here, in the form of 1 Peter, a "diaspora" (dispersion) letter written to Christians living in Asia, Bithynia, and other provinces of Asia Minor. John, the Jewish prophet of the Apocalypse, communicated his visions regarding the destinies of God's people and Satan's people to congregations in seven cities of Asia, Ephesus among them. There are also strong traditions that place the Johannine communities—as represented in the Gospel of John and the epistles (1–3 John)—in western Asia Minor.

The importance of this region for early Christianity is not limited to the New Testament. It was precisely to Christian assemblies living in Ephesus, Smyrna, Magnesia, and elsewhere that Ignatius, bishop of Antioch, wrote his letters in the early second century. The renowned bishop Polycarp lived

1

his long life in Smyrna before it ended in martyrdom in his eighties (c. 160 C.E.). So it is worthwhile investigating social and cultural life in western Asia Minor, including cities like Ephesus, since this is the world in which many Christians lived and breathed, and in which many New Testament documents were produced and read. Yet this is certainly not the only reason why research in this area is valuable.

Asia Minor was a lively center of activity for another closely related set of communities in the first centuries. Christianity began as a movement within Judaism in Palestine, and networks of Jewish communities dispersed throughout the Roman Empire, including Asia Minor, continued to be important for this new-born movement as it made its way into the Greco-Roman world. Much of our evidence for Judaism in the dispersion, both literary and archeological, pertains to Jewish groups living in Asia Minor (perhaps second only to Alexandria in Egypt and the city of Rome itself). Evidence for these "gatherings" or "synagogues" (*synagōgai*) comes partly from Josephus, who refers to civic and imperial decrees concerning Jews at Ephesus, Sardis, Pergamum (Pergamon), and elsewhere (in the late 1st century B.C.E.). Yet our knowledge is greatly enriched by archeological discoveries dating to the first centuries C.E. Most impressive, perhaps, is the synagogue building within the bath-gymnasium complex at Sardis (dating to the 3d century), but numerous monuments and plaques with inscriptions also give us glimpses into the lives of Jews at various locales, including Ephesus, Smyrna, Hierapolis (near Colossae), and Akmoneia.

From a bird's-eye view of culture in the Roman Empire, Jewish synagogues and Christian assemblies stand together as *minority cultural groups*, primarily due to their shared monotheism (and devotion to the same God) in a polytheistic culture. Yet a closer look at the diversity of these groups in the light of other local, unofficial religious groups may draw attention to the complexities involved in understanding the place of synagogues and assemblies within Greco-Roman society.

Christian assemblies and Jewish synagogues were by no means alone as unofficial gatherings within this cultural landscape. Their Greek and Roman neighbors likewise joined together in informal groups, guilds, or "associations" (*koina, synodoi, thiasoi, mystai, phratores, synergasiai, collegia*) under the patronage of deities like Zeus, Dionysos, and Demeter. Associations gathered together regularly to socialize, share communal meals, and honor both their earthly and their divine benefactors. In fact, cities like Ephesus were saturated with such groups, which, as we shall see, open a new window into the context of early Christianity and diaspora Judaism.

In many ways, these associations provide us with close social analogies for both assemblies and synagogues. Moreover, although for the sake of clarity in discussion I often use the terms "assemblies" or "congregations" for Christians, "synagogues" for Jews, and "associations" for others, we shall see that synagogues and assemblies *were associations* in important respects. Various associations in the ancient Mediterranean world expressed their identity in similar terms (using "synagogue" and "assembly," for instance). Ancient observers ("pagans"), Jews, and Christians alike recognized this parallelism, sometimes describing synagogues and assemblies in terms of association life in the Greco-Roman world.[1] Investigating the evidence for associations on its own terms and then proceeding to the task of comparison will advance our understanding of the place of Jews and Christians within social realities of life in the cities.

A journey into cities like Ephesus, therefore, brings us into direct contact with the real world where congregations and synagogues (and their individual members) lived and developed, and we shall see that Roman emperors, officials, and imperialism were part of this reality. Paying close attention to archeological evidence or artifacts from cities like Ephesus, Sardis, Smyrna, and Pergamum may bring this world to life and provide a new—even revolutionary—angle of vision on the lives of both early Christian congregations and Jewish synagogues, as well as their Greek and Roman neighbors.

A Visit to Roman Ephesus

Traveling through a city like Ephesus in Roman times, one would encounter an array of monuments, statues, and other structures indicative of social and religious life among the populace (see fig. 1). Among the messages communicated by this cultural landscape would be the significance of the Roman emperors and officials—and honors for them—within the life of the *polis* (Greek city or city-state), but also within the lives of local socioreligious groups or associations. A brief visit to Ephesus in the second century with an eye for small-group life will draw attention to neglected issues concerning group-society relations and imperialism that will occupy us throughout this study of Christians, Jews, and others in the first two centuries.

Docking at the harbor of Ephesus, we cannot help but notice the nearby fishery toll office, where an impressive monument of blue marble lists the donations by members of an association of fishermen and fish

FIGURE 1: Theater at Ephesus showing Harbor Street ending at what was the ancient harbor (where the fishery toll office was located). To the left of Harbor Street is the ancient marketplace, where the silversmiths had a place reserved for them.

dealers, along with their families (*IEph* 20; see fig. 2). Among those honored by this construction are Emperor Nero and members of his family, as well as both the Romans and the Ephesians. Together with his wife and children, the man who was responsible for overseeing the construction paid to have two altars dedicated within a room devoted to the deities of the Samothracian mysteries. These "great gods" (Cabiri) were especially known for protecting devotees against the hazards of seafaring. Looking closer, one discovers another deity watching over and protecting those who engage in business here, the Egyptian goddess Isis. The statue of Isis was donated to "the workers" in the toll office by a wealthy woman, who dedicated it to Ephesus's patron deity, Artemis, and to the emperor (*IEph* 1503).

FIGURE 2: Marble monument from the fishery toll office near the harbor at Ephesus (*IEph* 20). (Source: Keil 1930:50, Abb. 24. Österreichischen Archäologischen Institut. Selcuk Museum. Negative no. II 423.)

Walking along harbor street toward the theater, we happen upon a stall near the market reserved for the guild of silversmiths (*IEph* 547). The author of the Acts of the Apostles (19:23-41) relates a story when the silversmiths and other craftsmen at Ephesus gathered in the theater in defense of the city's patron deity, Artemis (see figs. 3 and 4). The prominence of the silversmiths' guild at Ephesus becomes clearer as we encounter several

FIGURE 3: Theater at Ephesus, facing out toward the harbor with Harbor Street on the right.

monuments during our visit, including gravestones (epitaphs) and honors (cf. *IEph* 585, 586, 636, 2212, 2441). Among them is an honorary plaque for T. Claudius Aristion, an important official of the city who was also high priest in charge of the worship of the emperors at the provincial imperial cult of Asia (*IEph* 425 + 636). This plaque was erected during the principate of Domitian (81–96 C.E.), when an imposing provincial temple was built in the upper section of Ephesus for the "revered ones" (Greek *Sebastoi*, Latin *Augusti*), the emperors and members of the imperial family.

If we had made a similar visit to Akmoneia, further inland in Asia, we might have noticed two monuments set up by a local elders' organization and a Jewish synagogue respectively in honor of another prominent person who was also an imperial cult functionary (*MAMA* VI 263–64). Alongside other benefactors, the synagogue honored Julia Severa, a wealthy woman who was also high priestess in the local cult of the imperial gods. These Jews were not alone in engaging in such imperial connections or honors, as a plaque displayed within the provincial imperial cult temple at Pergamum would show, this one involving Jews' honors for Emperor Augustus (Josephus, *Ant.* 16.165).

Returning to Ephesus, we encounter another monument from about the same time period as the silversmiths' honors. This marble structure

FIGURE 4: Statue of Artemis the huntress from the Louvre (early modern copy of a Hellenistic original).

reveals that an association of Demeter worshipers had written a letter to the governor of Roman Asia (*IEph* 213). They had requested and received special recognition of a yearly celebration in which they performed "mysteries and sacrifices" not only for their patron deity but also for the revered imperial gods, the emperors.

Unless we happened to be acquainted with local, inconspicuous groups of Christ devotees, we would not know that (also in the late 1st century) two leaders had written to congregations living in Ephesus and elsewhere in Asia Minor. One exhorted them to "honor the emperor" (1 Pet 2:17) and the other warned them against the dangers of "worshiping the beast" (Rev 13). Attention to how these contrasting Christian approaches compare to the range of concrete practices among other associations and synagogues tells us something important about the place of diverse congregations within society.

Purpose and Scholarly Context of This Study

Our brief visit to Ephesus provides glimpses into the cultural world in which Jewish synagogues and Christian assemblies lived and developed alongside many other associations. This visit raises subjects that will occupy us throughout this study, which is concerned with assessing and comparing the place of diverse associations, synagogues, and assemblies within the framework of the Greek city, or polis, under Roman rule in Asia Minor. More specifically, it focuses on the significance of imperial cults, honors, and connections in the external relations and internal life of these groups. In the process we will shed light on Jewish and Christian literature, including the writings of Josephus, the *Sibylline Oracles*, 1 Peter, John's Apocalypse, the Pastoral Epistles, Ignatius's epistles, the *Martyrdom of Polycarp*, and the *Acts of Paul*. Attention to the role of imperial honors, cults, and connections among these local groups reveals something about where they fit within society, but it also tells us something about the nature of society, religion, and culture in Roman Asia from the time of Augustus to that of Antoninus Pius (27 B.C.E.–161 C.E.).

The central argument of this study is that associations in Roman Asia, including some synagogues and assemblies, could in varying ways participate within certain areas of life in the polis under Roman rule, including involvements in imperial honors and connections. Associations were not, as often assumed, subversive groups in consistent tension with polis and empire. Rather, despite occasional involvements in civic disturbances, there was ongoing positive interaction between these groups and society. Comparing imperial dimensions of group life among associations with those of synagogues and assemblies draws attention to both similarities and differences in practice. This aids us in locating these groups within the social and cultural framework of the polis. Moreover, one of the most important contributions of this study pertains to its extensive use of inscriptions and artifacts in order to compare actual Greco-Roman associations with synagogues and assemblies, rather than merely theorizing in a vacuum when it comes to understanding the relationships between such groups and various dimensions of society.

The manner in which both Jewish and Christian groups are often categorized as "sects" in conflict with society acts as a hindrance to perceiving the more complex spectrum of possibilities in interactions between groups and society. There was a range of perspectives and practices among Jews and Christians with regard to separation from or involvements in various aspects of society, including imperial honors and connections. Virtually all Jews and Christians, it seems, rejected active participation in cultic honors or worship of the emperors (involving rituals and sacrifices that presumed the place of the emperors in the realm of the gods). There was variety, however, with regard to involvements in other aspects of civic life (life in the polis), including other noncultic forms of imperial honors or connections.

On the one hand, the author of the Apocalypse clearly condemned any form of honoring the emperor (the beast in league with Satan in his view), and he also took a sectarian stance in speaking against other social, religious, and economic contacts with imperial aspects of civic life. On the other hand, the Nicolaitan and other opponents of John (Rev 2:14-16, 20-25) were more open toward participating within some areas of life within the polis, including communal meals with fellow inhabitants and some imperial-related practices.

Many other Christians and Jews likewise took a more moderate position with regard to participation in other forms of imperial honors and connections. Inscriptional evidence shows that some synagogues did maintain connections with and honor imperial functionaries and emperors. In contrast to the Apocalypse, the authors of 1 Peter and the Pastoral Epistles encouraged the Christians in Asia Minor to honor or pray for the emperor. Attention to these and other imperial dimensions of group life among associations, synagogues, and assemblies informs us about how these groups claimed a place within polis and empire.

This study fills a significant gap in research and works to resolve problems that present themselves at the intersection of several areas of scholarship on social and religious life in the Greco-Roman world. There are three main areas of study to consider here. First, associations (or *collegia*) have drawn some attention from scholars since the height of their study around the turn of the twentieth century, which witnessed the production of the foundational studies of Paul Foucart (1873), Wilhelm Liebenam (1890), Erich Ziebarth (1896), Jean-Pierre Waltzing (1895–1900), Franz Poland (1909), and Mariano San Nicolò (1912–13). Until recent years, however, most studies by scholars of ancient history have focused on the legal situation and organizational characteristics of associations. Few have approached these groups with sociohistorical questions concerning group-society relations in mind, and there is a lack of local or regional studies.[2] Although associations have drawn the attention of scholars of early Christianity (esp. since the 1970s), few have studied associations on their own terms and none has attempted a comparative, sociohistorical study with a focus on group-society relations and imperial aspects of society.

Moreover, when it comes to questions of how such groups related to society and culture in polis and empire, widespread assumptions within

scholarship presuppose antagonistic relations. Scholars say far less, if anything, of what we encountered in our walk through Ephesus–the involvement of groups in imperial honors and connections of various
types–than they do of the occasions when associations became involved
in disturbances that sometimes brought controlling actions by authorities. Most common are notions that associations were subversive and that
their relationships with civic or imperial society were predominantly negative. For instance, G. E. M. de Ste. Croix includes associations among
the lower-class means of social protest, discussing them only in terms of
their involvement in civic unrest and stressing the authorities' suspicion
and control of them (1981:273, 318–20). He says nothing of evidence
concerning the participation of these same groups within society, including positive interactions with Roman officials. We shall see that de Ste.
Croix is by no means alone in focusing on incidents such as civic disturbances and imperial control to the neglect of other dimensions of group-
society relations among associations.

Second, some ancient historians tend to neglect or downplay the actual significance of the emperors within the social and religious life of the
populace, especially when it comes to assessing imperial cults (or worship
of the emperors). For example, M. P. Nilsson (1961:384–94) and G. W.
Bowersock (1965:112–21) characterize imperial cults as solely political
phenomena, lacking genuine importance within the lives of the populace
in areas like Asia Minor. The present study is indebted to S. R. F. Price's
foundational work, *Rituals and Power* (1984), which marks a turning point
in the study of imperial cults in Asia Minor. Price and others, such as
Steven Friesen (1993, 2001) and Stephen Mitchell (1993, 1:100–117), challenge previous assumptions and emphasize the significance of the emperors within intertwined social, political, and religious aspects of life among
various social levels of the population.

Still, these scholars have not given special attention to associations in
this regard. The evidence of associations will provide a new vantage point
from which to consider the significance of rituals and other honors for the
emperors at the local level. Participation or nonparticipation in such cultic activities (acts of worship) will help us locate various groups on a cultural map of the Roman Empire. It will also serve to correct the picture of
associations as primarily subversive or anti-Roman groups.

One of the reasons for the unbalanced picture of associations within
ancient Mediterranean society relates to a scholarly focus on literary and
legal sources to the neglect of archeological and epigraphic evidence (material remains, buildings, monuments, and inscriptions). Some scholars
have not adequately addressed the inscriptions that provide important

glimpses into the actual ongoing lives of such groups in specific regions and localities. Attention to this evidence will create a more balanced picture of association life, allowing us to perceive the ongoing engagement of many groups in imperial connections and cults within the polis. Artifactual evidence will also provide an important comparative framework for considering both Jewish and Christian groups living within these contexts.

This brings us, thirdly, to one of the most important contributions of the present study. Scholars interested in Jewish and Christian groups or literature of Asia Minor have touched on social questions regarding the relationship between these groups and surrounding society. When it comes to assessing the place of synagogues and assemblies within society or local culture, however, there is a tendency to stress conflicts, tensions, and separation to the neglect of other aspects of group-society relations (much like the conflict-centered approach of those who have studied other associations).

Some scholars interested in synagogues of the diaspora have viewed these groups as isolated and introverted communities living in a hostile environment. In this view, Jewish groups were sects in the sense that they were in a consistent state of tension with the surrounding society. For instance, Victor Tcherikover (1966:29) emphasizes the exclusivity of synagogues that ensured their protection from the syncretistic influences of an alien, Greco-Roman environment.

However, some recent studies of synagogues in Asia Minor specifically are beginning to draw a more complicated picture regarding the relationship between these groups and their civic contexts. For example, A. T. Kraabel (1968, 1978) and Paul R. Trebilco (1991) draw attention to neglected evidence that suggests some degree of interaction between diaspora Jews and their Greek neighbors. These scholars point toward areas of participation on the part of some synagogues within civic life in Roman Asia. They argue that some degree of integration within the polis did not necessarily mean the dissolution of the group or the loss of Jewish distinctiveness, and I would suggest that similar insights should at least inform our approach to Christian assemblies. These scholars emphasize that some, perhaps many, synagogues could find the polis to be a home in important respects; yet they do not focus on the evidence for Jewish groups' involvements in imperial aspects of civic life specifically, including imperial honors and connections. Attention to these activities will tell us more about the place of these groups within society.

Unfortunately, the revised picture of diaspora Jewish groups within the polis is not usually taken as a cue for reassessing Christian assemblies' places within Greco-Roman society. Recent years have seen a growing interest in the social world of Christian literature pertinent to Asia Minor, including 1 Peter, John's Apocalypse, the Pastoral Epistles, Colossians, Ephesians, and Ignatius's epistles.[3] Yet those who consider the issue of group-society relations are often preoccupied with the characterization of congregations as sectarian in a sociological sense, stressing separation from and nonparticipation in most or all areas of civic life. The result has been a concentration on the ways in which such assemblies were in tension with surrounding society to the neglect of evidence concerning how they continued to live *within* the polis and empire.

John H. Elliott's (1990) approach to the social situation and strategy of 1 Peter is in some respects representative of this sectarian-focused position. Employing a sociological model developed by Bryan R. Wilson, Elliott categorizes Christian groups in the provinces of Asia Minor as "sects," suggesting that 1 Peter's strategy is to heighten further the sectarian stance of these groups. Harry O. Maier (1991:163–68) takes a similar approach to the assemblies addressed by Ignatius, emphasizing the "sectarian identity of the Asian churches." For Elliott, the most important characteristics of these sects are their *tensions* with and *separation* from society. He stresses that the typical Christian assembly in Asia Minor was an exclusive "community set apart from the routine affairs of civic and social life" (Elliott 1990:79). In this regard, Elliott's characterization of Christian assemblies stands in continuity with the traditional portrait of group-society interaction among synagogues.

Despite the contributions scholars such as Elliott make, there are difficulties with this sort of approach. Elliott correctly emphasizes the distinctive identity of the Christians: they distinguished themselves from the surrounding society in many respects and refrained from participation in certain areas of life within the polis, especially religious life associated with Greco-Roman gods and goddesses. There were also clear tensions between some Christian assemblies and society. However, the way in which Elliott applies the sectarian model leads him to oversimplify the complexities of group-society relations and to neglect other evidence that does not so readily fit the sectarian model. Although 1 Peter advocates separation from certain aspects of society and culture, there are other values, conventions, and practices of civic life that the author apparently does accept and even promote. Challenging Elliott's approach, David L. Balch's studies (1981, 1986), for example, draw attention to some degree of acculturation evident within 1 Peter. This includes the use and adaptation of commonly accepted Greco-Roman values concerning relationships within the household between master and slave, and husband and wife (1 Pet 2:18–3:7).

Furthermore, there is 1 Peter's advocation of respecting and honoring the emperor and others in authority (1 Pet 2:11-17). This is a potential area of participation in civic life that Elliott does not adequately address due to his focus on sectarianism. Looking at this advice to Christians in Asia Minor in light of the concrete practices of many other associations and synagogues in the same region may draw a more complicated picture regarding the range of possibilities in group-society interactions among Christian assemblies. This will show that the usual sectarian-focused approach does not do justice to all the evidence.

There are similar difficulties with the way in which some scholars approach John's Apocalypse and its social context. This document is clearly concerned with issues regarding the relationship between Christians and society and about imperial cults and connections specifically (esp. Rev 13, 17–18). The traditional approach to the Apocalypse views the hostile and sectarian perspective of the author as *representative* of the actual viewpoints and relations of most Christians living in the cities of Roman Asia. For instance, Elisabeth Schüssler Fiorenza (1985) views the futuristic visions involving enforced worship of the beast and martyrdoms as reflective of actual conditions faced by Christians in Asia during the time of Domitian (81–96 c.e.). She argues that the Apocalypse's invective against Rome and the emperors is a "fitting response" to this sociopolitical situation. In this view, the majority of the recipients of this writing would have identified with John's hostile and sectarian perspective in relation to imperial and other dimensions of society. Most Christians, she suggests, would have remained removed from participation in imperial honors and connections within civic life. This understanding of the Apocalypse also finds expression in common assumptions within scholarship concerning a fundamental antagonism between early Christianity and the Roman Empire generally. Often this is expressed in terms of a conflict between the "cult of Christ" (*Christkult*) and the "cult of Caesar" (*Kaiserkult*; cf. Deissmann 1995; R. Horsley 1997).

However, this approach to the Apocalypse and to early Christianity generally is problematic. Studies by scholars such as Adela Yarbro Collins (1984) and Leonard L. Thompson (1990) suggest a more complex relation between rhetoric and reality. The futuristic visions of the Apocalypse do not directly represent the actual conditions in Roman Asia in the time of Domitian. There is a lack of evidence for any extensive, imperial-initiated persecution of Christians during this period. Nor is there evidence that Domitian's principate witnessed an increase or fundamental change in the promotion or significance of imperial cults in Asia Minor.

We need to reassess the relationship between John's Apocalypse, life within the congregations, and sociocultural realities within the cities. This is especially important when it comes to issues concerning imperial cults and their significance for early Christianity. We can no longer simply assume that the sectarian stance and hostile perspectives of the Apocalypse represent actual relations between most congregations and various dimensions of surrounding culture. Instead, we need to look at a range of evidence concerning the actual imperial-related practices among Christians, viewing this in light of the activities of both synagogues and other associations in the same region. We shall see that group-society relations were quite complex. Moreover, there was a range of possibilities among both Christian assemblies and Jewish synagogues with regard to interaction with, participation in, or separation from specific social and cultural aspects of life within the polis and empire.

Overall, then, the problem is that many scholars do not pay adequate attention to the concrete and complex ways in which local associations, synagogues, and assemblies found a place in polis and empire. When scholars do address the subject of group-society interaction or questions of imperialism, quite often they focus on issues of tension and sectarianism without sufficient regard for other evidence concerning positive interaction. Few have tapped into the vast reservoir of archeological evidence concerning association life for what it can reveal about the range of concrete possibilities in the interaction between groups and the societies in which they lived. None has attempted to compare the practices of associations with those of synagogues and assemblies in this regard. A variety of resources and methods will assist us in qualifying and rectifying these unbalanced portraits.

Methods, Sources, and the Use of Archeological Evidence

This study finds its home where the disciplines of Christian origins, Jewish studies, ancient history, epigraphy, and religious studies meet, and its methods and sources reflect this interdisciplinary character. The overall approach of this study is sociohistorical, which means several things. First, I am interested in the actual social and religious life of persons and groups (from various levels of society) living within a particular region of the Roman Empire. Social historians approach their subject with an attentiveness to the fact that all within society, not just the rich and powerful, could be significant actors and players within history. Material remains and inscriptional evidence provide an important window into social history. Second, I am concerned with social relations and, more specifically, with issues regarding the relationship between groups and surrounding sociocultural institutions and values. This encompasses a variety of issues concerning interactions between groups (associations, synagogues, or assemblies) and others within the structures of society, including the elites. It also encompasses the relation of groups to various social and cultural structures, values, symbols, practices, and institutions within society.

Another sociohistorical dimension of this study is its use of methods and insights from the social sciences, which can aid us in better comprehending society and culture in the ancient Mediterranean. Sociological studies of social networks, for instance, will shed light on both the formation of associations and on the significance of connections between groups and individuals within society. Anthropological insights will help to clarify the meaning of rituals for the emperors within associations. Social-scientific studies of acculturation and assimilation among minority cultural groups will clarify the complicated nature of group-society interactions in the case of synagogues and assemblies in antiquity. Yet I will also need to address difficulties in how some scholars of early Christianity employ sociological models of sectarianism, for instance.

It is important to make a few preliminary observations concerning the use of these social-scientific methods here.[4] I employ insights from the social sciences in a *heuristic* manner. By this I mean that they aid in the formation of questions that help us discover what might otherwise remain unnoticed. They provide an alternative lens through which to observe ancient society and culture, furthering our understanding of phenomena within it. But they certainly do not serve as substitutes for evidence.

Furthermore, my use of social-scientific methods and concepts remains attentive to the fact that many are developed within modern societies, and that our use of them needs to be cross-culturally sensitive and flexible. We need to modify or shape them in ways that avoid anachronistic approaches to studying ancient society. We also need to remain aware that evidence for social relations in ancient societies is fragmentary in comparison to the data available to a sociologist studying a modern society, for instance. What we get, at best, is snapshots of social relations at a particular time and place. It is not always clear how (or whether) we can generalize from these snapshots about the moving picture that is social reality. Despite these unfortunate circumstances concerning the nature of the sources, however, social-scientific insights assist us in making better sense of the evidence we do have.

The principal sources for this study are literary, archeological, and epigraphic. Although evidence for association life derives primarily from inscriptions, there are some references to these groups in literature, especially pertaining to the involvements of associations in what upper-class authors in the ancient world considered noteworthy historical incidents (e.g., civic disturbances and control of them). Evidence for synagogues in Roman Asia is also primarily epigraphic, though documents preserved by Josephus and other writings such as the *Sibylline Oracles* also give us some useful information. In the case of Christians, the evidence happens to be solely literary, and I discuss the reasons for this lack of material remains concerning early Christianity in chapter 8. Early Christian literature pertinent to this region, including John's Apocalypse, 1 Peter, the Pastoral Epistles, Ignatius's epistles, the *Acts of Paul*, and the *Martyrdom of Polycarp*, will occupy us primarily in the third part of this study.

Archeological sources and methods are fundamental to this study. Buildings, monuments, plaques, and other artifacts are an essential source of information concerning ancient social and religious life, providing an alternative perspective to that of literary sources (which are often produced by the elites). Most information about associations, as with local social and religious life generally, comes from extant Greek and Latin texts inscribed in stone for various purposes (epigraphy).[5] These inscriptions include gravestones (epitaphs); decrees or regulations of cities or groups; official decisions and letters of local magistrates, governors, or emperors; and, most ubiquitous, various kinds of monumental honors presented by individuals, groups, and civic institutions for benefactors (whether humans or gods) in response to benefits conferred or desired. These could include dedications of altars, plaques, statues, and buildings (see the figures throughout this study for visual examples). Epigraphic evidence provides a vital window through which to view concrete, and otherwise obscure, aspects of life. "Though we must always be conscious of how much inscriptions will *not* tell us, it is still the case that inscriptions, read in bulk, provide the most direct access which we can have to the life, social structure, thought and values of the ancient world" (Millar 1983:81).

Documented inscriptions from Asia Minor are accessible through various periodicals and collections. The most extensive multivolume series that collects inscriptions from the Greek cities of Asia Minor is *Inschriften griechischer Städte aus Kleinasien* (IGSK), commissioned by the Austrian Archeological Institute (Österreichisches Archäologisches Institut) in Vienna. Also very important are the multi-volume series *Tituli Asiae Minoris* (Inscriptions of Asia Minor), produced by the Austrian Academy of Science, and *Monumenta Asiae Minoris Antiqua* (Ancient Monuments of Asia Minor), now produced by the Society for the Promotion of Roman Studies. Several periodicals or series focus on gathering together recent epigraphic discoveries and discussions, including *L'Année épigraphique* (*AE*), *Supplementum epigraphicum graecum* (*SEG*), and "Bulletin épigraphique" (*BE*) in *Revue des études grecques*. Another very useful series, particularly for those new to inscriptions, is *New Documents Illustrating Early Christianity*, produced by the Ancient History Documentary Research Centre of Macquarie University in Australia. This series provides a more popular avenue into the world of inscriptions.

The value and significance of artifacts and monuments is certainly not limited to textual elements. This study remains attentive to the visual and symbolic messages of archeological remains. For instance, the building remains of associations that have been uncovered communicate something about what these groups did and what they felt was important. Paul Zanker's study of the *Power of Images in the Age of Augustus* (1988:3) vividly demonstrates how visual imagery and the pictorial language of monuments, statues, buildings, ceremonies, and other objects "reflects a society's inner life and gives insight into people's values and imagination that often cannot be apprehended in literary sources." At various points in this study I draw attention to the symbolic significance of monuments and buildings, regarding both the messages that they could communicate and their visual impression on the viewer. *Monumentalizing* (as I call the activity of erecting such monuments and inscriptions) could involve a concrete statement or assertion regarding the place of an individual, group, or community within society and the cosmos, as we shall see.

Having noted the great evidential value of inscriptions, it is important to remain aware of the difficulties involved in using such sources. First, there is the paucity and partial nature of inscriptional evidence. Only certain types of activities, mentioned above, were recorded in stone. Added to this is that inscriptions that have been discovered and published represent only a small portion of those that did exist or that may be discovered in the future. There are difficulties, then, in deciding whether a particular piece of evidence is representative of common practices or relations. Moreover, the material remains we do possess reflect only a small portion of social and religious life in antiquity; they certainly do not provide a complete picture. A second related difficulty is that quite often there is a lack of context for interpreting a specific inscription. Information for a particular person or group may derive solely from one fragmentary and partially reconstructed inscription, and quite often this may lack indication of date and context. This is why inscriptions should be studied in bulk with attention to regional factors. Studying groups of inscriptions can tell us something about social and religious life that an individual gravestone cannot. Finally, we should not imagine that the problems of interpretation disappear when we are working with such concrete remains, presuming that these sources speak to us in an uncomplicated manner.

In some important respects, my approach differs from some other scholars who have used material remains from the Greco-Roman world to shed light on early Christian history and literature. Colin J. Hemer's (1986) study of the opening letters of John's Apocalypse illustrates a common approach to archeological evidence among some scholars of early Christianity (cf. Scobie 1993). Hemer systematically works through the opening letters of the Apocalypse attempting to correlate references in the literary evidence to the concrete local contexts of the seven cities. Archeological materials are often removed from their broader contexts. Moreover, for Hemer the Christian literary evidence dictates the selection and interpretation of artifacts from the Greco-Roman world.

By contrast, I attempt to approach artifactual evidence concerning social and religious phenomena in local contexts *on their own terms* before turning to questions of how this might shed light on early Christianity or Judaism. Epigraphic and archeological evidence should not be interpreted in light of literary evidence. Rather one should understand it on its own terms, realizing that it can provide alternative views of social reality.

Outline

The book is divided into three main parts: associations in Roman Asia (part one); associations and imperial aspects of society (part two); and synagogues and congregations in Greco-Roman society (part three). Part one addresses some preliminary issues regarding associations, their internal life, and their context, laying the groundwork for parts two and three. First I outline the extensive inscriptional evidence for associations in Roman Asia, clarifying what groups are encompassed by this study (chapter 1). I use the term "associations" to refer to small, unofficial groups that met together on a regular basis for a variety of social, religious, and other purposes. Chapter one elaborates the definition and provides a *typology of associations*, focusing on social networks and issues of composition.[6] I then turn to a general outline of the *internal life* of these groups, discussing interconnected social, religious, and funerary functions that provided members of these groups with a sense of belonging (chapter 2). In the process, I challenge a tradition within scholarship that tends to stress the social side of association life to the neglect of religious dimensions. Chapter 3 considers the *civic framework* and the place of associations within the context of the polis in the eastern part of the Roman Empire, the Greek East. It is quite common for scholars to speak of associations (including the mysteries) as symptoms of decline, as compensatory phenomena in a period of social, cultural, and political degeneration within the polis. Yet this approach is problematic as the evidence for associations in Roman Asia clearly shows.

Part two focuses on associations and imperial aspects of society and culture in Roman Asia. These chapters provide extensive evidence concerning the interactions of associations within society and culture under Roman rule, which forces us to reevaluate the predominant tension-centered approach of most scholarship. This evidence of group-society relations sheds light on the concrete ways in which these groups claimed and maintained a place for themselves in the polis and empire. First, I address the significance of the emperors and cultic honors (acts of worship) for these "revered ones" *within* the religious life of associations (chapter 4). Contrary to a common scholarly paradigm, imperial cults were not solely political phenomena of little significance for the populace at the local level. These religious activities for the emperors or imperial gods (as I sometimes call them) also tell us something about how associations and their members understood their place within the webs of relations of society and the cosmos. Second, I focus on *external relations* of associations. The extensive evidence regarding ongoing *positive interactions* between associations and officials (local or provincial) and emperors (chapter 5) should lead us to reevaluate *areas of tension*, such as the intermittent involvement of associations in civic unrest and the intervention of imperial officials or emperors (chapter 6). Moreover, these imperial connections among associations illustrate some of the mechanisms that linked inhabitants to the civic community and to Roman imperial power, holding the empire together. I also assess the symbolic significance of monumentalizing in the Greco-Roman world, suggesting that these actions could be concrete claims about one's place within society and the cosmos.

Part three focuses on various Jewish synagogues and Christian assemblies that lived alongside these other associations within the cities of Roman Asia. As with the chapters on associations, I reevaluate the place of diverse groups within the social and cultural framework of polis and empire. I begin by addressing theoretical and methodological issues in the *comparison of socioreligious groups in antiquity* (chapter 7). It is quite common for scholars to categorize Jewish and Christian groups as "sects" in a sociological sense, stressing their separation from and conflict with surrounding society. This approach does not adequately account for variations among these groups and often obscures evidence regarding complexities in the interactions between groups and society. Insights from the social sciences regarding acculturation and dissimilation among minority cultural groups will provide a more fruitful approach to the question. Archeological and inscriptional evidence for synagogues within the polis in Roman Asia will serve as a case in point, challenging the sectarian portrait and preparing the way for an extensive treatment of other primary evidence regarding imperial honors in relation to both synagogues and congregations.

Comparing varied associations with both synagogues and assemblies draws attention to areas of participation and nonparticipation, positive interaction and tension, among Jews and Christians in relation to imperial and other aspects of civic life under Roman rule. There is substantial primary evidence concerning the *participation* of a significant number of synagogues and assemblies in imperial honors or connections (chapter 8). Rereading this evidence of positive interaction within society in light of the discussion of associations in earlier chapters suggests that a broadly sectarian understanding of many synagogues and assemblies is no longer overwhelmingly plausible. Moreover, there was a spectrum of perspectives and practices among both Jewish and Christian groups (and individuals or leaders) regarding what degree of participation in imperial and other aspects of civic life was acceptable, ranging from the more open or moderate approaches of the Nicolaitans, 1 Peter, and the Pastorals to the clearly sectarian approach of John's Apocalypse.

In light of this evidence for positive interaction, we need to reconsider other areas of tension, particularly regarding Jews' and Christians' *nonparticipation* in worshiping the Greco-Roman gods, emperors included (chapter 9). There has been a tendency within scholarship to inflate the importance of imperial cults specifically in regard to issues of persecution and negative group-society relations. The result has been a portrait of early Christianity that wrongly sees imperial cults or worship of the emperors as the heart of a conflict between Christianity and Roman society. It seems that most, or virtually all, Jews and Christians did avoid active or full participation in worship of the emperors as gods. But proper attention to the actual nature of imperial cults and persecution (drawing on incidents from the times of Trajan, Hadrian, and Antoninus Pius) suggests that this area of nonparticipation was a potential source of group-society tensions only insofar as imperial cults were part and parcel of religious life in the cities more generally. Finally, rereading the Apocalypse of John in light of all of this furthers our comprehension of its audience and its author's rhetorical strategy. This shows how John (a *Jewish* Christian) perceived and reacted to some of the realities of life in the cities and in the congregations devoted to Christ, responding in a way that was quite different from the approach of other fellow Jews and Christians in the same region.

Overall, this study draws attention to the ways in which diverse associations, synagogues, and congregations found a place for themselves within the polis under Roman rule, despite their individual or distinctive worldviews and practices in other regards. It also demonstrates the value in studying material remains from local contexts of the ancient Mediterranean. Doing so can provide new perspectives on the social history of various groups and communities in specific localities, bringing to life the diversity of the Greco-Roman world. This can also transform our perceptions of early Christianity and Judaism within that world.

PART 1

ASSOCIATIONS IN ROMAN ASIA

1

Associations and Guilds

Varieties and Social Makeup

Introduction

Reviewing the evidence of association life from an ancient city like Smyrna, one immediately notices gatherings among goldsmiths, porters, hymn singers; devotees of Dionysos, of Demeter, of Caesar, and of Christ; Judeans; and others. Before considering the place of such groups within the polis, it is important to discuss their nature and internal makeup and to provide a framework (typology or taxonomy) for understanding the varieties or types among them. Here I outline the evidence for associations in Roman Asia and deal with the question of what social strata of the population were represented within such groups.

It is common for scholars to categorize associations based on their main purpose, be it religious, funerary, or otherwise. However, a more useful framework for outlining the evidence from Roman Asia is one that gives attention to the principal social network connections that formed the basis of an association's membership and that continued to inform a group's self-understanding. There were several types of associations based on network connections associated with the household, common ethnic or geographic origins, the neighborhood, common occupational activities, and common cult (regular attendance at the temple of a given deity). It is important to note that the typology I present here is exploratory and is not meant to be applied rigidly, for many associations drew membership from more than one of these social networks. Nevertheless, there are also many cases when we can detect the principal set of linkages that formed a key basis of a given association, and the typology helps us to make sense of the diversity of groups.

Variety was also reflected in the internal composition of membership in associations. Many scholars characterize the majority of associations as socially homogeneous groups, consisting principally of the poorest segments of society. But evidence from Roman Asia suggests that association life often spanned the social spectrum of society generally. Composition differed from one group to the next, ranging from homogeneous to heterogeneous membership in terms of social status and other factors. This has important implications regarding the social makeup of early Christianity, too, as we shall see.

Social Stratification in Greco-Roman Society

A brief discussion of social stratification in the Roman Empire will provide a context in which to understand the social makeup of associations. The official social structure can be illustrated in terms of a steep pyramid of hierarchy, with an extremely small portion of the population at the top (probably about 10 percent) and the rest at the bottom (cf. MacMullen 1974b:88–121; Alföldy 1985; Garnsey and Saller 1987:107–25; Hopkins 1998). There were four main official orders of Roman society: senatorial, equestrian (knights), decurion, and plebeian.

At the very top of the hierarchy were those belonging to the senatorial and equestrian orders, which I refer to as the *imperial elites* (probably about 1 percent of the total population). The emperor and his direct family members were at the peak of power and influence. The senatorial aristocracy consisted of a few families (there were a total of about 600 members, all men, in the Roman senate) that were expected to possess property worth about one million sesterces.[1] The supreme patron, the emperor, chose senators from among these families. There was a typical career path (*cursus honorum*) through which a senator could pass, culminating (sometimes) in the position of consul (the highest, annually elected official at Rome) and then proconsul (governor) of one of the more prestigious provinces (such as Asia).

Membership in the equestrian order required a minimum of 400,000 sesterces, and these knights filled the important offices within the army and sometimes moved into the more prestigious administrative positions in Rome and the provinces. Equestrian standing was also hereditary. Patronage connections within networks, especially with the emperor himself, were an essential factor in advancement through the ranks appropriate to one's official order. There were occasions when these connections together with success within a family from one generation to the next could mean movement from the equestrian to the senatorial order.

This group of imperial elites had its counterparts, though usually on a more modest scale, in the decurions or *civic elites* (probably about 10 percent or less of the city population). These were the aristocratic families of the provincial communities who assumed the more important positions in the cities, including membership on the council, on the board of leaders (archons), or other important civic positions (e.g., director of contests). They, like the imperial elites, also played the social role of benefactors within the cities. From the mid- to late first century, a very small number of these provincial families with imperial connections began to attain equestrian and, eventually, senatorial standing over the course of generations.

Below the imperial and civic elites lay the vast majority of the population (about 90 percent), the plebeians or nonelite strata, including both rural peasant farmers and urban dwellers. The majority of the masses were peasant farmers in the countryside and villages, since the Roman economy was primarily agricultural (cf. MacMullen 1974a; S. Mitchell 1993, 1:165–97). The city population is our central focus here, since this is where we find most evidence for associations, synagogues, and assemblies. There was a range of possibilities in social and economic status among these (formally) nonelite segments of the city populations, and at least some potential for mobility. A variety of informal factors affected one's social standing at the local level, including family, ethnic background, legal standing (free, freed or slave), occupation (artisans, traders, physicians, etc.), citizenship (civic or imperial), education, skill, and especially wealth (cf. Hopkins 1965:14; Meeks 1983:54–55). There were, therefore, occasions of inconsistency between one's position within the official Roman orders (i.e., plebeian) and one's actual status within a local, civic context (see Hopkins 1965). Sometimes those formally low on the social ladder, including traders and artisans, attained positions in important city boards or offices, for instance.

Scholars who attempt to place the evidence for social composition among associations within these broader social structures often engage in generalizations that fail to account for some of the distinctions and variations I observe here. For example, Jean-Pierre Waltzing (1895–1900), E. Kornemann (1901), and George La Piana (1927) give the impression that the majority of associations ("burial clubs") were socially homogeneous, consisting of the poorest and most deprived strata of society. Wayne A. Meeks (1983:78–80) and other scholars of early Christianity likewise generalize about the supposed homogeneous social makeup of associations, contrasting this with the socially inclusive or heterogeneous character of

(Pauline) congregations. For Meeks this is one of several differences that make associations less than adequate models for comparison with Christian groups.

These approaches do not do justice to the range of possibilities regarding the social composition and varieties of associations in Roman Asia. Social status is a complex phenomenon that is difficult to measure, especially considering the fragmentary nature of our evidence from antiquity. Nonetheless, throughout this chapter I remain alert to several indicators of social standing among the members of various associations, including wealth, family background, occupation, legal standing (free, freed, slave), gender, citizenship (civic or imperial), and roles in civic or imperial positions. Recognition of such factors points toward a spectrum of possibilities in the social composition of associations, with variety among types and from one group to the next. Some could be more homogeneous, others heterogeneous, in terms of the social standing and gender of members.

Typology of Associations: A New Framework

Issues of social composition have often been bound up in discussions of the types of associations. Most commonly, scholars of associations propose a threefold typology based on apparent primary purpose: (1) occupational, (2) cultic (*collegia sodalicia*), and (3) burial (*collegia tenuiorum*; cf. Waltzing 1895–1900, 1:32–56, 114–54; Kornemann 1901:386–403; La Piana 1927:239–44). Waltzing, La Piana, and others argue that the majority of associations were of the burial type (*collegia tenuiorum*), consisting primarily of the poorest social strata of society who could not otherwise afford burial. Echoing views of Theodor Mommsen (1843), Waltzing can state that "many private associations, originally founded in order to honor a divinity, ended up regarding religion as an accessory and the funeral as their principal aim" (1895–1900, 1:46 [trans. mine]; cf. La Piana 1927:243, 272). These views are based, in part, on an assumption that the Roman authorities strictly controlled associations (from the time of Augustus) and that only burial clubs for the poor (*collegia tenuiorum*) were exempted from such laws.

There are several problems with purpose-centered typologies. Waltzing's categories, especially the so-called burial associations, rest on a questionable reading of legal sources. The topic cannot be discussed fully here, but recent studies by Frank M. Ausbüttel (1982:22–23) and John S. Kloppenborg (1996a:20–23) point out the lack of evidence even for the existence of associations devoted solely to burial, the so-called *collegia tenuio-rum* or *funeraticia* that are so integral to this typology. Furthermore, sorting of these groups based on purpose can obscure other evidence that suggests that associations of various kinds could serve similar social, religious, and funerary functions. Franz Poland strikes to the heart of the matter: "every association is in some sense a cult association" (Poland 1909:5 [trans. mine]; cf. Dill 1956:262–63). Evidently, we need a more adequate framework in which to understand the nature and variety of these groups.

Kloppenborg's (1996a) work in this area provides a useful starting point. Recognizing the problems with traditional typologies, he suggests that it is more helpful to categorize associations based on the profile of their membership. In his view there were three main sources of membership based on common household connections, shared occupation, and common cult, and all three types of associations served a variety of interrelated purposes. This focus on membership bases, rather than purpose, is fitting for our present aims.

An approach that pays special attention to the role of social networks in group membership provides a useful framework for considering the range of associations in Roman Asia. Sociological studies since the 1960s have increasingly recognized the importance of preexisting social network connections for understanding the formation and growth of social and religious groups or movements of various kinds, and this chapter is informed by such insights (see Stark and Bainbridge 1985:307–24 for discussion and bibliography). Relationships and interpersonal bonds established through social networks help to explain how persons come to associate with one another in particular group settings, as well as pointing toward sources for growth in membership.

Familial, ethnic, occupational, cultic, and other spheres of social ties help to account for the kinds of groups found in the cities of Roman Asia. These webs of connections certainly overlap, and several can play a role in the membership of a particular association. Still, it is possible to distinguish five common types of associations according to their principal social network basis. There were groups that drew primarily on (1) household connections, (2) ethnic or geographic connections, (3) neighborhood connections, (4) occupational connections, and (5) cult or temple connections. These sets of social linkages are often interrelated with issues concerning the self-understandings or identities of particular associations, and they also provide clues regarding the economic and social standings of their members.

Household Connections

Household connections or familial relationships account for the membership, existence, and identity of a significant number of associations. Family networks encompassed a far greater set of relations in the ancient
context (including slaves and other dependents) than in most modern
Western societies. The family of Agrippinilla, which originally lived in
Mytilene on the island of Lesbos (opposite Pergamum) and emigrated to
Torre Nova in Italy, provides an excellent example of a household-based
association exhibiting Asian influence. In about 160 c.e., an association of
four hundred "initiates" (*mystai*) in the mysteries of Dionysos (an exceptionally large group) honored Pompeia Agrippinilla, their priestess, with a
statue (*IGUR* 160). Achille Vogliano's study (1933) shows that many of the
main functionaries come from the families of Agrippinilla and her husband, M. Gavius Squilla Gallicanus, who was consul in 150 c.e. and proconsul of Asia in 165 c.e. The rest of the members, including both men
(292) and women (110) of free, freed, and servile status (many originally
from Asia Minor), reflect dependents associated with that household (see
Scheid 1986; cf. *SEG* 36 [1986] 925). This family-centered group has its
parallels elsewhere, as is evident in the dedication of an altar by the head
of the household near Bizye in Thracia "on behalf of his children and *his
own initiates* whom blessed Dionysos saves" (*IGBulg* 1865). Once such familial associations were formed, however, membership could presumably
expand somewhat to include others less directly affiliated with the household through friendship, occupation, or other relations within the network connections of individual family members.

An analogous household focus is apparent in the case of a group in
Philadelphia, Asia (*ILydiaKP* III 18 = Weinreich 1919 = *SIG*³ 985 = Barton and Horsley 1981 [with trans.]; early 1st century b.c.e.). A man named
Dionysios, who was head of the family, received a set of rules regarding
the entrance of "men and women, free people and slaves" into his "household" (*oikos*) by way of a dream from Zeus (cf. *IG* X.2 255 = *NewDocs* I 6).
There was probably a designated room within the household where the
sacrifices and mysteries were to be performed regularly "in accordance
with ancestral custom," especially in honor of Zeus and Agdistis (a sometimes androgynous deity associated with the Anatolian Great Mother, Cybele). The inscription (based on the dream) outlines numerous purity
regulations for entrance and closes with a prayer calling on Zeus to be well
disposed to Dionysios and his family. Once again, as with the Agrippinilla
association, membership in such household-centered groups could be

quite heterogeneous, reflecting the spectrum of social status levels of both genders that would naturally be associated with the household. Similar situations where members of a particular family constitute the group (or at least a significant portion of the group) could be cited from various cities or villages in Asia (cf. *IStratonikeia* 845–46; *TAM* V 817 [Attaleia, near Thyatira]; *IPhrygR* 30–31 [Thiunta, near Hierapolis]).

Family networks and structures played a key role in the formation and expansion of some early Christian assemblies as well, which in this regard are not dissimilar from the household association (cf. Filson 1939; Klauck 1981). A pattern of "conversion" and communal gathering portrayed in Acts, but also substantiated elsewhere, is indicative: again and again an entire family of dependents was baptized along with the head of the household and the home was subsequently used as a meeting place (e.g., Acts 11:14; 16:15; 18:8; cf. 1 Cor 1:16; 16:19; Phlm 2; Rom 16:10–16; Col 4:15). As with the association founded by Dionysios at Philadelphia, household origins could be reflected in the relatively heterogeneous makeup of some Christian groups, including masters and slaves, men and women, in their ranks.

Before going on to the second category of ethnically based associations, it is important to note that many associations of various types, even if they were not primarily family based in membership or organization, could be influenced by the household with regard to (1) organizational structures and (2) the language of familial affection. First, the influence of the organizational structures of the household can be concretely illustrated in architecture. L. Michael White (1996) shows that there was a pattern among groups, whether "pagan," Christian, or Jewish. Many such groups adapted local houses for communal use, frequently depending on the generosity of a head of the household to supply the house (or rooms therein) or the funds needed to adapt the building. In light of such architectural and corresponding social origins, it is not surprising to find heads of households becoming the leaders. In this respect, the leadership and organization of many associations, synagogues, and congregations were heavily influenced by the household and conventions of benefaction in the Greek East.

Second, contrary to Meeks's contention, the language of familial affection (e.g., "mother," "father," "brothers," or "sisters") does occur in connection with a significant number of associations (and in other Greco-Roman religious contexts) that do not involve actual families. Meeks's influential study suggests that familial or affectional language (esp. "brother" terminology) was rare within associations or "clubs," and that the use of such language in (Pauline) Christian groups, on the other hand, illustrates their unique and "sectarian" character (Meeks 1983:85–88; 225 n. 73; cf. Burkert 1987:45; Schmeller 1995:16–17). There is no reason to discount the following evidence for such familial language when it does occur within associations while doing the contrary with respect to Christian assemblies.

It was quite common for groups that were not actually related to express their gratitude toward benefactors or leaders with titles reflecting familial affection. Thus an all-female association of initiates of the Great Mother (Cybele) at Serdica in Thracia referred to its leader as "mother of the tree bearers," and similar uses of "mother" (*mētēr*) or "father" (*patēr*), as well as "son" (*huios*), are attested within associations of various kinds elsewhere.[2] For example, a Jewish group at Stobi in Macedonia honored the "father of the synagogue" for his donation of rooms in his own house for banqueting (a *triclinium*) and religious activities of the group (*CIJ* 694; late 2d–early 3d century C.E.). One wonders whether some of these "mothers" and "fathers," if they were to personally address members, might refer to them as "children," an address we find in some Pauline and Johannine Christian circles.

Finally, there are indeed cases where fellow members of an association, who appear to be unrelated in a literal sense, address one another or name themselves in familial terms, using the term "brother" (*adelphos*). Some of our epigraphic evidence comes from Asia Minor, including an inscription from Halicarnassus (south of Miletos) that involves priests of a particular temple who refer to one another as "brothers" (*IGLAM* 503; cf. *IAsMinLyk* I 1). At Lamos in Cilicia several inscriptions pertain to an association of craftsmen from Selge; in one, Rhodios prepares the collective tomb for the members of the association whom he also calls "the brothers" (*IKilikiaHW* II 193–202, esp. 201). It is quite possible that the "brotherly-loving" shippers near Iasos included members who were not literally brothers (Cousin and Deschamps 1894:21, no. 11). A monument dedicated to "god Most High" (Theos Hypsistos) at Sinope in Pontus refers to "the praying brothers" (*hoi adelphoi euxamenoi*; Doublet 1889:303–4, no. 7), which may very well be an association. Outside Asia Minor we find an association at Tanais in the Bosporus (north of the Black Sea) referring to itself as "the adopted brothers worshiping god Most High" (*isopoiētoi adelphoi sebomenoi theon hypsiston*; *IPontEux* II 449–52, 456; 212–240 C.E.). A Jewish connection, involving Gentiles who worship the Jewish God as Hypsistos, is quite possible in this case (cf. Levinskaya 1996:111, 244–45; S. Mitchell 1999:116–17).

Not surprisingly, this sort of "brother" language is attested more often in cases of personal address. Most of it comes from Egypt, since only there do we find climates suitable for the survival of personal letters on papyrus (the paper of antiquity); it is precisely in the context of letters that we find Christian authors like Paul using such language too. Robert W. Daniel (1979) devotes some attention to this practice of familial address among association members, discussing two papyri. In one letter, the leaders of an athletic association refer to several members as "brother" and "friend" (*PRyl* IV 604 [probably Antinoopolis]; *PSI* III 236 [Oxyrhynchus], both 3d century C.E.); in a second letter an undertaker writes to a fellow undertaker, addressing him as "brother" (*PPetaus* 28). In another papyrus from Oxyrhynchus (3d century C.E.), a man makes an oath pertaining to initiation into mysteries, making mention of both the leader of the group, "father Sarapion," and his fellow initiates, the "brothers," perhaps "mystical brothers" (*mystiko]us adelphous*) according to Ulrich Wilcken's reconstruction (*PSI* X 1162; cf. Wilcken 1932:257–59). Further examples of similar use could be cited, some from an earlier era.[3]

So there was common ground among some associations, synagogues, and assemblies in the use of familial language to express identity and feelings of belonging and community. In this connection, it is worth mentioning the use of the language of friendship to express belonging (esp. *philoi*). There are numerous cases of association members referring to one another as "friends" in inscriptions, often as a self-designation or title of the group itself.[4] Similar language was used by some Christian congregations in the region, at least those addressed by the epistles of John (cf. 3 John 15).

Familial structures and terminology were influential for associations of all kinds, then. Yet there were also specific household-based associations (like those of Agrippinilla in Italy and of Dionysios at Philadelphia) whose membership consisted principally of family members, including men and women as well as dependents, such as slaves and freedpersons.

Ethnic or Geographic Connections

A second basis of association relates to foreigners or persons of a common ethnic background or geographical origin, who could express their shared identity by joining together regularly (cf. Baslez 1988). A lively attention to ethnic or geographic origins and identity could be maintained while also finding a new home within the city or town of residence, however. In Asia there were many immigrants from Italy or from the city of Rome (often representing a mixture of merchants or traders) that joined together in societies, for instance.[5] Membership could include Romans or Italians involved in different forms of trade with varying socioeconomic status; some of these immigrants from Italy could assume local citizenship, attain considerable wealth, and become well known as benefactors within their city of residence (see Hatzfeld 1919:101–31, 148–74, 297–309; Broughton 1938:544). Several associations on the island of Rhodes consisted of persons of common geographic origin, such as the Samothracians, Cretans, Sidonians, and Pergaians (*IGR* IV 1114, 1128; *IG* II.5 1335b; *IG* XII.1 867; *ILindos* 391.31–32, 392a.12–13 and 392b.15–16; cf. MacKay 1990:2059–60), or a mixture of immigrants (see Poland 1909:317–21). There was an association (*symbiōsis*) of men from Dioscurias (in Colchis) that met together in Pergamum (*CIG* 3540). Immigrants from Egypt, like the "house" (*oikos*) of Alexandrians at Tomis in Thracia, also formed associations, probably choosing Isis, Serapis, or other deities of the homeland as patrons (*IGLSkythia* II 153; cf. *IGR* I 392 [Ostia], 446 [Neapolis], 800 [Heraklea-Perinthos, Thracia]; *SEG* 47 [1997] 2325).

In light of the tendency of Italians, Pergaians, Alexandrians, and others to congregate together, it is not surprising to find Judeans (*Ioudaioi*) in the cities of Asia (and "Israelites" or Samaritans on the island of Delos, for instance) forming similar groups, sometimes using terminology common to other associations.[6] Besides the many epitaphs referring to individual Jews and their families, there is literary or archeological evidence for gatherings at numerous cities including Akmoneia, Aphrodisias, Ephesus, Hierapolis, Laodicea, Miletos, Pergamum, Philadelphia, Priene, Sardis, Smyrna, Thyatira, and Teos.[7] It is worth noting that in some cases these Judeans had lived for decades and sometimes centuries at a particular locale, something that should caution us in overemphasizing their "alien" or "immigrant" status (cf. Josephus, *Ant.* 12.147–53); this also meant that Gentiles with varying levels of attachment could begin to affiliate with a given synagogue (slaves of Jewish families, proselytes, God-fearers).

Occupational and neighborhood networks sometimes help to explain why a particular Jew associated with one synagogue rather than another in cities where several existed. For example, of the eleven attested synagogues in the city of Rome (some of which existed simultaneously), it appears that three derive their name from the district where they lived: the Calcaresians probably from the lime-burners' district, the Campesians from the Campus Martius, and the Siburesians (*sic*) from the Subura district. Two others may very well have been founded by Jews initially from cities elsewhere: the Tripolitans from the city of their namesake either in Phoenicia or

North Africa, and the "synagogue of Elaia," perhaps consisting of some members formerly residents or citizens of Elaia (south of Pergamum) in Asia (see Leon 1995:135–66). Both neighborhood and occupational factors played a subsidiary role in the organization of the Jewish population at Alexandria in Egypt: there were certain streets and districts known for the presence of Jews (cf. Philo, *Against Flaccus* 55; *CPJ* III 454, 468) and some synagogues included subgroups organized by occupation, including goldsmiths, silversmiths, and clothing workers, according to a passage in *Tosefta Sukkah* (4.6; cf. Applebaum 1974b:476; Kasher 1985:352–53).

There are some indications of the socioeconomic makeup of synagogues. Although much of the evidence for Jewish civic citizenship in the first two centuries is notoriously complex and ambiguous (cf. Applebaum 1974a; Trebilco 1991:167–85), it seems that individual Jews could sometimes gain local citizenship (and attain civic office at least after 212 C.E. [*Digest* 50.2.3.3]); we also know of cases where Jews were Roman citizens, including the apostle Paul (according to Acts). Evidence for diaspora Jews suggests a range of occupational possibilities similar to those of non-Jews, including artists, physicians, workers in food production or sale, workers in clothing production or sale, and smiths (in gold or bronze).[8] But there were also wealthier Jews or Jewish families, women included, who owned slaves and could afford to provide a local synagogue with a place to meet or the funds to decorate one that existed (cf. *CIJ* 738 = *DFSJ* 13 [Phokaia]; *ISmyrna* 295 = *CIJ* 741 [Rufina]; Trebilco 1991:104–26).

Turning from immigrants to emigrants, similar associational tendencies were at work among those from Asia Minor who moved elsewhere in the empire for business or other reasons (including enslavement, military service, etc.). There were associations of Lycians (from both Kaunos and Pinara) and Pisidians (from Termessos) living in Sidon in Syria in the Hellenistic era (Macridy 1904:549–56 [*politeuma*]), and there were associations of Lycians, Cilicians, and Ionians (some of them soldiers) in Hellenistic and Roman Egypt (*SB* 6025, 6664, 7270 [*politeuma*]; *OGIS* 145–48, 157 [*koinon*]; *SB* 8757 = *IGR* I 1078; cf. Lüderitz 1994). There was a substantial community of immigrants from Miletos living in Hellenistic and Roman Athens (*IG* II.2 1996, 2024, 2026, 2271).

Several groups of this type are known in Rome and other cities of Italy (La Piana 1927). A group of Sardians met regularly at Rome (*IGUR* 85, 86, 87), as did the Ephesian shippers and merchants, for instance (*IGR* I 147; cf. *IGUR* 1355, 1491, 1563). The "corporate body" (*politeuma*) of Phrygians devoted to the Great Mother at Pompeii (*IGR* I 458; cf. Kayser 1994:232–36, no. 74) had its counterparts at Rome, where these associations consisted, in part, of freedmen and slaves of Phrygian background who belonged to the imperial household (cf. La Piana 1927:289–302).

Asians who emigrated to regions such as Macedonia, Thrace, and Italy were especially likely to gather together in the form of the Dionysiac mystery societies so familiar to them at home (cf. Edson 1948:154–58; Nilsson 1957:50–51). There was a Dionysiac "company (*speira*) of Asians" both at Dionysopolis and at Montana in Moesia; a benefactor named Marcus supplied the pillars for a "Baccheion of Asians," dedicating his gift on behalf of the emperors and the civic institutions of Perinthos in Thracia.[9] Several inscriptions from Thessalonica attest to a "cult society (*thiasos*) of Asians" there (*IG* X.2 309, 480; Edson 1938:154–58, no. 1). In such cases it seems that regional identity played a fundamental role in origins and membership, though certainly such a group might also begin to include locals among its numbers as the social network connections of native Asians expanded in their new home (cf. Edson 1948:154–55).

Contrary to a tradition in scholarship, extralocal links could play a significant role in the lives of some associations, especially those for whom ethnic, civic, or regional identity persisted (cf. Ascough 1997a). When the civic institutions of Nysa (east of Ephesus) passed a decree honoring their influential benefactor, T. Aelius Alkibiades, they were also sure to single out for mention his benefactions to an association (*kollegion = collegium*) of Nysaians living in Rome, who evidently maintained contacts with the aristocracy and institutions of their homeland (c. 142 c.e.; Clerc 1885 [side B]; cf. *IEph* 22 [side A only]). It is significant that Alkibiades was also a patron to both the Roman and Asian branches of the "worldwide" Dionysiac performers (actors, musicians, and dancers), groups that clearly maintained contacts with one another throughout the empire. Similar examples of the continuation of interregional contacts could be cited for various other associations, including the settlement (*katoikountes*) of Tyrian merchants (from Syria) at Puteoli in Italy who, after about a century of existence, wrote to their homeland for financial assistance in paying their rent (100,000 denarii a year). The city of Tyre responded by asking another group of Tyrian merchants, the one at Rome, to help those at Puteoli (*OGIS* 595 = *IGR* I 421 = *CIG* 5853; cf. MacMullen 1974b:84–85; La Piana 1927:255–59 [with trans.]; c. 174 c.e.).

Neighborhood or Locational Connections

Neighborhood networks form a third basis of membership for associations. Inhabitants of a particular street, district, or neighborhood (sometimes coinciding with occupational background) could act together corporately, sometimes becoming an ongoing group with social and religious purposes comparable to other types of associations. What interests us here are those groups that continued to *identify themselves* primarily in terms of locational considerations. There are three main terms used by such groups: "settlement" (*katoikountes*), "neighborhood" (*geitosynē, geitniasis*), and "street" (*plateia*).

Thus at Pergamum a "settlement of the acropolis" set up honorary inscriptions on more than one occasion, once for Nero (cf. Josephus, *J.W.* 7.73). At about the same time, another group that called itself "the settlement of Paspareitai street," including one dyer and perhaps a mixture of other artisans in its number, honored L. Cuspius Pactumeius Rufinus, a Roman consul who was also priest of Zeus Olympios (c. 140–150 C.E.; *IPergamon* 393, 424, 434; *IGR* IV 425; cf. *IStratonikeia* 536, 539–40). Though location-based groups could include a mixture in terms of occupation or gender, persons living or working in a particular area were more likely to reflect similar social brackets.

There were similar "neighborhood" associations in the region of Phrygia in Asia. At Saittai (east of Thyatira) a neighborhood honored a member on his epitaph (*TAM* V 90 [198 C.E.]). At Orkistos "those from the neighborhood of the adjacent countryside," who are also called members of a brotherhood (*phratorōn*), set up an offering for a god in fulfillment of a vow after their prayer had been answered (*IGR* IV 548; cf. *IGR* III 21 [Kios]). A Christian epitaph from third-century Akmoneia involves another association of this type. Aurelius Aristeas promises "the neighborhood of those by the gateway" provisions for regular banquets if they fulfill their obligation by putting roses on his wife's grave once a year (*IPhrygR* 455–57). Although of a later period, this inscription shows that Christians, like others, could follow the usual practice in including (neighborhood) associations or guilds among the recipients of funerary foundations. Similar neighborhood associations are attested in other provinces of Asia Minor, as at Prusa in Bithynia and Termessos in Pamphylia.[10]

A discussion of groups whose membership consisted of those who lived (or worked) on a particular "street" will serve as an appropriate transition to occupation-based associations. For example, numerous associations at Phrygian Apameia (northeast of Colossae) identified themselves by the colonnaded street where they worked. On several occasions in the mid-second century, the civic institutions (council and people) joined with the settlement of Romans to honor prominent civic functionaries and priests. In each case one of three different street-based associations set up the honorary decree "from their own resources": those from Bath (Thermaia) street, the artisans (*techneitai*) from Shoemaker street, and the traders (*ergastai*) from Bath street (*IGR* IV 788–91 = *IPhrygR* 294–96, 299). Similar street associations, some of them clearly of an occupational nature, are known at Ephesus, Mylasa, Saittai, and Smyrna in Asia, as well as Sura in Lycia and Canathai in Arabia (*IEph* 454, 3080; *IMylasa* 403; *TAM* V 79–81; *ISmyrna* 714; *IGR* III 711–13, 1230; cf. Robert 1937:529–38).

Occupational Connections

One's occupation and the networks of relations it entailed were in many ways a determining factor in socioreligious affiliations. Membership in an occupation-based association or "guild" (*synergasia*, the most common designation) was less than "voluntary" in the sense that, if one was a dyer or merchant, one naturally or by default (so to speak) associated with one's fellow workers in the guild of dyers or merchants. Still, it was possible to maintain simultaneous affiliations with, or memberships in, more than one association at a time (cf. Meiggs 1960:321–22; *Digest* 47.22.1.2). In considering occupation-based associations as a separate category, we must not forget the important role of familial factors here as well. It was common practice in antiquity for sons to follow in their father's footsteps when it came to profession, so it would not be surprising to find particular families at the forefront of certain guilds from one generation to the next. On the other hand, there were times when one's professional affiliations created family ties, as when a goldsmith at Laodikeia Combusta (in Galatia) married the daughter of the head goldsmith (*MAMA* I 281).

A wide range of these occupational associations existed in the cities and villages of Asia (see fig. 5). We find associations of those who supplied the necessities of life, including bakers, fishers, and farmers, as well as builders and physicians. Associations of clothing producers are well attested throughout Asia, especially in Phrygian towns such as Thyatira, where there were guilds of clothing cleaners, leather cutters, leather tanners, linen workers, and dyers. Producers and sellers of other amenities, such as potters, smiths in copper, silver, and gold, and merchants and shippers who dealt in various goods likewise formed associations. Entertainment in the form of festivals was an essential aspect of the social and religious life that is reflected in the prominence of guilds of Dionysiac performers and athletes devoted to Herakles, whose position and prestige relative to many other guilds was quite high, and some were more officially recognized than the groups we concentrate on here.

Clothing or Weaving-Related Groups

IEph 454 (hemp workers, linen weavers, wool dealers), 727 (wool dealers), 3063 (clothing sellers), 3803 (wool dealers).

IHierapJ 342 (carpet weavers); *IPhrygR* 8 (Laodicea, clothing cleaners); *IHierapJ* 50, *SEG* 41 (1991) 1201 (dyers); *IHierapPenn* 45 (linen dealers); *IHierapJ* 41, 42, 133, 195, 227, 342 (purple-dyers); *IHierapJ* 40 (wool cleaners).

Pergamum area: IGR IV 425 (dyers?); *IGR* IV 1169 (Attaleia).

Philadelphia: IGLAM 656 (leather tanners); *IGR* IV 1632 (wool workers).

ISaitt 26, *TAM* V 86 (clothing cleaners); *ISaitt* 31 (felt makers); *TAM* V 79, 80, 81, *ISaitt* 25 (leather workers); *TAM* V 82, 83, 84, *ISaitt* 30, *SEG* 40 (1990) 1088 (linen workers); *TAM* V 85, *ISaitt* 32 (wool workers).

ISmyrna 218 (hemp workers?).

Thyatira: SEG 40 (1990) 1045 (clothing cleaners); *TAM* V 935, 945, 965, 972, 978, 980, 989, 991, 1029, 1081 (dyers); *TAM* V 1002, *SEG* 41 (1991) 1033 (leather cutters); *TAM* V 986 (leather tanners); *TAM* V 1019, 933 (linen workers).

ITralles 79 (linen weavers).

Food Related Groups

IEph 215 (bakers); *IEph* 728, *SEG* 35 (1985) 1109-10 (wine-tasters); *IEph* 20, 1503 (fish-sellers); *IEph* 3216 (measurers).

IHierapPenn 25 (farmers); *IHierapPenn* 7 (water-millers).

ISmyrna 715 (fishermen); *LSAM* 17 (fishermen?).

Thyatira: TAM V 966 (bakers).

Potters, Smiths, and Artists

IEph 2402 (potters); *IEph* 425, 457, 585, 586, 2212, 2441 (silversmiths).

IHierapJ 133 (coppersmiths).

ISmyrna 721(goldsmiths and silversmiths).

Thyatira: TAM V 914 (potters); *TAM* V 936 (coppersmiths).

Building- and Service-Related Groups

IEph 2213 (bed builders); *IEph* 2115, 3075 (carpenters, builders); *IEph* 3216 ("workers").

IHierapJ 133 (nail workers).

IMagnMai 239 (assistant builders).

ISaitt 28 (carpenters).
ISmyrna 204, 205, 713 (porters).
ITralles 162 ("workers"); *IGLAM* 1666c (stone cutters).

Bankers, Merchants, and Traders (Excluding "Romans")
IEph 454 (bankers); *IEph* 800, 3079 (merchants and traders).
ISmyrna 642 (bankers?).
Thyatira: TAM V 862 (businessmen); *TAM* V 932 (slave merchants).

Physicians
IEph 719, 1161-67, 2304, 4101a-b.

Entertainment- and Festival-Related Groups
IEph 22 (Dionysiac performers); *IEph* 1084, 1087, 1088, 1089, 1098,
    1122 (athletes of Herakles); *IEph* 3055, 3070, *IGladiateurs* 200,
    201, 202, 204-208 (gladiators).
IHierapJ 36 (athletes).
IMagnMai 237 (flutists and acrobats).
ISmyrna 217, 709 (athletes); *IGladiateurs* 225, 240, 241; *ISmyrna* 598,
    599, 639 (Dionysiac performers).
Thyatira: TAM V 977, 984, 1097 (athletes); *TAM* V 1033 (performers).
ITralles 50, 65 (Dionysiac performers); *ITralles* 105, 109, Robert
    1937:412-13, no. 3 (athletes).

FIGURE 5: Some occupational associations in Roman Asia

Social networks associated with occupation and trade were a key factor in the formation and ongoing life of some Christian groups (cf. Humphries 1998). When a leader like Paul traveled to cities such as Ephesus, Corinth, or Thessalonica, the workshop and social connections based on occupation seemed to play a significant role (cf. Acts 18:2–3; Malherbe 1983:89–91 on Acts 19:9; Hock 1980). Although we should not take at face value Celsus's predominantly lower-class characterization of the Christian movement as a whole (he was a strong critic of Christianity), there is truth in his observation, about a century after Paul, that attachments through workshops of wool workers, shoemakers, and clothing cleaners continued to be a key resource for newcomers to some Christian groups (in Origen, *Against Celsus* 3.55). In light of the importance of work settings, then, it is not surprising to find that there were some Christian assemblies whose membership seems to derive primarily from networks associated with occupation or trade, such as those at Thessalonica (cf. Ascough 1997b, 2001). Paul emphasizes his own handwork in identifying with these particular Christians, even mentioning that he and his companions "worked night and day . . . while we preached to you the gospel of God" (1 Thess 2:9, 4:9–12; cf. 2 Thess 3:6–15). In cases where a congregation drew its membership primarily from occupational or business networks, the makeup of the group could be more homogeneous both in socioeconomic level and gender makeup than was the case with some other associations.

This brings us to issues pertaining to the composition of occupational associations more generally. The social status of craftsmen and traders is especially important here since we find such persons within many types of associations beyond just guilds, including Christian assemblies and Jewish synagogues. The upper-class disdain for work of any kind, especially manual labor but also trading or commerce generally, is abundantly clear in literary sources spanning the centuries from Herodotus (5th century B.C.E.) to Lucian (2d century C.E.), though there were exceptions to this among some philosophers.[11] A statement by Plutarch is indicative of views among upper-class writers: "[while] we delight in the [artistic] work, we despise the workman . . . it does not necessarily follow that, if the work delights you with its grace, the one who wrought it is worthy of your esteem" (*Pericles* 1.4–2.2 [LCL]). Similarly, Cicero includes all work involving manual labor among the "vulgar" (*sordidus*) means of livelihood, "for no workshop can have anything liberal about it." He gives special mention to the vulgarity of "fish-dealers, butchers, cooks, poulterers, and fishermen." Other professions, he admits, involved a "higher degree of intelligence," such as physicians, architects, and teachers, and therefore were less undesirable. Still, the true gentleman was supposed to derive his wealth not from trade or manual labor but from "agriculture," that is, landownership (*On Offices* 1.150–51; cf. Finley 1985a:35–61; D'Arms 1981). The status of workers of any occupation was extremely low, "vulgar," from the perspective of many upper-class authors, with some exceptions (cf. Dio Chrysostom, *Orations* 7.113–17).

In spite of this expression of general disdain in literature, however, it seems that workers' understanding of their own occupation and status in relation to the civic community where they lived was often very different. Alison Burford's study stresses that workers and artisans "shared to some extent a positive attitude towards their profession, which gave them all a certain confidence and independence of mind in the face of whatever pressures the rest of society saw fit to bring to bear upon them" (1972:27;

cf. Joshel 1992). Artisans often identify themselves by occupation on gravestones, sometimes depicting their tools or a workshop scene in relief (see Burford 1972, figs. 3–24, 41, and 46–48). The very existence of guilds is a testimony to the identity and pride that characterized workers of many trades such that they would attempt (and succeed, as we will discover) to find a place as a group within the polis, even maintaining contacts with the civic and provincial elites. The aristocracy's actual benefactions and other positive relations with guilds did not necessarily reflect the disdain expressed in literary sources.

Although craftsmen and traders were primarily among the nonelite segment of society, there was nevertheless a range of possibilities of wealth and status within the strata from which the guilds (and other associations) drew much of their membership. Certain occupations might be considered more desirable or conducive to gaining wealth than others. For instance, shippers or traders could hope to attain greater wealth and prestige within the wider community than, say, local tanners whose work involved undesirable odors and clothing cleaners whose labor by nature involved the burning of sulphur and urine (see Lucian, *Navigation*; Philostratus, *Life of Apollonios* 4.32; D'Arms 1981). In the case of clothing production, the status of those involved in the preparation of the more luxurious clothing, such as the purple-dyers, might exceed that of the regular clothing workers and dyers involved in the production of daily clothing for locals, though any of these occupations could also include ex-slaves (cf. Pleket 1983:139–40; *NewDocs* II 3). Silversmiths or goldsmiths who produced the statues that were necessary for appropriately honoring the gods, as well as the luxury items purchased by the rich, might hope to attain greater wealth or prestige within the polis in comparison with some other occupations, at least in cities such as Ephesus. There one silversmith was on the Artemis sanctuary's board of management (*synedrion* or *synagōgē* of *neopoioi*), a fairly well-respected civic position in the first century (*IEph* 2212 = *NewDocs* IV 1; cf. Acts 19:23–41). Physicians, who possessed some degree of education, would often be viewed as a step above many other occupations in terms of social status (cf. *NewDocs* II 2; Nutton 1977; *SEG* 44 [1994] 1713; *GCRE* 38 [74 C.E.]). The physicians' association at Ephesus, for example, included civic councillors in its membership (*IEph* 946). So guilds could reflect a range of status within local society, and some occupations were viewed more positively than others.

Many craftsmen and traders, as citizens of the polis, commonly played a role as participants in the civic assemblies (also see chapter 3). There were even a few cases when individuals of particular occupations achieved local prestige and wealth that led to the assumption of other important civic positions, such as the slave merchant (*sōmatemporos*) and the dyer at Thyatira who each assumed the relatively important position of market overseer (*agoranomos*; cf. *TAM* V 932, 991; 2d–3d centuries C.E.). There are also cases of craftsmen, traders, or other workers attaining membership in the civic council (*boulē*): shippers at both Ephesus and Nikomedia (Bithynia), a member of the purple-dyer's guild at Hierapolis, goldsmiths at Sardis (who are also Jews), and even a baker at Korykos in Cilicia (*IEph* 1487–88; *SEG* 27 [1977] 828; *IHierapJ* 156; *DFSJ* 22–23; *MAMA* III 756; 1st–3d centuries C.E.).

In light of the discussion thus far, the membership in most occupational associations might be described as relatively homogeneous, consisting primarily of men from a common socioeconomic bracket. However, some important qualifications should be made here. Although certainly not widely attested, it is possible that some occupational guilds included women in their number, particularly in the case of occupations for which there is evidence of women's engagement (cf. Wilhelm 1932; Kampen 1981; van Minnen 1986; Saavedra Guerrero 1991; von Drexhage 1992). One wonders whether Lydia the purple-dyer from Thyatira (Acts 16:11–15) or Elpis the purple-dealer at Kos, buried alongside a fellow worker (*CIG* 2519), would have affiliated with an association of others who shared their professions. This was the case with two women at Athens in the fourth century B.C.E. who joined with their fellow clothing washers in dedicating a monument to the nymphs and all the gods (*IG* II.2 2934). This being said, the most widely attested links between women and guilds are cases where the woman in question was a wealthy benefactor or the recipient of honors rather than an ordinary member.

Another important point that should caution us in assuming that all guilds were homogeneous are cases where a range of wealth and social status is evident in a particular group, despite the members sharing a common profession. The case of the fishermen and fish dealers (*hoi halieis kai opsariopōlai*) at Ephesus is instructive (*IEph* 20 = *NewDocs* V 5). This association consisted of approximately one hundred members (89 are legible in the inscription) who, together with their families, contributed toward the building and dedication of the fishery toll office in the mid-first century. The contributors are listed in order of the size of donation ranging from the four columns donated by Publius Hordeonius Lollianus with his wife and children to those who gave five denaria or less. This range of donations evidently represents the spectrum of wealth among the members' families.

In the same inscription, there are other indications of heterogeneous membership in this association. Studies by G. H. R. Horsley (1989) and Steven Michael Baugh (1990) demonstrate that the membership included Roman citizens of freed and free status (43–44 members; approximately 50 percent of the legible names), persons of nonservile status (between 36 and 41 members; about 45 percent), and several slaves (between 2 and 10 members; 3 percent or more). The presence of so many members possessing Roman citizenship, some of whom have sufficient wealth to build several columns, should caution us in assuming that Cicero's view of fish dealers as "vulgar" necessarily represents the actual socioeconomic and citizenship possibilities for such workers. It is more than likely that some other guilds, for which we lack such a list of membership, included such a mix of members of free, freed, and servile status with differing levels of wealth (cf. Kampen 1981:31).

Cult or Temple Connections

Appropriately honoring gods and goddesses through offerings and rituals (sacrifices, prayers, singing, mysteries) in a group setting was a concern of virtually all types of associations, as we shall see. Nonetheless, there are associations whose membership appears to draw primarily from social networks connected with a specific cult or sanctuary, and whose continuing group identity, both in the view of members and of outsiders, was expressed in terms of devotion to the deity or deities.[12] Here we are concerned with ongoing, unofficial groups of what we could call laypersons, not with official boards of temple functionaries. Even so, these unofficial associations could sometimes continue to meet within a sanctuary and occasionally participate as a group within the activities of a larger cult officially connected with the polis.

There was an array of such associations in Asia during the Roman era, including those devoted to Apollo, Aphrodite, Artemis, Asklepios, Cybele and Attis, Zeus, and the emperors as gods (*Sebastoi*), as well as messengers of the gods ("angels") or heroes, to name just a few.[13] Here I discuss for illustration those devoted to the following gods and goddesses: Men and Sabazios, Isis and Serapis, Demeter and Kore, Dionysos, and the Israelite or Jewish God (including Christians). Although the social status and gender makeup of many of these associations is elusive, there are some indications that are worth noting. E. N. Lane's study (1971–76) of those who dedicated monuments to the god Men (a native Phrygian deity associated with the moon) in Asia Minor suggests that they were primarily free persons or peasants from a variety of occupations, but a few were slaves. Associations dedicated to Men that we do know of in Phrygia were either solely male or a mixture of both men and women.[14] In cases where we can discern the membership in associations devoted to Sabazios (another native Phrygian deity, sometimes associated with Dionysos), men predominate, though the Sabaziasts at Teos honor a woman named Eubola on her grave. If the poor writing on the monuments for Sabazios is any indication, many worshipers of this god were of lesser economic means and little education.[15]

There were also many associations of initiates (*mystai*) in "the mysteries" in Asia Minor, including those devoted to Isis and Serapis, the Great Mother (Cybele), Demeter and Kore, and Dionysos. Alongside the staple ritual of sacrifice, "mysteries" (*mystēria, orgia, teletē*) were among the most respected ways of honoring the gods in various contexts (cf. Burkert 1987). The term "mysteries" could encompass a variety of practices, including sacrifice, communal meals, reenactment of the myths of the gods, sacred processions, and hymn singing; most important for initiation into such associations was the unveiling of sacred symbols (associated with a particular deity) by the "revealer of the sacred objects" (*hierophantēs*), often in lamplight. There was also a range of possibilities in the social and gender makeup of these mystery associations, so it is worth sketching out what we do know about the status of their members.

Associations devoted to Egyptian deities, especially initiates in the mysteries of Isis and Serapis, are attested in Asia.[16] Apuleius's famous description of a procession in honor of Isis suggests the importance of groups of women in the worship of this goddess (*Metamorphoses*, book 11). As Sharon Kelly Heyob (1975:81–110) warns, however, we should not exaggerate the role of women, for of the 1,099 inscriptions in Ladislav Vidman's catalogue (1969), for example, only 200 or 18.2 percent happen to mention women who were priestesses, members of associations, or devotees of the goddess.

Initiates devoted to Demeter (the Grain Mother) and Kore (the Maiden)—deities initially associated with the sanctuary at Eleusis, near Athens—were quite prevalent in some cities of Asia, especially at Ephesus, Smyrna, and Pergamum.[17] Worshipers of Demeter Karpophoros ("fruit bearer") are known at Ephesus and its vicinity from several inscriptions from the first and second centuries (cf. Herrmann 1998 [Sardis]).[18] Several inscriptions from the vicinity of the sanctuary of Demeter at Pergamum (mostly from the early 2d century) attest to initiates in the mysteries of the goddess as well as female hymn singers, and there was at least one "company" (*speira*) that included women in its membership.[19] At Smyrna we find a group of initiates of Kore (*ISmyrna* 726) and a synod of initiates of Demeter Thesmophoros ("lawgiver"; *ISmyrna* 653–54, 655). Groups devoted to Demeter could consist of both men and women as leaders and members, and some were solely women. In terms of social status, it seems that they included at least some wealthy members in their number, especially as priests and priestesses, alongside the more general membership, which would probably include a range of possibilities.[20]

By far the best-attested mystery associations in Asia are those devoted to Dionysos or Bacchus (associated with Thrace or Phrygia in some mythology), so it is worth giving a bit more attention to them (see the list in the appendix; cf. Nilsson 1957; Henrichs 1978, 1983; Cazanove 1986; Merkelbach 1988). Setting aside official guilds of Dionysiac performers (*technitai* = actors, musicians), we find unofficial associations in many cities and villages. A very important inscription from Magnesia on the Maeander River (set up in the mid-2d century c.e.) relates a myth concerning the introduction of maenads ("frenzied" female followers of the god) and cult societies to that city (*IMagnMai* 215; see Henrichs 1978). In the mid-third century b.c.e., so the story goes, a miraculous sign—an image of Dionysos—appeared after a tree was hit by lightning, and the people of Magnesia sent messengers to consult the oracle at Delphi about the meaning of this sign. Apollo's response was quite clear, calling on the people to dedicate temples to Dionysos and to "come unto Thebes' holy ground, so that you may receive maenads . . . who will give to you good rites and customs and will consecrate Bacchic cult societies (*thiasous*) in the city." This foundation story, whether true or not, was still important to groups of initiates in the Roman era, which, unlike the associations in the story, included men in their ranks. In the early second century, a similar mixed group of initiates met in a "sacred house (*oikos*)" in the nearby district of Klindos (*IMagnMai* 117; cf. *IErythrai* 132). This group consisted of both male and female leaders and members, including a chief initiate, two men that are each called "foster father" (*appas*), a "nurse" (*hypotrophos*) of Dionysos, a "revealer of the holy objects," and a priestess.

A similar association of initiates apparently met outside the city walls of Ephesus. During the reign of Hadrian, M. Antonius Drosos was their superintendent (*epimelētēs*) along with other leaders with Roman citizenship, one of whom, T. Claudius Romulus, was also one of the presidents of the polis (*prytanis*; *IEph* 275, 1020, 1601; cf. *IEph* 293, 434, 1595; Merkelbach 1979). At Smyrna there was a synod of initiates devoted to Dionysos Breseus. This group had its origins in the first century and even

FIGURE 6: Statue of Silenos holding the baby Dionysos, now in the Louvre (early modern copy of a Hellenistic original).

maintained some diplomatic contacts with emperors in the mid-second century (*ISmyrna* 731–32 [c. 80s–90s C.E.], 600–601, 622, 639). A separate group devoted to Dionysos in Smyrna met under the leadership of a "revealer of the god" (*theophantēs*) in the second or early third century; these initiates had a series of purity regulations—some reflecting the influence of Orphic dietary practices[21]—concerning entrance into their "sanctuary of the Thunderer (Bromios)" (*ISmyrna* 728; cf. Nilsson 1957:133–43).

Dionysos Kathegemon ("the leader") held a prominent position within religious life at Pergamum and in some of the cities most directly influenced by it (e.g., Philadelphia), so it is not a surprise to find abundant evidence for Dionysiac associations here (cf. von Prott 1902; Ohlemutz 1968:90–122; Athanassakis 1977; Burkert 1993). The bacchants who dedicated an altar to King Eumenes in the second century B.C.E. find their successors in the "dancing cowherds" (*hoi choreusantes boukoloi*) of the Roman era. The precise origin of this designation of male followers as herdsmen is not certain. In Euripides' version of the myth (late 5th century B.C.E.), the shepherds and cowherds stand in awe of the maenads of Dionysos and are somewhat helpless when the ecstatic women begin to tear apart their herds (*Bacchae* 714–75). In light of this display of the great power of the god, one of the herdsman (the messenger) urges the king to welcome Dionysos to Thebes (*Bacchae* 768). In Roman Asia Minor, the title "dancing cowherds" is clearly used for those who said prayers, sang hymns, and danced in honor of Dionysos (cf. the Orphic hymns in Athanassakis 1977; Artemidorus, *Dream Interpretations* 4.39). Around the turn of the first century, the cowherds at Pergamum consisted primarily of men (though at least two women are mentioned as members), some of them Roman citizens (up to 35 percent of membership).[22] Lucian of Samosata mentions that cowherds who performed Bacchic dances (in Ionia and Pontus) could include "men of the best birth and first rank," as was the case with at least some at Pergamum, though certainly not all (*On the Dance* 79; cf. C. P. Jones 1990). At Philadelphia (a Pergamene foundation) we find several references to a "revealer of the sacred objects" of Dionysos Kathegemon.[23] There were at least two associations, one a "company" (*speira*) with a chief cowherd at its head (*ILydiaB* 8) and another the "initiates gathered around Dionysos Kathegemon" (*ILydiaKP* I 42; 2d century C.E.).

Concerning Dionysiac associations I have not yet mentioned the prominence of children in the mysteries, which corresponds to the prominence of Dionysos's childhood (and his foster father, Silenos) in his myths (see fig. 6; cf. Nilsson 1957:106–15; Henrichs 1983:149–50). We know from several epitaphs—a couple from Asia Minor and others from Italy—that those as young as seven, ten, or seventeen could "speak the rites of Dionysos" or "lead the cult society (*thiasos*) in dances."[24]

As this brief survey of some of the evidence shows, there was a variety of possibilities in the gender and social makeup of Dionysiac groups in Asia Minor. Some consisted solely of women, especially groups of maenads; others in the later Hellenistic and Roman eras began to include a mixture of both men and women or, in some cases, solely men (e.g., the followers of Dionysos Bacchus, "Iobacchoi," at Athens). M. P. Nilsson's overall characterization of Dionysiac associations as consisting primarily of the wealthy (based on evidence from Italy and the Iobacchoi at Athens) is somewhat misleading, at least for Asia Minor. Dionysiac associations of varying economic means could count on benefactions from the wealthy for the construction, modification, or decoration of their meeting places or other provisions for activities. The presence of wealth or influential members does not necessarily exclude a range of socioeconomic standing among the other members of the group.

Similar diversity in composition is evident in the case of associations in Asia that were devoted to the Israelite or Jewish God. The social and gender makeup of associations of Judeans or Jews could vary from one city to the next and even among synagogues at a particular locale, as we saw in the earlier discussion of ethnic-based associations. Yet another phenomenon that deserves discussion here is associations that consisted principally of non-Jews (Gentiles) who adopted at least some Jewish practices and who worshiped the Jewish God in some way. This is a topic that is sometimes discussed in connection with the so-called God-fearers (as they are called in Acts), those Gentiles who, to various degrees, were attracted to the Jewish God or the synagogue and who could potentially become converts (proselytes; cf. S. Cohen 1989). There are indications in literature (besides Acts) that at least some Gentiles as early as the first century adopted practices associated with the Jewish God, especially observance of the Sabbath (cf. Josephus, *Ag. Ap.* 2.282, who is nonetheless exaggerating the point in this apologetic context). Evidence of Gentile associations of this sort does not necessarily imply Jewish "missionizing" in any way.

The group of "associates" (*hetairoi*) at Elaiussa in Cilicia (southwest of Tarsus), calling itself the Sabbatists (*Sabbatistai* or *Sambatistai*), seems to be such an association devoted to the Jewish God with practices relating to the Sabbath (time of Augustus).[25] The decree of this association, which was inscribed on a rock, includes an invitation for members to make offerings to "god Sabbatistes," a proposal to crown the "synagogue leader" (*synagogos*), and the association's statutes. Among these statutes is a rule that members are to swear that they will not entertain strangers in their homes on the day of the group's gathering (probably to prevent such visitors from attending). Suggestions that Sabbatistes was a "pagan" deity (e.g., Schulze 1966; Ziebarth 1896:61, Youtie 1944; Nilsson 1961:665–66) suffer from a lack of evidence confirming the existence of this god. The inscription nowhere mentions *Ioudaios/oi*, so an identification of the group as actual (syncretistic) Jews or Judeans is problematic (e.g., Hicks

1891:235–36; Dittenberger in *OGIS*). The most likely option remains that this is an association of Gentiles who engaged in practices relating to the Sabbath and who worshiped either the Jewish God (under the name Sabbatistes) or, possibly, the Jewish Sibyl (prophetess) Sambathe (see Tcherikover 1964:84; Feldman 1993:360, 368; Schürer 1973–87, 3:622–25 [F. Millar]). Like the Erythrean Sibyl, the Chaldean-Hebrew-Jewish Sibyl, who was named Sambathe or Sabbe, was sometimes revered among Gentiles (see Schürer 1973–87, 3:618–25; cf. Pausanius, *Description of Greece* 10.12; *Sib. Or.* 3.809).

Other evidence for Gentile associations worshiping the Jewish God comes from associations devoted to "god Most High," or "the Highest god" (Theos Hypsistos), in the Bosporan kingdom, north of Asia Minor on the Black Sea. In the second and third centuries (from 155 C.E.) there were numerous associations (*thiasoi, synodoi*) devoted to "Most High" (Hypsistos) in the cities of the Bosporus, especially at Tanais (cf. *IPontEux* II 437–56). The leader of these associations was commonly called a "synagogue leader" (*synagogos*). Though certainly not all associations that identified their god as "Most High" have Jewish connections (or even quasi-monotheistic tendencies), both Irina Levinskaya and Stephen Mitchell argue that some of these groups at Tanais, in particular, were associations of Gentiles worshiping the Jewish God.[26] Later on, several church fathers of the fourth century (including Epiphanius and Gregory of Nazianzus) complain of the existence of similar "prayer houses" (*proseuchai*) or gatherings of Gentiles ("pagans") that were offshoots of neither Christianity ("heresies") nor Jews (by ethnicity). The associations discussed by these church fathers focused their worship on the Jewish God as Pantokrator ("All-Powerful") and adopted practices relating to the Sabbath and some dietary practices (for the evidence see S. Mitchell 1999:92–97).

There are far more certain cases than these, however. Christian congregations in Asia were devoted to the Jewish God, some of them consisting principally of Gentiles (cf. 1 Pet 1:14–19; 4:3–4; Eph 2:11–12) and others including a mixture of both Gentiles and Jews. Christian literature pertinent to the province of Asia attests to such groups in various cities (and perhaps villages) including Ephesus, Magnesia on the Maeander River, Pergamum, Philadelphia, Sardis, Smyrna, Thyatira, Tralles, and the cities of the Lycus Valley: Colossae, Hierapolis, and Laodicea. There was considerable diversity among congregations of this region in the first two centuries, including Johannine, Pauline, Montanist, Marcionite, docetic/proto-Gnostic, and other forms of Christianity.

It used to be quite common for scholars to speak of early Christianity as, in the words of Adolf Deissmann (1995:8–9), "a movement of the lower classes." The notion that most, if not all, early Christian groups drew their membership primarily from the poorest segments of society has also heavily influenced some studies of Christian literature relevant to Asia. For example, John H. Elliott's study of 1 Peter assumes that the "vast majority" of its recipients were literally "aliens" from the "working proletariat of the urban and rural areas" of Asia Minor (Elliott 1990:59–100, esp. 70–72). He goes on to portray the social situation of this "proletariat," "the ignorant and exploited masses," in harsh terms, citing a study by Samuel Dickey (1928). A corollary of these harsh socioeconomic circumstances and experiences of deprivation, Elliott suggests, was a milieu most conducive to the success of a sectarian movement with an apocalyptic message. Such an understanding of Christian assemblies generally, as well as the nature of conditions in Asia Minor under Roman rule, is problematic.

Beginning especially in the 1980s scholars have shifted away from this sort of characterization toward an acknowledgment that Christian congregations were "more nearly a cross section of society than we have sometimes thought," as Floyd V. Filson (1939:111) observed long ago. Studies by Abraham J. Malherbe, Meeks, and others emphasize that although we lack sufficient information to provide detailed profiles of the social level of Christians, there are indications that many groups reflected a mixture of socioeconomic levels (cf. Judge 1960; Malherbe 1983:29–59; Theissen 1982; Meeks 1983:51–73; Lampe 1989; Holmberg 1990:21–76). Within this mixture, Meeks (1983:73) suggests that the "typical Christian" was a "free artisan or trader," though, as I said earlier, there was certainly a range of possibilities in wealth and status within such segments of society.

Evidence for Christianity in Asia Minor specifically also reflects a cross section of society. The Christians brought before Pliny the Younger (Roman governor of Bithynia-Pontus), represented "individuals of every age and class, both men and women," among them some Roman citizens and two female deaconesses (*Epistles* 10.96.4, 8–9). In a more general sense, the inclusion of household codes giving advice to both husbands and wives, masters and slaves in 1 Peter, the Pastoral Epistles, and Ignatius's epistles implies that some of each were present in the groups addressed. The Pastoral Epistles' guidelines on the selection of leaders reflects the presence of some persons of considerable wealth, and the epistles of Ignatius and of John likewise mention wealthier figures, such as Diotrephes and Polycarp, who assumed leadership within congregations (see Maier 1991:155–56; *Mart. Pol.* 5.1; 6.1–2; Ign. *Pol.* 4.3).

Having made these generalizations regarding composition, we must remain aware of the possibilities of differences in the makeup of Christian groups from one city to the next in the same region or even from one group to another in a particular locality. For instance, while the congregation at Smyrna in the late first century may have drawn the greater part of its membership from those of limited financial means, the Christians in nearby Laodicea appear to include a relatively high proportion of those with considerable wealth, probably gained through trade (Rev 2:9; 3:17). I have already noted the probability that some congregations might be better described as more homogeneous, occupational guilds, drawing membership from a similar socioeconomic level and gender (as at Thessalonica), while others might rest on household connections, reflecting the social spectrum associated with that institution.

Conclusion

Many unofficial associations in Asia Minor drew their membership primarily from among the nonelite population, rather than from the upper strata that could boast of senatorial or equestrian rank or of holding the most important civic positions (though there were certainly some elite associations such as the Arval Brothers at Rome). The civic and imperial elites were important for associations primarily as benefactors or leaders, even though there were some that did act as leaders of associations. Furthermore, we must also beware of imagining that the nonelite segments of the population were homogeneous, that they were predominantly poor and deprived, for instance; instead, there was a range in levels of wealth and social status within these strata of society, and the membership of many associations reflects this range.

When we consider associations in terms of the principal social networks that informed their membership, here identifying five types, we begin to draw a better picture of variety in composition. An association deriving from networks associated with a particular household could reflect the spectrum of dependents associated with such familial structures, both men and women of free, freed, and servile origins. While some geographic-ethnic groups could consist solely of men (sometimes of a common profession), others included both men and women in their number as members or leaders. Location-based associations could consist of a mixture of occupations, depending on the neighborhood in question. On the one hand, many occupational associations could be somewhat homogeneous, consisting of men of a common level of wealth and status. On the other, there were cases when a particular guild reflected a social spectrum with respect to citizenship, wealth, legal standing, and status overall.

Variety, rather than uniformity, is also the case with those groups that appear to be based on social connections associated with a particular deity or sanctuary. While an association devoted to the god Men in a village of Lydia might include both men and women of modest means in its number, another devoted to Dionysos or Serapis elsewhere might include a member or leader wealthy enough to pay for a new mosaic, and one who was perhaps also a Roman citizen or civic functionary. Jewish synagogues and Christian assemblies, too, could differ in composition from one locality to another, some reflecting the social spectrum of society more fully than others.

Here I have focused primarily on Roman Asia, but it is worth briefly noting that other studies of the composition of associations elsewhere in the empire come to similar conclusions, despite regional variations and diversity. In studying associations (*collegia*) in the West, Ausbüttel (1982:34–48) challenges the common portrait of these groups as consisting of only the poorest in society. Instead, he shows, "the composition of the *collegia* was just as heterogeneous as that of the *plebs* [nonelite classes]," closely reflecting the social structure of the population in towns generally (1982:37, 40 [trans. mine]; cf. Kampen 1981:31). Such issues regarding the range of social strata represented within associations will be of continuing relevance when we assess the involvements of associations in imperial and other aspects of civic life. But first we need to give attention to the internal life of associations and their purposes.

2

Internal Activities and Purposes

Honoring the Gods, Feasting with Friends

Introduction

The new typology provided in the previous chapter sets the stage for a reevaluation of the purposes that various associations served. There has been a tendency among some scholars to downplay the religious purposes of many groups. Moreover, as I argue here, all types of associations served a variety of interconnected social, religious, and funerary functions for their members. The evidence strongly suggests the importance of honoring gods and goddesses within associations of all types. Overall, these functions helped to provide members with a sense of belonging and identity.

The present chapter does not attempt to provide a comprehensive discussion of all activities. Nor does it claim that all associations served the same purposes in precisely the same way. Instead, acknowledging variety, I give a broad overview of the internal life of such groups so that we cannot be misled into believing that imperial dimensions of group life (part two) stood in isolation or that they were the only important aspect of group life. Indeed, we will find that imperial aspects were embedded within the internal life and external relations of associations. In this sense, the portrait of association life here, together with the following chapter on the civic context, provides an essential framework within which we can begin to understand the place of such groups within society in Roman Asia.

The discussion here also begins to sketch out, in broad strokes, similarities between the general functions of associations—social, religious, funerary—and those of both Jewish synagogues and Christian congregations.

FIGURE 7: Monument from Panormos dedicated to Zeus Hypsistos and depicting the meeting of an association (*GIBM* IV.2 1007). (Source: Perdrizet 1899, figure IV).

It was for this reason, in part, that both synagogues and assemblies could be described by ancient observers (including certain Christians and Jews) in terms of association life, despite the peculiarity of monotheism in a polytheistic context.

Visualizing Association Life

Several monuments from Mysia (northwestern Asia Minor) capture in visual form the central thesis of this chapter concerning the interconnected purposes of associations. On them are reliefs depicting something we rarely encounter in surviving evidence: an actual picture of the activities of associations and related scenes that communicate to us something of how these groups understood themselves. One monument from Panormos near Kyzikos, now in the British Museum, was dedicated "to Zeus Hypsistos and to the village by Thallos," a member of the association (see fig. 7; *GIBM* IV.2 1007).[1] The relief consists of three parts that reveal the interrelated purposes of the association and the importance of the gods for group life overall. Immediately beneath the text of the dedication are depicted in a preeminent manner the deities to whom this association granted particularly appropriate honors: Zeus, Artemis, and Apollo. Zeus stands in the center holding a spear in his left hand, and all three hold out the customary libation bowl in their right hands.

Under the beneficent protection of the gods we find on a much smaller scale a depiction of six members of the association reclining to share in a banquet (cf. *CIG* 3699 = Lolling 1884:25–26). This is a scene not unlike what we might imagine for various guilds and associations, such as the Dionysiac cowherds at Pergamum who met in a hall ideal for banqueting, as we shall see. For other associations, especially those devoted to Serapis, members might be very much aware of a deity's presence with them as they offered sacrifice and reclined on benches to eat the accompanying meal. The fusion of social and religious dimensions of group life is completed by the lower panel of the relief, depicting the group's entertainment. On the left a seated man plays a Phrygian double flute while a woman performs a circular dance, likely in honor of the gods. To her right a man uses sticks or reeds to provide percussion while another man oversees the mixing bowl for the wine that accompanied the meal (cf. Hasluck 1904:36–37, no. 58).

Other reliefs demonstrate the prominence of sacrificial offerings for the gods and other forms of rituals or worship. On one occasion, the men

FIGURE 8: Monument from Triglia, near Bithynian Apameia, dedicated in honor of Stratonike, priestess of Cybele and Apollo and depicting the meeting of an association. (Source: Pfuhl and Möbius 1977–79, vol. 2, pl. 332. Deutsches Archäologisches Institut, Athens. Negative no. N M 919.)

and women belonging to a cult society (*thiasos*) near Apamea in Bithynia (Triglia) honored Stratonike, a priestess of Mother Cybele, and Apollo, by setting up a monument with reliefs in the "synagogue of Zeus" (see fig. 8; *IApamBith* 35; likely 85 C.E.).[2] Like the monument I described above, the upper panel depicts the realm of the gods. In this case Stratonike is pictured on the same plane approaching an altar with upraised hands in adoration of both Apollo (who stands beside the altar) and Cybele (who remains seated to the right).[3] This priestess is accompanied by a girl playing a double flute and a boy bringing a sheep for sacrifice (cf. *IApamBith* 33 = Robert 1949a:42, no. 2). Beneath the sacrificial scene ten members of the association gather for a banquet, consuming food and drink while they are entertained by flutists, seen on the left. Beside the musicians is a youth carrying a basket toward two others who are managing the mixing bowls for the wine as some souvlaki roasts to the far right.

Questioning a Tradition in Scholarship

This picture of associations eating and drinking as they gather together under the protection or even in the presence of the deities whom they honor regularly is further confirmed by archeological evidence from throughout Roman Asia. One scholarly tradition, which is apparent in the works of M. P. Nilsson, Ramsay MacMullen, and Nicholas R. E. Fisher, tends to separate the social from the religious in arguing that most associations were primarily concerned with conviviality and other social concerns, in some sense lacking genuinely religious dimensions. Similar views are evident among scholars who have considered imperial cults in the past.

    The gatherings of almost all associations in the Roman era were more an excuse to have a party than a genuine attempt to honor gods, according to Nilsson: "the Dionysiac mystery associations resemble the other very numerous associations of the Hellenistic and following age, which, under the pretext of honoring some god after whom the association was named, assembled in order to enjoy themselves and to feast" (1957:64; cf. Ferguson and Nock 1944:123). For Nilsson, many mysteries performed by groups in the Roman era, including those associated with imperial cults, were merely "pseudo-mysteries."[4] Nilsson is right to compare Dionysiac groups with other associations in that all of them certainly included conviviality among their purposes, but he is mistaken in downplaying religious dimensions in this way. Further on, in connection with his upper-class characterization of most Dionysiac groups, Nilsson's value judgments become even clearer: "These people were not in earnest about religion" (1957:147).

Nilsson does not consider the possibility that in antiquity even social aspects of life, such as banquets, could be infused with religious significance for those who participated. We need not agree with such a view wherein enjoyment of participants is viewed as a telltale sign that they were not interested in genuinely honoring the gods.

Although more balanced in his views, it is more than a coincidence that MacMullen's book on *Roman Social Relations* (1974b) discusses guilds extensively while his book on *Paganism in the Roman Empire* (1981) gives far less attention to them. In the former he discusses the various purposes of occupational associations, including their civic role. But he stresses that it was their social function above all else—"pure comradeship" and feasting— that were important: "if piety counted for much, conviviality counted for more" (1974b:71–87, esp. 77, 80). It is only when he turns to "cult associations" and groups of foreigners that he considers the religious side of life to be of more significance. Yet even his discussion of associations devoted to Mithras (1981) is revealing of these tendencies to downplay religious dimensions of group life. MacMullen emphasizes the down-to-earth aspects of feasting and friendship as the main objectives of such groups to the neglect of the cosmological significance of their communal meals. He disregards that meals could replicate "in the life of the Mithraic community something originally enacted on the divine plane by the cult's gods," as Roger Beck demonstrates (1992:4–5; cf. Burkert 1987:73, 109–11). A similar tradition of scholarship to that of Nilsson and MacMullen is echoed in Fisher's (1988b:1222–23) statement that "although the *collegia* had religious functions, they were above all concerned with status, solidarity, sociability, and aspects of social security."

These scholars are correct in acknowledging the social side of association life. But their corresponding neglect of its religious dimensions, often intertwined with what we might call "social," is problematic. It appears that they are working with a view of religion that distinguishes it rather sharply from feasting and other aspects of life. Modern, Western definitions of religion along the lines of those offered by William James (1902) and Rudolf Otto (1923) focus on the feelings and personal experiences of the individual in relation to the divine as the most important indicators of "genuine" or "true" religion. Some scholars have approached the study of antiquity with similar conceptions. Within this framework, religion is more concerned with solemnity, asceticism, and mysticism than with conviviality and enjoyment, and the focus is on the individual rather than the group or community, on feelings and attitudes rather than activities and rituals.

The present study takes a more open-ended and cross-culturally sensitive approach to the subject. We need to realize that in employing terms such as "religious" and "religion" we are dealing with abstractions that allow us to conceptualize our subject; we are not dealing with objective realities that the groups and persons we are studying would necessarily isolate from other aspects of life. The modern compartmentalization of life into the political, economic, social, and religious does not apply to the ancient context, where "religion" was very much embedded within various dimensions of the daily life of individuals, whose identities were inextricably bound up within social groupings or communities. Within the Greco-Roman context, we are dealing with a worldview and way of life centered on the maintenance of fitting relations among human groups, benefactors, and the gods within the webs of connections that constituted society and the cosmos. To provide a working definition, "religion" or piety in antiquity had to do with appropriately honoring gods and goddesses (through rituals of various kinds, especially sacrificial offerings) in ways that ensured the safety and protection of human communities (or groups) and their members. Moreover, the forms that such cultic honors (or "worship" to use a more modern term) could take do not necessarily coincide with modern or Western preconceptions of what being religious should mean.

Intertwined Social, Religious, and Funerary Dimensions of Association Life

This understanding of ancient religion and of Greco-Roman society and culture specifically will become clearer as we proceed throughout this study. As I argue here, what we would call religious, social, and burial functions of associations were very much interconnected. There is no reason to question the genuineness of their religious dimensions in the sense that appropriately honoring the gods in a variety of ways was a real concern of virtually all types of groups and their members.

Religious Activities

We have already encountered gods and goddesses—and honors for them—in the discussion of various types of associations. The family-based association at Philadelphia performed mysteries in honor of Zeus, Agdistis, and other deities. Phrygians living at Pompeii worshiped Cybele, the Great Mother; and groups of Asians living in Moesia and Macedonia often chose Dionysos as patron. The Roman businessmen at Assos were engaging in typical activities for such groups when they dedicated monuments both to god Augustus's wife, Livia, the "new Hera," and to Roma, "the benefactor of the cosmos" (*IAssos* 19, 20; both early 1st century C.E.). So was the neighborhood association at Prusias who dedicated monuments to Savior Zeus.

Inscriptional evidence, by its very nature, limits the degree to which we should even expect to find rituals and other honors for the gods revealed to us in any detail, if mentioned at all (with the exception of inscribed cult regulations, of course). Inscriptions rarely state what was taken for granted as customary practice. The majority of extant inscriptions pertaining to associations are gravestones (epitaphs) or honorary inscriptions for benefactors (including deities), not cultic guidelines or prescriptions for group life. Nonetheless, it seems that most, if not all, associations chose particular deities as patrons and included rituals in honor of gods or goddesses among their regular activities. Quite often it is not possible, however, to measure the degree to which religious aspects were important for a particular group in comparison with other groups. What is clear is that such practices were significant to virtually all associations. I begin with occupational associations since it is with them that religious aspects are most neglected by scholars such as MacMullen.

The dream books of Artemidorus of Daldis (who resided in Ephesus in the 2d century) supply the social historian with indispensable information regarding social and religious life (cf. Pomeroy 1991), especially revealing the genuine importance of gods and goddesses for members of guilds. It is significant that throughout his guidebook on interpreting dreams he frequently associates workers and craftsmen with the gods whom they worshiped (esp. *Dream Interpretations* 2.33–44). With respect to artisans who appear in dreams he states: "People who have professions that are associated with particular gods signify the gods who are the patrons of the professions in question" (2.44; trans. R. White 1975). It was common knowledge—not only to Artemidorus but also to the social spectrum of persons for whom his dream interpretations were supposed to work—that those of a common occupation frequently devoted themselves to honoring particular deities.

Yet even for artisans themselves, Artemidorus states, "it is more auspicious to see gods who are compatible with the professions of the dreamers than to see gods who are incompatible. For gods who do not assist men in their work are inauspicious" (4.74). This and other commonsense statements (at least to Artemidorus and his readers) are particularly significant since, especially in this case, he is actually revealing what he perceives to be the self-understanding of the artisans themselves (i.e., artisans are the dreamers). The gods were a regular part of the landscape of the populace's dream life as well as waking life, and for workers of many trades appropriately honoring the gods was important (cf. Burford 1972:164–83). The silversmiths of Ephesus who, according to the author of Acts (19:23–41), gathered together a crowd of craftsmen and others in defense of the reputation of Artemis, patron deity of their hometown, would not be exceptional in this regard: "Great is Artemis of the Ephesians!" they shouted.

Sometimes we catch glimpses of these concerns to honor the gods working themselves out in the corporate lives of occupation-based associations in Roman Asia and elsewhere, despite the limitations of archeological evidence. Cases of professional guilds honoring the gods by dedicating altars or other monuments to them could be cited from throughout the Roman world.[5] There were also cases when guilds expressed their devotion to a deity by honoring a religious leader associated with the god, as was the case with both the "fleet" (*stolos*) of fishermen and the guild (*station*) of gardeners that honored Ulpius Karpos of Miletos, who was prophet and priest of "the Most Holy and Most High god (*tou hagiōtatou theou hypsistou*)" (*OGIS* 755–56; 140s C.E.; cf. *IMilet* 205a-b = *SIRIS* 286).

Building remains also clearly communicate the importance of religious aspects among the purposes of occupational associations. Though we lack excavated guild halls in Asia specifically, several halls (*scholae*) used by guilds of builders, shippers, shipbuilders, grain measurers, and others have been excavated at Ostia (a port city of Rome) in Italy. Both Russell Meiggs (1960:324–30) and Gustav Hermansen (1981:55–89) point out that the remains of these buildings, which often included both sanctuaries and banqueting facilities, disclose the intertwined religious and social activities of the guilds. The building of the grain measurers' guild included a general meeting room, a courtyard with a well, a latrine, and a temple dedicated to their patron deity, Ceres Augusta (see the photo of the main meeting room in fig. 9 and building plan in fig. 10; Hermansen 1981:65–66; 2d–3d century C.E.). The meeting hall was decorated with a mosaic floor that proudly depicts members of the guild engaging in their profession (see photo in fig. 11).

Built in the time of Hadrian, the builders' meeting place at Ostia consisted of a central courtyard surrounded by several rooms on all sides (see

FIGURE 9: Main meeting room of the guild of grain measurers at Ostia.

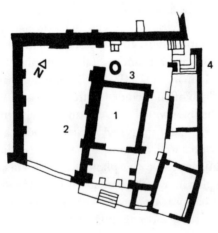

Seat of the grain measurers' guild. 1. Temple of Ceres Augusta. 2. *Schola* of the guild. 3. Yard with well. 4. Latrine. Scale 1:500.

FIGURE 10: Building plan of the grain measurers' meeting place. (Source: Hermansen 1981:65, fig. 14. University of Alberta Press.)

FIGURE II: Mosaic floor depicting a member of the profession carrying grain. (Photo by Teresa Harland.)

the building plan in fig. 12). Most conspicuous was the central room encountered immediately on entering the building, which was the sanctuary where rituals were performed regularly in honor of the guild's patron deities. In the southwestern corner was the kitchen and four other rooms on the east were dining rooms with built in couches (*triclinia*) for reclining to eat (see the photo in fig. 13).

The meeting place of an ethnic-based guild of an earlier era on the Greek island of Delos is also indicative of the importance of cultic purposes. The buildings of associations of various types have been excavated on Delos, including those of the comedian actors, Israelites (Samaritans), Judeans, and Serapis devotees.[6] There is also inscriptional evidence for

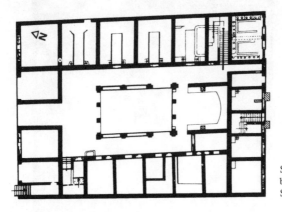

Seat of the house
builders' guild.
Scale 1 :550.

FIGURE 12: Building plan of the builders' meeting place. (Source: Hermansen 1981:63, fig. 12. University of Alberta Press.)

many other ethnic- or geographic-based associations on the island, including the Tyrian merchants and shippers devoted to Herakles (likely identified with the Tyrian god Melkart; cf. *IDelos* 1519), and various groups of Italians or Romans (see Rauh 1993:29–41). The group that concerns us here is the ethnic-based association of Poseidon worshipers from Berytus in Syria, consisting of a mixture of merchants, shippers, and traders (*to koinon berytiōn Poseidōniastōn emporōn kai nauklērōn kai egdocheōn*; cf. *IDelos* 1520, 1772–96; Bruneau and Ducat 1983:174–79, no. 57). This guild met in a residential-style building that had been constructed or adapted sometime before 152 B.C.E. and was used by the guild until the building's destruction in 69 B.C.E.

This guild's concern to honor gods and goddesses alongside its other activities is clearly communicated by the remains that have been unearthed. The building consisted of a large courtyard in the style of a household (F), which the guild dedicated to "the gods of the homeland" (*theois patriois*; *IDelos* 1774; see the building plan in fig. 14). This was the location of various statues and other honorary monuments for benefactors and deities. A well-preserved statue of Aphrodite and Pan (god of the wild, half man and half goat) was also found within the building (see photo in fig. 15). Another courtyard (E) may have been used for commercial activities, and there were several other smaller rooms, some of which were probably used for storage (G-T). One of these rooms (G) may have been used for banquets. An honorary inscription erected by the guild for a Roman benefactor and banker, Marcus Minatius, happens to

FIGURE 13: One of the dining rooms (triclinia) in the builders' meeting place.

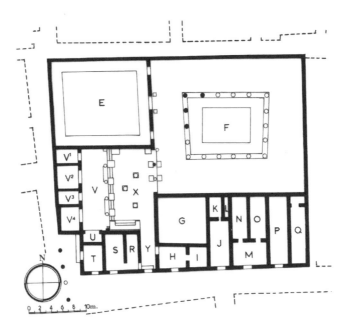

FIGURE 14: Building plan of the meeting place of the merchants, shippers, and traders from Berytus on the island of Delos. (Source: Bruneau and Ducat 1983:175, fig. 46. L'École française d'Athènes.

FIGURE 15: Sculpture of Aphodite and Pan from the meeting place of the merchants, shippers, and traders from Berytus. (Source: Bruneau and Ducat 1983:176, fig. 47. L'École française d'Athènes.)

describe one of the guild's festivals in honor of Poseidon (*IDelos* 1520). This festal gathering under the leadership of the chief of the cult society (*archithiasitēs*) involved a sacrificial procession, offering of an ox, and accompanying meals.

The religious activities of this guild also took place in the sanctuary area in the southwestern section, which consisted of a foyer (pronaos V) along with several shrines (cf. Picard 1920; Bruneau 1978; H. Meyer 1988; Bruneau 1991). Although there is some debate concerning their building history, there were at least three (perhaps four) shrines. By the early first century (88 B.C.E. at the latest) one of these shrines (V^1) contained a statue with an inscribed base for Roma, the guild's "benefactor" (*IDelos* 1778). Another shrine (V^2) was devoted to the patron deity, Poseidon (*IDelos* 2325). A third (and perhaps fourth) was likely dedicated to some of the other "gods of the homeland" often mentioned in the inscriptions, probably including Astarte and perhaps Herakles-Melkart (cf. *IDelos* 1774, 1776, 1781, 1783, 1785, 1789). Here the members of the guild could regularly honor the deities who protected them on a daily basis, ensured their success in business, and contributed to the well-being of their distant homeland. We can imagine similar rituals in honor of the gods taking place within other guilds and ethnic-based associations about whom we happen to know far less.

Returning to occupational guilds in Roman Asia, we sometimes get momentary glimpses of what were common, ongoing internal practices in honor of gods and goddesses. Thus on one epitaph from Teira, near Ephesus, a grain measurer (*prometrēs*) by profession makes provisions for a guild of workers (*ergatai*) to hold a yearly wine banquet in connection with celebrations in honor of Poseidon, apparently their patron deity (*IEph* 3216; cf. van Nijf 1997:60–61). The well-attested "sanhedrin" (*synedrion*) of physicians at Ephesus incidentally reveals in only one of its surviving inscriptions what was central to its ongoing internal life—sacrifice and accompanying ritual feasts—in referring to itself as the "physicians who sacrifice to ancestor Asklepios and to the *Sebastoi*," the revered emperors as gods (*IEph* 719; early 2d century C.E.).

The importance of the gods can be assumed for other occupational associations as well. An association of merchants (perhaps fish dealers) at Kyzikos dedicated a monument to Poseidon and Aphrodite Pontia with a relief depicting a sacrificial scene so familiar to them in their group life (Mordtmann 1885:204–7, no. 30; 1st century B.C.E.). There were two altars in a special shrine dedicated to the great gods (Cabiri) of Samothrace (*Samothraki[o]n*) in the fishery toll office at Ephesus (*IEph* 20.70–71; 54–59 C.E.). These divine protectors of those at sea were evidently the patron deities of the fishermen and fish dealers who made donations to build the structure; some of the members may well have been initiates in the mysteries of these gods. When a guild of builders had doubts about whether they should engage in certain construction work on the theater at Miletos, they turned to the god Apollo at Didyma for advice (c. 120 C.E.):

Should the builders (*hoi oikodomoi*) associated with . . . Epigonos—that is, the contractors (*ergolaboi*) for the section of the theater in which the prophet of the god, the late Ulpianus, was superintendent of works (*ergepistatei*) and the architect, Menophilos, assigns the work—fashion and produce the arches and the vaults over the columns or should they consider other work?[7] The god answered: "For good uses of wise building techniques, it is expedient to consult a skillful man for the best suggestions, performing sacrifices to thrice-born Pallas and strong Herakles."[8]

Apollo's rather vague response regarding their architectural work (suggesting that they consult an expert) is accompanied by a clear prescription that these craftsmen perform sacrifices to Athena and Herakles (cf. Burford 1972:194–95). Offerings of sacrificial victims, other foods, and libations with accompanying banquets were the touchstone of corporate religious piety in the Greco-Roman world, and we can assume that they were a regular part of the lives of all types of associations.

Regular festivals and gatherings associated with honoring the gods were a common feature of group life in other types of associations and could involve a variety of rituals and practices, including mysteries. As Walter Burkert's (1987) study emphasizes, mysteries were not a separate religion to be defined over against the religious life of the city. Rather, mysteries could be incorporated within cultic life in various contexts, including associations. Mysteries were integral for entry into some groups, especially those devoted to Dionysos, Demeter and Kore, Isis and Serapis, or others who called themselves "initiates" (*mystai*). Partially because of the element of secrecy, little is known concerning these rites, but these rituals often involved revelation of objects considered sacred to a particular god—a phallus in a basket for Dionysos and images of gods in other cases.

For other groups, such as the association meeting in the house of Dionysios at Philadelphia, certain states of morality or purity could be required before participating in ritual activities. In this case members were not to deceive one another, use contraceptives, or cause abortions, and the statutes also outline some guidelines as to acceptable sexual relations. The list of requirements concludes with a call for obedience to the gods, stating that "the gods will be gracious to those who obey, and always give them all good things, whatever gods give to men whom they love. But should any transgress, they shall hate such people and inflict upon them great punishments" (*SIG*[3] 985 = *LSAM* 20, lines 46–51; trans. Barton and Horsley 1981:9). The Christians brought before Pliny in Pontus apparently had similar expectations for those participating in their rituals. These

Christians, Pliny states, "bind themselves by oath, not for any criminal purpose, but to abstain from theft, robbery, and adultery, to commit no breach of trust and not to deny a deposit when called upon to restore it" (*Epistles* 10.96.7 [LCL]).

Appropriately honoring the gods by way of rituals was taken very seriously by both individuals and groups. In one of the so-called confession inscriptions (*Beichtinschriften*) of Asia Minor, a man from Blaundos (east of Philadelphia) lamentingly tells of frequent and enduring punishment from the god "because he did not want to come and take part in the mystery when he was called" (*MAMA* IV 281 = Petzl 1994:126, no. 108; 1st–2d century C.E., from Dionysopolis). Although not widely attested, there are even cases when some degree of exclusivism accompanies participation in such rites, as with the worshipers (*therapeutai*) of Zeus at Sardis who were "not to participate in the mysteries of Sabazios . . . and of Agdistis and Ma" (*ISardH* 4 = *NewDocs* I 3; 2d century C.E.).

There is evidence for a variety of other religious practices that were ongoing features of life within associations in Asia. Myths of the gods could be an important component within rituals (cf. Burkert 1987:66–88). At Smyrna, for instance, the initiates of Dionysos Bromios included among their activities an exposition of the story of the Titans (who in some versions of mythology tore apart the child Dionysos), probably done by the functionary called the god-revealer (*theophantēs*; *ISmyrna* 728; 2d–3d century C.E.). The initiates of Demeter thanked two female "theologians" (*theologoi*) who gave expositions or recited hymns in praise of the deity's virtues (like the one for Isis found at Kyme) on the greatness of the goddesses in question (*ISmyrna* 653–54; 1st–2d century C.E.; M. Meyer 1987:172–74). Among the rituals of the worshipers of Dionysos Bacchus (Iobacchoi) at Athens was the priest's pronouncement of a sacred discourse (*theologia*), his sermon. They also engaged in some sort of sacred drama in which members were assigned roles as Dionysos (their patron deity), Kore, Aphrodite, and others, reenacting stories of the gods (*IG* II.2 1368, esp. lines 44–46, 64–67, 121–27; cf. Poland 1909:269–70). Here we are dealing with more than simply a group of "drinking buddies" (*Zechkumpane*), as Engelbert Drerup (1899:357) misleadingly calls them.

Prayers, singing, music, and dancing were also among the means by which the membership in associations fittingly honored the gods. Communities, groups, and individuals sought concrete favors, guidance, or protection from the gods through prayers. In response, votive offerings or gifts for the gods (*euchai*) were one way of recognizing fulfillment of a prayer request, expressing gratitude for the deities' benefactions (cf. van

Straten 1981). For example, an association that met in a sanctuary of Zeus at Philadelphia in Egypt regularly included in its practices a prayer, along with libations and "other customary rites on behalf of the god and lord, the king" (*PLond* 2193 = Roberts, Skeat, and Nock 1936; 1st century B.C.E.). Although the nature of our sources means that we rarely have record of an association actually praying corporately (but see Apuleius, *Metamorphoses* 11.17, cited in chapter 8), we do possess monuments that were set up in connection with a group's earlier prayer request for a favor from a god and the accompanying vow.[9]

Singing and music could be important within various associations (cf. Poland 1926; Quasten 1983). Hymns were an elaborated, sung prayer that also honored the deities whose help was requested, as J. M. Bremer (1981) points out. Quite common in Asia were organizations of boys, girls, or youths who regularly sang in the context of civic cults and festivals.[10] There were also functionaries associated with the composition or performance of hymns in honor of the gods in connection with both the mysteries of Demeter and of Dionysos at Pergamum, for instance (see Hepding 1910:457–59, no. 40; Ippel 1912:287, no. 16; *IPergamon* 485; cf. *IEph* 275, 973–74; *ISmyrna* 758). The so-called Orphic hymns, which likely come from western Asia Minor (probably Pergamum), refer frequently to the Dionysiac initiates and cowherds who sang them (Athanassakis 1977). There were other associations who called themselves "hymn singers" (*hymnōdoi*), like those devoted to Cybele near Thyatira and to Dionysos at Histria in Moesia (*TAM* V 955, 962; *IGLSkythia* I 57, 100, 167, 199, 208, 221).

It is worth mentioning a similar importance for singing within congregations and synagogues. After questioning the Christians brought before him in Pontus, Pliny characterizes their gatherings in terms familiar from association life: they "met regularly before dawn on a fixed day to chant verses alternately amongst themselves in honor of Christ as if to a god" (*Epistles* 10.96.7 LCL). Philo's discussion of the "contemplative life" of the Jewish *therapeutai* in Egypt likewise provides a similar picture concerning the prominence of singing (alongside prayer, meals, and other activities) within worship:

> After the supper they hold the sacred vigil. . . . They rise up all together and standing in the middle of the refectory (*symposion*) form themselves first into two choirs, one of men and one of women. . . . Then they sing hymns (*hymnous*) to God composed of many measures and set to many melodies, sometimes chanting together, sometimes taking up the harmony antiphonally, hands and feet keeping time in accompaniment, and rapt

with enthusiasm reproduce sometimes the lyrics of the procession, sometimes of the halt and of the wheeling and counter-wheeling of a choric
dance. Then . . . having drunk as in the Bacchic rites of the strong wine of
God's love they mix and both together become a single choir. . . . [The]
end and aim of thoughts, words and choristers alike is piety. Thus they
continue till dawn, drunk with this drunkenness in which there is no
shame. (*On the Contemplative Life* 83–89; trans. Colsen 1941–62 [LCL]; cf.
Richardson 1993:348–53)

Philo's description alludes to the analogy of Dionysiac mysteries. His
mention of ritual dancing in honor of God brings us to another aspect of
internal group practices.

We have already encountered musicians and dancers in the earlier discussion of reliefs depicting the meetings of associations devoted to Cybele, Zeus, and others. Lucian's discourse *On the Dance*–set in the form of
a dialogue in which a Cynic, Crato, is convinced of the value of pan-
tomimic dancing by Lycinus–emphasizes the close connection between
dancing and worship of the gods, even suggesting that "not a single ancient mystic rite (*teletēn*) can be found that is without dancing" (*On the
Dance* 15 [LCL]). Along with the discussion of dances associated with
cults in honor of Zeus, Aphrodite, Orpheus, and others, Lucian has Lycinus note the following in connection with Dionysiac mysteries in Asia
Minor:

the Bacchic dance that is especially cultivated in Ionia and in Pontus . . .
has so enthralled the people of those countries that when the appointed
time comes round they each and all forget everything else and sit the
whole day looking at Titans, corybantes, satyrs, and cowherds. Indeed,
these parts in the dance are performed by the men of best birth and first
rank . . . with great pride. (*On the Dance* 79; trans. Harmon 1925 [LCL]; cf.
Artemidorus, *Dream Interpretations* 4.39; *ISmyrna* 728)

The association of "dancing cowherds" at Pergamum was not the only
Dionysiac group that honored the gods and portrayed their myths by way
of dance (including the myth of the Titans' dismemberment of the child
Dionysos), and we know that dancing could also play a role in the rituals
of other associations, such as those devoted to Serapis.

So honoring gods and goddesses in a variety of ways was a common
concern for virtually all types of associations and their members. By participating in such religious activities, the members of associations were

helping to maintain appropriate relations between human communities and the deities who protected and provided benefactions for people in their everyday lives. Sacrifices or offerings of animals, foods, and drink were often at the focal point of these honors, and these offerings were almost always accompanied by a meal among the participants in worship.

Social and Feasting Activities

An element of group life that is often discussed in connection with social purposes pertains to the eating and drinking that went on at associations' festivals and banquets. However, we should be wary of accepting wholeheartedly the opinions of Jewish or Christian apologists, such as Philo or Tertullian, for instance. Philo spends a good part of his discourse on the Jewish *therapeutai* near Alexandria contrasting the "mysteries" of their sanctified, ascetic life to the "frenzy and madness" of Greco-Roman banquets and associations (*On the Contemplative Life*, esp. 40ff.; cf. Seland 1996). According to him, most associations, in contrast to Jewish gatherings, of course, were "founded on no sound principle but on strong liquor, drunkenness, intoxicated violence and their offspring, wantonness" (*Against Flaccus* 136–37 [LCL with adaptations]; cf. *Embassy to Gaius* 312–13). Writing a couple of centuries after Philo, Tertullian clearly has in mind "pagan" associations when, in defending and promoting the virtues of the Christian association (*factio, corpus*), he states that the financial contributions of Christians are "not spent upon banquets nor drinking-parties nor thankless eating-houses," but on helping the poor and ensuring their burial (*Apology* 39.5–6 and 38–39 generally [LCL]). Of course, Philo and Tertullian were not alone in describing meetings of *others* in such negative terms for apologetic or entertainment purposes. That they chose associations as the object of their rather one-sided comparison, however, shows how both Jews and Christians (as well as outsiders) could express their identities in terms of association life.

Stories of secretive, nocturnal, and uncontrolled banquets involving drunkenness and, at times, somewhat extreme rituals—incestuous sex, ritual murder, and cannibalism among them—were the mainstay of mudslinging and a source of novelistic shock value among upper-class authors in antiquity. A novel by Lollianos (of which only fragments survive), for example, depicts an association engaging in ritual infanticide followed by a cannibalistic communal meal and promiscuous sexual activity (Henrichs 1970, 1972). Jack Winkler (1980) discusses such ritual depictions in novels, which sometimes involved villain bandit associations.[11] Challenging Henrich's views of Lollianos's novel (which suggests that the story derives from knowledge of actual rituals as practiced by some groups), Winkler argues that it is in *inverting* what was commonly assumed to be normal or acceptable religious practices within associations that these episodes found their shock and entertainment value. One wonders how much of Livy's description of the subversive and secret meetings of Dionysiac groups (Bacchanalia) in republican Rome, involving sexual excesses, murder, and other crimes (written in the time of Augustus), corresponds more with such novelistic stereotypes and upper-class pretensions than with the reality of what happened in 186 B.C.E. (Livy, *History of Rome* 39.8–19; cf. Gruen 1990; see discussion in chapter 6).

Some outsiders' accusations against Christian groups—Thyestan feasts (cannibalism) and Oedipan unions (incest), for instance—drew on the same stockpile of fantastic popular lore, as did many "orthodox" attacks against "heretics" (cf. Eusebius, *H.E.* 5.1.14; Tertullian, *Apology* 9.9; Benko 1980:1081–89; M. J. Edwards 1992). Yet the reasons for such accusations could be quite different in the case of Christians and Jews, pertaining to their failure to fully participate in local religious life, especially sacrifices for Greco-Roman deities. Moreover, we must refrain from accepting descriptions of wild "impious" meetings of associations, whether Jewish, Christian, or other, at face value, as though they realistically describe actual practices among a significant number of the groups in question.

Though there is truth in the observation that eating and drinking were important parts of group life, and sometimes this might be interpreted as disorderly behavior in the eyes of some (cf. Paul's comments on Christian assemblies in 1 Cor 11:17–34), we should not reduce the purposes of associations to mere conviviality or exaggerate the uncontrolled nature of meetings. First of all, there was a set of socioreligious expectations and values concerning behavior, sometimes set in stone as statutes, which helped to maintain order during the meetings and banquets of associations. The regulations of the association devoted to Zeus Hypsistos in Egypt and the Bacchic worshipers (Iobacchoi) at Athens, for instance, both included rules (with accompanying punishments) regarding obedience to the leaders, as well as proscriptions against members causing disturbances or attempting to take the seat of other members during gatherings (*PLond* 2193). The inscribed column of the Iobacchoi (*IG* II.2 1368) actually includes the minutes of the meeting in which the rules of the association were confirmed, along with the rules themselves. It is worth quoting portions of this inscription as an example of rules and their enforcement (for another translation of the full text see Tod 1932):

> The officers (*hoi proestōtes*) shall be empowered to prevent any of the inscribed decrees from being violated. . . . It is not lawful for anyone in the gathering to sing, cause disturbances or applaud. Rather, members shall speak and do their parts (in the rituals) with all good order and quietness, as the priest or the chief bacchant gives directions. . . . Now if anyone begins a fight, is found disorderly, sits in someone else's seat, or is insulting or abusing someone else, the person abused or insulted shall produce two members (*iobacchoi*) as sworn witnesses, testifying that they heard the insult or abuse. The one who committed the insult or the abuse shall pay to the common treasury 25 light drachmae. If someone comes to blows, let the one who was struck file a report with the priest or the vice-priest, who shall without fail convene a meeting; the members shall make a judgment by vote as the priest presides. . . . Let the penalty be the same for the officer in charge of good order (*eukosmos*) if he does not expel those who fight. . . . The officer in charge of good order shall be chosen by lot or be appointed by the priest, laying the *thyrsos* [reed or wand] of the god on anyone who is disorderly or creates a disturbance. Now if the *thyrsos* is laid on anyone—and the priest or the chief bacchant approves—let the violator leave the feast. If he refuses to leave, let those who have been appointed by the priests as "horses" [bouncers] take him outside of the door and let him be liable to the punishment for those who fight. (lines 30–31, 60–90, 94–95, 135–46)

Behavioral norms could be upheld in more subtle ways than this. A dream retold by Artemidorus reflects a member's feelings of falling short of the expectations of other fellow members of an association. His dream involves a radical violation of unstated rules: "Someone dreamt he lifted up his clothes in front of his fellow members (*symbiōtais*) in an association (*phratria*) to which he belonged and urinated upon each of them. He was expelled from the association for being unworthy of it. For it is understandable that those who commit such vile deeds would be hated and expelled" (*Dream Interpretations* 4.44; trans. R. White 1975). Apparently his dream reflected his failure to live up to other social or religious standards of the group (that resulted in his actual expulsion); his violation of standards was probably less drastic than the one he dreamt (one would hope).

That banqueting activities could be infused with varying degrees of religious significance for the participants, being viewed as a means of honoring or communing with the gods, further suggests caution in reducing the purposes of associations to the social, as Nilsson and others do. The inseparable nature of the social and religious dimensions of feasting is illustrated in Dio of Prusa's (Chrysostom) remarks: "What festivity could delight without the presence of the most important thing of all [friendship]? What symposium could please without the good cheer of the guests? What sacrifice is acceptable to the gods without those celebrating the feast?" (*Orations* 3.97; trans. Stowers 1995:298–99). It is important to note that, for virtually all associations and guilds, sacrifice or libations in honor of the gods accompanied or preceded the banquet. Jewish synagogues (at least in the diaspora) and Christian assemblies did not engage in actual sacrifice, however, though the Christian concept of the Lord's Supper was certainly expressed in sacrificial terms (cf. Mark 14:12–25; 1 Cor 11:23–26).

For some groups food and drink or the meal itself could be an essential element in the myth and ritual of the deity in question. For example, how could a worshiper of Dionysos appropriately honor or identify with the god of wine without making the consumption of that beverage a central part of his or her activities? Gods such as Serapis could also be considered present with the association in its festal gatherings, as a passage in Aelius Aristides of Smyrna shows:

> And mankind exceptionally makes this god [Serapis] alone a full partner in their sacrifices, summoning him to the feast and making him both their chief guest and host, so that while different gods contribute to different banquets, he is the universal contributor to all banquets and has the rank of mess president for those who assemble at times for his sake . . . he is a participant in the libations and is the one who receives the libations, and he goes as a guest to the revel and issues the invitations to the revelers, who under his guidance perform a dance. (*Orations* 45.27–28; trans. Behr 1981)

In one of several invitations to such banquets found in Egypt, Serapis himself is the host who bids his guests to attend (*PKöln* 57; cf. *NewDocs* I 1). Conviviality was not the antithesis of religion—of fittingly honoring the gods—in antiquity, and we need to set aside restrictive conceptions of religion that would suggest otherwise. A brief look at some architectural remains will further illustrate the interconnected social and religious dimensions of association life.

The earlier discussion of buildings at Ostia and Delos suggested that the remains of buildings could bring to life the purposes of associations. Rarely have the remains of actual buildings or banqueting halls of associations been discovered or identified in Asia, so it is worth giving some attention to one that has: the meeting hall of the Dionysiac cowherds at Pergamum, the so-called *Podiensaal* or "Hall of Benches" (see figs. 16–17; Radt 1979:321–23; 1988:224–28; 1999:196–99; Schwarzer 2002; cf. Mellink 1979:340–41). This building, which was excavated and restored in 1978 by Wolfgang Radt, lies in a residential area on the southern slope of the acropolis, almost directly north from the sanctuary of Demeter. Also nearby was a sanctuary with a cult hall and small odeion that was dedicated to a hero named Diodoros Pasparos of Pergamum; this "Heroon" building was most likely used as the meeting place of another cult association in the Roman period (Radt 1999:249–54; Schwarzer 2002). The identification of the hall of benches as the cowherds' meeting place is virtually certain. The building was set back from the street behind a row of shops with an alley leading to the hall's courtyard on the south side. At the west end of the courtyard were two running fountains and a small vestibule entering into two small rooms, perhaps small service rooms or storage areas.

The hall proper was largely symmetrical, measuring 24 meters from west to east and 10 meters from north to south, and it was ideal for the religious and banqueting activities of the cowherds (see photo in fig. 16). There was a large bench (1 meter high and 2 meters deep), seen in the photo, running alongside all four walls, except at the central entrance on the south and the cult niche opposite it on the north. Members of the association (up to 70 persons) reclined on the benches with their feet toward the wall and their heads toward the center of the room, where an altar for sacrifices stood. A small marble slab or shelf ran along the length of the benches, being designed for the banqueters to set down their food and drinks. Excavators found bone remnants of beef, swine, and poultry ground into the floor, some of them the remains of sacrificial victims offered to the god. Under the benches, at regular intervals, are niches, which probably served as storage areas for cultic implements, as Radt suggests.

The entire hall was plastered and painted. The decoration and other objects found there attest to the importance of the patron deity and his myths for the association. Dionysiac scenes—only a small portion of which

FIGURE 16: Hall of Benches at Pergamum, meeting place of the "dancing cowherds." (Source: Radt 1979: 322, Abb. 8.)

were still visible when excavated—were painted on the main walls, one section depicting an altar with fire and a *thyrsos*, the holy reed or wand of the god. A painting with Dionysiac connections was also still visible on the western wall of the cult niche. This depicted wine leaves and grapes against a red background, along with a man dressed in sacrificial garb as Silenos. We hear of members with the title "Silenos" in other inscriptions pertaining to the cowherds (*IPergamon* 485). Though the mythology varies, this Silenos (sometimes described as chief of the satyrs who accompanied Dionysos and who could also be called *silenoi*) was often viewed as an old and cheerful drunkard and foster father of the child Dionysos. A mosaic from another building in Pergamum depicts this Silenus holding Dionysos as he offers a cup of golden wine to the child (compare the statue in fig. 6 in chapter 1). Finally, two altars were found in or near the

FIGURE 17: Altar from the Hall of Benches dedicated to Dionysos Kathegemon by Herodes. (Source: Radt 1979: 323, Abb. 10.)

building, one of which depicts a wine cup and garland (see fig. 17). These had evidently been damaged in an earlier meeting place, perhaps by an earthquake, and subsequently reused in this building. Both were set up by Herodes, a chief cowherd (*archiboukolos*) during the reign of Augustus; one was dedicated to Caesar Augustus and the other to Dionysos Kathegemon (Radt 1999:199; cf. *SEG* 29 [1979] 1264).

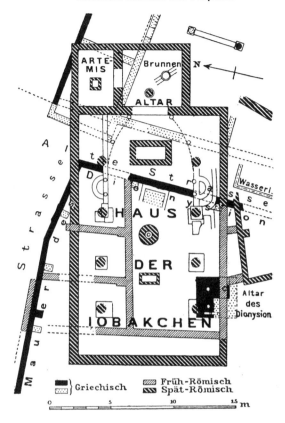

FIGURE 18: Plan of the meeting place of the Iobacchoi at Athens. (Source: Judeich 1931:291.)

Before I go on to the funerary purposes of associations, it is worth saying a few words about another building that has been unearthed, this one at Athens in Greece. Wilhelm Dörpfeld's excavations of the late 1880s in an area west of the Athenian acropolis, between the Pnyx and the Areopagus, uncovered the site of an ancient triangular precinct that, although not necessarily the famous Dionysion in the Marshes, as originally thought (Hooker 1960), was probably dedicated to Dionysos (Dörpfeld 1894, 1895; cf. Harrison 1906:88–91). Some time before mid-second century the devotees of Dionysos Bacchus (Iobacchoi), which we have already encountered in connection with their rules, decided to construct a meeting place within this ancient sacred space. The building or Baccheion,[12] as it is called, measured about 11 meters wide by 18 meters long, consisting of a

FIGURE 19: Sketch of the inscribed column containing the rules of the Iobacchoi. (Source: Harrison 1906:90, fig. 25.)

large hall with two rows of columns, which divided the structure into a central nave and two aisles (see the plan in fig. 18). It was here that they gathered for their socioreligious activities including a sacred play reenacting stories of the gods and the priest's sacred discourse, his sermon.

Several artifacts found within the structure point to the importance of honoring the gods among those who used the building. At the eastern end of the building, within an apse, was found an altar decorated with Dionysiac motifs, including a sacrificial goat, a satyr (horned male attendant of the god), and a maenad (female attendants of the god). A small shrine devoted to Artemis appears to have been located in a room just north of this apse. Also near the Dionysiac altar were various sculptural objects including a head of Dionysos, a statue of Pan, several reliefs depicting Cybele, and statuettes of Aphrodite and of Hekate (Dörpfeld 1894:148).

Most interesting here is the inscribed column found alongside the altar, including a Dionysiac scene depicting the head of a bull above two panthers on either side of a large drinking vessel (see the sketch in fig. 19). This column identifies the building as the meeting place (Baccheion) of the association; it happens to be one of the most extensive inscriptions concerning an association of the Roman era (IG II.2 1368).[13] It relates the minutes of a meeting in which the leaders and members of the association decided to have their rules more permanently inscribed in stone, some of which I quoted earlier. The members' pride and sense of belonging become quite evident when they shout: "Long life to the most excellent priest, Herodes! Now you have good fortune! Now we are the best of all Bacchic societies!" Their recently appointed priest, Claudius Herodes, can be identified with the extremely wealthy and influential Claudius Herodes Attikos, and the events recorded in the inscription pertain to a time shortly before his death in 178 C.E. (Rotroff 1975; Kapetanopoulos 1984:184–87; not the 3d century, as originally thought). The inscription provides information concerning the meetings and rituals of the group and the roles and responsibilities of members and leaders (priest, vice priest, and chief bacchant). The group gathered quite frequently, "on the ninth of each month, on the annual festival, on Bacchic holidays and if there is any occasional feast of the god." When they did, participants were expected to "speak, act, or do some honorable deed" (lines 42–46). Besides the religious practices already mentioned, the group performed customary libations and sacrifices along with accompanying feasts in honor of Dionysos. They also engaged in wine feasts at the death of a member (lines 159–63).

Funerary Activities

The connection between the socioreligious functions of associations and
funerary ones could be quite direct. A passage from Artemidorus illustrates this well:

> A man dreamt that his fellow members in an association (*phratria*) to
> which he belonged suddenly appeared and said to him, "Receive us as
> guests and entertain us at dinner." He replied, "I do not have the money
> nor the means to receive you." Then he sent them away. On the next day,
> he was in a shipwreck. He faced extreme danger and barely escaped with
> his life. . . . It is customary for the associates to go to the house of the de-
> ceased members and to dine there, and the reception is said to have been
> given by the deceased because of the honors paid to him by his fellows.
> (*Dream Interpretations* 5.82; trans. R. White 1975)

It was common practice for associations of all kinds to hold similar funerary feasts or wine banquets in memory of deceased members, including
customary burial rituals.

Several other practices associated with death and burial can be mentioned here (cf. Fraser 1977:58–70; van Nijf 1997:31–69). First, associations could provide burial for their members, often collecting
contributions or fees that went toward the cost of the funerary rituals or
the actual burial of members. There were numerous epitaphs throughout
Asia set up for the deceased by the association he or she belonged to, and
at Saittai alone, for instance, there were dozens of epitaphs erected by
guilds or associations of "friends" (*TAM* V 79–93). Christian congregations, too, could serve a similar purpose, providing burial and related funerary honors for their members, especially the less fortunate (cf.
Tertullian, *Apology* 39.5–6).

Ensuring burial could be of greater or lesser importance depending on
the economic circumstances of the members. For example, the regulations
of the association (*collegium*) devoted to Diana and Antinoos at Lanuvium
in Italy give extensive attention to issues relating to the death and burial of
members, presumably because the lower-class members might not otherwise have been able to afford proper burial (*CIL* XIV 2112). Among them
are rules regarding procedures for burial if a member happens to die further than twenty miles away from town, as well as a stipulation that if a
member commits suicide the right to burial by the association would be
forfeited. On the other hand, the rules of the Iobacchoi at Athens—a group

consisting of a notable number of wealthier members—say little of the procedures for ensuring actual burial, mentioning only the funerary wine banquet: "If an Iobacchos dies, let there be a wreath up to the cost of 5 drachmae and let a single jar of wine be set before those who attend the funeral. But do not let anyone who was absent from the funeral itself have any of the wine" (*IG* II.2 1368, lines 159–63). Although from an earlier era in Egypt, it is worth mentioning two papyri in which family members (a sister in one, a brother in another) register a complaint with the king regarding the failure of a cult society (*thiasos*) to abide by its own rules in paying for the burial of a member (*PEnteuxeis* 20, 21; c. 220 B.C.E.).

Second, some associations could have a communal cemetery or collective tomb. This was the case with the guild of flax workers at Smyrna who received a vault as a donation (*ISmyrna* 218; cf. *IEph* 2213). The Selgian craftsmen living at Lamos in Cilicia likewise had their own collective tomb, with each member owning a share that could not be sold to nonmembers (*IKilikiaBM* II 190–202; cf. van Nijf 1997:46–49). P. M. Fraser (1977:58–70) discusses the extensive evidence for communal burial plots among associations on the island of Rhodes, where burial boundary markers have been found (cf. *IKosPH* 155–59).

A third funerary-related issue pertains to individuals or members who either granted a financial donation to an association for specific purposes or made provisions for a group to be among the recipients of fines for violation of the grave. Regarding the former, it was common for associations of various kinds to receive benefactions from a wealthy individual provided that they take care of the grave regularly or commemorate the patron's death day (cf. Polybius, *Histories* 20.6.5–6). Thus, associations of Jews, silversmiths, physicians, and hemp workers at Ephesus were assigned responsibility for the upkeep of graves (*IEph* 1677, 2212, 2304; *SEG* 43 [1993] 812). In a Jewish epitaph from Hierapolis the owners follow common conventions in making provisions for the guilds of purple-dyers and carpet weavers to crown the grave on certain religious festivals, commemorating the death of the deceased (Ritti 1992–93, revising *CIJ* 777; cited in chapter 7). The Christian tradition of gathering at the grave of a well-respected member or "witness" (on the anniversary of his or her death), which became increasingly important, is closely related to this funerary function (cf. *Mart. Pol.* 18.1–3).

Frequently, associations (along with other groups and civic institutions) were made the recipients of fines for violation, often administered by institutions of the polis (cf. Strubbe 1997). At Kyzikos alone, for example, guilds of marble workers, clothing cleaners, and porters were named in epitaphs as recipients of any fines incurred for violation of the grave (*IKyzikos* 97, 211, 291). When Rufina, the head of the synagogue at Smyrna, prepared a common tomb for her household (3d century c.e.), she made the fines for violation payable to the Jewish association (*ethnos*), and a copy of the inscription was put into the civic archives (*ISmyrna* 295 = *CIJ* 741). Many Jews and Christians of Asia apparently followed suit in adopting similar funerary-related customs, as J. H. M. Strubbe points out (1994, 1997; cf. *SEG* 44 [1994] 1088).

These funerary functions were an integral part of the varied social and religious purposes of associations that helped to provide members with a sense of belonging and community. A poetic memorial from the vicinity of Magnesia Sipylos illustrates well the feelings of allegiance that continued to the grave among fellow members of associations:

> I, who at one point honored the leader of the cult society with a monument, lie here, I who first observed zealous faith (*spoudēn [p]eistin*) toward the cult society. My name was Menophilos. For honor's sake these men have set up this memorial plaque. My mother also honored me, as well as my brother, children, and wife. (*IManisa* 354; trans. Malay 1994, with adaptations; 180 or 234 c.e.)

Conclusion

The purposes of associations outlined here are by no means exhaustive, but they begin to give a general picture of various interrelated dimensions of group life that we will need to keep in mind as we turn to other aspects of associations in Asia. Evidently, the gatherings of such groups were occasions for ongoing social interaction and conviviality. Although, inseparable from this, they were also a place where members could fittingly honor the gods (including emperors) who protected them as groups and as individuals or families in daily life, at work and at home. Intertwined social and religious functions continued to the grave as associations honored members on an epitaph, gathered for a funerary banquet, or regularly adorned the grave of a benefactor or member. If one were to inquire what it was that such groups offered their members, then, the answer would be manifold. Certainly, however, through a combination of purposes, associations could offer their members a sense of belonging and identity (contrast Burkert 1987:43–53, regarding cult societies). When we turn to the external relations of these groups, we will begin to see how group identity could be expressed within a broader civic and imperial context, less in terms of conflict or opposition than in terms of integration and participation.

Associations did provide their members with a sense of belonging, but this does not necessarily mean, as many scholars assume, that such groups were therefore principally a compensation for decline in other social or religious structures of belonging within the polis. Joining and feeling at home within the association was not necessarily a response to deficiencies elsewhere. Nor was it incompatible with a continuing sense of belonging within the structures of the polis, which were part of the larger world of province and empire.

3

Associations in Civic Context

Symptoms of Decline or Participants in Vitality?

Introduction

As small groups offering their members a sense of belonging, associations have had a significant role to play within many scholarly theories regarding the nature of civic life and society in the Hellenistic (from 323 B.C.E.) and Roman (from 27 B.C.E.) eras. More specifically, one prominent scholarly tradition explains associations as compensatory phenomena in a period of civic decline. From this perspective, these groups offered a replacement for the attachment that the populace had previously, but no longer, felt in relation to the social, cultural, and political structures of the polis. Closely related to this are approaches that focus on the supposed incompatibility or even opposition between most of these groups and civic or imperial structures under Roman rule. Yet such approaches are problematic.

The purpose of this chapter is to consider in broad strokes how we should understand the place of associations within the polis while also outlining some key structures of urban life in Roman Asia. Challenging common scholarly characterizations of associations as symptoms of decline or as substitutes for membership in the polis, I argue that the actual evidence for associations' relations within cities in Roman Asia provides a very different picture. Instead of fitting associations into broader theories of decline, which are questionable in themselves, we need to look at the concrete ways in which associations related to the polis and its social, cultural, and political structures. Doing so provides a picture of associations as participants in civic vitality alongside other persons, groups, and institutions. My discussion here prepares the way for a better understanding of the participation of associations in imperial cults and connections specifically while also shedding light on the place of such groups within society in the Greek East more generally. One should remember that these are the same social and cultural structures in which Jews and Christians lived.

I begin by outlining and challenging common theories regarding the place of associations within the polis in the Hellenistic and Roman eras. This is followed by a section on the civic framework and developments in the Roman era, especially regarding social networks of benefaction. Finally, I deal with primary evidence regarding the actual relations between associations and the polis in Roman Asia, pointing out three main interrelated realms of participation (political, social, and cultural).

Assessing Scholarly Theories:
Associations as Symptoms of Decline?

The characterization of associations as symptoms of civic decline or as compensations for lack of attachments to the political, social, and cultural structures of the polis is common in scholarship since the late nineteenth century and it is still repeated today.[1] Associations are often placed within a broader theory of decline that emphasizes the "failure" of the polis in the fourth century B.C.E. followed by a steady degeneration of political, social, and cultural facets of civic life in the Hellenistic and Roman periods (see, e.g., Tarn and Griffith 1952:47–125; Mossé 1973; Kreissig 1974; de Ste. Croix 1981). According to Erich Ziebarth (1896:191–93), the origins and continued success of associations can be attributed to these radical social changes within the polis. Associations were a response to individuals' feelings of detachment. They were a replacement for the sense of belonging formerly felt in relation to the polis's structures.

One particular version of this theory regarding the place of associations within culture in this period is worth outlining in some detail. It is important to note that not all who suggest that associations were compensations for civic structures would necessarily subscribe to all aspects of this particular characterization of cultural and religious developments. Nonetheless, W. S. Ferguson's overview of the "leading ideas" of the Hellenistic age in the first edition of the *Cambridge Ancient History* (1928) reflects widespread views that are evident in the works of influential scholars of Greco-Roman religion including M. P. Nilsson (1964, 1961), André-Jean Festugière (1972, 1960), E. R. Dodds (1959:179–206, 236–69), and those who depend on them, such as Peter Green (1990:382–413, 586–601).

According to these scholars, the vitality of traditional Greek religion was bound to the effectiveness of the autonomous and democratic polis of the classical era (5th–4th centuries B.C.E.). With its decline from the late fourth to third centuries came the downfall of the polis's religious system, leaving an "empty shell" with little vestige of "genuine religion"; the "ancient gods were tottering," in Nilsson's words (see Nilsson 1964:260–62, 274–75, 285; cf. Murray 1935:106–8, 158–63; Martin 1987:3). These scholars claim that although individuals continued to participate in the outward ceremonies of communal religious activities, their feelings and attitudes were no longer evoked by them.[2]

In this view the decline of the polis's structures also led to other important trends including the rise of "individualism," which was the "dominant feature of the age" (Ferguson 1928:4; cf. Nilsson 1964:282–83, 287; Farnell 1912:137, 140–41, 147–50; Guthrie 1950:256, 334). Moreover, as traditional structures of belonging broke down, individuals in the Hellenistic era (unlike the classical era, it is supposed) suffered from a general malaise characterized by feelings of detachment, isolation, and uncertainty. Feelings of "loneliness and helplessness in a vast disintegrating world" (Ferguson 1928:35) led them to seek substitutes for the attachments they had previously felt to the polis and its structures (cf. Martin 1987:3, 23, 58). Among these substitutes that filled a social or cultural vacuum were new "private" forms of socioreligious life, especially associations.

One of the most important responses to feelings of dislocation was the rise of what Nilsson and Festugière call "private" or "personal" religion. This was a replacement for the outward and increasingly artificial "public" religion. As traditional civic religious structures declined, clubs, associations, and mystery societies, which involved the individual's voluntary choice in joining, were the most successful socioreligious unit (cf. Festugière 1960:40; Dodds 1959:243). They provided a replacement for the sense of belonging and attachment that individuals previously felt toward the civic community and its religious structures.

More recent scholarship that continues to hold some, though not all, of the views outlined above tends to define associations as phenomena over against society, sometimes expressing this in subversive terms. In some respects J. K. Davies's survey of cultural features of the Hellenistic world (in the second edition of the *Cambridge Ancient History*) qualifies aspects of the above outlined theory of decline. Yet he still suggests that several new forms of religious life in this period challenged declining traditional civic religion. Among them he includes associations that, he asserts, "ran counter to city-based religion and society" (Davies 1984:318).

In a similar manner, Richard Gordon (1990:240, 245–52) still speaks of the "oriental" religions and private mystery associations as "forms of resistance" against both the civic model of religion and elite culture.

G. E. M. de Ste. Croix emphasizes the political background to the antagonistic relationship between associations and society. In the classical period, democracy by means of the assembly (*ekklēsia*) of the people (*dēmos*) permitted the real participation of all strata of the population, giving the lower classes an avenue of political activity and a sense of belonging. However, there was a disintegration of democracy in the Hellenistic and Roman eras that led to the detachment of the majority of the population from the structures of the polis (de Ste. Croix 1981:300–326, 518–37). Within this framework, de Ste. Croix considers the activities of guilds and associations (e.g., civic disturbances) among the means of social protest or resistance that compensated for the lower classes' lack of participation in the life of the polis (1981:318–20). From this perspective, associations offered a substitute structure of belonging and participation to that of the polis and its political assembly. One can understand how scholars who hold such views would tend to pay far more attention to the tensions between these groups and society, neglecting the ways in which associations were participants within the polis.

There are several difficulties with approaches that see associations as compensatory phenomena in a period of civic decline. These theories do not adequately address the extensive primary evidence concerning actual relationships between associations (and their members) and the polis, which I discuss at length below. For now it is important to note several theoretical shortcomings of these views and difficulties with the assumptions involved.

First, the last part of the twentieth century has seen the beginning of a shift away from the overall paradigm of decline in the study of the polis, which should caution us in simply plugging associations into these theories. Thus Louis Robert, whose knowledge of the inscriptions of Asia Minor remains unparalleled, states that "the Greek city did not die at Chaironeia, nor under Alexander, nor during the course of the entire Hellenistic epoch" (Robert 1969b:42 [trans. mine]). Furthermore, P. J. Rhodes (1994), Walter Eder (1995), Mogens Herman Hansen (1993, 1994a–b, 1995), and Erich Gruen (1993) question key interpretations of previous scholars concerning the early crisis and decline, reaffirming instead the continued importance and vitality of the polis despite changes and developments (cf. Gauthier 1985, 1993). Regarding Asia Minor specifically, Stephen Mitchell (1993, 1:199) argues that, despite the loss of complete autonomy, the cities continued as effective centers of administration, and they "were, in a very positive sense, communities."

Theories regarding the decline of the polis broadly are often based on a particular and questionable interpretation of two main issues: autonomy and democracy. Hansen's studies challenge the notion that autonomy was the central ingredient of the polis without which decline was inevitable. Every "city-state would of course have preferred to be autonomous, but . . . a city-state did not lose its identity as a polis by being subjected to another city-state or, for example, to the king of Persia, or Macedon, or a Hellenistic ruler, or Rome" (Hansen 1993:19; cf. Hansen 1994a, 1995; P. Brunt 1990:272). Furthermore, some adherents of decline theories overstate the degree to which Hellenistic kings and Roman emperors or officials actively interfered in the affairs of the cities. Fergus Millar (1967, 1977, 1984), G. P. Burton (1975), and P. A. Brunt (1990) point instead to the passive and re-active character of Roman rule in the imperial period. Seldom did the emperors or other Roman authorities actively interfere in the affairs of the cities unless public disorders could not be handled locally or action was requested from below (cf. Oliver 1954, refuting Magie 1950:641, 1504 n.21). As Brunt states, "it was not the practice of the Romans to govern much. The governor had only a small staff, and he did little more than defend his province, ensure the collection of the taxes and decide the most important criminal and civil cases. *The local communities were left in the main to run their own affairs*" (1990:116–17 [emphasis mine]).

Another basis of the theory of decline that is in need of qualification is the degree to which the typical polis of the Hellenistic and Roman periods represents a degeneration from an earlier form of democracy. Some scholars tend to idealize classical Athenian democracy and allow modern conceptions of democracy to shape the discussion, resulting in a picture of full participation of the people in the classical era that does not accurately reflect the reality of the situation (cf. Saxonhouse 1996:1–29, esp. 7; Bradeen 1975:405; Rhodes 1994:566, 573). Furthermore, as Rhodes (1994:189 n.102) states in reference to de Ste. Croix's theories, "the failure of democracy would not be the same thing as the failure of the polis, and it is not obvious that either occurred." There is evidence that the assembly (*ekklēsia*) of the people (*dēmos*) could continue to play a significant role in the legislative and judicial aspects of government in the polis in the Hellenistic and Roman eras, despite the prominence of the wealthy in civic affairs and in the council (*boulē*; cf. Gruen 1993:354; Quass 1993:361–62). Guy MacLean Rogers (1992) and Stephen Mitchell (1993, 1:201–4) also question the commonly stated view that in the Roman era the council completely usurped the role of the people to such an extent that the latter institution possessed very little (if any) real power, being reduced to simply approving the lists of candidates for office (contra A. H. M. Jones 1940:177; Magie 1950:640–41). Further below I discuss primary evidence that members of various associations, including artisans and traders, could be citizens involved in the activities of the civic assemblies. Participation in associations did not necessarily reflect a compensation for lack of political or other participation within civic structures.

A second theoretical caution regarding the view of associations as symptoms of decline concerns the manner in which scholars emplot cultural and religious developments within this framework. One often hears of the degeneration in traditional religious life that accompanied the supposed deterioration of the polis. Simon Price's (1984:14) study of imperial cults in Asia Minor challenges the "conventional model, which has been applied to both Greek and Roman cults, [that] posits an early apogee followed by a long and continuous decline, until the last embers were extinguished by Christianity." Some important studies of civic religious life from those of Johaness Geffcken in 1920 (1978) to those of Ramsay MacMullen (1981), Robin Lane Fox (1986), and S. Price (1999) interpret the evidence quite differently. Moreover, far from showing signs of deathly illness in the third century B.C.E., the weight of the evidence demonstrates that Greco-Roman religion–"traditional" and otherwise–thrived at least into the third century C.E., even though there were certainly changes and differences from one region to another.

Robert Parker's recent study of *Athenian Religion* (1996) in the classical and Hellenistic periods specifically is worth mentioning in this connection. Parker's case study of Athens convincingly argues that scholars have exaggerated the contrast between the classical era and the Hellenistic era with regard to the supposed decline of religion, and he also issues extreme caution in the use of the "private" vs. "public" distinction in the study of ancient religion (1996:4–7). Instead, he points to evidence that suggests considerable *continuities* over a broad span of time (from the archaic to the Hellenistic periods and beyond) in religious life at this locale, despite areas of development (Parker 1996:256; cf. S. Price 1999:7–8). Most interestingly for us here, Parker seriously qualifies the widespread notion that unofficial associations were a completely new and "distinctively Hellenistic phenomenon, a symptom of the collapse of the city as organizing centre of religious life" (1996:333; see also 333–42; contrast N. Jones 1999:4–7, 307–10).

The third century B.C.E. certainly witnessed an expansion of noncitizen groups or associations of foreigners at Athens (as Parker points out) and the evidence for occupational guilds specifically in the classical era is meager, at best. But the very partial nature of our evidence for associations in the classical era—which is only beginning to be fully addressed—should steer us away from making clear-cut statements of fundamental disjuncture with regard to the nature of association life generally, or from asserting that the phenomenon of associations was completely "new" or "late."[3] Moreover, as I discuss below, the "epigraphic habit" (the practice of monumentalizing) was of increasing importance in the Hellenistic and, especially, Roman eras (more so than the classical era). This means that the inscriptional record (including evidence for associations) swells as a result. This should caution us in too readily assuming that "the production of inscriptions is a reliable index of [associational] activity" (as does N. Jones 1999:307) when comparing different periods of history. Nor should we presume that the number of associations attested in surviving evidence for a particular place and time (e.g., the meager evidence for the classical era, especially outside Athens) is necessarily an accurate measure of the nature and importance of association life.

Furthermore, the traditional view of religious decline and the rise of associations sometimes reflects an anachronistic approach that reads history through the lenses of subsequent developments. The civic cults of "paganism" did eventually lose out to the adopted religion of empire, Christianity; thus, according to this view, such cults must have been inadequate in addressing the needs of people and were inevitably declining long before. Any religious activity during this age of decline that can be interpreted as personal or individualistic religion involving genuine feelings or notions of salvation (esp. the mysteries)—that is, as approaching what such scholars understand Christianity to have been—is viewed as more vital or superior to other traditional forms of religious life.[4] The cult societies devoted to the mysteries and any other associations that closely approximate the small-group settings of Christian congregations are in some sense preparatory for the success of Christianity from this problematic perspective.[5] Giulia Sfameni Gasparro (1985:xiii–xxiii) and Jonathan Z. Smith (1990) correctly question such christianizing interpretations of the mysteries that were previously so prevalent within scholarship.

A third theoretical problem relates to the imposition of concepts and models of historical development borrowed from the modern era that are inappropriate in studying the ancient world, including notions of "private religion" and "individualism." Nilsson, Festugière, and Dodds claim to find in the Hellenistic age the rise of "individualism" and corresponding feelings of detachment, loneliness, and uncertainty. However, a developed

concept of "individualism" (and related concepts of "private" vs. "public")
did not emerge until the sixteenth century and only fully developed during the Enlightenment. These concepts are inappropriate for studying pre-
modern societies like the Greco-Roman world, which was very much
collectivistic. The developments that Ferguson, Festugière, Dodds, and
others claim to find in the ancient world and emphasize most are precisely
those which came a millennium and a half later with the impact of modern individualism and the Enlightenment: the individual's detachment
from the larger community, freedom of choice, cultural mobility, critique
of traditional forms of religion, and the tendency to privatized religion (cf.
Hazelrigg 1992).

Even without the concept of "individualism" there are difficulties with
the social and religious conditions presupposed for this period. Louis
Robert, Paul Veyne, Peter Brown, and others challenge notions of widespread rootlessness in the Greco-Roman world.[6] As Peter Brown (1978:
2–3) observes,

> many modern accounts of religious evolution of the Roman world place
> great emphasis on the *malaise* of life in great cities in Hellenistic and
> Roman times. Yet the loneliness of the great city and the rapid decultura-
> tion of immigrants from traditionalist areas are modern ills: they should
> not be overworked as explanatory devices for the society we are studying.
> We can be far from certain that [as Dodds states] "such loneliness must
> have been felt by millions."

There is truth in the observation that associations could provide their
members with things they might not otherwise get in precisely the same
way elsewhere. However, we should not speak of widespread feelings of
economic, religious, or social deprivation (e.g., exploitation, alienation,
loneliness) as the principal factor or cause of associations as socioreligious
groups or movements in the ancient context.[7] As Stephen G. Wilson
(1996:14) also observes, it would be "a mistake to suppose that the motive
for joining these groups was always compensatory, making up for something otherwise lacking in family or political life."

Evidently, theories that have been offered to explain the relations between associations and the polis in terms of decline are problematic in several respects. These theories should be left aside if we hope to gain a better
understanding of the nature of society and culture and the place of socioreligious phenomena, such as associations, within them. Yet the most
fundamental problem with the notion that associations were symptoms of

decline is the primary evidence regarding the actual relations between such groups and the polis, which I fully address below. First, a few words are in order about the nature of the polis in Roman Asia, about the civic framework within which associations, Jewish synagogues, and Christian congregations found themselves.

The Civic Framework
and Social Networks of Benefaction

There are significant continuities with regard to the political, social and cultural institutions of the polis from the classical period into the Hellenistic and Roman eras. Institutions such as theaters, baths, marketplaces, and stadia remained prominent into the Roman era. The constitution of cities in Asia Minor founded on the model of the Hellenic polis still consisted of the two main bodies of civic authority, the council (*boulē*), which usually numbered between two and five hundred members, and the people (*dēmos*). The people (as an institution) consisted of the citizen body (men only), often divided according to tribes (*phylai*; see N. Jones 1987:295–384).

Yet one of the most significant developments in the structures of the polis in the late-Hellenistic and Roman eras pertains to the emergence of a systematic pattern of benefaction ("euergetism") that was dependent on social networks and involved a particular cultural worldview. By the time the regions of western Asia Minor were incorporated into the Roman province of Asia (c. 133 B.C.E.), this system of benefaction—an elaboration of conventions that characterized Greek society in earlier times—had become a, important structural element with special relevance to the social and economic well-being of the polis.[8] Integral to this system of relations were the pursuit of honor (*philotimia*) and the avoidance of shame (*aischynē*), which were central cultural values in the ancient Mediterranean, values also shared by both Jews and Christians (cf. Malina 1981; Elliott 1993, 1995). This system involved reciprocal relations within networks marked by a clearly differentiated hierarchy. The most prominent characteristic of these relations was the exchange of benefits or gifts of numerous kinds (protection, financial contributions for various purposes, legal or other assistance) in return for appropriate honors. Relations were reciprocal in the sense that both the benefactor and the beneficiary (be they gods, individuals, groups or institutions) had something to gain from the exchange, whether tangible or otherwise. The system was also self-perpetuat-

ing in that a benefaction was followed by fitting honors in return. Honors
would then ensure the probability of further benefactions from the same
source in the future, as well as benefactions from others who might seek to
outdo competitors in the pursuit of honor.

The definition of appropriate honors depended both on the benefits
conferred and on the positions of the benefactor and the beneficiary
within the overall hierarchy of relations. Failure to fittingly honor a benefactor resulted in shame (*aischynē*), and this might be viewed as analogous
to impiety (*asebeia*) toward the gods (the ultimate benefactors), as Dio
Chrysostom suggests (cf. *Orations* 31.57, 65, 80–81, 157). Correspondingly,
failure of the upper classes to provide appropriate benefactions was a
threat to the position and status they strove to maintain within society. In
this sense, benefaction became a duty or obligation, not simply a voluntary action. The provision of benefactions and granting of honors reaf-
firmed the relative positions of the benefactor and beneficiary within the
social system and hierarchy of the polis and cosmos.

According to this worldview, gods and rulers, whose ongoing protection and benefaction ensured the well-being of the civic community and its
constituent groups, were at the top of this hierarchy as powers external to
the polis. The deities' protection of the polis and its inhabitants, holding
off earthquakes, famine, and other natural disasters and providing safety,
stability, and peace, was deserving of the utmost honors, especially cultic
ones (cf. Dio, *Orations* 38.20 [on natural disasters]). By the Roman era, in
the Greek East the emperor's relation to the polis was more often than not
considered parallel to that between gods and the polis; rulers whose beneficence and insurance of stability was comparable to the gods likewise became deserving of cultic honors. As Aristides of Smyrna states, "there is no
reproach in writing to [the emperor] in the same fashion in which we address the gods" (Aristides, *Orations* 19.5; cf. Artemidorus, *Dream Interpretations* 3.13; Dio, *Orations* 32.26). The massive building programs in the cities
that accompanied and followed the establishment of the principate were
perhaps the most conspicuous evidence of the beneficence of the distant
emperors. The imperial presence marked the architectural landscape of the
cities in Asia under Roman rule (see S. Price 1984:249–74 for a catalogue of
imperial structures; cf. Rogers 1991:128–35; Friesen 1993).

Yet those scholars who cite cultic honors for (or worship of) rulers as
the epitome of the failure of the polis, as a sign of the utter debasement of
its ideals and values, fundamentally misunderstand the meaning and function of such honorary activities within society of the time (cf. Friesen
1993; S. Price 1984). Instead, as I elaborate in part two, the integration of

emperors within the framework of the civic social system and ideological framework actually served to reinforce the ideals, values, and structures of the polis, rather than to undermine them (cf. Wallace-Hadrill 1990:152–53; S. Price 1984; R. Smith 1987). What this incorporation of the emperors also means is that, as Fergus Millar (1993) stresses, the relation to the emperor was very much part of what the polis was in Roman times.

Gods and emperors may have been at the top of the networks of benefaction, but they were certainly not the only important players. Imperial officials in the provinces also held an important position in this hierarchy. The local aristocracy, the institutions of the polis, and other groups (including associations) were sure to maintain contacts with these powerful figures within social networks (see part two).

Perhaps more important for the everyday life of the average polis, wealthy individuals or groups in the cities were expected to provide various services and benefactions for the well-being of the polis and its inhabitants as a matter of course. Such contributions could take the form of official civic positions (liturgies or magistracies) that required considerable financial output. Apart from these official roles, inhabitants could also make benefactions in the form of financial contributions for the establishment of buildings, festivals, statues, and other structures that were often dedicated in honor of the polis, gods, or emperors. Benefactions could also take the form of banquets or food distributions in times of famine, as when a wealthy woman named Atalante made such provisions for the inhabitants at Termessos in Pamphylia (*TAM* III 4, 62). The beneficiaries of such actions were expected to reciprocate with appropriate honors, such as the erection of an inscription of gratitude or another monument or statue in honor of the benefactor. Gratitude for a festival could be shown in less tangible ways as Petronius sums up, "He gave me a spectacle, but I applauded it. We're even: one hand washes the other" (cited in Veyne 1987:113).

This leads to the question of what prompted such contributions, thereby ensuring the stability of this systematic pattern of benefactions. Motivations may have differed from one person to the next and depended on the situation, but three main components stand out in explaining why such benefactions were made. First, there is no reason to discount the role of genuine feelings of civic pride in many such benefactions. Second, honor in and of itself was highly valued in this culture. As well, the desire to have one's benefactions or deeds remembered after death, to preserve one's reputation for posterity, also played a role (cf. Woolf 1996:25–27).

As Dio Chrysostom puts it, "many in time past have even given up their lives just in order that they might get a statue and have their name announced by the herald or receive some other honor and leave a succeeding generation a fair name and remembrance of themselves" (*Orations* 31.16 [LCL]; cf. Polybius, *Histories* 20.6.5–6; Laum 1964).

A third motivating factor, however, must not be forgotten: fear of what might happen if conspicuous donations were not made. Cultural values of the day virtually made such benefactions a duty. Failure to meet expectations, especially at critical times, could result in shame and, more concretely, angry mobs seeking revenge against wealthier inhabitants. It was at times of food shortage that the socioeconomic inequalities between the strata of the population, often lying dormant, could manifest themselves in social unrest or open conflicts. The food shortage at Prusa in Bithynia in the late first century led crowds of rioting inhabitants to attempt a siege on the houses of wealthier inhabitants, Dio and his neighbor included, who were thought to be hoarding grain (*Orations* 46). According to Philostratus (*Life of Apollonios* 1.15), a similar situation happened at Aspendos in Pamphylia when the corn dealers there, who were considered among the powerful (*dynatoi*), were suspected of hoarding grain during a famine in the time of Tiberius. Hungry, rioting crowds directed their anger toward the leading civic magistrate, who sought refuge from their plans to burn him alive by "clinging to the statues of the emperor." Publicized contributions by the wealthy to the polis and its inhabitants ensured the maintenance of a person's position and prestige within the city, while also staving off the potential for such conflicts (cf. S. Mitchell 1993, 1:206).

It is not hard to see how both competition and cooperation played an important role within this social system and culture. Competition for preeminence among the prominent families was matched by competition among the potential recipients of such benefactions. The constituent groups of the polis were in many ways competitors with one another in their attempts to maintain contacts with and receive ongoing support from influential persons. Beneficiaries also had something to gain from publicly advertising their connections in the form of an honorary monument: the advantage that such contacts accrued to them in their competition for prestige within the civic context. In setting up an honorary inscription, an association or guild was not only praising the benefactor, but also making a claim regarding its own place within society, reaffirming its ties within the networks of the polis in a concrete way (cf. Woolf 1996:29).

Cooperation was essential to this system, too. Individual inhabitants of the nonelite social strata—a purple-dyer on her own, for instance—were far less likely, if at all, to gain the attention and benefaction of an imperial or civic official. By cooperating together in the form of an association, the united purple-dyers could ensure the possibility of such relations in the polis and empire. Within a wider context, a sense of civic pride and identity meant that the inhabitants of the polis as a whole, including constituent groups such as associations and guilds, cooperated together within the larger arena of competition and rivalry with other cities (cf. Dio, *Orations* 38–39; Tacitus, *Annals* 14.17).

Associations as Participants in Civic Vitality

Primary evidence concerning associations and the polis speaks strongly against the notion that these groups were symptoms of decline within this civic context, at least in Roman Asia. Many of these small groups represent the nonelite strata of society that so many scholars of the decline theories see as most removed from civic identity and participation. Strong feelings of civic pride and identity in relation to the polis or "homeland" (*patris*) are clearly evident among associations and their members, as was also the case with upper-class authors.[9] There is substantial evidence for the participation of associations and their members within several areas of civic life, including political structures, networks of benefaction, and other social or cultural structures.

Participation in Political Life

A discussion of citizenship will provide a context for considering the potential participation of members of associations within political structures, further challenging the notion that guilds or associations were necessarily substitutes for membership in the polis. Our knowledge of demography and of citizenship specifically is in many respects meager for the cities of Roman Asia, but some general remarks can be made.[10] Officially, only citizens (*politai*) had civic rights as members of the people (*dēmos*), participating in the governance of the polis through the assembly (*ekklēsia*). Citizenship and considerable wealth were required in order to assume civic offices or membership in the council (*boulē*). Citizenship was generally limited to native-born men of nonservile status; women and slaves were excluded. We know very little concerning freedpersons (ex-slaves), but there are some cases involving a freedperson who achieved citizenship, as well as important civic positions (e.g., C. Julius Zoilus at Aphrodisias; see Reynolds 1982:156–64). A clear distinction remained between the rural dwellers of the surrounding countryside (*chōra*), who were not citizens, and city dwellers, who were.

In some respects, notions of citizenship became somewhat less restricted in the Roman era. It became quite common for a polis to confer citizenship as a means of honoring outsiders, especially distinguished performers and athletes. So there were many instances of persons holding citizenship in more than one polis and some cases of wealthier individuals with membership on more than one civic council in Roman Asia Minor.[11]

Immigrants or resident foreigners as groups, at least, were normally excluded from citizenship. This is partially why some scholars view membership in geographic- or ethnic-based associations as a substitute for membership in the polis in the Hellenistic and Roman eras. For instance, P. M. Fraser (1977:60) states the following concerning these associations of foreigners in Hellenistic Rhodes:

> with their grandiloquent titles, their own magistrates, priesthoods, assemblies, cults, and social services, they provided foreign residents . . . with the same type of social environment, the same modes of advancement, and the same opportunities for lavish benefactions, as were provided by the civic organization for Rhodian *demesmen*,[12] who themselves rarely, if ever, belonged to [associations]. They were, so to speak, a microcosm of the state, and loyalty that they evoked in their members was rewarded with honors similar to those awarded by the state.

There is some truth in the suggestion that ethnic- or geographic-based associations offered their members what was not totally accessible to them within the polis due to lack of citizenship. It is also certainly true that these associations reflect and replicate the conventions and values of the polis context.

Yet several qualifications regarding this view need to be made. There were cases when particular resident foreigners, especially wealthier benefactors, were granted citizenship. A decree of the assembly of Aspendos (probably from the early 3d century B.C.E.) involved the grant of citizenship and membership in the civic tribes to men of various ethnic or geographic origins (see Magie 1950:263, 1135 n.9). We simply do not know whether or when nonelite immigrants acquired citizenship in their polis of residence in the cities of Asia Minor in the Roman era. Furthermore, even noncitizen foreigners could participate within the social and cultural activities of the polis. Ethnic- or geographic-based associations and their members could quite often find their polis of residence to be a home, regardless of whether they were actual citizens participating in the assembly of the people. Inscriptional evidence discussed in the sections below concerning other areas of involvement by associations of Romans, Judeans, and others further confirms this (cf. *IGR* I 787, 800; *ILindos* 391–92).

Even more problematic is the suggestion that (nonethnic) occupational guilds were, in some sense, substitutes for political participation in the polis, that is, that guilds were replacements for active membership in the citizen body and the assembly. A central issue in this regard pertains to whether the members of guilds, especially artisans and traders of the lower social strata, were usually citizens who participated in the assemblies of the cities in Roman Asia.

Some scholars tend toward the view that many members of guilds were commonly excluded from citizenship and participation in the life of the polis (cf. C. P. Jones 1978:80–81; Finley 1985a:136–38; Rogers 1991: 71–72). For instance, C. P. Jones (1978:81) cites the case of the linen workers at Tarsus as representative of the situation in many other cities of the Greco-Roman era: "[the passage in Dio's speech to the Tarsians] illustrates a less well known feature of Greek city life, the restriction of full citizenship to those of at least moderate wealth [i.e., those who could pay 500 drachmae]. . . . It must have excluded an ordinary artisan from citizenship."[13] The reference to 500 drachmae in Dio's oration need not be interpreted this way even for Tarsus. More importantly, though, C. P. Jones's and M. I. Finley's (1985a:136) suggestion that the linen workers' situation is representative of the circumstances in most cities does not adequately account for Dio's overall approach to the case (cf. Sartre 1991:128–29; Quass 1993:355–56; van Nijf 1997:18–20).

In his speech delivered before a gathering of citizens at Tarsus, Dio Chrysostom addresses several problems of discord, including divisions between the council and the people and between the organizations of elders and of youths. He then goes on to another perceived problem involving the exclusion of certain artisans from participation in the polis:

> there is a group of no small size which is, as it were, outside the constitution (*politeias*). And some are accustomed to call them linen-workers (*linourgous*), and at times the citizens are irritated by them and assert that they are a useless rabble and responsible for the tumult (*staseōs*) and disorder (*tarachēs*) in Tarsus, while at other times they regard them as part of the city (*ekklēsiais*) and hold the opposite opinion of them. Well, if you believe

them to be detrimental to you and instigators of insurrection and confusion, you should expel them altogether and not admit them to your popular assemblies; but if on the other hand you regard them as being in some
measure citizens, not only because they are resident in Tarsus, but also because in most instances they were born here and know no other city, then
surely it is not fitting to disfranchise them or to cut them off from associations with you. . . . "What then, what do you bid us to do?" I bid you en-
roll them all as citizens (*politas*)—yes, I do—and just as deserving as
yourselves, and not to reproach them or cast them off, but rather to regard
them as members of your body politic, as in fact they are. (*Orations* 34.21-
23; trans. Cahoon and Crosby 1940–46 [LCL])

Dio goes on to point out the irony in that the Tarsians would readily accept foreigners as citizens upon payment of a fee of 500 drachmae while
excluding from the citizen body some members of guilds who had actually been born in Tarsus (and whose fathers and forefathers had been as
well).

As Maurice Sartre argues, the exclusion of the linen workers from participation in the citizen body at Tarsus stems from issues other than simply that they were artisans or that they could not afford to pay an entrance
fee for citizenship (Sartre 1991:128–29; cf. Quass 1993:355–56). Most importantly for present purposes, Dio's overall approach to the exclusion of
linen workers, arguing that they should be included, suggests that it was
not normal practice among cities in Roman Asia to exclude artisans or others of similar occupations from participation in the polis, including its assembly. Dio sees this situation as an anomaly caused by the specific
troubles and discord at Tarsus. Further on he refers to the fact that even at
Tarsus artisans of other occupations—dyers (*bapheis*), leather workers (*sky-
totomoi*), or carpenters (*tektones*), for instance—were not excluded in the
same way. We simply do not know why the linen workers were excluded
here, but this passage is far from suggesting that such exclusion was common within the cities of Asia Minor. In contrast to their counterparts at
Tarsus, the guild of linen workers (*linourgoi*) at Saittai were apparently included within the citizen body, perhaps even forming one of the tribes
(Kolb 1990), as was the case with guilds at Philadelphia.

It seems that (native- and freeborn) artisans and those of other occupations usually did possess citizenship and participate in the assemblies in
Asia, sometimes playing significant roles (see Quass 1993:355–65; van Nijf
1997:18–21). This was the situation that Cicero had in mind when, in defending Flaccus, he complained that the political assemblies in Asian cities

(like Pergamum and Tralles) were dominated by the mob and the "dregs" of society, by cobblers, belt makers, craftsmen, and shopkeepers (*sutores, zonarii, opifices, tabernarii; For Flaccus* 17–19, 52–61). Similarly, Strabo relates the case of Hybreas at Mylasa, who, although of humble origins, achieved local prestige including the position of market overseer (*agoranomos*). The growth of his power in the polis is attributed, in part, to his relations with "the people of the market" (*hoi agoraioi*), namely, craftsmen and merchants (Strabo, *Geography* 14.2.24; cf. van Nijf 1997:21, citing L. Robert).

Further evidence that guilds and their members (artisans, workers, merchants) were involved in the life of the polis as citizens, and that the guilds were not a substitute for attachments to the civic institutions, comes from two cases of civic unrest at Ephesus (cf. S. Mitchell 1993:1.201–2). The author of Acts (19:23–41) describes the spontaneous gathering of silversmiths, craftsmen, and other workers (*argyrokopoi, technitai, ergatai*) in the theater at Ephesus as an "assembly" (*ekklēsia*, vv. 32, 41), and those who attempt to resolve the problem address the gathering as the "people" (*dēmos*, v. 33). Furthermore, the account assumes that such craftsmen were citizens who could resolve such grievances within the context of the regular assembly of the people (v. 39; cf. Quass 1993:358; van Nijf 1997:20–21). The second-century proconsular edict dealing with disturbances caused by bakers in the marketplace of Ephesus likewise seems to presume that these workers were part of the citizen body with some influence on the activities of the political institution of the people: "sometimes the people (*dēmon*) falls into confusion and uproar (*tarachēn kai thorybous*) because of the gatherings and insolence of the bakers at the market" (*IEph* 215 = Buckler 1923:30–33, no. 1).

Inscriptional evidence points to the importance of the guilds within the actual civic organization of some cities in Asia. The suggestion of W. M. Ramsay (1895–97:105–6) and A. H. M. Jones (1940:43–44, 162) that the citizen bodies of *many* cities in Lydia and Phrygia consisted of a "primitive" organization according to guilds, rather than regular tribes, is generally unsubstantiated. Subsequent epigraphic discoveries have shown that some of the cities formerly suggested as candidates (e.g., Akmoneia, Smyrna, and Hierapolis) were in fact organized according to the usual tribal structure, not guilds (cf. N. Jones 1987:358, 381 n.6; G. Cohen 1995:306–7). However, the case of Philadelphia remains. An inscription from that city involves honors granted to a benefactor by the homeland, the elders' organization, and seven "tribes" (*phylai*), one of which is explicitly named as "the sacred tribe of wool-workers (*eriourgōn*)" (*IGR* IV

1632 = *IGLAM* 648). Another inscription from the same city involves a group called "the sacred tribe of leather tanners (*skyteōn*)" (*IGLAM* 656). Evidently, the members of guilds in Philadelphia, at least, were included as a group among the civic tribes (i.e., they were active citizens).

It is quite common for scholars discussing the organization and activities of associations to note the fact that associations and guilds mimic civic structures. For instance, Jean-Pierre Waltzing (1895–1900, 2:184) observes that associations were, in many ways, "a veritable city within the city, a small country within the large one" (cf. Foucart 1873:50–51; Dill 1956:269; Lane Fox 1986:85). Thus, for example, the internal organization of many associations and guilds mirrors civic organization, with positions of leadership including secretary (*grammateus*), treasurer (*tamias*), president (*epistatēs*), and superintendent (*epimelētēs*; cf. Poland 1909:376–87). The self-designations of some groups also reflect the vocabulary of the polis, such as the associations that called themselves an "assembly" (*ekklēsia*) at Aspendos in Cilicia and on the island of Delos (*IGLAM* 1381–82; Foucart 1873:223–25, no. 43 = *CIG* 2271) and, of course, many Christian gatherings. Furthermore, the activities of associations reflect those of civic institutions: passing decrees, granting honors, voting on decisions, electing leaders (cf. *IG* II.2 1368), and engaging in the conventions of diplomacy, for instance.

Overall, in light of the discussion throughout this chapter, evidence of associations as cities writ small can be understood as a sign of the continuing vitality and influence of the polis, not as a sign that associations were a substitute for declining participation in various areas of civic life. The close involvements in the political, social, and cultural structures of the polis that did exist help to explain how civic structures came to influence association life so heavily. Belonging within an association and belonging within the polis were by no means mutually exclusive.

Participation in Social Networks of Benefaction

Some degree of involvement in the political structures of the polis was by no means the only significant area of participation in society by members of many guilds and associations. There were other important ways in which associations *as groups* expressed belonging within and attachment to the polis. Identification with the civic community could be expressed through involvement in benefactions for or dedications to the polis or homeland (*patris*). The guild of silversmiths and goldsmiths at Smyrna expressed both its piety toward the goddess Athena and the civic pride of its members by repairing her statue "for the homeland" (*ISmyrna* 721; c. 14–37 C.E.; *IEph* 20, 1501). And the dyers at Hierapolis who set up a statue of Lady "Council" (*boulē*) in personified form evidently identified with the institutions of their polis (*SEG* 41 [1991] 1201; c. 100–150 C.E.). Several civic officials and some groups at Smyrna, including theologians, an association of hymn singers, and a group of Judeans (see chapter 7), displayed civic-mindedness in joining together to provide financial donations for the polis in the early second century (*ISmyrna* 697; c. 124 C.E.).

Ethnic- or geographic-based associations could also be involved in honorary activities that indicate attachments to the polis of residence. At Heraklea-Perinthos (opposite Kyzikos) in Thracia, for instance, a man erected a pillar for the local Baccheion of Asians, dedicating it on behalf of the emperors and, most importantly here, "the sacred council and people of the Perinthians" (*IGR* I 787; c. 196–198).

Civic inhabitants and associations might also express their identification with the polis by honoring an individual who demonstrated goodwill (*eunoia*) and acted as "benefactor of the homeland."[14] An inscription from Smyrna, for example, involves the sacred guild (*synodos*) of performers and initiates of Dionysos Breseus honoring Marcus Aurelius Julianus, a civic crown bearer, "leader of Asia" (Asiarch, probably a civic functionary),[15] temple warden of the *Sebastoi* and benefactor, "because of his piety toward the god and his goodwill toward the polis" (*ISmyrna* 639; mid-late 2d century C.E.).

Perhaps even more telling concerning the involvement of associations within these networks of civic life is the cooperation between such groups and important civic and imperial functionaries or institutions. There is abundant evidence for associations on their own honoring important civic officials, thereby maintaining connections with powerful citizens, as when the *therapeutai* of Zeus honored a "foremost leader of the polis" for his piety toward the deity (*ISardBR* 22; c. 100 B.C.E.).[16] Associations also maintained important links with Roman officials of equestrian or senatorial rank (see part two). The connections of associations with both local and imperial functionaries attests to some of the ways these groups confirmed their relationship with the polis, identifying with its interests.

There are numerous examples of various types of associations collaborating together with civic institutions, especially the council and the people, in honoring eminent citizens or benefactors. This is true of ethnic- or geographic-based associations. Associations of Romans throughout the cities of Asia commonly joined with the council and the people in honoring civic functionaries and benefactors of their polis of residence.[17] On more than one occasion the council and the people of Lindos (on the island of Rhodes) joined together with various associations, some of which were groups of foreigners (e.g., the Pergaians), to honor the priest of Athena Lindia and Zeus Poleus, protector of the polis (*ILindos* 391–92; time of Augustus). When a benefactor built or renovated the temple of Tyche at Hereklea-Perinthos, the council and the people honored him with a monument; an association of Alexandrians also played a key role by setting up a statue in his honor (*IGR* I 800). Ethnic- or geographic-based associations could maintain such connections not only with their polis of residence but also, of course, with their homeland, as the case of the political institutions of Nysa and the Nysaians at Rome showed.

Occupational and other associations also joined with political institutions in honoring benefactors. The council and the people at Smyrna joined with a synod of initiates in honoring two female theologians for their display of piety toward the goddess (probably Demeter or Kore) in providing their services at a festival by singing praises for the deity (*ISmyrna* 653; 1st–2d century C.E.; cf. *TAM* V 1098 [Thyatira]). At Erythrai (west of Smyrna), the sacred theatrical synod joined with the "homeland" in honoring Antonia Tyrannis Juliane, the director of games devoted to Hadrian (*IErythrai* 60; 124 C.E.; cf. *ITrall* 65; 1st century C.E.). It was also common for associations to set up honors for a benefactor *on behalf of* the council and the people, often in accordance with a specific provision in a decree or decision of the polis.[18] At Ephesus, for example, "the council and the people of the first and greatest metropolis of Asia . . . honored Publius Vedius Antoninus," the civic secretary and ambassador to the emperors; "those who are engaged in the taste [i.e., a guild of wine tasters] put up the statue" (*IEph* 728; 160s C.E.).

Participation in Social and Cultural Life

Attachment to civic institutions and an accompanying sense of civic identity or pride is evinced in various other ways alongside involvement in political structures and civic networks of benefaction. Among the principal sociocultural institutions of the hellenized polis were the marketplaces, baths, gymnasia, stadia, and theaters. Here too there is clear evidence of active participation by associations and their members. The various official age-group organizations of boys (*paides*) or girls, youths (*ephēboi*), young men (*neoi*), and elders (*gerontes, gerousia*) were a prominent feature of life in the gymnasia (cf. Forbes 1933; Jaczynowska 1978). Guilds of Dionysiac performers and athletes devoted to Herakles were also active in the gymnasia, stadia, and theaters, competing during festivals held in honor of gods or emperors.

Yet ordinary associations and guilds also had a place (often in a literal sense) within these institutions of the polis. For example, the stadia at Aphrodisias, Didyma (near Miletos), and Saittai included bench reservations for guilds and associations of various kinds (*IAphrodSpect* 45; *IDidyma* 50; Kolb 1990; see photo in fig. 20). Several latrines at the Vedius bath-gymnasium complex at Ephesus were set aside for groups of bankers, hemp workers, wool dealers, and linen weavers, who evidently frequented the place (*IEph* 454; cf. Yegül 1992:217–19, on associations in North Africa). Quite well known is the synagogue contained within the bath-gymnasium complex at Sardis in the third century, which I discuss in chapter 7. Various such groups could also have special seats reserved for them in the theater where the assembly of the people, as well as various theatrical and other performances, took place. The theater at Miletos included reservations for guilds such as the "emperor-loving goldsmiths" and the "Jews (Judaeans) and God-fearers," who sat just a few rows from the front, right next to the benches reserved for the "friends of the Augusti" (see photos in figs. 21a and 21b; cf. Kleiner 1970:18–20). The theater at Aphrodisias included reserved benches for the butchers alongside others (*IAphrodSpect* 46).

FIGURE 20: The stadium at Aphrodisias.

21a

21b

FIGURES 21a and 21b: Reserved seating for the "Jews and God-fearers" and for the "friends of the Augusti" in the theater at Miletos.

Discussion of cultural institutions leads to another important aspect of the polis and its socioreligious life: festivals, processions, and related activities in honor of the gods (cf. S. Price 1984:101–32; Wörrle 1988; S. Mitchell 1993). As we noted earlier, the gods and rulers were an integral part of the relations and hierarchies that characterized the system of benefaction. Festivals were one means by which appropriate honor could be shown to these "godly" benefactors who sat atop the web of networks and protected the polis and its inhabitants. Plutarch, who was quite emphatic about the need for moderation in the pursuit of honor, felt that the best pretext for benefaction was one "connected with the worship of a god [which] leads the people to piety; for at the same time there springs up in the minds of the masses a strong disposition to believe that the deity is great and majestic, when they see the men whom they themselves honor and regard as great so liberally and zealously vying with each other in honoring the divinity" (*Morals* 822b; trans. Helmbold and Harold 1957 [LCL]). The proliferation of associations of athletes and performers in the Hellenistic era and, even more so, the Roman era is just one clear indication of the continuing popularity and importance of festivals and the gods and goddesses (including emperors) they honored.

There are clear signs of the continuing importance of the gods and goddesses of the civic cults for the members of many associations, along with civic pride. The relation between the community and the gods was taken seriously, and any threat to this relationship was a grave offense. The Acts account of the silversmiths' riot at Ephesus realistically portrays the attachment that inhabitants of a polis, including the membership of guilds, felt for their patron deity (Acts 19:23–41). In this case, silversmiths and other craftsmen were involved in a disturbance not as a consequence of opposition to local structures or of being distanced from civic identity, but rather in defense of them. The more important of the motives Acts mentions relates to the need to appropriately honor the goddess: "there is danger . . . that the temple of the great goddess Artemis will be scorned, and she will be deprived of her majesty that brought all Asia and the world to worship her" (19:27; cf. *IEph* 24 [c. 160 C.E.]; cf. Oster 1976).

The official patron of a polis was not the only deity to whom honor was due, however, as we saw in regard to the range of deities honored within associations of Asia. The foundation and continuation of associations or cults in honor of gods other than the polis's patron deity could also be bound up in civic identity and well-being. The myth of the introduction of Dionysiac cult societies (*thiasoi*) to Magnesia, which I have already mentioned, clearly shows this (*IMagnMai* 215). The well-being of the Magnesian people, whose patron deity was Artemis Leukophryene, was also dependent on the proper fulfillment of the wills of other gods, Apollo and Dionysos, who called for the foundation of associations and temples devoted to Dionysos. Those who belonged to a Magnesian Dionysiac association in the Roman era (whose leader set up this monument) evidently felt themselves to be part of this polis and its history.

Conclusion

The inscriptional evidence from Asia provides a concrete illustration of the continuing importance of the polis and its structures as a locus of identity, cooperation, and competition for members of many associations and guilds, reflecting various social strata of society. These groups were often participants in civic vitality, not symptoms of decline. We should not assume that they were naturally inclined to be in opposition to the polis or its structures.

Moreover, inhabitants who joined together on a regular basis to form associations could find the polis to be a home. The level and nature of participation or identification within the civic context could vary from one association to the next, however. Each group could find its own individual way of living within the polis despite commonalities with the ways of other associations. The involvement of associations in imperial facets of civic life, to which I now turn, was another factor involved in a group claiming its place within society.

PART 2

IMPERIAL CULTS AND CONNECTIONS
AMONG ASSOCIATIONS

4

Imperial Gods within Religious Life

Cultic Honors

Introduction

In assessing the relationship between associations and society, especially the imperial dimensions, scholars often stress tensions. One hears far more of involvements in disturbances and strict controlling actions by imperial authorities than of the extensive evidence for associations' participation in other imperial facets of society and culture. This and the following chapter begin to correct the unbalanced picture of association life entailed in these common scholarly approaches. I do this by looking at evidence concerning the place of the emperors and imperial family within the internal religious life of many associations (chapter 4) and the involvements of associations in external relations with emperors and imperial-connected individuals and families (chapter 5).

So as to avoid the pitfalls of previous scholarship, which has seen conflict and control as the focal point of association life, I reserve evaluation of civic disturbances and the intervention Roman authorities until the end of part two (chapter 6). There I put this evidence of group-society tensions into perspective in light of ongoing positive interaction. Since much of the evidence for associations' involvements in disturbances and imperial intervention pertains to Rome or Italy, this order of discussion also prevents us being sidetracked from the principal focus on Roman Asia.

Moreover, the evidence relating to cultic honors (or worship) for the emperors and participation within social networks of benefaction helps to provide a clearer picture regarding the place of associations within culture in Asia Minor. It also provides a fitting framework within which to compare the participation and nonparticipation of both Jewish synagogues and Christian assemblies in imperial dimensions of civic life in the same region. By looking at manifestations of Roman imperialism within society we witness an important part of the world in which Jews and Christians lived their lives.

The cultural landscape of Roman Asia was permeated by festivals, rituals, and temples that included the emperors and imperial family or *Sebastoi* ("revered ones"), and there are associations that reflect this context in their internal ritual life. Alongside provincial and civic imperial cult institutions and temples stood unofficial forms of rituals in honor of the revered ones, some within smaller group settings. The evidence for these local associations throws into question many common scholarly views concerning rituals for the emperors, or imperial cults. Overall, cultic honors for these *imperial gods* (as I often call them) could be a significant and integral part of association life, telling us something about the self-understanding of such groups and their place within society and the cosmos. Insights from the social sciences and ritual studies help us to evaluate the meaning of this evidence.

The Case of Demeter Worshipers at Ephesus

An association of Demeter worshipers at Ephesus will serve as a foray into the issue of imperial cults and scholarly approaches to them. Unfortunately, we do not usually have sufficient evidence to discuss in any detail the general history of a particular association in a specific locality, let alone the place of the *Sebastoi* within that history. In many cases we are lucky if we even have two or three extant, though incomplete, inscriptions pertaining to a particular group. So it is significant that in the case of the Demetriasts of Ephesus we at least get momentary glimpses of their history from the beginning of the first to the mid-second century. Two inscriptions reveal, among other things, the ongoing importance of the emperors or imperial family within the religious life of this association (*IEph* 213, 4337; cf. *IEph* 1210, 1270 [c. 90–110 c.e.], 1595; *IMagnMai* 158 [c. 38–42 c.e.]). The case of the Demetriasts, which is not isolated, suggests that imperial gods could be an important aspect of group identity and practice, revealing to us something about how members of such associations felt about their place within society and the cosmos.

The earliest evidence we have for this group dates to the time of Tiberius, between 19 and 23 c.e. (*IEph* 4337 = Keil 1928:61–66; cf. Oster

1990:1671–73). The inscription, whose beginning is missing, preserves for us a decree of the Demetriasts concerning honors for particular benefactors who were also priests or priestesses. One of them, probably the man named Bassos, had assumed liturgies associated with the management of the gymnasium and the night watch, besides being priest of Artemis. In connection with the civic institutions' acknowledgment of these services, the Demetriasts decided that they, too, would grant these persons special honors both for their contributions to the life of the city and for their goodwill toward the association specifically, which probably took the form of specific benefactions. They arranged to have images or statues of these benefactors made and set up in a prominent place.

Especially significant for our present purposes, however, are the imperial cult connections associated with the priesthoods of the honorees. Along with the priest of Artemis (Bassos) is mentioned Proklos, who is called priest of the "new Dioskoroi," the sons of Drusus Caesar (cf. Tacitus, *Annals* 2.84). There was evidently a cult devoted to the twin sons of Drusus Caesar and Livilla identifying them as the sons of Zeus, perhaps alongside other members of the imperial family identified as gods. The third honoree, Servilia Secunda, is referred to as the priestess of "Sebaste Demeter Karpophoros." Here we have the Demetriasts honoring prominent persons who had assumed priesthoods associated with cults for the imperial family alongside traditional deities. More importantly here, the Demetriasts identify their own patron deity with a member of the imperial family, Sebaste (Augusta), most likely Livia Drusilla Augusta (the third wife of Augustus). This suggests that rituals for such members of the imperial family were integrated within traditional practices for Demeter within group life.

There are further indications that religious rites for members of the imperial family were an integral and ongoing part of the life and identity of this group at Ephesus. Another important inscription from the time of Domitian confirms this, and it is worth quoting what has survived of this letter in full (*IEph* 213; c. 88–89 C.E.):

> To Lucius Mestrius Florus, proconsul (*anthypatō*), from Lucius Pompeius Apollonios of Ephesus. Mysteries and sacrifices (*mystēria kai thysiai*) are performed each year in Ephesus, lord, to Demeter Karpophoros and Thesmophoros and to the revered gods (*theois Sebastois*) by initiates with great purity and lawful customs, together with the priestesses. In most years these practices were protected by kings and revered ones, as well as the proconsul of the period (*apo basileōn kai Sebastōn kai tōn kat eniauton anthy-*

patōn), as contained in their enclosed letters. Accordingly, as the mysteries are pressing upon us during your time of office, through my agency the ones obligated to accomplish the mysteries (*hoi ōpheilontes ta mystēria epitelein*) necessarily petition you, lord, in order that, acknowledging their rights . . . [lacuna][1]

It does not seem that this group is asking permission, as though they would otherwise be unable to engage in their celebration. Instead, they are seeking the prestige that further acknowledgment by important officials could give to them. As G. H. R. Horsley also points out, the manner in which the association's representative addresses the proconsul and emphasizes the precedents for such recognition—even including copies of previous correspondence—would make it hard for the official to deny what they wanted (see *NewDocs* IV 22). After all, there was a long history of prestige attributed by kings, emperors, and proconsuls long before Florus arrived on the scene during the time of Domitian.

The manner in which this history is cited suggests that the rituals for imperial gods were not something new added to simply appease a Roman official. Instead, they were a continuation of the sort of cultic practices hinted at in the inscription from the time of Tiberius. This group included "sacrifices and mysteries" dedicated not only to Demeter but also to the *Sebastoi* gods in one of its most important yearly celebrations, and there is no clear distinction made in the inscription between the godly recipients of these honors. The "revered ones" found themselves alongside the likes of Demeter in the realm of the gods. The offering of sacrifices "to" (not just "on behalf of") the emperors as gods was not at all limited to this particular association, as we shall soon see. Where such sacrifices were made to these gods we can assume that the customary banquets involving the consumption of sacrificial food would follow.

Also significant here is the incorporation of the imperial gods within the ritual life or mysteries of this group. Alongside the central ritual of sacrifice, mysteries were among the most respected and revered acts of piety in the Greco-Roman world; few human actions so effectively maintained fitting relations between the realm of humans and that of the gods, ensuring benefaction and protection for the individual, group, or community in question. Unfortunately, the inscription does not give us any information concerning the actual content of these mysteries, so we are left wondering what exactly the rituals entailed. This gap in our knowledge about the precise nature of the mysteries and related rituals, though never completely filled, will diminish somewhat when we turn to other evidence for

imperial mysteries further below. Contrary to what many scholars who ad-
here to the traditional paradigm of imperial cult would be inclined to assert, this example of imperial mysteries and sacrifices is not simply an
isolated exception. Rather, it is indicative of similar practices that were important within the internal socioreligious life of other associations too, at
least in Roman Asia.

Questioning a Scholarly Tradition

When the influential scholar A. D. Nock (1972a:248) encounters this evidence for the Demetriasts he discounts it, stating that it "is hardly likely
that the Emperor or the Empress identified with Demeter figures in the
mysteries. . . . The promoters of a secret rite were perhaps eager to avoid
any suspicion of cloaking disloyalty under secrecy." M. P. Nilsson (1959)
also briefly considers the evidence for rituals such as imperial mysteries
within small-group settings, but he readily categorizes them as politically
motivated clichés or "pseudo-mysteries" (cf. Nilsson 1961:370–71). Writing before both Nock and Nilsson, Franz Poland's (1909:234–35) sum-
mary statement regarding associations specifically does not come as a
surprise in light of the commonly held assumptions within scholarship:
"the cult of the emperors appears relatively seldom [within associations]
and, where it does occur, has little independent meaning." Moreover, he
asserts, such cultic activities had little significance for an association's
"self-understanding" (Poland 1909:532).

    These assessments of imperial rituals within associations should be un-
derstood within the context of a common paradigm of imperial cults generally. The central conviction of the traditional view is that imperial cults
were *not* well integrated within religious life. Rather, they were fundamentally different in kind from other cultic forms in the Greco-Roman world.
Scholars such as Nock, Nilsson, G. W. Bowersock, and Paul Veyne emphasize that imperial cults were political, not religious; public, not private. According to Nilsson (1948:178), imperial cult "lacked all genuine religious
content." The cult's "meaning lay far more in state and social realms,
where it served both to express loyalty to the rule of Rome and the emperor and to satisfy the ambition of the leading families" (Nilsson
1961:385; cf. Bowersock 1965:115; 1983; de Ste. Croix 1981:394–95).
Moreover, from this viewpoint imperial rituals were merely ceremony, "a
purely mechanical exercise" that failed to evoke the feelings or emotions
of the individuals who participated (Fishwick 1978:1252–53; cf. Veyne

1990:315). No one actually believed that the emperors were gods, and this is reflected in the lack of any "private" forms of religious life, such as votive offerings (reflecting prayers to the emperors) and mysteries.[2]

Underestimating the social and religious significance of imperial cults for the populace is partially the result of the imposition of modern viewpoints and assumptions onto ancient evidence (cf. Harland 1996). First, the traditional view reflects modern distinctions between politics and religion that, as Simon Price also stresses, do not fit the ancient context, where the social, religious, economic, and political were intricately interconnected and often inseparable. Second, the view involves the imposition of modern notions concerning "individualism," "private" vs. "public," and related definitions of religion onto ancient evidence. Some modern definitions of religion (such as those offered by William James 1963:50 and Rudolf Otto 1923) stress emotions or feelings of the individual as the heart of religion, emphasizing an equation between "personal" or "private" and genuine religiosity, and there is a tendency among some scholars to apply this to antiquity, as we have seen in chapter 2 (cf. Festugière 1954:1–4; Dodds 1959:243; 1965:2; Nilsson 1961:711–12; Green 1990:588). However, such individualistic and (sometimes) antiritualistic definitions of religion are problematic when applied to non-Western (or even non-Protestant) religious phenomena, modern or ancient. Though there were certainly some cases when religious feelings were strongly expressed by individuals in antiquity (cf. Apuleius, *Metamorphoses* book 11), piety and religiosity were often more concerned with the performance of rituals within group or community settings in order to maintain fitting relations between communities and the gods rather than with the inner feelings of the individual. This does not make such activity any less "genuinely" religious within that context. Even so, there is neglected evidence that imperial cults were important within contexts that many of these scholars would consider "private," including the associations that I discuss at length.[3]

This scholarly view that emphasizes a fundamental difference between cults for emperors and those for other gods is not without opponents (cf. Robert 1960c:321–24; Will 1960; Hopkins 1978; Momigliano 1987a). Fergus Millar's (1973:164) overall impression is that imperial cults were not essentially different from other cults, but rather "fully and extensively integrated into the local cults of the provinces, with the consequence that the Emperors were the object of the same cult-acts as the other gods." "Unless we deny the name 'religion' to all pagan cults," he states, "our evidence compels us to grant it also to the Imperial cult" (Millar 1973:148).

H. W. Pleket's article (1965) on the evidence for "imperial mysteries" draws attention to certain instances of what he would call genuine piety in relation to the emperors, to which I will return in connection with a group at Pergamum.

Recent research on imperial cults in Asia Minor specifically likewise provides an alternative understanding to that of the traditional paradigm. Studies by S. Price (1984), Steven J. Friesen (1993), and Stephen Mitchell (1993, 1:100–117) point to the integration of imperial cults within civic life in this region, with political, social, and religious significance for various social strata of the population. And R. R. R. Smith's (1987:136) work on the symbolic significance of the reliefs of the temple of the *Sebastoi* at Aphrodisias shows how emperors were "added to the old gods, not as successors or replacements, but as a new branch of the Olympian pantheon" (cf. Reynolds 1981, 1986, 1996). Although such scholars present compelling evidence with respect to the varied significance of imperial cults (beyond the political), they do not devote special attention to the inscriptional evidence for associations specifically, to which we now return.[4]

Rituals for the *Sebastoi* within Associations

Taking a closer look at associations in Roman Asia provides a convincing illustration of the integration of the emperors and imperial cults within political, social, and religious dimensions of the populace's life on a local level. This investigation will shed more light on both the nature of imperial cults and the self-understanding of associations.

A few words of introduction are in order concerning the various forms that cults for the emperors took, so that we can place associations within this framework. It is useful to distinguish between four levels of imperial cults. First, there was the official cult of *deceased* emperors centered at the city of Rome itself. At the death of popular emperors (but not those that gained the *damnatio memoriae* of the Roman senate), a special ceremony took place that involved the senate inducting the deceased emperor into the realm of the gods. Republican and Augustan traditions clearly stopped short of "worshiping" a living emperor as a god, and this tendency was primarily reflected in imperial cults in the West or Latin speaking parts of the empire. In the Greek East, however, there was no such hesitancy in granting cultic honors to living rulers (esp. in the centuries following Alexander the Great, who died in 323 B.C.E.).

Second, there were *provincial* imperial cults and temples organized by institutions that claimed to represent the civic communities of a given province (cf. Friesen 2001). In Asia this central organization was known as the "*koinon* of Asia" or the "Hellenes of Asia," and the imperial cult temples founded by this organization were primarily under the direction of the "high priests of Asia" (*archiereis Asias*). Similar organizations existed in provinces like Bithynia-Pontus and Galatia as well. Temples established by this provincial council of Asia in the first century or so included those for goddess Roma and god Augustus at Pergamum (founded 29 B.C.E.), for Tiberius at Smyrna (23 C.E.), for Domitian at Ephesus (89 C.E.), and for Trajan at Pergamum (just before 113 C.E.).[5] The provincial temple at Pergamum included cult statues of Trajan and of Zeus Philios ("the friend"); later on, a statue of the emperor Hadrian was also placed within the sanctuary (see the photo in fig. 22; cf. Radt 1999:209–20). This cult for Trajan was also typical of provincial imperial cults in the sense that there were regular festivals and games in honor of the emperor in connection with the temple (*CIL* III Sup 7086). An influential benefactor of Pergamum, C. Antius Aulus Julius Quadratus, contributed a substantial amount of funds to establish these games, and we shall soon encounter this important imperial official in connection with associations in the next chapter. In Asia Minor it became common in various contexts, including provincial cults,

FIGURE 22: Temple for Trajan (Trajaneum) and Zeus Philios on the acropolis at Pergamum. Partially reconstructed by archeologists.

to refer to a given emperor as "god *Sebastos*," and to refer to the emperors (and some other members of the imperial family) collectively as the "*Sebastoi* gods," "the revered gods."

Third, there were *civic* imperial cults that were devoted to honoring the *Sebastoi* (or a particular emperor) and that maintained close connections with other institutions of the polis. These cults, which were established using donations from local benefactors or prominent families, could involve a newly built temple or could take place within existing civic buildings. A good example of such a civic temple is the Sebasteion at Aphrodisias, which was dedicated to "Aphrodite, the *Sebastoi* gods, and the people" (Reynolds 1981:318, no. 2) or, alternatively, to the "Olympian *Sebastoi* gods" (see R. Smith 1987; Reynolds 1981, 1986, 1996). There were similar civic cults with their own priesthoods and other functionaries at various locales, including Akmoneia, Ephesus, and Laodicea. Civic and provincial imperial cults were not mutually exclusive. The same persons could serve as functionaries in either context or even both at the same time, as we will see in the next chapter.

Fourth, there were other *local* shrines, monuments, and expressions of honor for the emperors as gods in unofficial settings (e.g., small groups, families, individuals), which brings us back to associations. Despite the limitations of epigraphic sources, there is considerable evidence of imperial cult activities from various cities of Roman Asia concerning associations of different types. The nature and extent of the practices we encounter in these various settings suggest that a similar range of activities probably took place within other associations about whom we happen to know far less. Overall, cultic honors for imperial gods (*Sebastoi*) could be a significant component in the internal life of associations, proposing something to us about the self-understanding or identity of these groups, about how they understood their place within the context of polis, empire, and cosmos. Contrary to the traditional view, such practices were not merely expressions of political loyalty. Rather, they were religious expressions in the same sense that one could speak of religious expressions toward the traditional gods, all of which were intertwined within social, political, and other dimensions of life in the polis.

Official Settings

Some associations could participate in official civic or provincial celebrations and festivals in honor of emperors. Such participation was primarily limited to the organizations of the gymnasia and professional associations of Dionysiac performers or athletes devoted to Herakles, which are not the primary focus of this book.[6] For instance, a decree of the worldwide Dionysiac performers found at Ankyra involves this group thanking a benefactor for his contributions to the "mystery" (*mystērion*) and for supplying funds for the performers' competition in a "mystical contest" (*mystikos agōn*) involving sacred plays in honor of both Dionysos and Hadrian, the "new Dionysos" (*IAnkyraBosch* 128, esp. lines 10–11, 20–25; see Buckler and Keil 1926; cf. *IAnkyraBosch* 127, 129–30).

Nonetheless, there were some other, less official, associations that could also on occasion participate in provincial or civic imperial cult celebrations in Asia. Associations called "hymn singers" (*hymnōdoi*) in Asia, such as those at Pergamum, provide a good example of this (cf. Poland 1926; Friesen 2001:104–16). Hymn singers dedicated to the imperial gods are attested in several places. At Ephesus there seems to have been more than one group using this self-designation, one being connected with a temple of Hadrian. At Smyrna there were two groups by this name, one a subgroup of the elders' organization and the other calling itself "the fellow hymn singers of god Hadrian," a group that continued long after that emperor's time.[7] Unlike associations of Dionysiac performers, however, it seems that these groups were not usually professionals.

We know of the group at Pergamum from several inscriptions of the first and early second centuries. By the beginning of the second century, at least, the membership consisted primarily if not solely of Roman citizens, some of whom were wealthy (*IPergamon* 374).[8] There is earlier evidence from the time of Claudius concerning the Pergamene and other hymn singers (*IEph* 3801 = *IGR* IV 1608c; cf. *IEph* 18d.4–24 [c. 44 c.e.]; Keil 1908; Buckler 1935). The first part of the inscription reveals that the hymn singers had previously received a letter from Claudius himself acknowledging the decree that they had sent to him, probably honoring the imperial household (only the beginning is legible). They decided to monumentalize this instance of contact with an emperor.

More importantly here, the second part of the monument preserves a document concerning a provincial celebration held at the temple of god Augustus and goddess Roma at Pergamum. It is a resolution of the provincial assembly (*koinon*) or council of Asia (also known as the "Hellenes of Asia"). The provincial council thanks the hymn singers for their participation in celebrating the emperor's birthday:

> Since it is appropriate to offer a visible expression of piety and of every intention befitting the sacred to the revered household, the hymn-singers

from all Asia, coming together each year in Pergamum for the most sacred
birthday of god *Sebastos* Tiberius Caesar, accomplish a magnificent work
for the glory of the association (*synodos*), singing hymns to the revered
household, accomplishing sacrifices to the revered gods, leading festivals
and banquets. (*IEph* 3801)[9]

It seems that on some important occasions associations of hymn singers
from various cities of Asia, perhaps including those we hear of at Ephesus
and Smyrna, joined together with the more prominent group at Pergamum to honor imperial gods at official celebrations. The provincial civic
communities, who bore the cost involved (cf. *IEph* 18d, lines 4–24; 44
c.e.), appreciated the hymn singers' piety in this regard.

Unofficial Group Settings

By far the majority of evidence for the participation of associations in imperial cult activities pertains to internal group life, though these groups
were certainly, in part, reflecting the civic and provincial context when
they engaged in these activities. The names of some associations suggest
that members of the imperial household could be chosen as patron deities
of a group, being recipients of regular cultic honors (cf. Pleket 1958:4–10;
S. Price 1984:118; Robert 1960b:220–28). We have numerous examples
from throughout Asia: the "friends-of-Agrippa" (*philagrippai*) association
at Smyrna (*ISmyrna* 331; cf. *IG* VI 374 [Sparta]; *IXanthos* 24; *CIL* VI 37847
[Rome]); the "friends of the *Sebastoi*" (*philosebas[toi]*) at Pergamum (*IPergamonAsklep* 84); the "friends-of-Caesar brotherhood" (*phratraōn philoke-
sareōn* [*sic*]) at Ilion (Pleket 1958:4, no. 4); and the Tiberians (*Tibeireiōn*) at
Didyma, who sat near a group of hymn singers (*IDidyma* 50.1a.65).[10]

We also encounter similar groups outside the walls of the polis. For instance, the Caesarists (*kaisariastai*) in a village near Smyrna (Mostenai)
honored a man for his contributions to the association (*koinon*) in connection with its sacrifices for the *Sebastoi* and accompanying banquets
(*IGR* IV 1348; cf. *IEph* 3817, from the village of Azoulenon). In these cases
we clearly see the importance of the emperors, and rituals for them, in the
self-understanding of the groups in question.

There are indications that ethnic-geographic and occupational associations engaged in similar rituals for imperial gods. For example, Dio Cassius refers to the fact that groups of Romans resident in Ephesus and in
Nikaia granted cultic honors to both Roma and Julius Caesar in connection with the sanctuaries established for these deities around 29 b.c.e.

(*Roman History* 51.20.6–7). Several statues of imperial figures were dedicated by associations of Romans or Italians in Asia (cf. *IEph* 409, 3019; *MAMA* VI 177 [Phrygian Apameia]). The guild of shippers at Nikomedia in Bithynia dedicated its sanctuary (*temenos*) to Vespasian, indicative of rituals in honor of that emperor (*TAM* IV 22; 70–71 c.e.).

Unfortunately, remains of guild halls in Asia Minor have seldom been found or identified, but those that have been discovered elsewhere suggest a similar picture regarding the importance of the emperors within group life. For example, on the island of Delos, the meeting place of the merchants and shippers from Berytus contained a sanctuary with a shrine for goddess Roma, set up "on account of her goodwill towards the association and the homeland" (*IDelos* 1778; 2d century b.c.e.; also see chapter 2). Certainly this group returned her goodwill with the appropriate honors, especially sacrifice. Elsewhere, several of the guild halls at Ostia in Italy contained portrait heads, busts, and statues of members of the imperial household. Russell Meiggs (1960:325–27) concludes that "some form of imperial cult [was] common to all guilds." I would suggest that we can imagine a similar integration of the emperors within the religious life of other occupational or ethnic-geographic associations, and we do in fact encounter more direct evidence in Asia that includes guilds.

Sacrifices

The religious activities of other associations suggest a parallelism between honors addressed to the traditional gods and those addressed to the revered imperial gods. I have already mentioned the performance of sacrifice, the most important cultic honor in antiquity, within associations. Sacrifices or other forms of offerings for the gods inevitably involved a set of other ritual activities including prayers, hymns, libations, burning of incense, and, of course, the accompanying meal.

Recent studies regarding the meaning and function of sacrifice, which often employ insights from the social sciences, emphasize two main elements or functions of sacrifice within the ancient Greek context.[11] On the one hand, sacrifice was a setting in which the bonds of human community were expressed and reinforced, revealing the nature of social relations and hierarchies within society. On the other hand, sacrifice was a means of relation with the gods in order to solicit protection and avoid punishment for the group or community. Sacrifice was a symbolic expression of the nature of the cosmos and fitting relations within it. In other words, sacrifice, like other forms of ritual, encompassed a set of symbols that communicated, among other things, a certain understanding of relations between humans within the group and between human groups and the gods. The incorporation of the emperors in the Greek system of sacrifice, therefore, tells us something about both group identity and the place of imperial gods within the worldview of the members of associations.

There is considerable evidence for the importance of sacrifice for imperial gods among various groups. Associations sometimes dedicated altars to the *Sebastoi* gods generally or a particular member of the imperial family, or had benefactors that did so for them.[12] For example, the hymn singers at Pergamum, whose internal activities definitely involved various rituals for the emperors including sacrifices, dedicated an altar to Hadrian, "Olympios, savior and founder" (*IPergamon* 374). These dedications of altars are indicative of the inclusion of imperial gods in at least sacrifice and perhaps other rituals of the groups in question. It is not a far stretch to imagine that associations who dedicated other structures to the "*Sebastoi* gods," such as the guild of merchants at Thyatira (*TAM* V 862), would also engage in sacrifices or other rituals for these same gods in their internal life as well.

There is also more direct evidence that sacrifices were made to the imperial deities alongside other gods (or alone). We have already encountered this in the practices of the Demetriasts at Ephesus. Another inscription from Ephesus (*IEph* 719), this one involving an occupational association, reveals the customary practices of the group in referring to the "physicians who sacrifice to the ancestor Asklepios and to the *Sebastoi*" (*hoi thyontes tō propatori Asklēpiō kai tois Sebastois iatroi*). Compare also an earlier reconstructed inscription that mentions an imperial freedman dedicating money to a synod, perhaps Roman businessmen, "in order to perform the sacrifice to Roma and the goddess" (*epitelesth[eisan tēi Rōmēi kai] tēi theōi thysian*; Engelmann 1990:93–94, revising *IEph* 859a; c. 27 B.C.E.).

These inscriptions pertaining to sacrifice are particularly relevant in regard to one of S. Price's claims. Despite his recognition of the varied importance of imperial cults (beyond the political), Price argues that, in general, sacrifices were consciously made "on behalf of" the emperors rather than "to" the emperors (using the dative in Greek), and that the majority of the evidence from Asia Minor reflects a conscious effort to use the former terminology (S. Price 1984:207–33; cf. Nock 1972a). This argument, coupled with other claims regarding imperial statues, is fundamental to his overall suggestion that in ritual practice the emperors were not equated with the gods but rather ontologically located "at the focal point between human and the divine" (S. Price 1984:233).[13]

The above inscriptions involving local associations, as well as the evidence for the Demetriasts and the hymn singers discussed earlier (both of which use the dative of sacrifice), are examples where no such distinction is made between the revered ones and other gods. As Friesen (1993:149) states, "there is quite a bit of evidence from Asia and not cited by Price that equates the gods and the emperors in a sacrificial context. In fact, the vast majority of evidence does not distinguish gods from emperors." Once again, this stresses that the emperors could function as gods within religious life at the local level in Roman Asia.

It was customary for a communal meal to follow such sacrifices in which some of the foods offered to the gods, in this case the imperial gods, would be consumed by the members of the association. The banquets of associations were among the most common small-group settings where a person living and working in Ephesus, Pergamum, or Thyatira would encounter on a regular basis sacrificial food that had been offered to the gods (*ta hierothyta*), including the imperial gods. This observation will become particularly relevant when we consider early Christian debates on the eating food offered to idols (*ta eidōlothyta*).

Mysteries

There was a range of other possibilities in the ritual practices of associations, some of which can be discussed in connection with mysteries in honor of the imperial gods (cf. Robert 1960c:321–24; Pleket 1965; S. Price 1984:190–91; Harland 1996:328–33; Herrmann 1996:340–41). These imperial mysteries deserve special attention since scholars like Nock and Nilsson are concerned with downplaying their significance in order to argue that rituals for the imperial gods were not genuinely religious.

A few words of introduction regarding imperial mysteries will be useful before looking at associations. Sometimes mysteries could be performed within civic or provincial cult contexts (cf. *IG* XII.2 205 [mysteries for Tiberius at Mytilene on Lesbos]). For instance, there were mysteries and related rituals in connection with cults of "god Antinoos" (the beloved teenage companion of Hadrian) at various locations in the empire, including Mantineia in Greece, Antinoopolis in Egypt (named after Antinoos), and Claudiopolis in Bithynia (Antinoos's hometown).[14] Comparable mysteries were practiced in honor of other imperial gods in some of the official civic and provincial cults of Asia Minor as well. In the inscriptions of Asia, Bithynia, and Galatia, for example, we come across functionaries called sebastophants, that is, "revealers of the *Sebastoi*" in imperial mysteries.[15] This is a functionary that we find in unofficial mysteries as well. Evidence of this kind from official cults shows how, in some regards, associations that engaged in imperial mysteries also reflected the polis context. Through participating in similar religious practices in a small-group setting the members of an association could feel a sense of belonging not only within the group, but also within this broader civic or imperial framework. But to say that associations' practices were, in part, a reflection of their surroundings is not to undermine the significance of these rituals for participants.

Egyptian papyrological evidence provides important background information concerning imperial mysteries and associations. One papyrus fragment from Antinoopolis, perhaps from a novel, refers to royal mysteries in Egypt from an earlier period: "Triptolemus . . . , not for you have I now performed initiation; neither Kore abducted did I see nor Demeter in her grief, but kings in their victory" (*PAntinoopolis* I 18; late 2d century C.E.; trans. Burkert 1993:269; cf. Nilsson 1960). Reference to royal mysteries in Egypt, this time in connection with Dionysiac mysteries, also appears in an honorary poem for the king by Euphronios, which refers to celebrants in the mysteries of "new Dionysos," that is, Ptolemy IV (Burkert 1993:268–69). J. Tondriau (1946) traces the history of a continuing connection between Dionysiac mysteries and the royal court, including evidence for a *thiasos* within the court during the reigns of Ptolemy IV Philopater (221–203 B.C.E.), Ptolemy XII Auletes (80–51 B.C.E.), and Cleopatra and Mark Antony (42–20 B.C.E.; cf. Plutarch, *Antony* 24).[16] Here we have various references to mystic rites, akin to the traditional mysteries of Demeter, Kore, Dionysos, and others, associated with Hellenistic royalty in Egypt, foreshadowing the sorts of practices we encounter during the Roman era.

Another papyrus fragment found at Oxyrhynchus brings us into the Roman era and provides an interesting link between Egypt and Asia Minor in regard to imperial mysteries. The papyrus, which dates to the third century C.E., preserves part of a novel in which a character condemns what he sees as the imitation of Demeter's Eleusinian mysteries in the performance of mysteries to magnify "Caesar" in Egypt. The critic attributes the origins of such rites to Bithynia in Asia Minor: "It was not we who originally invented those rites, which is to our credit, but it was a Nikaian who was the first to institute them . . . let the rites be his, and let them be performed among his people alone . . . unless we wish to commit sacrilege against Caesar himself, as we should commit sacrilege against Demeter also, if we performed to her here the ritual used there; for she is unwilling to allow any rites of that sort" (*POxy* 1612 [with trans.]; cf. Deubner

1919:8–11). The critic seems concerned with impiety against both Caesar and Demeter, but we know too little to assess precisely why he objects to these rituals. Nonetheless, this papyrus further demonstrates that mysteries were performed in honor of rulers or emperors in regions of the Greek East such as Egypt and Asia Minor, and that they could closely mirror the mysteries in honor of deities such as Demeter.

Now that we have some background on royal and imperial mysteries we can turn to the practices of associations in Asia. We have already discussed at some length the mysteries of the Demetriasts at Ephesus, who, similar to those critiqued by the character in the novel, integrated the emperors within mysteries of Demeter. Yet there were comparable practices within other groups as well, which suggest that imperial mysteries were not uncommon within associations, though probably not as widespread as were sacrificial rituals for "the revered ones."

Imperial gods could be incorporated within the mysteries of Dionysos. We find Hellenistic precedents for the importance of ruler cults for these groups in Asia Minor as well. In one inscription from Pergamum, for instance, "the bacchants of the god to whom you call 'euoi!' [i.e., Dionysos]" dedicate an altar "to King Eumenes, god, savior, and benefactor" (von Prott and Kolbe 1902:94–95, no. 86; 197–159 B.C.E.).[17] In light of this context, it would not be far-fetched to suggest the continuing importance of similar cultic honors involving the *Sebastoi* alongside Dionysos within the association of cowherds in Roman Pergamum, though this is not directly attested (cf. von Prott 1902:182–86).[18]

There are other indications of the integration of imperial gods within the mysteries of Dionysiac and other groups. According to a fragmentary inscription from the time of Commodus found at Ephesus, for instance, mysteries were performed there in honor of Dionysos, Zeus Panhellenios, and Hephaistos (*IEph* 1600 = *GIBM* IV.2 600 = Merkelbach 1979:155–56, no. 4). More importantly, it seems that those who led the mysteries—most likely the Dionysiac initiates we encounter in other inscriptions—also included the emperor identified as "new Dionysos" (line 46) in the mysteries and sacrifices (cf. *IEph* 293 [Commodus as "new Dionysos"]). Hicks (*GIBM*) even suggests the possibility that the list of participants and priests along with names of deities may indicate that the festival involved the impersonation of the gods (including imperial personages) in some sort of dramatic play—similar to those of the Iobacchoi at Athens and the Dionysiac performers at Ankyra—though this is not certain.

Further evidence of imperial mysteries is worth mentioning. Peter Herrmann discusses a quite heavily reconstructed inscription from Sardis, which may refer to a revealer of the *Sebastos* and a revealer of the sacred objects (hierophant) in the mysteries of an association (Herrmann 1996:340–41 on *ISardBR* 62; 2d century C.E.). We happen to lack evidence regarding imperial mysteries among associations devoted to Isis or Serapis in Asia; but it is noteworthy that a "company" (*taxis*) of paean singers (*Paianistai*) at Rome (probably consisting of members originally from the Greek East) chose both Serapis and the *Sebastoi* gods as its patrons, suggesting rituals for the imperial gods as a normal part of this group's life (*IG* XIV 1084; 146 C.E.).

Unfortunately, due to the nature of the evidence, mysteries and other related practices of the Demetriasts, Dionysiac initiates, and others are mentioned only in passing, telling us little of the actual details of what was involved. Still, one monument from Pergamum may help to clarify some of what was involved in the various internal rituals for the imperial gods, serving as an appropriate conclusion to this section.

Besides their occasional participation in singing during civic or provincial celebrations, the association of hymn singers at Pergamum engaged in imperial mysteries and sacrifices internally. One monument, which was dedicated to Hadrian, contains an inscription that outlines the provision of food and wine for the group's calendar of meetings, including the celebrations of the birthday of Augustus and the mysteries that lasted several days (*IPergamon* 374, B lines 10, 16). The celebrations and mysteries included sacrifices to Augustus and Roma (part D, line 14) and accompanying banquets, as well as the use of sacrificial cakes, incense, and, notably, lamps for the image of the "revered one (*Sebastos*)" (part B, lines 18–19). Further on, "images of the revered ones (*Sebastoi*)" (part C, line 13) are mentioned again which, as Pleket also suggests, were a significant component of this group's mysteries. Apparently images of Augustus or other imperial gods were revealed in the lamplight by a sebastophant, the equivalent of the "revealer of sacred objects" in Demeter's mysteries at Eleusis. This scenario concerning the nature of imperial mysteries also coincides with the case of a Dionysiac company (*speira*) in Thracia where there were functionaries responsible for lamps and several sebastophants alongside other titles associated with Dionysiac mysteries (*IGBulg* 1517; Cillae, 241–244 C.E.). It is quite possible that the mysteries of the Demetriasts at Ephesus, or of other associations, included similar rituals to those of the hymn singers.

Pleket (1965:346) concludes from his study of imperial mysteries that Nilsson's use of the term "pseudo-mysteries" to refer to such rites is unwarranted since "the mysteries at Pergamum as far as their rites are concerned were true copies of the traditional mysteries; both include hymns, glorification . . . , showing of the image" (cf. S. Price 1984:191). Nilsson's assertions that these imperial mysteries, like other cultic activities associated with the emperors, were merely "a public demonstration of loyalty" and were "really devoid of any mystical content" (Nilsson 1961:370), is based less on evidence than on his own presuppositions and overall paradigm with regard to the nature of imperial cults generally.

The Significance of Imperial Rituals within Associations

The traditional view of imperial cults corresponds to a particular theoretical trajectory in the modern study of religion, a trajectory that favors the personal feelings of the individual over communal actions or rituals (e.g., sacrifice) in defining what it accepts as meaningful religion. From this perspective corporate ceremonies are often merely outward or mechanical actions ("empty shells") with little significance to the essence of religion. As Mary Douglas (1973:19–39) points out, this modern tendency to devalue ritual as synonymous with meaningless and mechanical forms of religion has its roots, in part, in the antiritualist tradition of the Reformation. This theoretical framework does not do justice to the function and meaning of ritual actions, including "political" rituals, by which I mean rituals closely associated with power relations within society.

A brief discussion of some of the insights of sociologists and anthropologists concerning ritual will help to clarify the significance of imperial cults in antiquity, including rituals within associations. Here I use the term "ritual," as do many others in this field, to refer to "symbolic behavior that is socially standardized and repetitive," as "action wrapped in a web of symbolism" (Kertzer 1988:9; cf. Douglas 1973:26–27; Geertz 1973:112–14).

Clifford Geertz's influential studies of religion from an anthropological perspective provide useful insights here. Geertz is in many ways representative of a now common approach that understands religion as a cultural system of symbols or inherited conceptions, analogous to language, which communicates meanings (Geertz 1973:87–141; cf. Vernant's similar view of Greek religion, cited in Zaidman and Pantel 1992:22–23). A symbol in this sense is "any object, act, event, quality, or relation which serves as a vehicle for a conception—the conception is the symbol's meaning" (Geertz 1973:91). As a system of symbols, religion acts to coordinate and maintain both the way of life (ethos) and the worldview of a particular group, community, or society: "Religious symbols formulate a basic congruence between a particular style of life and a specific (if, most often, implicit) metaphysic, and in so doing sustain each with the borrowed authority of the other" (Geertz 1973:90).

According to Geertz, ritual plays a very important role in sustaining the interplay between social experience and worldview, or notions of the overall cosmic framework. As concrete actions performed in the realm of lived reality, rituals reinforce the apparent truth of the worldview:

> For it is in ritual . . . that this conviction that religious conceptions are veridical and that religious directives are sound is somehow generated. It is in some sort of ceremonial form . . . that the moods and motivations [ethos] which sacred symbols induce in men and the general conceptions of the order of existence [worldview] which they formulate for men meet and reinforce one another. In a ritual, the world as lived and the world as imagined, fused under the agency of a single set of symbolic forms, turn out to be the same world. (Geertz 1973:112)

Ritual, then, plays an important role in reinforcing a set of conceptions and symbols concerning the order of the cosmos and society. Another related point is that ritual actions can be concrete expressions or even performances of what people think of the world and their place within it. As Catherine Bell (1997:xi) puts it, "the fundamental efficacy of ritual activity lies in its ability to have people embody assumptions about their place in a larger order of things."

Some of these insights have been applied in studies of rituals associated with power and politics, worth discussing since our present focus is on imperial cults that are often dismissed as meaningless political ceremonies. Social-scientific and cross-cultural studies in this area show that even those public rites and ceremonies that we as moderns categorize as "political" can have meaningful and even cosmological significance (cf. Cannadine and Price 1987; Kertzer 1988). It is in Geertz's cross-cultural study of royal rituals in Elizabethan England, fourteenth-century Java, and nineteenth-century Morocco, for example, that he speaks of "the inherent sacredness of sovereign power" (Geertz 1977:151). He goes on to argue that royal ceremonies "mark the center as center and give what goes on there its aura of being not merely important, but in some odd fashion *connected with the way the world is built.* The gravity of high politics and the solemnity of high worship spring from liker impulses than might first appear" (Geertz 1977:152–53 [emphasis mine]).

Other instructive generalizations come from Maurice Bloch's anthropological case study of the royal bath ceremony in nineteenth-century Madagascar, in which he proposes a dual understanding of royal rituals. On the one hand, they function to legitimate authority by "making royal power an essential aspect of a cosmic social and emotional order"; and on the other, the effectiveness of this function is rooted in how royal rituals employ symbolism from the rituals of the everyday life of ordinary people (Bloch 1987, esp. pp. 294–97). As Bell (1997:135) states: "Political rituals display symbols and organize symbolic action in ways that attempt to demonstrate that the values and forms of social organization to which the ritual testifies are neither arbitrary nor temporary but follow naturally from the way the world is organized. For this reason, ritual has long been considered more effective than coercive force in securing people's assent to a particular order."

S. Price's study of imperial cult rituals in Roman Asia Minor specifically reflects insights similar to those I have just outlined. He rejects the conventional approach of many scholars of Greco-Roman religion who have focused on the mental states of individuals. Instead, he approaches imperial rituals as a "way of conceptualizing the world," as part of a "system whose structure defines the position of the emperor" (S. Price 1984:7–11). This system involving imperial rituals, he suggests, was important for all levels of society and functioned in various ways: "Using their traditional symbolic system [inhabitants of Asia Minor] represented the emperor to themselves in the familiar terms of divine power. The imperial cult, like the cults of the traditional gods, created a relationship of power between subject and ruler. It also enhanced the dominance of local elites over the populace, of cities over other cities, and of Greek over indigenous cultures. That is, the cult was a major part of the web of power that formed the fabric of society" (S. Price 1984:248). The broadly based nature of Price's insightful analysis of imperial cults did not allow him to focus attention on the significance of rituals within small-group settings or associations, however.

In light of recent studies on ritual, we can better understand imperial rituals within associations. Contrary to what Poland and others suggest, we need to realize that imperial gods were an important component within the self-understanding or identity of many associations. The performance of sacrifices, mysteries, or other rituals for emperors in the group setting was not simply an outward and meaningless statement of political loyalty. This was a symbolic expression of a worldview held in common by those participating. Within this cosmic framework, the *Sebastoi* were placed at the height of power alongside other gods in a realm separate from, though in interaction with, humans and human communities. Concrete ritual actions not only expressed this conception of reality but also reinforced the participants' sense that this conception corresponded to the way things actually were in real life.

As we have observed, imperial rituals were closely bound up in and reflect the system of symbols associated with cults for the gods more generally. This close link between symbols within imperial rituals and those of the everyday life of persons living within cities in Roman Asia suggests the meaningfulness of both for the participants. This helps to explain the effectiveness of symbolism associated with the imperial gods for legitimating the existing structures of power or authority. Yet it is important to stress the grassroots or spontaneous nature of these honors and ritual actions. They served to legitimate the authority and ideology of Roman rule within a developing ideology or worldview of the polis and its inhabitants. It seems that there was not always a need for Roman authorities systematically to propagate or enforce an ideology that legitimated their position of power within the Greek East. They simply had to take advantage of and encourage aspects of a developing symbolic framework that already existed.

Rituals within associations functioned and expressed cultural meaning in a variety of ways. The understanding of the cosmos (including the revered emperors) that was expressed in ritual strengthened the sense of belonging within the group. Yet it simultaneously made a statement regarding the place of that group or community within the societal and cosmic order of things. It said something of how the members of such a group regarded their relation to the most important figures of power in the Greco-Roman world. The group could be viewed as playing a part in the overall maintenance of fitting relations within the webs of connections that linked individuals (of all social strata), groups, civic or provincial communities, imperial functionaries, and the gods. In doing so, an association was also reflecting, often unconsciously, many features of cultural life in the polis context.

Conclusion

Overall, the evidence from Asia suggests that religious rites for imperial gods, which paralleled the sacrifices, mysteries, and other rituals directed at traditional deities, were a significant component within numerous associations. There is no reason evident in the inscriptions themselves to suggest that these rituals were any less meaningful, mystic, or religious than those connected with worship of the traditional gods in that context. Furthermore, insights regarding the function and meaning of ritual should steer us even further away from common assumptions held by scholars of imperial cults in the past.

Alongside interactions with civic and imperial officials, cultic honors for the *Sebastoi* gods were a means by which such groups engaged in what was considered by their contemporaries as fitting relations with those at the pinnacle of the networks and hierarchies of society and the cosmos. The imperial external relations and internal activities of these groups tell of their tendency toward integration within society and evince one of several factors involved in their finding a home within the polis.

Positive Interaction

Imperial Connections and Monumental Honors

Introduction

When Trajan received a letter from Pliny, then governor of Bithynia-Pontus (a province in northern Asia Minor), requesting that an association (*collegium*) be formed to fight fires at Nikomedia, the emperor cautioned that "we must remember that it is societies like these which have been responsible for the political disturbances in your province, particularly its towns. If people assemble for a common purpose, whatever name we give them and for whatever reason, they soon turn into a political club (*hetaeriae*)" (*Epistles* 10.34 [LCL]). The initial impression one might get from reading this passage in Pliny's correspondence, Livy's account of the senate's suppression of Dionysiac associations in republican Rome (written in the Augustan era), or most of modern scholarship, for that matter, is that there was a strong suspicion among the elites regarding associations, which often led to strict controlling action. One might think that the reality of relations between such groups and imperial functionaries in the day-to-day life of a Roman province like Asia would primarily reflect such tensions. In light of such views, one would not expect to find Roman officials like Pliny or other civic and imperial functionaries interacting with such apparently subversive groups, let alone actively supporting, say, a Dionysiac association at Pergamum or a lower-class guild of clothing dyers at Thyatira. Yet this impression is quite misleading.

When we turn from the scant literary references regarding upper-class views of these groups to look at the actual ongoing relations that could exist between the elites–Roman officials and governors included–and associations of various kinds in Roman Asia, a very different picture emerges. This picture involves a fair degree of positive interaction and beneficent behavior that scholars have not sufficiently recognized in the past. Associations were very much involved in the webs of relations that characterized civic life and linked polis to empire. In many respects, we can speak of the overall integration of many associations within society rather than an ongoing opposition to it.

The involvement of associations in imperial aspects of the honorific system further attests to ways in which these groups cemented their relationship with the polis, identifying with its interests. Attention to the significance of connections between associations and the elites in social networks, using insights from the social sciences, will help us to better understand the place of these groups within society. Two specific case studies—one focusing on an influential Julian family of Asia Minor and the other looking at connections from the perspective of a guild of dyers at Thyatira—will set the stage for a survey of connections between associations and those who assumed imperial positions both locally and provincially. Participation in monumental honors for the emperors or imperial family specifically communicates something about how such groups understood and expressed their own conception of where they fit within society and the cosmos. All of this helps to put into perspective the often overemphasized evidence for tense relations and the intervention of authorities in association life, which is discussed at length in the next chapter.

Social Network Analysis

The *metaphorical* use of "networks" to speak of social relations that exist among individuals and groups within a social system or society is a common one. Yet since the mid-1950s social scientists have come to use the term "social network" as an *analytical* tool for studying specific phenomena within society.[1] The social anthropologist J. Clyde Mitchell (1969:2) defines the social network "as a specific set of linkages among a defined set of persons [or groups], with the additional property that the characteristics of these linkages as a whole may be used to interpret the social behavior of the persons [or groups] involved." Several sociological insights regarding patterns of ties that make up a social network serve as helpful exploratory tools here. Scholars such as L. Michael White (1992a-b), John K. Chow (1992), and Harold Remus (1996) suggest the value in employing such tools in the study of antiquity and early Christianity. Moreover, these insights may help us to better understand the nature and significance of the interactions between associations and benefactors within the social structures of the polis and empire, providing us with a firm basis on which to establish the place of these groups within society.

Both J. Clyde Mitchell (1969) and Barry Wellman (1983) discuss several dimensions of social network analysis that are of importance to the following discussion of associations. Mitchell uses the term "interactional dimensions" to speak of the characteristics of the links themselves, which are "crucial in understanding the social behavior" (1969:20).[2] Among interactional dimensions are the following: *content* pertains to the original purpose of a particular link, be it economic assistance, kinship, religious, or occupational; *directedness* pertains to the direction of the flow of interaction, be it reciprocal or otherwise; *durability* pertains to whether the ties are temporary or ongoing; and *intensity* regards the "degree to which individuals are prepared to honor obligations, or feel free to exercise the rights implied in their link to some other person" (Mitchell 1969:27). All of these play a role in shaping the social behaviors and interactions of the actors, and we shall soon see how this provides a framework for discussing some of the connections of associations.

Wellman (1983) identifies several other key principles that are pertinent here. First, ties in a social network are often asymmetrically reciprocal, involving the exchange of resources that may be either material or intangible (e.g., honor, being liked). Thus, although the members of a bakers' guild differed greatly in status from the wealthy civic or imperial official, relations between them involved an exchange of resources. The association gained financial support and the prestige of links with a prominent person. An official gained honor and nonfinancial forms of support, bringing advantage in competition with other members of the aristocracy. Second, ties can directly or indirectly link the members of a local network with larger network structures. For example, connections between an association and a Roman proconsul involved a link between the local social networks (in which the association was a clear participant) and larger networks that linked the polis to province and empire.

Finally, Wellman discusses how networks structure collaboration and competition to secure scarce resources (whether material or otherwise). This principle is particularly apt for our present discussion. We have seen that associations themselves were groups based, in part, on particular spheres of social network connections, allowing collaboration among members to secure resources, such as benefaction from the wealthy. On the other hand, associations could compete with one another for access to the limited resource of benefactors within broader social networks. Correspondingly, the elites could compete with one another for the prestige and honor, as well as nonfinancial forms of support (e.g., political support), that accompanied patronage of various groups and institutions in the civic context.

Two Case Studies: Views from Above and Below

We will begin to see how these various characteristics of networks worked themselves out in the reality of association life presently through two case studies: one from the perspective of an elite Julian family in Asia Minor and the other from the perspective of a guild of dyers at Thyatira. Riet van Bremen's study of women in Asia Minor stresses the importance of the family context for understanding many facets of civic life, including elite behavior. As she states, "to fulfill all one's civic duties loyally and, if possible, splendidly, and to be seen to do so from generation to generation, was one of the crucially important ideologies that shaped the self-image of Greek civic elites" (van Bremen 1996:46). Family traditions of beneficent excellence, whether to the polis or to its constituent groups, reflect a competitive ethos that shaped relations between elite families and influenced behavior among members of particular families. Associations could be among the beneficiaries of such family traditions, maintaining important contacts with the provincial imperial elites.

The case of a certain Julian family of Asia Minor is illustrative. These were descendants of Galatian and Attalid royalty who entered into imperial service as equestrians and then senators by the late first century. Scholars who engage in the study of names and family lineages (prosopography) in the Roman world have given some attention to members of this family. Most of the family tree connections outlined in figure 23 are certain, a few are probable.[3] Members of this family habitually included associations as recipients of their benefactions. Julia Severa was an important figure in Akmoneia in the mid-first century, acting as director of contests (*agōnothetis*) and high priestess in the local temple of the "*Sebastoi* gods." She was a benefactor not only to the local elders' organization (*gerousia*) but also to the synagogue of Jews, for whom she supplied a meeting place (*MAMA* VI 263, 264; *PIR*² I 701; Halfmann 1979, no. 5a). A generation or so later, several others who may have been freedmen associated with Severa's family renovated the building by decorating the ceiling and walls and adding shutters to the windows.

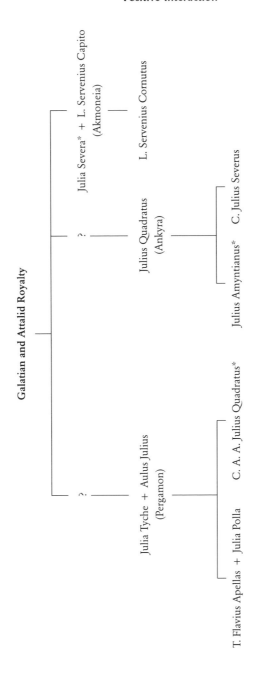

FIGURE 23: Family tree of a Julian family of Asia Minor

Severa's relative, C. Antius Aulus Julius Quadratus, was a prominent Pergamene and senator who assumed the Roman consulate in 94 and 105 C.E. He held numerous provincial offices in the Greek East, including legate in Asia, Bithynia-Pontus, Lycia-Pamphylia, and Syria, and proconsul of Asia in 109–110 C.E. (*PIR*[2] I 507; Halfmann 1979, no. 17). Quadratus's mother, Julia Tyche, was also a prominent figure at Pergamum, being both "queen" of the precincts of goddess Roma and priestess of Demeter (Ippel 1912:298–301, no. 24). It is worth mentioning that Quadratus was a member in the elite association of "Arval Brothers" at Rome from about 72 C.E. Numerous cities honored him for his services and benefactions including Laodicea in Syria, Ephesus in Asia, Side in Pamphylia, and, of course, his hometown of Pergamum (*IEph* 614, 1538; *ISide* 57; *IPergamon* 436–51). Yet he was also the benefactor of local associations at home including the synod of young men (*neoi*) and, on more than one occasion, the Dionysiac "dancing cowherds" (*IPergamon* 440; Conze and Schuchhardt 1899:179–80, nos. 31–32). These "cowherds," whose meeting hall we have already discussed, came into contact with him directly when he was priest of Dionysos Kathegemon. Another relative, Julius Amyntianus, probably Quadratus's cousin, was a member in the Panhellenion institution of Athens, but also the priest of Isis and Serapis at Tralles for a time, for which an association of initiates of these Egyptian deities honored him with a monument (*ITrall* 86; post-131 C.E.; see *PIR*[2] I 147; Follet 1976:133).

Considering interactional dimensions of these links in social networks between members of this family and associations can help us understand the nature of connections. First, the content or purposes of all these instances of interaction—"the meanings which the persons in the network attribute to their relationships" (J. Mitchell 1969:20)—are similar, though not necessarily identical. Furthermore, the directedness of all links is reciprocal, though certainly not equal. Both Julia Severa and the Jews at Akmoneia, for instance, would clearly understand the link in terms of a benefactor-beneficiary relationship: the exchange of tangible financial aid (donation of a meeting place) for the far less tangible, though extremely valuable, return of honors.

The purposes of the interaction between both Quadratus and Amyntianus and associations at Pergamum and Tralles likewise pertain, respectively, to benefaction and honors, but there is a further religious element to the content of these contacts. Both men are priests of the deities to whom the associations are devoted, and this would have been a key factor in ensuring benefaction in the first place. The service of these men as priests—thereby bringing about fitting honors for the gods in question—would on its own warrant reciprocation from the associations, so the content of the link is not limited to the financial.

Owing to the partial nature of inscriptional evidence, it is difficult to assess the durability of connections between a certain person and a given association. Still, if Quadratus's relations with the cowherds are any indication, there was often potential for ongoing links over time. In such cases, the social pressures on both the wealthy person to make further benefactions and on the association to respond with appropriate honors (i.e., the *intensity* of the link) would be considerable. Failure of an association to respond to a benefaction with clearly visible honors in return would be disastrous in its hopes of maintaining contacts with this or any other influential person. As such, an element of competition among associations, groups, and institutions in securing the benefaction of wealthy inhabitants helped to maintain this asymmetrically reciprocal system of honors. From this elite family's perspective, such links with local associations were part of a larger set of connections with various institutions, groups, and individuals within the context of polis and province. These helped to ensure the family reputation of beneficence in competition with other aristocratic families, securing family members' high position and degree of honor within Asian society.

What happens to be missing from the material evidence that has survived regarding this Julian family is information regarding relations with occupational associations. Yet there is plenty of evidence that guilds also maintained similar ongoing interactions with members of other prominent families. The case of the guild of dyers at Thyatira provides us with the view from below at a particular locality, revealing the continuing interactions that helped to cement a particular group's position within the networks that linked polis to province and empire.

We get momentary glimpses of these ongoing links at several points in the group's history, which can be partially reconstructed from ten extant inscriptions (many pertaining to the same guild), five of which involve imperial connections (*TAM* V 935, 945, 965, 972, 978, 980, 989, 991, 1029, 1081). Figure 24 provides an illustration of the various connections that existed between the dyers and various benefactors over the span of about two centuries. Around 50 C.E. the dyers set up an honorary monument for Claudia Ammion, a priestess of the *Sebastoi* (probably a civic cult) and high priestess of the polis who had also been director of contests "in a brilliant and extravagant manner with purity and modesty" (*TAM* V 972; cf. Buckler 1913:299–300).

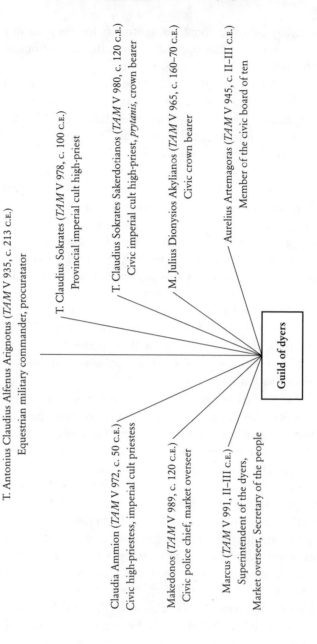

T. Antonius Claudius Alfenus Arignotus (*TAM* V 935, c. 213 C.E.)
Equestrian military commander, procurator

T. Claudius Sokrates (*TAM* V 978, c. 100 C.E.)
Provincial imperial cult high-priest

T. Claudius Sokrates Sakerdotianos (*TAM* V 980, c. 120 C.E.)
Civic imperial cult high-priest, *prytanis*, crown bearer

M. Julius Dionysios Akylianos (*TAM* V 965, c. 160–70 C.E.)
Civic crown bearer

Aurelius Artemagoras (*TAM* V 945, c. II–III C.E.)
Member of the civic board of ten

Claudia Ammion (*TAM* V 972, c. 50 C.E.)
Civic high-priestess, imperial cult priestess

Makedonos (*TAM* V 989, c. 120 C.E.)
Civic police chief, market overseer

Marcus (*TAM* V 991, II–III C.E.)
Superintendent of the dyers,
Market overseer, Secretary of the people

Guild of dyers

FIGURE 24: Diagram of some connections of the guild of dyers at Thyatira

Claudia Ammion belonged to an aristocratic family in Thyatira with kin in other cities of Asia (see the family tree in fig. 25). For instance, her brother, Andronikos, was a civic president (*prytanis*) and priest of the goddess Roma. Some of her other relatives were also benefactors of associations or gymnasium clubs. Claudia's kinsman, C. Julius Lepidus (probably a cousin once removed), was a high priest in the provincial imperial cult like his father (see *ISardBR* 8.99), and he had been a benefactor of an athletic club that met in the "third gymnasium" in Thyatira just decades earlier (*TAM* V 968; c. 25 C.E.). Claudia's husband, T. Claudius Antyllos, was honored by a gymnastic association, the "partners" that met in this same gymnasium; he had supplied them with oil (*TAM* V 975; c. 50 C.E.). Another kinsman of this Lepidus family, T. Julius Lepidus of Sardis, was secretary of the provincial council of Asia in the late first or early second century; he was honored with marble plaques by both the organization of youths (*ephēbes*) and "those engaged in business in the slave-market (*statariō*)" at Sardis (see *BE* [1997] 568–69, no. 516; *SEG* 46 [1996] 1523–24, revising *ISardBR* 46; cf. *TAM* V 932).

Around the turn of the second century in Thyatira, we find the dyers honoring a member of another family, T. Claudius Sokrates. Sokrates was the founder of several civic building projects and director of contests. He had held a prestigious position as high priest of Asia in the provincial imperial temple at Pergamum (*TAM* V 978; before 113 C.E.). The dyers were by no means the only occupational association at the time seeking the support of such imperial-affiliated citizens; at about the same time the leather cutters were honoring another man, T. Flavius Alexandros, the curator of the association (*conventus*) of Romans and Thyatira's ambassador to Rome (*TAM* V 1002).

Connections with local associations continued in the Sokrates family. The guild of dyers also honored his son Sakerdotianos, a high priest of the *Sebastoi* who had displayed "love of honor since he was a boy" toward the polis, conducting himself "in accordance with his ancestors' love of glory" (*TAM* V 980; c. 120–130 C.E.; cf. *TAM* V 979). Yet the dyers' allegiance was not limited to this particular family, for at about the same time the guild joined with civic institutions of Thyatira in honoring Makedonos, the police chief (*eirēnarchos*) and market overseer (*agoranomos*; *TAM* V 989). The dyers honored other persons in influential civic positions of Thyatira in the following decades, including two who were also members or leaders of the guild (cf. *TAM* V 945, 965 [c. 160–70 C.E.], 991).

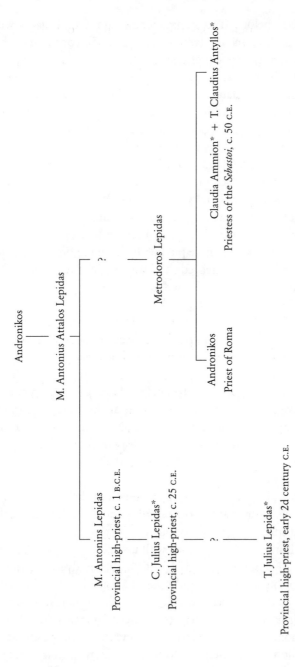

FIGURE 25: Family tree of Claudia Ammion

We get a final glimpse of imperial connections when about 213 C.E. the dyers honor T. Antonius Claudius Alfenus Arignotus, a military commander of the equestrian order who reached the office of procurator and had served in various parts of the Greek East (*TAM* V 935; *PIR*[2] A 821).[4] Arignotus had also been priest of Thyatira's patron deity, Apollo Tyrimnos, not to mention temple warden of the *Sebastos*, the revered emperor. The inscription is sure to point out that his father and grandfather were high priests of Asia in the provincial imperial cult.

As with the contacts between members of the Julian family and associations, the content of the connections between the dyers and various influential persons in imperial positions pertains primarily to benefactor-beneficiary (or patron-client) relations, and it is reciprocal in directedness. As an ongoing group formed from occupational social network connections, the dyers were able to secure access to limited resources of financial assistance from the wealthy, furthering their own interests in competition with other associations, groups, and individuals within Thyatira. Thus exchange of material assistance for honors is once again a key purpose of a particular link.

I have not yet emphasized enough some of the less tangible or symbolic purposes behind such connections from the perspective of a local association like the dyers. An association's maintenance of ongoing relations with influential persons, some of whom also had important imperial ties, was not only a source of material assistance; this was also a means by which an association could increase its own feeling of importance within the polis. Associations set up an honorary monument or statue for a benefactor not only because such was required of them by the social conventions of benefaction, but also because advertising their own connections with highly respected individuals or families within the civic context was a way of claiming their place within society, a point I return to further below.

Overall, then, these connections tell us something about how the dyers found a place for themselves within the networks and hierarchies of the polis. Imperial connections within civic life were a very important component in the external relations of associations, directly or indirectly connecting them with the social, religious, and political structures of polis, province, and empire. This point will become clearer as we consider the range of evidence for the interactions of other associations with imperial officials and, further on, with emperors.

The Range and Forms of Participation in Networks

The picture of associations interacting with persons in a variety of imperial positions is not at all limited to the cases I have just outlined. There is a range of evidence for many associations interacting with influential persons, from those who assumed high priesthoods in civic or provincial imperial cults to those of the equestrian and senatorial orders. Figure 26 provides an illustration of the range of connections, discussed here, between associations and persons at various levels within the civic and provincial elites.

Associations could have connections with functionaries of imperial cult temples. Most cities and towns of Asia included local civic temples or shrines devoted to the imperial family with accompanying priesthoods (often called "high priesthoods" [*archiereis*], as in provincial imperial cults) or other offices taken on by the wealthier families. As I have noted, these temples were usually built under local initiative using funds donated by prominent families, and they were quite separate from those founded in connection with the provincial council of Asia.

Associations could honor officials connected with these municipal imperial cults, as the case of Julia Severa already demonstrated. In the first years of the Common Era, for instance, the civic institutions of Iasos (southeast of Miletos) joined together with both the organizations of young men and elders and the Roman businessmen to honor the priest of a local cult devoted to Agrippa Postumus (son of Augustus and Julia; *IIasos* 90). Associations of worshipers of Hermes, Aphrodite, and Dionysos on the island of Nisyros (south of Kos) crowned Gnomagoras, a civic magistrate and "priest of the *Sebastoi* in Nisyros" who had also made various benefactions to the polis and its inhabitants (*IGR* IV 1110). There are similar connections with civic imperial priests and priestesses attested with initiates at Tralles, initiates of Dionysos Kallon ("the beautiful") at Byzantion, and a guild of linen workers at Thyatira (*ITrall* 74; *IByzantion* 34 [late 1st century C.E.]; *TAM* V 933). This practice of praising priests was certainly not limited to civic cults in the province of Asia, as shown by inscriptions involving leather workers at Termessos in Pamphylia, Roman businessmen at Isaura in Galatia, and dyers at Sagalassos in Lycia (*IGR* III 114, 292, 360).

More prestigious than the local or civic priesthoods in imperial cults were those organized and founded in connection with the provincial council of Asia. The earliest of these cults was dedicated to Augustus and Roma at Pergamum (by 27 B.C.E.) on the initiative of the provincial communities

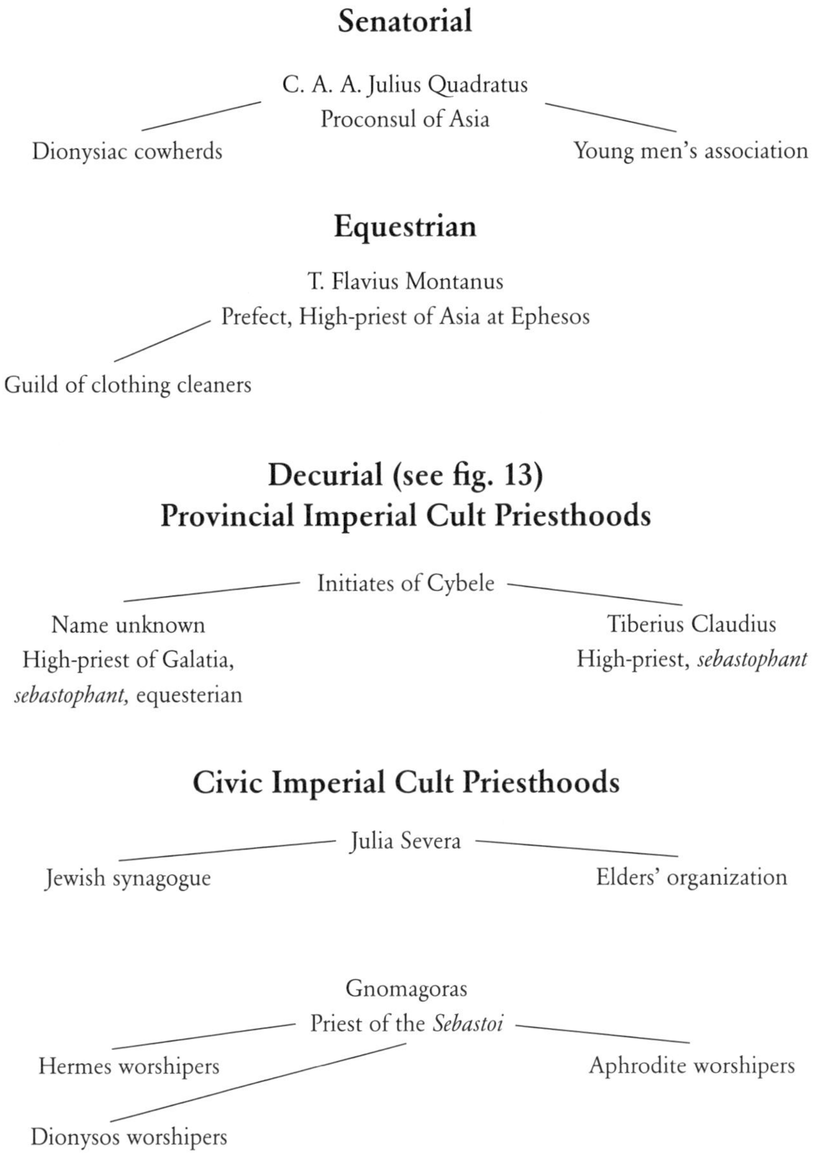

Senatorial

C. A. A. Julius Quadratus
Proconsul of Asia

Dionysiac cowherds

Young men's association

Equestrian

T. Flavius Montanus
Prefect, High-priest of Asia at Ephesos

Guild of clothing cleaners

Decurial (see fig. 13)
Provincial Imperial Cult Priesthoods

Initiates of Cybele

Name unknown
High-priest of Galatia,
sebastophant, equesterian

Tiberius Claudius
High-priest, *sebastophant*

Civic Imperial Cult Priesthoods

Julia Severa

Jewish synagogue

Elders' organization

Gnomagoras
Priest of the *Sebastoi*

Hermes worshipers

Aphrodite worshipers

Dionysos worshipers

FIGURE 26: Diagram of associations' connections with elites at various levels of society

with recognition from Rome, as was customary. By the end of the first century of the principate there were similar temples at Smyrna (founded under Tiberius) and Ephesus (founded under Domitian). We have already encountered provincial celebrations associated with these cults in connection with the hymn singers of Pergamum.

Once again, it was not uncommon for associations to maintain contacts with these provincial high priests or priestesses. For example, the silversmiths at Ephesus honored T. Claudius Aristion, who was a high priest of the imperial cult in the time of Domitian and also the secretary of the Ephesian people (*IEph* 425 + 636 [with corrections]).[5] Similarly, at Pessinos (near the border of Galatia and Asia) we find a group of initiates in the mysteries of Cybele honoring on more than one occasion aristocrats who were high priests of the Galatian assembly, "revealers of the *Sebastoi*," and priests of Cybele or Attis (*CCCA* I 59, 60; late 1st century C.E.).

An inscription from Thyatira involving C. Julius Xenon is worth discussing here. It reveals that a hero cult had been founded in honor of Xenon after his death in view of his many contributions to Thyatira and the province during his life; and it seems that his time as high priest in the provincial imperial cult at Pergamum was a key factor (cf. *IEph* 3334; S. Price 1984:49–50). Putting Thyatira on the provincial and imperial map in such an exceptional manner made this man deserving of heroic honors after his passing. The association devoted to him, the Juliasts, set up a monument that clearly praised his roles as both benefactor and high priest of Caesar Augustus and goddess Roma, stating that "he has done the greatest things for all Asia, being savior, benefactor, and founder in every way and father of the fatherland, first among the Hellenes" (*TAM* V 1098; early 1st century C.E.). Most often, however, associations maintained relations with imperial officials who had not yet departed from the scene.

A monument from Akmoneia (early 2d century) involving a high priest serves as a fitting transition to associations' contacts with those of the equestrian order. It reads as follows: "To good fortune. The guild of clothing cleaners erected this monument for T. Flavius Montanus, son of Hiero of the tribe of Quirina, prefect of the craftsmen, high priest of Asia for the Asian council's temple in Ephesus, revealer of the *Sebastoi*, and director of contests for life" (Ramsay 1967 [1941]:33, correcting *IGR* IV 643; cf. *IEph* 2037, 2061, 2063; Kearsley 1988:43–46). As his prefecture suggests, Montanus was of the equestrian order and we also know that he belonged to an aristocratic family centered at Kibyra (south of Colossae, near the border with Lycia). Montanus's sister, Flavia Lycia, married into a family with a long history of high priesthoods in the provincial imperial cult (see Kearsley 1988). Her father-in-law, T. Claudius Polemo, was a well-known rhetor and "leader of Asia" (Asiarch) of the equestrian order. Another guild, the leather workers at Kibyra, honored Polemo in connection with a decree of the civic institutions (*IGR* IV 907; on Polemo see *IGR* IV 883, 909; *PIR*² C 963).

Other associations in Asia, especially occupation-based groups, could maintain similar contacts with officials of the equestrian order, including army officials, legates, and procurators. We have already encountered links with several equestrian officials in connection with the dyers at Thyatira, but there are other cases as well. The guild of clothing cleaners in first-century Temenothyrai (west of Akmoneia), for instance, honored as "founder" and "friend of the homeland" L. Egnatius Quartus, an equestrian military commander who had been prefect of a cohort and of military wings, as well as tribune of a legion (*AE* [1977] 227–28, no. 802; late 1st century C.E.). As assistants to the proconsul, the procurator (*epitropos*) of provincial Asia was an important official, and we find both the physicians at Ephesus (*IEph* 719; early 2d century C.E.) and the purple-dyers at Hierapolis (*IHierapJ* 42 = *IGR* IV 816) honoring a procurator.

The connections of associations could even extend to the senatorial order, that extremely small segment of society who, in theory, possessed the most power and influence. In the first years of the Common Era, for example, the people of Assos (northwest of Pergamum) joined together with the association of Roman businessmen to honor Augustus's grandson Gaius, who was also consul (*IAssos* 13; 1 B.C.E.–4 C.E.). On several occasions neighborhood associations at Pergamum set up an inscription for L. Cuspius Pactumeius Rufinus (*PIR*² C 1637), a senator who was consul in 142 C.E., priest of Zeus Olympios at Pergamum, and also a member of the elite association of "Arval Brothers" at Rome, as was Quadratus decades earlier (*IPergamon* 424, 434; *OGIS* 491). At Ephesus we find an association of businessmen honoring a praetor of the Roman people and legate of Caesar (*IEph* 738; 1st century C.E.) and another group of merchants joining with the civic institutions to honor a senator of the famous Vedius family (*IEph* 3079; 2d century C.E.; cf. *IEph* 727–28, 3075). Both the leather tanners and a gymnastic organization at Thyatira honored as benefactor of the homeland a man of consular rank, M. Gnaius Licinius Rufinus (*TAM* V 986–87; *PIR*² L 236; Robert 1948).

As the case of Quadratus and the Dionysiac cowherds showed, patronage connections could even extend to the highest and most influential Roman provincial official, the proconsul (*anthypatos*) of Asia, a position taken on only by senators who had reached the consulship in Rome. "The merchants (*empo[roi]*) who are engaged in business in Ephesus" honored the proconsul Gaius Pompeius Longinus Gallus as "their savior and benefactor" in the mid-first century (*AE* [1968] 153, no. 485; cf. *IEph* 800; Magie 1950:1421 n.72). A few years earlier, the merchants of the slave market at Ephesus had set up a similar monument for their patron, C. Sallustius Crispus Passienus, who was proconsul in 42–43 C.E. (*IEph* 3025; *PIR*[1] P 109; cf. *SEG* 34 [1984] 1094). Later we will see that some groups of Jews in Asia also maintained important contacts with such imperial officials of the equestrian and senatorial orders, sometimes following usual custom among associations in setting up monuments in their honor.

Other Tangible Benefits of Connections

Now that we have some idea of the range of evidence concerning the possibilities for connections between associations and Roman officials, a few words on the nature of these positive interactions are in order. Besides the symbolic significance of monumental honors (which I elaborate below), there were also other more concrete aspects to these relations within social networks. We have already seen the most basic content of these links, namely a patron-client or benefactor-beneficiary relationship involving the exchange of assistance for appropriate honors. Such reciprocal yet asymmetrical exchanges helped to ensure the maintenance of hierarchies within the social structures of society.

There is evidence from Asia Minor, however, that gives us hints as to some of the other nonfinancial, though tangible, purposes or benefits of such contacts from the perspective of associations. Alongside other factors, these benefits help to explain why these connections existed. At the local level, for example, a guild's connections with a market overseer or another official responsible for the distribution of shops could have very tangible benefits, such as assignment of a shop in a preferable location (e.g., *IEph* 444–45, 2076–81; 3d century C.E.; see Knibbe 1985).

Positive links with influential persons were a potential source of other forms of support, including legal and other assistance for an association (cf. van Nijf 1997:82–100). We know from several papyri of Egypt that guilds might require a legal advocate for a variety of reasons. One case of this involves the clothing cleaners and dyers of Tebtunis hiring a lawyer to protest overtaxation by an official (*PTebtunis* I 287; 161–169 C.E.). Another case involves the linen merchants attempting to gain a higher price from the city of Oxyrhynchus for their provision of supplies for the making of vestments (*POxy* 1414; 270–275 C.E.).

Several instances in Asia Minor apparently involve an association honoring an influential person who did or would act as such an advocate for the group, furthering its interests in legal or other contexts. Thus the coppersmiths at Nikaia in Bithynia honored T. Flavius, "leader of Asia" (Asiarch), high priest, property assessor, and "just advocate" (*p[r]oēgoran dika[ion]*; *INikaia* II.1 addend. 73*; 1st–2d century C.E.). Similarly a neighborhood association at Prusias set up a monument in the early second century for its benefactor and "avenger," or legal representative (*egdikos*), "because of everything he had done," probably relating to his success in a legal case on the association's behalf (*IGR* III 50; between 102 and 114 C.E.). On more than one occasion a guild of porters devoted to Demeter at Tarsus honored a patron, one a Roman consul, who had evidently been their helpful advocate (*syndikos*) in some matters (*IGR* III 883; *SEG* 27 [1977] 947; 2d–3d century C.E.; cf. Robert 1949b; 1977:88).

The maintenance of positive relations with Roman officials possessing considerable power and influence, such as a proconsul, might also come in handy in furthering particular aims of an association. We have already encountered the Ephesian Demeter worshipers, who repeatedly sought and gained recognition of their rites from officials, and I will discuss diplomatic practices among Jews soon. Here an interesting inscription from Kyme will illustrate well the nonfinancial, though tangible, content of interactions between officials and associations.

A few words of background on the inscription are in order before going on to see how the legal power and influence of the proconsul were solicited by a local Dionysiac association of Kyme (*IKyme* 17).[6] The wars that preceded the victory of Augustus at Actium and the heavy taxation levied by Brutus, Cassius, and Antony were quite devastating economically to the cities of western Asia Minor (Magie 1950:418–40). One consequence of these circumstances was that sacred places and other properties in the cities were sometimes sold to individuals for their commercial value. It seems that as conditions in Asia stabilized after 31 B.C.E., partially by way of imperial aid, the Asian cities became aware of just how many sacred places or other properties had passed into individual possession, as Robert K. Sherk (1969) suggests. In the hopes of restoring these properties to the ownership of the gods or cities in question, cities in Asia, perhaps collectively, registered a complaint and sought a ruling from the Roman authorities, likely the senate. The official response to these requests from below was a ruling in 27 B.C.E. by Augustus and Marcus

Agrippa, then consuls, to the effect that sacred objects and places were not to be sold or given to any individuals; furthermore, any such transactions that had taken place in the past were to be reversed by the governor's restoring them to the possession of the god or city in question. A Greek translation of this document is preserved along with a proconsular letter in Latin ruling on a particular case (*IKyme* 17).

This brings us to the situation at Kyme specifically, where one such sacred place, previously used by the members of a cult society (*thiasitai*) devoted to Dionysos (Liber Pater), had passed into the possession of a man named Lysias. The circumstances that led to this transaction, as H. W. Pleket (1958:56–57) argues, most likely involved the association seeking a loan from Lysias (cf. Atkinson 1960:250–51). Securing loans with immovable property, this time a temple, was common practice (cf. Strabo, *Geography* 13.3.5, also regarding Kyme). Apparently the association failed to pay the loan on time and Lysias refused to accept late payment, retaining the temple.

Finally we come to the association's interactions with the Roman proconsul of Asia as administrator of justice, which resulted in a decision in the association's favor. This provides an excellent example of the more tangible benefits that could come to an association by way of positive contacts with Roman officials in high places. Yet in this case we do not know for sure whether positive relations existed beforehand or whether honors for the official followed (but we can certainly imagine such). The association sent a member, Apollonides, as its ambassador to the proconsul in order to present the group's request "to restore the sacred objects to the god, as Augustus Caesar has ordered, after having paid the price written on the temple of Liber Pater [i.e., Dionysos] by Lysias" (trans. Pleket 1958:50). Evidently, the association had heard of the official decision made by Augustus and Agrippa (probably within a year or two of its proclamation) and appealed to its provisions before the most powerful Roman official of the province.

L. Vinicius's favorable response in the case came in the form of a letter to the civic magistrates of Kyme, ordering that they look into the matter and, if the association's claims were correct, to ensure that Lysias received payment and handed over the sacred place into the possession of the god, Dionysos.[7] The members of the association, but likely others in Kyme also, once again had access to the place where they met to honor the god. Not surprisingly, they (or the city itself) had both Augustus's order and the proconsul's letter engraved on a monument that was set up at the temple in question for all to see. They were more than willing to follow the suggestion of the proconsul by inscribing the following: "Restored by Imperator Caesar, Augustus, son of the deified Julius." This brings us to the emperors and imperial family.

Monumental Honors for Emperors and the Imperial Family

The "connections" of associations could extend to some of the most important beneficent figures of power within the empire and cosmos, the emperors and members of the imperial household. It was common convention for individuals, groups, institutions, and cities to honor the emperors or imperial family by dedicating monuments, statues, altars, and buildings to them, and various types of associations took part in these honors. The evidence regarding associations that has survived for Asia includes dedications to specific emperors: Augustus (27 B.C.E.–14 C.E.), Tiberius (14–37 C.E.), Claudius (41–54 C.E.), Nero (54–68 C.E.), Vespasian (69–79 C.E.), Domitian (81–96 C.E.), Trajan (98–117 C.E.), Hadrian (117–138 C.E.), Antoninus Pius (138–161 C.E.), Marcus Aurelius and Lucius Verus (161–169 C.E.), Commodus (176–192 C.E.), and Caracalla (198–217 C.E.), but also dedications to the more general category of the "revered ones" (*Sebastoi* or *Augusti*). Here I focus primarily on monumental honors from the well-excavated site of Ephesus, making reference to similar material attested elsewhere in Asia that suggests that the associations of Ephesus were not an exception in honoring the emperors and imperial family.

Associations could be on the receiving end of benefactions that were dedicated to the emperors alongside other institutions and gods. In the mid-second century, a wealthy woman named Kominia Junia gave a statue of Isis to the workers in the fishery toll office, dedicating the statue to Artemis, the Ephesian polis, and Antoninus Pius (*IEph* 1503 [138–161 C.E.]; cf. *IEph* 586 [2d century C.E.]; *IGR* I 787 [196–198 C.E.; Perinthos, Thracia]). A few decades later in the city of Rome we find M. Ulpius Domesticus, a famous athlete and leader of an athletic association, erecting statues dedicated to Antoninus Pius and Marcus Aurelius and to a society of Ephesian shippers and merchants (*IGUR* 26).[8] Altars could also be dedicated to the emperors in connection with an association. An altar at Ephesus that was dedicated "to the *Sebastoi* gods and the initiates" by Sarapion and his family (*IEph* 1506) has its counterpart at Hierapolis, involving a "sacred cult society (*thiasos*)" (*AE* [1984] 250, no. 855; cf. *IGR* IV 468 [Pergamum; c. 215 c.e.]; *IErythrai* 132; mid-2d century c.e.).

Similar practices can be found outside the walls of the polis in the villages of the countryside. The village of Azoulenon, near Ephesus, honored the "joyful-celebration association" (*tēn synbiōsin tōn Euēmeriōn*) by dedicating a structure to both the ancestral gods and the *Sebastoi* gods (*IEph* 3817; see Robert 1937:65–66). The devotees of Zeus Bennios in a village near Aizanoi dedicated their altar on behalf of Emperor Trajan (*IGR* IV 603; see Drew-Bear and Naour 1990:1988–90), mention of which brings us to more proactive group involvement in such honorary activities.

Associations were not only among the recipients of benefactions dedicated to the emperors; they were also active initiators of monumental honors. The group (*conventus*) of Roman businessmen at Ephesus that set up two monuments (probably statues) for Claudius (*IEph* 409, 3019) was reflecting common practice among other associations of this type, as inscriptions from Assos, Sebaste, Akmoneia, Apameia, and Pergamum show.[9] Yet these honorary activities for the emperors were certainly not limited to these immigrants from Rome or Italy.

We have already encountered the association of fishermen and fish dealers who built the fishery toll office near the harbor at Ephesus and dedicated it to Nero, his mother, his wife, the Roman people, and the Ephesian people (*IEph* 20; 54–59 c.e.; cf. *IPergamon* 394). The practice of dedicating buildings and meeting places to the emperors is well attested elsewhere, too. At Thyatira, a group of merchants dedicated their workshops to the *Sebastoi* gods (*TAM* V 862), and the Nikomedian shippers in Bithynia dedicated their sanctuary and meeting place to Vespasian (*TAM* IV 22; cf. *ILydiaKP* III 19, from Philadelphia, late 2d century c.e.).

Years later at Ephesus we find another association dedicating a monument both to its patron deity, Dionysos, and to Trajan (*IEph* 3329). Here the emperor himself is referred to as "a member of the cult society (*thiasōtēs*)," an honorary member of the Dionysiac association; though it is doubtful whether the emperor was aware of this honor.[10] Apparently this association liked to think that it had a particularly close connection with Trajan, whose comments to Pliny opened this chapter. Other inscriptions from Ephesus involving Dionysiac initiates and both Hadrian and Commodus likewise show the importance of monumental honors for the emperors, not to mention cultic ones (*IEph* 275 [119 c.e.], 293). Dionysiac associations elsewhere engaged in similar practices. For instance, the initiates of Dionysos Breseus at Smyrna praisingly addressed Hadrian as "Olympios, savior and founder," in one of their inscriptions (*ISmyrna* 622; c. 129–131 C.E.).

The links implied in the monumental honors discussed thus far are primarily indirect. Often the association involved was far more aware of its "connections" than were the emperors named as recipients of the honors. This differs from what we found in the case of other Roman imperial officials and cultic functionaries, who were usually well aware of the honors set up for them, often in return for very specific benefactions, services, or actions of support. There were some occasions, however, when honors might be communicated to the emperor himself by way of the regular means of diplomacy, the sending of an embassy to the emperor, who might then reply with a rescript or letter (see Millar 1977). Diplomatic practices similar to those of cities and leagues were more common among somewhat official associations of athletes and performers (cf. Millar 1977:456–63; *IEph* 22; *GCRE* 27–28, 37 = *PLond* 1178 [Egypt]), which are not our present focus. Still, there were occasions when other associations, including Jewish groups, might engage in similar diplomatic conventions involving more direct relations with emperors.

The initiates of Dionysos Breseus at Smyrna provide an example of an association maintaining ongoing diplomatic ties with emperors. One inscription preserves letters of response to this "synod" from both Marcus Aurelius and Antoninus Pius (*ISmyrna* 600 = *GCRE* 157–58; cf. Krier 1980; Petzl 1983). Only the opening of the latter is legible. The former letter involves the future emperor Marcus Aurelius, then consul for the second time (c. 158 C.E.), responding to the initiates who had sent a copy of their honorary decree by way of the proconsul, T. Statilius Maximus. Aurelius's response to the decree, which pertained to the association's celebration at the birth of his son, acknowledges the goodwill of the initiates even though his son had since died. That these diplomatic contacts continued when Aurelius was emperor with Lucius Verus is shown in a fragmentary letter from these emperors to the same group around 161–163 C.E., perhaps in response to further honors (*ISmyrna* 601 = *GCRE* 168).

The associations that did maintain such direct diplomatic relations with the emperors themselves were sure to advertise these connections. Yet in many cases associations honored the emperors without expectation of such direct acknowledgment by way of correspondence with the honoree. This might lead us to ask what exactly was going on when associations set up a monument involving honors for the emperors or imperial family.

The Symbolic Significance of Monumentalizing:
Claiming a Place within Society and the Cosmos

Acts of monumentalizing also had symbolic significance, which further demonstrates the importance of the emperors within the social and religious life of associations. Since Ramsay MacMullen's article on the "epigraphic habit" (1982), some scholars are turning their attention toward explaining the nature and significance of the epigraphic phenomenon and the visual messages of monuments for what they can tell us about society and the behavior of actors within it, whether they be communities, groups, or individuals (cf. MacMullen 1982, 1986; Millar 1983; Meyer 1990; Woolf 1996). A discussion of the purposes and meanings of monumentalizing will help to clarify the nature of associations' relations with emperors, but also put into context aspects of the honorary activities for other imperial functionaries discussed earlier.

Greg Woolf's (1996) work on "epigraphic culture" provides a useful starting point with respect to the significance of monumentalizing. Woolf looks at the uses and significance of monumental inscriptions, arguing that they can be viewed as statements regarding the place of individuals and groups within society. We need not accept his theory regarding the social settings that led to the predominance of the epigraphic habit, however. He attempts to link the popularity of monumentalizing with supposed widespread feelings of social dislocation and anxiety that coincided with the "rise of individualism," depending on assumptions that I challenged in part one. Nevertheless, his observations on the meaning of acts of monumentalizing, seeing them as "claims about the world" (Woolf 1996:27), are insightful and applicable to situations involving associations.

According to Woolf (1996:29), "the primary function of monuments in the early Empire was as devices with which to assert the place of individuals within society." Those who set up a monument were in a concrete manner, literally set in stone, attempting to preserve symbolically a particular set of relations within society and the cosmos for passersby to observe. The visual and textual components of epigraphy "provided a device by which individuals [or groups] could write their public identities into history, by fixing in permanent form their achievements and their relations with gods, with men, with the Empire, and with the city" (Woolf 1996:39). The location of the monument could also be an important factor: most desired for visibility would be prestigious structures, such as theaters, marketplaces, and civic or provincial temples. Monumentalizing, then, was one way in which groups, such as associations, could express where they fit not only within society as we would understand it, but also within the broader cosmic framework that existed within the worldview of persons living in that society.

Closely related to this is the sense of belonging that these assertions of place could provide for those involved in setting up an inscription, altar, statue, or other monument. By participating in such honorary activities set in stone, MacMullen (1982:246) states, people "felt themselves members of a special civilization." More importantly with regard to the cosmic framework, Mary Beard (1991:37) points out that writing in the form of monuments symbolically "played a central role in defining the nature of human relations with the divine, and indeed the nature of pagan deities themselves." An altar, building, or other inscribed monument could be a statement of one's "position in relation to a deity [or deities]" (Beard 1991:48).

In light of all this, we can begin to see the symbolic meaning of *associations'* honors for and connections with both the emperors and other imperial-connected individuals and families. First, a few words about some of the cosmological issues peculiar to the emperors. Among the honorary inscriptions of Asia, there were cases where an association's dedication spoke explicitly of the emperors or imperial family in terms of their position within the cosmos as the *Sebastoi* gods. By participating in this aspect of life, associations were making claims regarding their own role in the upkeep of fitting relations within the cosmos, contributing toward the well-being of the larger civic community in which they belonged. Yet such monuments for the *Sebastoi* gods could also be an indirect assertion of belonging within broader religious contexts, within imperial cults at both the civic and provincial levels. In this connection, the relations with imperial cult functionaries likewise tell of how some associations could express in a concrete way their feelings of belonging within these specific contexts.

Monumental honors for the emperors also involved other more down-to-earth claims regarding an association's place within society. A monument erected by an association set in stone for all to see the group's connections, whether real or imagined, and advertised that group's role within the nexus of relations that linked inhabitants to the polis and the polis to province and empire. In this sense, it did not matter whether a particular emperor was aware that a guild of merchants at Thyatira dedicated its building to his family or that the head of a Dionysiac association at Pergamum set up an altar in his honor. What was more important was the association's own feelings of importance within society, and the perceptions that others in the civic context might begin to have regarding that group's status or prestige within the polis.

We have already discussed the more literal links between associations and imperial officials along with the various nonsymbolic characteristics of these connections. Yet some similar points regarding the symbolic significance of monuments could be said in these cases, too. For example, the dyers or Dionysiac cowherds literally maintained contacts with benefactors of the equestrian or senatorial order. Expressing these contacts in the form of a monument ensured that the prestige and social propriety implied by these momentous occasions would not be forgotten. It made a clear assertion regarding the association's active participation within the webs of sociopolitical relations and hierarchies of the polis under Roman rule.

Conclusion

The bulk of the epigraphic evidence that we do have from Roman Asia (which scholars have largely neglected) suggests that connections with and honors for both imperial officials and the emperors were a normal part of group life for many associations and guilds in the first two centuries. This evidence for positive interaction speaks of the tendency toward the integration of associations (representing various social levels) within the polis and helps to explain how the structures and hierarchies of society were maintained under Roman rule. Involvement in imperial dimensions of the polis was one of the ways in which an association could claim a place for itself within society and the cosmos. I soon turn to the issue of comparison regarding a diversity of synagogues' and congregations' participation, or lack thereof, in various imperial and other dimensions of civic life. This will tell us something important about their place, alongside other associations, within society in Roman Asia. But first, negative dimensions of group-society relations among associations need to be put into perspective.

6

Tensions in Perspective

Civic Disturbances and Official Intervention

Introduction

The preceeding discussion of the integration of many associations within society should not lead us to believe that the cities were totally free from social conflicts and disturbances, disturbances in which associations could occasionally become involved. By its very nature, epigraphic evidence often (though not always) preserves for posterity the positive dimensions of social relations, so we need to remain aware of negative interaction as well.

Yet there has been a tendency for scholars to give priority to literary or legal evidence, especially those few passages involving Roman officials' control over associations, to the neglect of the inscriptional evidence for association life that I have discussed.[1] For this reason, the impression one might wrongly get from reading scholarship in this area is that tensions, disturbances, and resulting imperial intervention were the be-all and end-all of association life generally. Assumptions that Roman officials strictly controlled associations throughout the empire—that their relations with such groups were primarily, if not solely, negative—can be found throughout scholarship unfamiliar with or uninterested in the ongoing interactions I have just presented, including influential scholars from Jean-Pierre Waltzing (1895–1900) to Francesco M. de Robertis (1971) to G. E. M. de Ste. Croix (1981).

This widespread characterization of associations in terms of conflict with society also finds expression among scholars of early Christianity. For instance, Paul J. Achtemeier (1996:25–26), although correctly looking to associations for understanding the social context of Christianity (1 Peter specifically), oversimplifies his portrait of associations in stating that they "were subject to official scrutiny" and were a "constant problem to the governing authorities."[2] Achtemeier, like other scholars, says little if anything of evidence concerning positive dimensions of group-society relations.

Contrary to the assumptions of many scholars, however, civic unrest involving associations that led to the intervention of Roman officials was intermittent, pertaining to the particularities of time and place. This fell far short of repression or strict enforcement of legislation. When such disturbances involving associations did occur, they would usually be handled locally, which was in keeping with the character of Roman rule more generally. Rarely would Roman imperial officials in a pacified province need to become directly involved in controlling actions against local associations.

Moreover, occasional disturbances involving associations and subsequent imperial control must be viewed in light of the evidence for associations' participation in networks of benefaction and the general desire to secure a place within the polis and empire. Sporadic incidents requiring resolution were a natural outcome of living within a competitively minded society, and we should not speak of associations as anti-Roman or subversive sects because of their occasional involvement in such incidents. Nor would Jewish synagogues and Christian assemblies, *as associations at least*, be automatically considered subversive or sectarian in this sense. The following discussion of incidents in Italy and Asia Minor will illustrate this point and further clarify the nature of Roman authorities' relations with associations, concluding with the Pliny correspondence mentioned earlier.

Politics and Associations
in Italy and the City of Rome

Most of the evidence for the occasional control of associations (*collegia*) by Roman authorities relates to Rome and nearby regions of Italy. Even then, it pertains to broader concerns regarding the maintenance of public order or other political issues, not the ongoing legal control of associations per se by Roman officials (on associations and politics also see Fellmeth 1987, 1990).

Livy's lively account of the Bacchanalian affair of 186 B.C.E., which we have already encountered in connection with exaggerated descriptions of wild banquets, was written in the time of Augustus (Livy, *History of Rome*

39.8–19). It relates the story of how politicians (consuls and the Roman senate) were distracted from their business by a "conspiracy at home" involving Dionysiac associations:

> [A] Greek of humble origin . . . was the hierophant of secret ceremonies performed at night. There were initiations which at first were imparted only to a few; but they soon began to be widespread among men and women. The pleasures of drinking and feasting were added to the religious rites. . . . When wine had inflamed their feelings, and night and the mingling of the sexes . . . had extinguished all power of moral judgment, all sorts of corruption began to be practiced. . . . The cult was also a source of supply of false witnesses, forged documents and wills, and perjured evidence, dealing also in poisons and in wholesale murders among the devotees. . . . The violence was concealed because no cries for help could be heard against the shriekings, the banging of drums and the clashing of cymbals in the scene of debauchery and bloodshed. . . . This evil, with all its disastrous influence, spread from Etruria to Rome like an epidemic. (*History of Rome* 39.8–9; trans. Bettenson 1976: 401–2; cf. Sage 1965 for Latin text)

Once in Rome, these "degraded and alien rites" started by a lower-class upstart spread and came to involve murder and intrigue within elite circles ("some men and women of rank were to be found among them"), which seems to be among Livy's (and the politicians') main concerns (cf. 39.13). The result was a special investigation by the consuls (the two highest, annually chosen officials for the city of Rome) followed by a decree of the Roman senate to the effect that "no one who had been initiated into the Bacchic rites should attempt to assemble or meet for the purpose of holding these ceremonies or to perform any such religious rite" (39.14), both in Rome and in the surrounding towns of Italy (cf. *ILLRP* 511). Once the initial investigations and punishments took place, Livy points out, those who wished to engage in Bacchic worship in Rome or Italy needed to gain permission to do so from a city official (praetor) and the senate (39.18).

We cannot fully deal with the nature of this incident here, which has been thoroughly researched by others (see, more recently, North 1979; Rousselle 1982; Gruen 1990:34–78; Walsh 1996). Suffice it to say that various factors, other than the control of associations as such, were at play in leading the senate to take action in controlling these groups. Among them were accusations of criminal activities (including attempted murder) on the part of specific members in these associations, issues regarding a foreign cult's inroads into the Roman aristocracy, and the senate's attempt to extend its political authority in Italy (cf. Gruen 1990). Most importantly here, Erich Gruen (1990:39) points out "how extraordinary and exceptional . . . the features of this episode [are] in Roman cultural and institutional history." The Roman officials' active suppression of Dionysiac associations during this Bacchanalian affair is *not* typical of ongoing Roman policy in relation to associations, Dionysiac or otherwise.

There is further evidence for the political involvement of associations in the late republican era (before the creation of the empire under Augustus from 27 B.C.E.). It is important to keep in mind the background of many of these earliest examples of Roman officials' involvements with associations, as well as the motivations and biases of those who happen to report these involvements to us. The last century of the republic was a particularly volatile age with regard to politics at Rome as various senators strove to secure power over against others, and there were times when the support of associations (*collegia*, the most common Latin term) was solicited by various politicians. Thus when Cicero and C. Antonius narrowly beat Cataline in elections for consulship (64 B.C.E.) the senate was sure to pass a decree abolishing "all guilds which appeared to conflict with public interest," namely, any that supported Cataline and other political opponents of the new consuls (Asconius, *Commentary on Against Piso* 7; cf. Cicero, *Against Piso* 9; *Speech Delivered to the Senate upon Return from Exile* 33; c. 57 B.C.E.).

Several years later, the tribune Clodius together with the consuls allowed or even encouraged the political use of *collegia* once again, probably because it was to their own advantage at the time (Cicero, *Against Piso* 8–9; *For Sestius* 33–34). Cicero condemns this action by Clodius, equating the *collegia* in question with bands of brigands or bandits. Yet this contrasts strongly to Cicero's own attitudes toward those *collegia* that happened to support him instead. Thus, in a speech after his return from exile, Cicero positively states that there "is no *collegium* in this city . . . that did not pass resolutions in the most generous terms supporting not only my restoration, but my dignity" (*On His House* 74; trans. Bailey 1991; cf. Quintus Cicero, *Handbook on Election Strategy* 8.29–30).

Similar motivations appear to underlie Julius Caesar's dissolution of "all *collegia* except those of ancient foundation" while securing his power in 47–46 B.C.E. (Suetonius, *Julius* 42; cf. Josephus, *Ant.* 14.213–16). As Jerzy Linderski argues, this action involved disbanding particular groups viewed as a threat to Caesar's maintenance of power in Rome. It did not involve a law that henceforth ensured the strict control of associations throughout the empire, as de Robertis and others assume (Linderski 1995; cf. Yavetz 1983:86, 94–95).

Evidently, associations could come into contact with Roman officials within the political arena at the capital, especially in the closing decades of the republic. But whether such involvement was considered subversive, requiring some intervention, was in the eyes of the beholder and subject to the political climate of the time. In these cases, as in others, we *cannot* say that most Roman officials were opposed to associations in general. Similar things can be said of the imperial period.

The actions of Octavian, soon to be Augustus, in the late 30s B.C.E. are worth some discussion here. According to Suetonius, Octavian made special efforts to eliminate the many "anti-social practices that endangered public order" in Italy that were a "legacy of the civil wars," especially brigandage or banditry (*Divine Augustus* 32). Suetonius relates that gangs of brigands roamed the countryside, and "numerous leagues (*factiones*), too, were formed for the commission of crimes of every kind, assuming the title of some new association (*titulo collegi novi*). Therefore to put a stop to brigandage, he stationed guards of soldiers wherever it seemed advisable, inspected the workhouses, and disbanded all associations (*collegia*), except such as were of long standing and formed for legitimate purposes" (32.1–2; trans. Rolfe 1913 [LCL], with adaptations).

Scholars who follow Waltzing interpret this passage as a reference to the institution of an actual law, the *lex Iulia* of Augustus. This law, they assert, made it necessary for associations in Rome, Italy, and even the provinces to gain official permission from the Roman senate in order to exist, a requirement that continued to influence control of associations for the next two centuries (Waltzing 1895–1900, 1:115–16; cf. La Piana 1927:239–45). In this view, the senatorial decree found in some inscriptions of Italy in the second century (e.g., *CIL* XIV 2112, c. 136 C.E.) was simply a reiteration of a system of control over such groups that had been in effect since the time of Augustus, even in the provinces.

This interpretation rests on slim evidence, however, and certainly reads far too much into the passage (cf. Radin 1910:91–94). Suetonius seems rather to indicate that Octavian, like others in the late republican period, was concerned primarily with controlling "brigandage" and, particularly, *so-called* associations (*collegia*). They were, in fact, gangs with ties to local men of power, engaging in activities subversive to Octavian's attempts to establish stability in the vicinity of Rome at this turbulent time. A comparison with Appian's account of the same period further suggests that brigandage is the main issue in this case (Appian, *Civil Wars* 5.132; see Shaw 1984:33–34). Nothing in the passages in Suetonius or Appian implies that Octavian was initiating some comprehensive law that involved control of ordinary guilds and associations in Italy, let alone the empire, henceforth.

Another specific disturbance that came to involve Roman authorities occurred during the principate of Nero, when a riot broke out between inhabitants from Nuceria and those of Pompeii during a gladiatorial show at Pompeii in 59 c.e. (Tacitus, *Annals* 14.17). Tacitus's account shows that some associations (*collegia*) played a key role in instigating the intercity battle, which was clearly a manifestation of the civic pride of those involved. Civic pride happened to escalate into violence on this occasion. The scene is depicted in a wall painting from Pompeii (see photo in fig. 27), in which various sets of spectators are shown battling one another in and around the amphitheater. A graffito engraved by a patriotic Pompeian in connection with this incident depicts a gladiator bearing the palm of victory with the caption: "Men of the Campania region, you were destroyed by us in the same victory with the Nucerians" (Tanzer 1939:72–74, with sketch).

This violent incident, which was clearly out of the control of the civic authorities, was considerable enough to warrant a special investigation on Nero's instruction. According to Tacitus, the Roman senate banned gladiator shows at Pompeii for ten years, dissolved the associations involved, and exiled the sponsor of the show and those who instigated the disorder. Once again, it was within the context of maintaining public order (as the Roman authorities understood it) that specific associations from Pompeii and Nuceria encountered such controlling action. Most associations would continue to function openly and undisturbed, as the involvement of associations (about a decade later) in supporting political candidates at Pompeii shows (c. 71–79 c.e.; cf. Franklin 1980). In the main, associations in the cities of Italy, as elsewhere, would not face such governmental repression on a day-to-day basis. Rather, intervention occurred only when associations were caught up in broader disorderly incidents that were not adequately dealt with locally. Incidents like this one do not reflect consistently enforced control of associations as such by Roman authorities in Rome or Italy, let alone the provinces.

The legal sources assembled in the sixth-century collection called the *Digest* provide further evidence concerning Roman law and associations, especially with regard to Italy. There are two main sections pertaining to

FIGURE 27: Wall painting from Pompeii depicting the riot in the amphitheater that involved some associations from Pompeii and from Nuceria.

associations or *collegia* (*Digest* 3.4.1–10; 47.22.1–4). Although we cannot fully discuss the history of this legislation, it is important to make a few observations here, particularly concerning the nature and dates of the documents and the extent of their application (or lack thereof). One difficulty that should be noted at the outset is that it is not clear to what degree the laws collected in the time of Justinian reflect the actual application of laws controlling associations in earlier years.

Furthermore, even the documents and laws that have been preserved are somewhat ambiguous concerning Roman policy on associations. In some respects they hint at the need for a considerable degree of control and in others they reflect greater freedom of association. The much-cited passage attributed to Marcian, a jurist of the early third century C.E., states the following:

> By the decrees of the emperors, the governors of provinces are directed to forbid the organization of corporate associations, and not even to permit soldiers to form them in camps. The more indigent soldiers, however, are allowed to put their pay every month into a common fund, provided they assemble only once during that time, for fear that under a pretext of this kind they may organize an unlawful society, which the Divine (Septimius) Severus stated in a rescript should not be tolerated, not only at Rome, but also in Italy and the provinces. (trans. Scott 1932)

Scholars often cite this passage as proof that there was a law controlling associations in Italy and the provinces, assuming that this reference to a source of the early third century is indicative of the actual existence and enforcement of laws in earlier years, even as early as the time of Augustus (the supposed association component of the *lex Iulia*). At least two points suggest that this should not be interpreted in such a general manner. On the one hand, the primary concern was clearly with the army; on the other, the time of Severus (193–211 C.E.), not the first or early second century, was, in many respects, a turning point in state control of associations. For example, the development of compulsory membership in the occupational guilds began following the time of Severus (cf. Kornemann 1901:442–80; Radin 1910:134–35).

Furthermore, scholars who discuss this passage often neglect what immediately follows (e.g., Cotter 1996:86–87): "To assemble for religious purposes is, however, not forbidden if, by doing so, no act is committed against the decree of the senate by which unlawful societies are prohibited." It is not clear which decree is being referred to here, though it may be the senatorial decree that is cited in some inscriptions from Italy, such as that at Lanuvium (*CIL* XIV 2112; c. 136 C.E.). Even the association at Lanuvium that quotes the senatorial decision clearly does not feel it needs to follow its prescriptions strictly: the group meets more often than once a month and for purposes other than just burial or cult. More importantly, this neglected passage from *Digest* suggests that the Roman policy toward associations with a religious character was relatively indifferent; they, too, alongside those organized for burial, were permitted to exist.

Other aspects of the documents in *Digest* indicate some degree of freedom of association, suggesting that Roman policy tolerated the existence of such groups without interfering in their lives. One document attributed to Gaius (early 2d century) cites the Greek law of Solon (6th century B.C.E.) as a precedent, assuming that associations exist and are "authorized to make whatever contracts they may desire with one another, provided they do nothing in violation of the public law" (*Digest* 47.22.4). Whether the decrees or precedents that did exist, such as those in the *Digest*, were actually employed is another question altogether. A discussion of Asia Minor will clarify the limited nature of imperial authorities' intervention in association life in the provinces.

Disturbances in the Provinces of Asia Minor

Intervention of officials in association life of the provinces was occasional, pertaining to the particularities of time and place and falling far short of comprehensive control (cf. Philo, *Against Flaccus* 4–5, concerning Egypt). When it comes to the province of Asia itself, we have absolutely no evidence of Roman officials dissolving such groups or applying laws regarding associations.[3] Instead we have civic disturbances that illustrate well the sporadic nature of controlling intervention of Roman officials in connection with associations.

The Acts account of a disturbance (*tarachos*) at Ephesus, whether a reminiscence of an actual historical event or not (and I would agree with scholars who suggest it is), vividly portrays the potential for unrest and how it was dealt with by authorities (Acts 19:23–41; cf. Stoops 1988:73–91; Molthagen 1991:42–76). Apparently in response to Paul's preaching that gods made with hands were not gods at all, the prominent guild of silversmiths gathered together a crowd of craftsmen and others in defense of the city's patron deity, chanting "Great is Artemis of the Ephesians" for hours in the theater (cf. *IEph* 425, 547, 585, 586, 636, 2212, 2441; *NewDocs* IV 1). As with the involvement of associations in the disturbance at Pompeii under Nero, it is civic pride (defense of the polis's patron deity here) that played a key role in instigating the incident.

This incident did not provoke Roman intervention. Instead it was settled by the civic authorities, in this case the secretary (*grammateus*; an important position). The secretary's speech to the crowd does warn of the potential involvement of Roman officials if the usual institutional procedures were not pursued to resolve disputes: "If . . . Demetrius and the craftsmen with him have a complaint against any one, the courts are open, and there are proconsuls; let them bring charges against one another. But if you seek anything further, it shall be settled in the regular assembly (*ekklēsia*). For we are in danger of being charged with rioting (*staseōs*) today, there being no cause that we can give to justify this commotion" (Acts 19:38–40). It was only when a disturbance reached such riotous levels and, even then, only when local civic mechanisms failed to solve the problem, that there was *potential* for a Roman proconsul to intervene, provided that he was not busy elsewhere on the judicial circuit.

We do know of another occasion at Ephesus when the proconsul did personally intervene in the form of an edict, in the case of disturbances (*staseis*) involving the bakers in the second century (*IEph* 215; cf. Buckler 1923:30–33 [with trans.]).[4] Unlike the silversmiths' riot, in this case the civic functionaries at Ephesus had been unable to resolve the unrest caused by the bakers in the marketplace, who were not producing the necessary bread for reasons we do not know (which should caution us against calling this a "strike," as Buckler does). As a result, control of the situation was turned over to the proconsul, apparently on the initiative of the civic council (as the inclusion of a now fragmentary civic decree also suggests). He responded with an edict attempting to put an end to the "disorder and tumults" (*tarachēn kai thorybous*) caused by the bakers in such a way, he stressed, that the welfare of the city was put first and the essential production of food continued. The bakers were not punished, or dissolved as a guild, but instead warned not to continue such factious meetings or disturbances (with the threat of future punishment). The issue as to whether associations were permitted to exist does not appear at all in the proconsul's edict. Nor does the document refer to any precedents that would suggest that such disturbances were consistently prominent in Asia or that laws controlling associations as such were regularly enforced by Roman officials there.

Of the incidents concerning associations in other provinces of Asia Minor, the best known are those involving Pliny as legate or governor of the province of Bithynia-Pontus during the time of Trajan (c. 110–111 C.E.; cf. Sherwin-White 1966; Wilken 1984:1–30). Pliny refers to associations at a few points in his letters. The first reference, with which I opened the previous chapter, is Trajan's reply to Pliny regarding the formation of an association of firemen at Nikomedia in Bithynia (*Epistles* 10.33–34). Second, Pliny refers to the free city of Amisos's petition to form "benefit societies" (*eranous*). In this case Trajan's response acknowledges Amisos's status of freedom that allowed them to do what was forbidden in other cities, provided that the groups were "not used for riotous and unlawful assemblies, but to relieve cases of hardship among the poor (*tenuiorum*)"

(10.93–94). Finally, when Christians were brought before Pliny in Pontus (perhaps at Amisos or Amastris), he told Trajan that these groups had obeyed Pliny's earlier edict pertaining to societies (*hetaeriae*; 10.96). Several scholars suggest that this edict encompassed some sort of restrictions on association (though we do not know any details), restrictions that coincided with some of the mandates given to him by Trajan.

Contrary to a common assumption in scholarship, the evidence from Pliny falls short of a consistently enforced "imperial policy" regarding associations in the provinces generally. We need to remember at least two things when reading about these incidents involving associations in Bithynia-Pontus. Both should caution us in taking this situation as normative for other provinces or times, or as necessarily reflecting the reality of association life even in this province.

First, the situation in Bithynia-Pontus around the beginning of the second century was exceptional in some respects. Trajan appointed Pliny as legate with consular power, giving him a "special mission" aimed at rectifying previous maladministration of the province, local political factionalism, and financial mismanagement of the cities (*Epistles* 10.18, 32; cf. Magie 1950:593–605; C. Jones 1978). We know that Roman proconsuls before this period had been accused of maladministration (Julius Bassus, proconsul c. 101 C.E., and Varenus Rufus, c. 105 C.E.; see Jones 1978:101–3). Furthermore, intercity rivalry and internal political factionalism were seen to be exceptionally bad at the time in the region. Dio of Prusa (late 1st century C.E.) refers to problems relating to parties supporting one aristocrat over against others, noting that there were times when politically motivated gatherings (*hetaireiai*) played a role in these partisan politics within the cities (*Orations* 45.8, 10; C. Jones 1978:95–103). Most importantly, despite general prosperity at the time, the financial management of the cities was perceived to be in utter disarray, which directly affected many building projects. There was a "need for many reforms," as Trajan states, and he wanted Pliny to take exceptional measures in order to correct the situation (cf. *Epistles* 10.18, 32). In this specific case, a specially appointed legate's (Pliny's) intervention in aspects of life in the cities, associations among them, might understandably exceed the norm.

Within this broader picture of a special mission to correct regional problems, we can better understand why it is that Trajan's instructions to Pliny include, among other things, a caution against the contribution associations could make toward political factionalism. This situation-specific nature of Trajan's advice to Pliny comes out clearly even in the case of the fire at Nikomedia. Trajan mentions that it is the specific problems in the cities of the province at the time that necessitate Pliny's disallowing what was not uncommon elsewhere (at least in the West): the formation of a group of craftsmen (*collegium fabrorum*) to also act as a voluntary fire brigade. Despite Trajan's concerns, however, there are even exceptions to this general tendency to disallow associations. As previously mentioned, a city with free status, such as Amisos, was to do as it pleased so long as no major disorders or political problems resulted. Concern to control associations would not be as prominent in other provinces at the time or even in the same province at times when the Roman authorities' perception of disorder and mismanagement was not as prevalent. We must also remember that the emperor's or governor's wishes, even at these exceptional times, were not necessarily consonant with day-to-day reality in many cities and towns.

The second thing to remember when considering the potential control of associations, then, relates to broader issues concerning the nature of Roman rule. There was a gap between the wishes of an emperor and the theoretical power of a governor, on the one hand, and the reality of life in hundreds of cities, on the other. However powerful a governor such as Pliny was in theory and however much Trajan wished to correct the specific problems in a particular area, there were "severe constraints on the effective exercise of their responsibilities by provincial governors and other elite officials" (Burton 1993:25). As Keith Hopkins (1980:121) plausibly estimates, in the second century there would have been approximately one Roman equestrian or senatorial administrator for every 350,000–400,000 persons. Added to this is the vast territory overseen by a sole Roman governor along with his small staff of procurators, legates, or others. In Asia, for example, there were at least three hundred constituent civic communities under a governor's jurisdiction, and a similar though lesser number would exist in Bithynia-Pontus. Finally, duties relating to the collection of taxes, the administration of justice (the assize circuit), and the overall maintenance of public order would more than occupy the governor and his assistants, leaving little room for ongoing strictly enforced control over all the cities and their populations. By virtue of the nature of Roman rule, control "could only be sporadic and discontinuous, and variable from district to district" (Burton 1975:105). This also applies, by extension, to the control of unofficial, local associations.

Furthermore, it is important to note that we are seeing things through the eyes of Pliny, who is concerned to give the impression of success, suggesting that he is thoroughly controlling the situations in the cities of the province as per Trajan's request. One wonders, for instance, whether Pliny projects onto the Christians a clear awareness and strict obedience to his earlier edict in order to impress upon Trajan the effectiveness of Pliny's actions in gaining the obedience of provincials. We also hear far more of situations in which Pliny is "reforming" successfully in the province, at the expense of the situations he is unaware of or unable to address.

In light of all this, it is likely that the average guild of coppersmiths or association of Dionysiac worshipers in Bithynia-Pontus, as elsewhere in the provinces, could go on meeting together relatively unnoticed by Roman authorities as they had before Trajan assigned Pliny to the province in about 110 C.E. As P. W. Duff (1942:130) states, "when the tradesmen and artisans of the little towns met to dine and honor their patrons, human and divine, they did not worry much about spies who might carry tales to the authorities." Though the partial nature of our epigraphic evidence from Bithynia-Pontus certainly does not provide us with a complete picture, there were associations of various kinds, both before and after Pliny, meeting in numerous cities including Amastris, Apameia, Kios, Nikaia, Nikomedia, and Prusa.[5]

Conclusion

Although intervention by Roman officials could occur on occasion within the broader context of civic disturbances, these incidents were not broadly representative of the ongoing external relations between associations and the aristocracy. In general, associations were not anti-Roman or subversive groups, let alone sects in tension with society generally. For some associations we simply do not have sufficient evidence to discern whether, or to what extent, there was involvement in imperial facets of social networks, so we must be cautious in assuming that all associations were involved in precisely the same way or to the same degree. Rather, it seems that there was a spectrum of possibilities for participation within these areas of civic life. Archeological evidence for cultic honors and imperial connections among many associations in Roman Asia strongly suggests relative integration in society. We can now turn to the task of comparing these associations with synagogues and congregations, thereby locating the place of many Jews and Christians within Greco-Roman society.

PART 3

SYNAGOGUES AND CONGREGATIONS
WITHIN SOCIETY

Comparing Socioreligious Groups in Antiquity

Introduction

Scholars with a sociohistorical interest in Christian congregations and Jewish synagogues within the Greco-Roman world have increasingly recognized the value of studying other groups, associations, or guilds. For example, Wayne A. Meeks is among those who acknowledge similarities between Jewish and Christian groups on the one hand and associations on the other. He draws attention to the fact that both were small, voluntary groups that gathered for communal meals and religious rituals on a regular basis (Meeks 1983:35, 77–78). To an outsider, a Jewish or Christian group could initially appear to be just another association, *thiasos*, *synodos*, or *collegium* within the polis.

Yet for Meeks and others, although there are similarities between such groups at first glance, there are fundamental differences that make associations less than satisfactory analogies, particularly regarding group-society relations. Most importantly here, both Jewish and Christian groups were utterly exclusive of other loyalties, and they were "sects" in a sociological sense of the word, whereas most associations were not. Scholars who focus on the Apocalypse, 1 Peter, or other literature pertinent to Christianity in Asia Minor also characterize Christian congregations in general as largely sectarian. In other words, scholars like John H. Elliott (1990), Harry O. Maier (1991), and Margaret Y. MacDonald (1988) stress congregations' separation from most, if not all, facets of society and they emphasize conflicts in group-society interactions. This particular depiction of Christianity and diaspora Judaism as a largely uniform set of exclusive and sectarian groups serves to obscure rather than explain other evidence that suggests more complicated scenarios regarding the relationship between particular groups and the surrounding society

Some recent studies of the Jewish diaspora are beginning to draw a more complicated picture of how the synagogues fit within the polis in areas such as Roman Asia. Moreover, the artifactual evidence concerning synagogues that I discuss sheds light on various areas of participation in civic life, such that a sectarian reading of these groups is inadequate. Like-wise, primary evidence for some Christian assemblies, including those re-flected in 1 Peter, the Pastoral Epistles, and Ignatius's epistles, points in a similar direction regarding areas of positive interaction. Insights from the social sciences regarding the complex processes of acculturation and as-similation among minority cultural groups, rather than sectarianism, may suggest more fruitful approaches to such issues of group-society relations. Moreover, there is a growing recognition among some scholars that social groupings in the ancient context, especially associations (rather than mod-ern "sects"), can serve as helpful comparative analogies for understanding some of the dynamics of group-society interactions among both syna-gogues and assemblies. The present chapter sets the stage for a more ex-tensive comparative study of evidence regarding Jews' and Christians' participation in imperial aspects of civic life. Mounting evidence makes a sectarian reading of many synagogues and assemblies implausible.

Associations and Early Christianity: Trajectories in Scholarship

Though scholars since Theodor Mommsen (1843) noted the importance of associations for understanding legal issues concerning early Christian-ity, it was the work of both Georg Heinrici and Edwin Hatch around the end of the nineteenth century that laid the foundation—upon which no structure was built for almost a century—for the comparison of Christian groups and associations (cf. Kloppenborg 1993a).[1] Heinrici, who focused on issues of the internal organization of Pauline communities, proposed that associations (more so than synagogues) should be considered as "his-torical analogies" to Christian congregations (Heinrici 1881:509; also Heinrici 1876, 1877; cf. T. Wilson 1927:120–35). Apparently independent of Heinrici's work, Hatch (1909) made a similar proposition regarding the comparability of organizational structures. What interests me far more here are some of Hatch's methodological concerns and their implications for sociohistorical approaches and comparisons.

Hatch is emphatic about the need for scholars to approach the study of early Christianity not with apologetic notions regarding its uniqueness and, hence, incomparability, but rather with the same set of historical methods that one would employ in studying any phenomena within that same society: "the facts of ecclesiastical history do not differ in kind from the facts of civic history" (1909:2, 13–20). Hatch emphasizes the need to approach the early Christian assemblies "as organizations in the midst of human society" (1909:32), paying close attention to the "relations of the early Churches to the social strain in the midst of which they grew" (1909:54).

A corollary of this approach is a concern to employ comparative methods in the study of social structures and organizations in the Greco-Roman world, and Hatch gives special attention to comparing associations and congregations in regard to leadership structures. However, both Hatch and Heinrici faced harsh criticisms from other scholars (often with apologetic overtones), the majority of whom emphasized Christianity's insulation from Greco-Roman influence and stressed the synagogue instead as the formative influence with regard to the organization of congregations.[2] Quite often, it seems, critics of comparison (and sometimes even Heinrici and Hatch) had in mind questions of influence or borrowing, of genealogy, rather than analogy. The comparative program implied by the works of Heinrici and Hatch gained little or no attention or elaboration within scholarship in the decades that followed.

Hatch's focus on understanding congregations in relation to the social groups and structures of surrounding society is, in some respects, a precursor to E. A. Judge's work on *The Social Pattern of the Christian Groups in the First Century* (1960). His sociohistorical approach and attention to associations, unfortunately, also went largely unheeded for some time. What interests us most here are Judge's observations regarding the relation of congregations and synagogues to the social structures and institutions of society, including the Greek city (polis), the household (*oikos*), and the association (*koinōnia*). He emphasizes that Christianity did not live in a vacuum, isolated from the rest of Greco-Roman society; rather, once established in the polis of the Roman Empire, the Christian group "belongs inevitably, as a social phenomenon, to the Hellenistic republics [i.e., *poleis*]. Its thinking and behaviour naturally reflect the social institutions of these states" (1960:14; cf. Winter 1994). Within the civic context, Judge suggests, associations provide a useful analogy to both congregations and synagogues, despite the differences and peculiarities among these groups. Indeed, "they were not distinguished in the public's mind from the general run of unofficial associations," nor would they be "unwilling to be thought of as forming an association of the usual kind" (Judge 1960:44, 45; cf. Wilken 1980:100). The implications of Judge's preliminary observations with regard to the fruitfulness of comparison are echoed two decades later when Malherbe optimistically states: if "we are interested in social relations . . . and in analogies rather than genealogical relationships, the material [regarding associations] may help to clarify some aspects of both the informal relationships within the church as well as the *church's relationship to the larger society*" (1983:89 [emphasis mine]; cf. Kloppenborg 1993a:230).

Now, two decades after Malherbe's statement, numerous useful studies have pursued comparison of associations with congregations or synagogues to some degree. The focus has often been primarily on internal life or organization rather than group-society relations.[3] Building on the insight that both congregations and synagogues might be viewed as associations, I pursue in chapter 8 a comparative study of certain aspects of group-society interaction. I explore in detail how the evidence for associations' participation in imperial honors and connections sheds light on the activities of both Christian and Jewish groups in Roman Asia in a way that makes a sectarian reading of many groups problematic. Part of the reason for a dearth in comparative studies regarding group-society relations specifically pertains to another trajectory within recent scholarship.

Meeks and other scholars contend that, overall, associations do *not* serve as useful models for comparison with Christian or Jewish groups. This contention rests on several supposed key differences between the groups that, in the view of these scholars, outweigh any similarities that would warrant deeper or more extensive comparison:

1. Christian groups were far more inclusive or heterogeneous in terms of social composition, while associations were more homogeneous.
2. Christian groups did not use the same terminology for the group or its organization and leadership structures.
3. Associations were a "self-contained local phenomenon," lacking the sort of extralocal linkages that the churches possessed.
4. Most importantly here, Christian groups, like Jewish ones, were fundamentally exclusivistic or sectarian while associations were not (Meeks 1983:78–80; cf. Schmeller 1995; McCready 1996).

This tendency to assert the *in*comparability of associations and Christianity also extends to some scholars of Greco-Roman religion (cf. Lane

Fox 1986:85–89, 324–25). Walter Burkert (1987:2–4) correctly refutes some common stereotypes concerning the mysteries. Yet he also devotes considerable attention to dismissing any possibility that cult societies (*thiasoi*) or associations of mystery initiates (*mystai*) were in any sense "communities" with ongoing "identities": "festive togetherness . . . does not outlast the festival" (Burkert 1987:43, 43–53, 110). The measuring stick, it becomes increasingly clear, is an *idealized* picture of early Christian "churches" as true communities; over against this caricature, other groups are considered inferior and lacking in a sense of belonging for their members. This becomes the basis of a problematic theory regarding why the mysteries were to "pass away" and Christianity was to succeed (Burkert 1987:45, 48–53).

Before fully addressing the issue of sectarianism (point 4), it is important to note some of the problems with Meeks's approach to the first three points. The main methodological problem is that in assessing the usefulness of comparison Meeks adopts a uniform picture of congregations (based primarily on social data from Corinth) that is contrasted to an artificially uniform picture of associations (based on something other than an extensive knowledge of the varied primary evidence for these groups). Yet these pictures do not actually reflect the more complex and diverse realities concerning both Christian assemblies and other associations. Furthermore, Meeks's understanding of each of the supposed fundamental differences is questionable, particularly since the evidence for associations—which is varied and deserving of study on its own terms—has not received the kind of attention that early Christian sources have. A few scholars more familiar with inscriptions have begun to challenge or qualify key aspects of each of these main points (cf. Kloppenborg 1993a; Ascough 1997; Harland 2000).

First, Meeks oversimplifies issues concerning the social composition of associations in antiquity. The evidence for the makeup of associations and guilds, like that for congregations, is in fact varied. Both types of groups could draw their membership from similar social network connections and could range from being relatively homogeneous (e.g., many occupational associations and the Christian handworkers at Thessalonica) to more heterogeneous or socially inclusive (e.g., the association of fishermen at Ephesus, many household or cultic-based associations, and the Christian groups at Corinth; cf. Kloppenborg 1993a:234–36).

Second, congregations and synagogues had in common with associations many organizational characteristics. Each could be heavily influenced by the structures of the household and by the common conventions of benefaction and honors in the Greek East, conventions that often meant that wealthier benefactors naturally became leaders of the group (cf. Klauck 1981; L. White 1996; Maier 1991; Rajak and Noy 1993). Furthermore, as Kloppenborg (1993a:232) also points out regarding the specifics of leadership positions, there "is no a priori reason to assume. that there was uniformity among the Pauline churches, any more than one should assume a uniform organizational structure in associations. On the contrary, titles were highly variable, local particularities abound, and in many instances we have no indication of how officers were designated." Contrary to what Meeks implies, there are in fact considerable crossovers in the varied terminology employed by different guilds, associations, and both synagogues and congregations. Thus, for example, self-designations used by Jewish groups in Asia are also used by other associations, including "synagogue," "household" (*oikos*), "settlement" (*katoikountes*), "synod" (*synodos*), and "associates" (*hetairoi*). At least some associations in Asia Minor refer to themselves as an "assembly" (*ekklēsia*; cf. *IGLAM* 1381–82 from Aspendos, Pamphylia; Foucart 1873:223–25, no. 43 = *CIG* 2271). Despite the variety in leadership structures among both associations and Christian congregations, there are also crossovers in titles such as "overseer" or "bishop" (*episkopos*), "elders" (*presbyteroi*), "servant"/"deacon" (*diakonos*), and "patroness" (*prostatis*).[4] Both types of groups could use familial language in reference to leaders or benefactors, as well as fellow members, as we have already seen.

Third, as Richard S. Ascough's (1997a) study clearly shows, Meeks exaggerates the extralocal character of Christian assemblies and underestimates the possibilities for these linkages among associations (cf. Harland 1996:327–28 n.33). We have already encountered such linkages in connection with ethnic-geographic and other associations. Yet the difficulties with Meeks's approach to the question of comparing Christian groups with other models in the environment is not limited to these few substantive points.

The Portrayal of Christian and Jewish Groups as "Sects"

Exclusivity and Sectarianism

Most pertinent to the issue of group-society relations is Meeks's claim that, like synagogues, "Christian groups were exclusive and totalistic in a way that no club nor even any pagan cultic association was" (point 4 above). While he admits that "the boundaries of the Pauline groups were

somewhat more open than those of some other early Christian circles"
(i.e., "gates" in community boundaries), he nonetheless stresses that all
Pauline groups involved a "thoroughgoing resocialization, in which the
sect was intended to become virtually the primary group for its members,
supplanting all other loyalties" (Meeks 1983:78; also see 35–39, 77–80, 85
[emphasis mine]).

In this respect, Meeks suggests, congregations were much like synagogues of the time, which were also fundamentally different from other associations in regard to their exclusivism and separation (Meeks cites
Smallwood 1981:123, 133–34, in this connection). He disregards considerable evidence regarding Jewish groups at locations such as Sardis, Miletos, and Aphrodisias, where there are clearly significant contacts or
relations between Jews and non-Jews within the civic context. Instead,
Meeks's concern is to emphasize the isolation of both Jewish and Christian groups from the Greco-Roman environment, asserting their uniqueness and incomparability to other groups.

Meeks's portrait of congregations as exclusive and sectarian and associations as entirely lacking in exclusivity is problematic. Although many
associations were not exclusive, some could make somewhat exclusive
claims on the allegiances of their members. Such was the case with the
therapeutai of Zeus in Sardis, who in the mid-second century reengraved a
Greek translation of an apparently ancient, Aramaic edict by the Lydian
governor (c. 404–359 B.C.E.; *ISardH* 4 = Robert 1975 = *CCCA* I 456 =
NewDocs I 3).[5] The edict instructs that the temple-keeping *therapeutai* of
Zeus "who enter the shrine (*adyton*) and who crown the god are not to participate in the mysteries of Sabazios . . . and the mysteries of Agdistis and
Ma"; moreover, "they instruct Dorates, the temple warden, to abstain
from these mysteries." What is most significant for us here is that the leaders or certain members of this group in the Roman era felt a need to reinforce the allegiances of members to the association, tending toward a view
that would limit participation in other groups or mysteries. Among the
statutes of the association devoted to Zeus Hypsistos ("Most High") in
Philadelphia, Egypt, is a prohibition against "leaving the brotherhood
(*phratras*) of the president for another" (*PLond* 2193 = Roberts, Skeat, and
Nock 1936:40–42, line 14). So although religious exclusivity was not the
norm in a polytheistic society, some associations did indeed have exclusivistic tendencies.

More problematic, though, is Meeks's assumption that most Christian
groups were exclusive in a comprehensive sense. In the case of the Christians at Corinth, for instance, he categorizes relatively open boundaries in-

cluding participation in legal institutions (i.e., courts), in social groupings, or in banqueting contexts as exceptions rather than the rule, and even here he stresses that Christian groups in this city were "sects" nonetheless (referring to Bryan R. Wilson's work). In the service of maintaining his focus on sectarianism, Meeks obscures the more varied nature of the evidence for Pauline and other groups. While Paul praises the Thessalonian Christians for turning from idols to God (1 Thess 1:9–10), for example, he knows and does not seem to disapprove of the practice among the Corinthians who know that "an idol has no real existence" and join with their fellow civic inhabitants at communal meals in some contexts, including an "idol's temple" (1 Cor 8–10; see 9:19–23).[6] Paul warns against the dangers of idolatry (10:1–22), but he also refers to the fact that some of the Corinthian Christians were invited to dinners by outsiders and that it would be acceptable in such cases to eat whatever food was put before them as long as it did not offend others (10:27–28).

The evidence of Paul's letter to Corinth suggests the strong possibility that some Christians were maintaining multiple affiliations or memberships within social groupings other than just the Christian assemblies. The language that Paul uses, speaking of outsiders actively inviting these Christians (*ei tis kalei hymas* . . . [10:27]), is reminiscent of the language of many actual invitations on papyri to dinners held in homes and temples, sometimes in connection with associations (cf. Youtie 1948; Gilliam 1976; *NewDocs* I 1; *POxy* 110, 523, 1484, 1755, 2592, 3693, 4339). In one of these the god Serapis himself calls on recipients of the invitation to attend: "The god calls you (*kalei se ho theos eis kleinēn*) to a banquet being held in the Thoereion tomorrow from the ninth hour" (*PKöln* 57; trans. *NewDocs* I 1). It is quite possible that some among the Christians at Corinth were considered to be full members of other associations, such that they would receive actual invitations to the dinners held by fellow members in homes or temples. This evidence for dual affiliations or "loyalties" (to use Meeks's term) on the part of Christians does not fit with a sectarian understanding of such groups and should not be passed off as an exception. Later on, I will adduce further evidence of such multiple affiliations in connection with both Jews and Christians.

Sectarian Depictions
of Groups Addressed by the Apocalypse

Similar sectarian-focused depictions of Christianity are evident among scholars who focus on literature pertinent to Roman Asia. I begin by discussing scholarly approaches to the Apocalypse, dealing with some issues of persecution, before going on to 1 Peter, Ignatius, and the Pastorals.

The traditional view of the Apocalypse is that the author's references to the death of Christians in the futuristic visions (e.g., Rev 6:9–11; 12:11; 14:13; 16:6; 17:6; 18:24) are references to the actual, current situation faced by most Christians; this involved a substantial and official persecution under Domitian (emperor 81–96 C.E.), who forced inhabitants to worship him as "lord and god" (cf. Beckwith 1967; Charles 1920; Hemer 1986:86–87; Schüssler Fiorenza 1985:192–97). Following the proponents of a Domitianic persecution (e.g., Keresztes 1979:257–72; Marta Sordi 1983:43–54), Elisabeth Schüssler Fiorenza argues that the author's invective against Rome and the emperors is a "fitting response" to this sociopolitical situation. The recipients of the Apocalypse were faced with a real threat of martyrdom if they did not worship Domitian and would have identified with the Apocalypse's strongly sectarian viewpoint (Schüssler Fiorenza 1985:6–8, 181–203; cf. deSilva 1991:186, who uses Bryan Wilson's sect typology). That is, in this view most of the Christian assemblies addressed by the Apocalypse were sectarian in their relation to society.

Such an understanding of the Apocalypse and, by implication, of the social situation of most congregations in Roman Asia suffers from several difficulties. The problems to be discussed relate to (1) whether there was an official and substantial Domitianic persecution (along with the related issue of Domitian's character); (2) how we should characterize persecution in Asia Minor more generally; and (3) whether the Apocalypse's sectarian stance means that we can categorize most Christian groups in Asia as sects in the sense that their relationship with society and empire was consistently in tension.

First, it is worth outlining the evidence often cited as support for a Domitianic persecution (first assembled by Lightfoot 1889–90:104–15; see the critique by J. Wilson 1993), focusing primarily on Asia Minor. The earliest direct reference to Domitian that concerns some negative relation to Christianity is the comment by Melito, bishop of Sardis (c. 170–180 C.E.), preserved by Eusebius: "The only emperors who were ever persuaded by malicious men to slander our teaching were Nero and Domitian, and from them arose the lie, and the unreasonable custom of falsely accusing Christians" (*H.E.* 4.26.9; cf. *H.E.* 3.17–20; Tertullian, *Apology* 5.4, both apparently depending on Melito). Other contemporary evidence from Asia Minor does not refer to Domitian at all.

The futuristic visions of the Apocalypse (dated to Domitian's time by Irenaeus) make frequent references to the "blood of the saints" and the slaughter of Christians, which John closely associates with the beasts in league with Satan, namely emperors and/or imperial officials (Rev 6:9–11; 12:11; 14:13; 16:6; 17:6; 18:24; 11:3–13). In the case of Christians in Pontus (c. 110 C.E.), Pliny the Younger states that some of the accused "said that they had ceased to be Christians two or more years previously, and some of them even twenty years ago" (*Epistles* 10.96.6 [LCL]). The figure of about twenty years coincides with the time when a Domitianic persecution would have occurred (if it did) and these, therefore, may have been apostates resulting from official persecution.

This evidence from Asia Minor falls short of suggesting an official persecution by Domitian or his officials, however. Melito's apologetic comment does not expressly refer to persecution at all. Rather it tries to suggest that only widely disliked emperors, Nero and Domitian, held negative attitudes toward Christian teaching (cf. Aune 1997–98, 1:lxvi). As T. D. Barnes (1971:150) points out, all "other authors who depict Domitian as a persecutor derive their information either directly or indirectly from Melito." The visions of the Apocalypse are explicitly set in the future and do not name Domitian. We cannot assume a direct relation between futuristic rhetoric and contemporary reality, as the discussion in chapter 9 clarifies. Finally, the apostates mentioned by Pliny could have been but were not necessarily the outcome of official persecution, and, indeed, this seems unlikely. Pliny's lack of familiarity with how to approach prosecutions against Christians suggests that he, at least, did not know of an earlier, official persecution of Christians on which to base his actions. This is particularly significant in view of the fact that much of Pliny's career during the principate of Domitian was spent at Rome; he first served as quaestor conveying messages from Domitian to the senate, then as tribune of the people, and then as praetor (cf. Sherwin-White 1966:72–82; Wilken 1984:4–5). No doubt he would have known of official actions taken by Domitian against Christians, either at Rome or in the provinces, if they had occurred.

Those who hold that there was a substantial Domitianic persecution also cite evidence from Rome as support. The letter of the Roman Christians to the church at Corinth, written in the 90s C.E., refers to "sudden and repeated misfortunes and calamities that have befallen us (*tas aiphnidious kai epallēlous genomenas hēmin symphoras kai periptōs*)," which can be interpreted as official persecution (*1 Clem.* 1.1). However, there is no explicit reference either to Domitian or to actions by Roman authorities, and this passage could refer to any number of troubles affecting the churches. Furthermore, the authors use similar language (*eris, stasis, diōgmos, polemos*) to describe the main problem at Corinth, which is not official "persecution" from outside; rather, it is the internal rebellion of youths against the elders (3.1–3). Overall, then, these bits of evidence do not add up to an official and substantial persecution by Domitian of Christians in Asia Minor.[7]

A final related point cited by scholars of the traditional view is that a substantial persecution fits well with our overall knowledge of Domitian's character. Our principal sources (Pliny the Younger, Tacitus, and Suetonius) unanimously emphasize the savage and tyrannical nature of Domitian's actions, including murders of senators and pretentious demands to be honored as "lord and god" (*dominus et deus*; cf. Suetonius, *Domitian* 13.2; Dio Cassius, *Roman History* 67.4.7; 67.13.4; Pliny, *Panegyricus* 33.4; 52.6). These references to Domitian being addressed as "lord and god" are often interpreted as a sign that Domitian actually promoted the imperial cult throughout the empire (including Asia Minor) in a way that differed from his predecessors.

However, other (many more recent) studies of Domitian's principate suggest that the picture of a savage and mad tyrant is not accurate. Portrayals of Domitian after his death and *damnatio* by friends of a new emperor are less than accurate measures of Domitian's rule. Pat Southern (1997) and Brian W. Jones (1992) point to the unreliability of the primary sources that harshly condemn Domitian and draw a very different picture regarding his principate (cf. Thompson 1990:95–115; Suetonius, *Domitian* 8.2). H. W. Pleket (1961) argues that a strained relationship between Domitian and the senate (not his character) underlies much of the hostility expressed by upper-class authors like Pliny, Suetonius, and Tacitus. The supposed murders of innocent senators were in fact the result of trials for treason involving senators who had actively conspired against Domitian (Pleket 1961:299). Furthermore, the suggestion that Domitian's supposed demands to be called "lord and god" meant that he also went out of his way to promote imperial cults in the provinces is unfounded (cf. Southern 1997:45–46). There is, in fact, no clear evidence of a significant change in imperial cults in Asia Minor at this time. A new provincial temple was built at Ephesus, but (as was customary) this was on the initiative of the provincial assembly, not the emperor (see Friesen 1993). The notion that imperial cult activity in a province like Asia was dependent on active promotion by particular emperors reveals an inadequate understanding of the spontaneous nature of worship of the emperors in the Greek East.

This brings me to my second point pertaining to the actual nature of persecution in Asia Minor, which is further elaborated in chapter 9. G. E.

M. de Ste. Croix (1963) and T. D. Barnes (1968; 1971:143–63) show that
there is a lack of evidence for any Roman-initiated, official persecution of
Christians in Asia Minor and the empire generally not only in the time of
Domitian but also in the first two centuries (cf. Thompson 1990:95–115;
A. Collins 1984:70–75; J. Wilson 1993:587–605; Aune 1997:lxiv–lxix). By
and large, Nero's slaughter of Christians at Rome (as scapegoats for the fire
that had devastated part of the city) was an exceptional incident, as Tacitus's (*Annals* 15.43–44) account clearly shows. Pliny's correspondence
with Trajan regarding the Christians in Pontus (c. 110 C.E.) and Hadrian's
rescript a decade or so later (c. 123 C.E.) with respect to Asia show that
there were indeed occasions when some inhabitants of the cities might
bring charges against Christians before Roman authorities. But nothing
suggests any active persecution of Christians in the provinces by Pliny or
other Roman officials or emperors before him, or any precedents to follow
in the matter. The relatively passive-reactive character of Roman rule also
speaks against an active or consistent role by Roman authorities in persecutions of or prosecutions against Christians.

Persecution of Christians in the first two centuries in Asia Minor is better characterized as *local and sporadic* (cf. van Unnik 1980d:95–96; Elliott
1990:78–82; Thompson 1990; Achtemeier 1996:33–36). This took the
form of various levels of social harassment and verbal abuse by some civic
inhabitants that could periodically lead to physical abuse or martyrdom,
especially when general socioeconomic conditions were at their worst
(e.g., famines, epidemics, natural disasters). In connection with the frequency of actual martyrdom, it is worth noting Origen's statement in the
third century: "For a few, whose number could be easily enumerated, have
died occasionally for the sake of the Christian religion by way of reminder
to men that when they see a few striving for piety they may become more
steadfast and may despise death" (*Against Celsus* 3.8; trans. Chadwick
1953). The circumstances of Christians could vary from one city to the
next and change over time.

There are few references in Christian literature from Asia to actual
Christians who were killed, which should further caution us in assuming
that martyrdoms such as those envisioned (for the future) in the Apocalypse, the incident involving Pliny the Younger, or the martyrdom of Polycarp in the 160s C.E. were extremely common. The Apocalypse refers to
Antipas as "my witness, my faithful one, who was killed among you"
(2:13), but we know nothing concerning the circumstances surrounding
his death. Ignatius, who is himself a prisoner on his way to Rome to face
death (he hopes), does not refer to any other Christians facing similar ar-

rest or persecution, let alone martyrdom in the Asian congregations (c. 108–110 C.E.).

The evidence of 1 Peter is particularly significant concerning the nature of persecution, since it pertains to Christian groups in Asia Minor during roughly the same time period as the Apocalypse. First Peter's characterization of the situation faced by Christians differs considerably from the martyrdoms of the Apocalypse's futuristic visions. The addressees were faced with "suffering" primarily in the form of verbal abuse: they are spoken against, blasphemed, reviled, and falsely called "wrongdoers" (1 Pet 2:12; 3:9, 15–17; 4:3–5; 5:9). The reasons for this suffering stemmed from the Christians' failure to participate in religious life in the same way as they had before: the Gentiles "are surprised that you do not now join them in the same wild profligacy, and they abuse you" (4:4). According to this author, this same sort of "suffering" was faced by the "brotherhood throughout the world" (5:9).

This brings us to the third point, which pertains to the issue of whether the congregations addressed by the Apocalypse were necessarily as sectarian as John was (at least in relation to empire). Evidently, the Apocalypse's visionary description of mass slaughter of Christians does not (nor does it claim to) represent the actual conditions faced by most Christians living in Roman Asia. The emperor and Roman officials were not engaged in systematic persecution of Christians in Asia Minor. We should be cautious, therefore, in assuming that John's sectarian stances regarding the relationship between the Christian assemblies and empire are representative of those of most other Christians—at least based on issues pertaining to persecution. Considerable primary evidence from Asia concerning the participation of Jewish and Christian groups in imperial honors and connections, for instance, would strongly suggest otherwise. While some Christian groups may have been more inclined toward the sectarian stances of the Apocalypse, many others clearly were not. It seems that one of John's purposes is to convince others (like the Nicolaitans and the followers of "Jezebel") to see, as he did, the problems with Roman imperial power and its social, economic, and religious manifestations in the cities of Asia.

Sectarian Depictions of Other Christian Groups in Asia

Some scholars who generally accept the revised understanding of the character of persecution in the first two centuries nonetheless argue for a sectarian understanding of Christianity in Asia Minor on other grounds, often employing Bryan Wilson's sociological typology. Wilson's sect typology, which substantially modifies the church-sect typologies of Max Weber and Ernst Troeltsch, was first developed out of his studies of divergent Christian religious movements in Western cultural contexts, and later broadened for cross-cultural study of developing countries in *Magic and the Millennium* (1973; cf. B. Wilson 1970, 1990). According to Wilson, a sect is a "deviant" religious movement primarily characterized by tension with society, and he suggests that there are seven main types based on their "response to the world" and a corresponding soteriological perspective. Most important for present purposes is the "conversionist" type of sect, for whom the world and those in it are corrupt and can be changed only through the "supernaturally wrought transformation of the self" that takes place through an "emotional transformation conversion experience" (B. Wilson 1973:22–23, also cited by Elliott 1990:76).[8] The modern, individualistic character of Wilson's model is quite evident here.

Elliott broadly categorizes Christian groups in Asia Minor as conversionist sects in this sense, stressing the fundamental separation and conflict between such groups and the society in which they lived. In reference to 1 Peter, Elliott states that the "sectarian features of the movement [in Palestine] continued to characterize the Christian communities of Asia Minor and *determine the nature of their interaction with society*" (1990:74 [emphasis mine]; cf. Elliott 1986a). Like the typical diaspora Jewish group, the Christian community "drew firm social and religious boundaries between its members and all 'outsiders'" (1990:79). The recipients of 1 Peter, who were literally aliens of the lower-classes faced with dire socioeconomic conditions (according to Elliott), had terminated all previous familial, social, and religious ties or loyalties in order to form "a community set apart and disengaged from the routine affairs of civic and social life" (1990:79). First Peter's strategy in addressing these sectarian groups, Elliott stresses, was to emphasize the identity of the Christians as the elect of God and the suffering that they faced in order to further *heighten* their separation from all aspects of the Greco-Roman context (1990:107, 148; cf. Achtemeier 1996:52–55).

Other scholars take a similar approach. Maier, for instance, also employs Wilson's typology in order to stress that the congregations addressed by Ignatius had a strong sense of separation from society, speaking of the "sectarian identity of the Asian churches." From their perspective, he suggests, Ignatius "would have appeared as an embodiment of separation from the world" (Maier 1991:163–68). Maier, like Elliott, is correct to point out the distinctive beliefs, practices, and self-understandings of the Christian groups (e.g., notions of election). However, his overemphasis on separation from society in a very broad sense, failing to distinguish the various aspects of life in the polis encompassed by his use of the term "society," does not do justice to the intricacies of everyday life in the cities of Roman Asia. In a similar manner, Margaret MacDonald categorizes most Pauline communities as conversionist sects. She still refers to those addressed by the Pastorals as a sect, even though she admits that there is a lack of any evidence of "world rejection" that may suggest "a movement away from the sect-type toward the church-type" (M. MacDonald 1988:163–66).

Problems with Sectarian-Focused Approaches

There are several difficulties with these sectarian-focused approaches to the social history of early Christianity or Judaism, only some of which can be discussed here. The most fundamental problem is that they do not adequately account for primary evidence indicative of more complex possibilities in group-society interactions. Nor do they fully acknowledge the diversity among both synagogues and congregations. Moreover, evidence from Ignatius's epistles, the Pastoral Epistles, 1 Peter, and the Apocalypse discussed here and in the following chapters shows the difficulties in speaking of all Christian groups in Asia Minor as sects. The case study of imperial honors and connections provides extensive data that do not fit the common sectarian portrayal of many synagogues and congregations; likewise in the case of archeological evidence from Roman Asia concerning the participation of synagogues within various other areas of life in the polis.

Before I address this primary evidence more fully, a general discussion of the difficulties with these scholarly approaches is in order (also see L. White 1988; Holmberg 1990:77–117; Barton 1993). The term "sect" has come to be used in a variety of ways, and there is little reason to question its applicability to many early Christian groups in the general sense that they were "divergent" cultural groups or "minority religious movements within the context of [other] dominant religious traditions" (B. Wilson 1973:11). What I question here is not whether such groups were in important ways "deviant" or distinctive in relation to many cultural norms in the Greco-Roman world (primarily with regard to their monotheism), nor whether they were in tension with aspects of society (or, better put, particular dimensions of civic life), both of which are true.

The problem is not necessarily with sect typologies as such. Rather it is with how scholars such as Elliott have applied them, overemphasizing exclusivity, separation, and tensions with "society" in a broad sense while obscuring other primary evidence concerning specific and more complex dimensions of group-society relations, including imperial dimensions of group life. Elliott's application of the model dictates what evidence is considered in the first place. For instance, only after he categorizes the Christian groups as sects does he consider the evidence for 1 Peter's apparently positive view of Roman authorities and of the "secular model" of the household, which are then taken as secondary. Elliott's application of the sociological model suffers from a problem also identified by some sociologists. For example, James A. Beckford points out how the application of church-sect typologies often involves categorizations based on limited contrasting dualities or oppositions—protest or accommodation, exclusivity or inclusivity—that fail to do justice to the subtleties of social realities, and he even calls for a moratorium on the use of church-sect typologies (Beckford 1973:94–104; for other critiques see Eister 1967; Knudsen, Earle, and Shriver 1978).

Some scholars interpret literary evidence for Christianity in Asia Minor quite differently from those who take a sectarian-focused approach, and draw a more complicated picture regarding the relationship between particular congregations and specific dimensions of society and culture. Here I provide an overview of some of these other studies, giving some brief concrete illustrations from primary evidence, including Ignatius's epistles, the Pastoral Epistles, and 1 Peter.

Unlike Maier, both Bruce J. Malina (1978) and William R. Schoedel (1980) suggest that Ignatius's letters reveal a positive outlook with respect to the place of Christians within civic life, despite distinctive Christian identities and worldviews. Schoedel can even state that Ignatius "has the popular culture of the Greek city in his bones" (cited by Carruth 1996:295). Malina (1978:87) uses Mary Douglas's idea that the relation of spirit and matter, mind and body, are "symbolic statements about the relation of society and the individual." In this way, he argues that Ignatius's use of binates—flesh-spirit, material help-spiritual help—suggests that spirit works through matter (corresponding to Ignatius's antidocetism) and that the individual is subordinate to society, finding his or her freedom *within* its forms (cf. Ign. *Eph.* 5.1; 7.2; 8.2; 10.3; *Magn.* 1.1; 13.1; *Trall.* 12.1; *Smyrn.* 3.3; 12.2; 13.2).

Several aspects of the evidence from Ignatius are indicative of the sort of material obscured by the common sectarian reading. Despite the clear distinction between the church (spirit) and the world (flesh), the Ignatian material has various indicators of noteworthy positive relations with out-

siders, both on the part of Ignatius and on the part of the Asian Christians.[9] The principal conflicts faced by the Christian assemblies in Asia
were internal (docetics and "judaizers"), not external, in Ignatius's view. In
those few passages that discuss outsiders, the attitude is quite positive. Ignatius points out praisingly that the bishop at Tralles commands great respect not only within the Christian assembly, but also among the
"godless" (*Trall.* 3.2).

It is in this same letter that Ignatius shows further concerns with the
image of the Christians in the view of those outside the group: "Let none
of you have a grudge against his neighbor. Give no occasion to the Gentiles, in order that the congregation of God may not be blasphemed for a
few foolish persons" (*Trall.* 8.2 [LCL]; cf. 1 Pet 2:12; Pol. *Phil.* 10.2–3).
Even when Ignatius encourages the congregation at Ephesus to pray for
outsiders, he employs familial language in calling on Christians to treat
these people as "brothers" (*Eph.* 10.1–3). One wonders how Meeks
(1983:85–88) would deal with this language of belonging that extends outside the boundaries of the Christian group. For in the case of the use of
this language *within* Pauline Christian groups he suggests that by "this
kind of [familial] talk members are taught to conceive of only two classes
of humanity: the sect and the outsiders" (Meeks 1983:86). Something
more complicated than this dualism is going on in the case of Ignatius.

There are similar indications of the more complicated nature of
group-society interactions among Christian groups of Asia in the Pastoral
Epistles, which further suggests the inadequacy of applying the sect
model. Labeling the Pastoral Epistles "bourgeois" (*bürgerlich*, as does Dibelius) is problematic in the least. However, the characteristics of the letters that led scholars to come up with the label do indeed suggest a
Christian leadership approach in Roman Asia that in some respects accepted or transformed some Hellenistic values of "good citizenship" and
other conventions of civic life.[10]

Evidence from the Pastoral Epistles should caution us against assuming that all congregations were sects. I discuss passages relating to imperial-
related issues extensively in chapter 8 (1 Tim 2:1–2; Titus 3:1–2), but it is
worth at least noting some other evidence here. As with Ignatius, the author of the Pastoral Epistles clearly emphasizes the distinct status of be-
lievers as "the elect" with a "holy calling" (cf. Titus 1:1; 2 Tim 1:9–10;
2:10) and he contrasts this with their pre-Christian status (Titus 2:12;
3:3–8). Yet, as in Ignatius's epistles, the principal threat or conflict that the
author perceives comes from those "unbelieving" opponents or false
teachers *within* the church (cf. 1 Tim 1:3–11; 5:13–16; 6:3–7; 2 Tim 4:3–4;

Titus 1:13–15), not from outsiders. There is, in fact, a continuing concern on the part of the author regarding the perception of the congregations in the eyes of non-Christians.

The Pastor's advice regarding proper behavior among Christians of varying status within the church reflects both his prevalent concern for the view of outsiders and his acceptance of certain values of Greco-Roman culture. The requirements for assuming leadership in the Christian assembly, "the household of God" (1 Tim 3:15), are expressed as follows: "Now a bishop must be above reproach, the husband of one wife, temperate, sensible, dignified, hospitable. . . . He must manage his household well, keeping his children submissive and respectful in every way; for if a man does not know how to manage his own household, how can he care for God's church? . . . Moreover he must be well thought of by outsiders, or he may fall into reproach and the snare of the slanderer" (1 Tim 3:2–7).

Christian slaves are also to behave in ways that are pleasing to non-Christian masters: "Let all who are under the yoke of slavery regard their masters as worthy of all honor (*timēs*), so that the name of God and the teaching may not be defamed" (1 Tim 6:1; cf. Titus 2:9–10). Young women, too, should live in a way that is acceptable to outsiders: "So I would have younger widows marry, bear children, rule their households, and give the enemy no occasion to revile us" (1 Tim 5:14). They should be trained "to love their husbands and children, to be sensible, chaste, domestic, kind, and submissive to their husbands, that the word of God may not be discredited" (Titus 2:3–5). These are cultural values that were widely accepted within the context of the polis. Overall, the Pastoral Epistles' approach to the role of women, which is limited primarily to the household, also reflects a concern with the perception of outsiders. Alternative trajectories in early Christianity in Asia Minor, such as those evident in the *Acts of Paul* and the Phrygian (Montanist) movement, suggest a far more prominent role for women. They also show that subversion of cultural values concerning marriage and the household could be among the accusations that outsiders made against Christians (cf. *Acts of Paul* 3; Origen, *Against Celsus* 3.55; D. MacDonald 1983:59–65; M. MacDonald 1996, throughout).

In contrast to Elliott's sectarian-focused approach is the picture drawn by other scholars regarding the social strategy and situation of 1 Peter. Thus W. C. van Unnik (1980d:101) states: "In every respect the relation with fellow-men is central, not retreat from the world, but a life in the given conditions."[11] Similarly, Leonhard Goppelt observes that the attempt to gain a place for Christians *within* Hellenistic society "shapes the theology of 1 Peter in a decisive way" (Goppelt 1993:161, 154–61; cf. Goppelt 1982; Winter 1994:11–40). David L. Balch's studies (1981, 1986), too, challenge Elliott's portrait of the social situation and strategy of 1 Peter, arguing instead that the household code, at least, represents some degree of acculturation in order to lessen group-society tensions.

In certain respects the author of 1 Peter advocates the adoption or continuation of *some* Hellenistic values and practices, including those pertaining to "good works" (or benefaction) and honors for authorities (1 Pet 2:11–17). The household code as a whole (2:11–3:7) suggests a concern with the positive view of outsiders and promotes the adoption of some Greco-Roman cultural values within congregations. Yet 1 Peter's advocation of certain values and practices does not mean that the author suggested an openness to all other aspects of that same society or culture, least of all the "futile ways inherited from your fathers" (1:18), that is, a lifestyle of "passions, drunkenness, revels, carousing, and lawless idolatry" (4:3; cf. van Unnik 1969).

Overall, the manner in which the sect typologies are often applied to early Christianity does not adequately account for all the evidence. Before considering further primary evidence to this effect, it is worth tapping into some other insights from the social sciences that may help us to recognize the complexities of group-society relations. Balch's study of the household code in 1 Peter points out the value of studies of acculturation, for instance: "Instead of the assumption that 'all Gentile modes of behavior' are sinful, anthropologists studying acculturation emphasize that there is a 'selection' by the receiving culture among cultural traits of the donor culture. Some foreign traits are accepted and/or adapted; others are rejected" (Balch 1986:86).

Assimilation and Acculturation

Anthropological and sociological insights concerning assimilation and acculturation, or culture contact, will be useful here.[12] Although these theories are developed primarily in connection with ethnocultural groups of the modern era, the insights they provide help us to better understand our evidence for group-society relations among ancient Jewish ethnic groups and also Christian groups in some respects. J. Milton Yinger's study (1981:249) defines assimilation as "a process of boundary reduction that can occur when members of two or more societies or of smaller cultural groups meet." At the same time, he stresses that assimilation need not lead to loss of boundaries between a group and society, or of group identity; instead, "assimilation can range from the smallest beginnings of interaction and cultural exchange to the thorough fusion of the groups" (1981:249; cf. Berry 1980:13).

Scholars often distinguish between subprocesses of assimilation, the most important here being (1) cultural assimilation (or acculturation) and (2) structural assimilation (cf. Yinger 1981; Marger 1991:116–29). First, *acculturation* refers to "the phenomena which result when groups of individuals having different cultures come into continuous first–hand contact, with subsequent changes in the original cultural patterns of either or both groups" (Redfield, Linton, and Herskovits 1936:149). Acculturation can involve the selection, adoption, and adaptation of a variety of cultural traits including language, dress, religion, and other cultural conventions, beliefs, and values that make up the way of life and worldview of a particular cultural group. Anthropologists and sociologists emphasize the selective and transformative character of intercultural transmission: "the patterns and values of the receiving culture seem to function as *selective screens* in a manner that results in the enthusiastic acceptance of some elements, the firm rejection of other elements"; furthermore, "the elements which are transmitted undergo transformations" in the process (H. Barnett et al. 1954 [emphasis mine]). At both the individual and group levels acculturation need not be substitutive, replacing a set of cultural traits or radically changing a worldview; rather it can be additive, allowing for the continuation of a particular individual's or group's identity and cultural framework despite acculturation (Yinger 1981:252).

Again, acculturation can progress a long way without the disintegration of a group's boundaries or existence in relation to a larger societal or cultural entity. John W. Berry (1980:13) emphasizes that there are various forms of adaptation in cases of culture contact, some of which can involve a twofold process that entails the "maintenance of cultural integrity as well as the movement to become an integral part of a larger societal framework." Similarly, it is also important, as Yinger points out, to remain aware of the processes of *dis*similation that can occur at certain points in a group's history. That is, certain levels of acculturation or assimilation in the case of a particular cultural group can also be accompanied by conscious efforts to reassert and strengthen specific intrasocietal differences: "powerful assimilative forces are matched by renewed attention to sociocultural differences" (Yinger 1981:257; see also 257–61).

The second main subprocess of assimilation of interest to us here is *structural assimilation*, which can be discussed in terms of both primary and secondary (or informal and formal) levels. At the primary level, individual members of a given ethnic or cultural group can interact with persons from other cultural groups through personal social network connections, including memberships in neighborhoods, clubs, and associations (cf. Yinger 1981:254; Marger 1991:118; Elise 1995:275). This will become relevant when we come to consider Jewish (or even Christian) individual's multiple memberships or interactions within other institutions and subgroups of society, including occupational associations. The occupational connections of Jews and Christians are especially important in this regard, for, as Yinger (1981:254) points out, incorporation within occupational networks "almost certainly leads to at least some acculturation, identification [i.e., psychological identification with occupation or fellow workers], and amalgamation [e.g., intermarriage]."

The secondary level of structural assimilation involves members of a particular cultural group becoming more evident and participatory in the formal political, legal, social, or economic institutions of society. Total assimilation at this level would entail equal access to power and privilege within the major societal institutions. Yet again there are a range of possibilities in the nature and degree of these secondary relations.

Now that we have some idea of the character and complexity of the processes of assimilation and acculturation, we can turn to the question of how this applies to the ancient context and to the issue of interactions between diverse synagogues and congregations and the surrounding society. Before addressing evidence for synagogues that are clearly ethnically based, it is important to explain how some of these social-scientific insights concerning acculturation might apply to Christians.

Though many congregations were not primarily Jewish in membership or ethnically based associations in the same sense that synagogues were, in some respects we can indeed approach them as minority cultural groups with a *distinctive cultural complex* (a specific configuration of various social and cultural factors, traits, values, and practices). This cultural complex derived, in part, from the Jewish worldview and way of life. Thus, for example, the author of 1 Peter (4:3–5) can expect his primarily Gentile Christian audience in Asia Minor to understand his characterization of them as "exiles" of the "diaspora" (1:1–2), drawing heavily on Jewish ethnic identity ("chosen people," "holy nation," "a people belonging to God"; cf. 2:9–10) to express their distinctiveness in relation to the surrounding society. The most distinctive cultural element that, in some respects, set both Jews and Christians apart as minority cultural groups was their peculiar monotheism (devotion to one god to the exclusion of others) in a predominantly

polytheistic society.[13] Thus in some ways we can accurately speak of both
synagogues and congregations (as well as some other ethnic-based associations, such as "Israelites," or Samaritans) as minority cultural groups even
though many of their members may have been lifelong inhabitants in a
polytheistic society like Roman Asia. Thus insights concerning acculturation can, if carefully adapted, provide a working framework for considering group-society relations among minority cultural groups such as these.

Assimilation is a complex, two-way process that works at both the individual and group levels in the ancient context. The entrance of a new individual member (e.g., a Gentile or a Jew) into a group with a distinctive
cultural complex could be part of this cultural exchange. All individuals,
social-scientific studies emphasize, are *culture carriers* who bring with them
a set of cultural traits pertaining to a particular way of life and worldview.
The case of a new (Gentile) member entering a Christian assembly will be
appropriate as an illustration here. Processes of acculturation would take
place even though many other members may also come from a similar
background (i.e., Gentiles who had lived their entire lives in a particular
city of Asia), since in some respects the group maintained a deviant or minority cultural configuration that differed from the surrounding society. A
potential or new member's cultural traits were profoundly shaped by and,
at some point, consonant with those of the surrounding culture, more so
than with the distinctive elements in the cultural complex of the Christian
(or Jewish-Christian) congregation. A person's experience in associating
with individual Christians (or Jewish Christians) and subsequently in joining a Christian group, then, would entail a process of culture contact or acculturation. The person would go through a process of *en*culturation into
the specific cultural complex of a particular group. Monotheism was a key
distinguishing factor in the case of Christian (and Jewish) cultural groups.
Enculturation would entail a selective process of continuation, rejection,
adoption, and adaptation of specific social and cultural elements by the
new member (both of her own cultural heritage and of the newly joined
group with its distinctive cultural elements). But this would also entail the
potential sociocultural modification of specific elements of the group as
well, especially as others joined and interacted with fellow members.

Presumably, though, the enculturation of a new member would vary
from one person to the next and would not necessarily involve complete
assimilation, so to speak, to a particular group's sociocultural matrix. Thus
the new member would not necessarily or even likely cut off all previous
social connections or affiliations within networks (including occupational
ones) in the polis even though membership in a such a minority cultural

group (the monotheistic congregation) could influence, to varying degrees, transformations in the nature of such contacts. My point is that we should not be surprised to find a certain degree of agreement in some of the social and cultural values and practices between members of congregations and other inhabitants within the civic context, despite the differences that would, perhaps increasingly, develop between a given new member and those within her previously principle social circles. These differences would be particularly present with respect to changes in the positions of God, the gods, and others (including emperors) in the cosmological framework or worldview of the member, which could also have significant impacts on behavior and practices. These circumstances concerning entrance of new members would also influence the dynamics of cultural or structural assimilation (or dissimilation) of the group in relation to society.

As minority groups, synagogues and congregations living alongside other associations within the structures of the polis would also be affected in various ways by contacts with the social and cultural institutions, conventions, practices, and values of surrounding society. Any given synagogue or congregation could adopt, adapt, and develop ways of finding a place within civic society akin to the ways of other socioreligious groups in that setting, as the case of imperial honors illustrates. It seems that many of the Jewish groups we find in Roman Asia had been living there for extended periods of time, sometimes even centuries, and this would play a role in the nature of culture contact or acculturation. For as Martin N. Marger (1991:127) points out, this temporal factor is often an important variable: "the more recent a group's entry into the society, the more resistance there is [both on the part of the group and of society] to its assimilation"; a corollary of this is that groups "with alien ways are seen differently after they have lived in the society for several generations." Certain levels of assimilation and the continuation of strong group identity (including processes of dissimilation) are not mutually exclusive.

The main point of this section has been to suggest that a complex scenario akin to acculturation, assimilation, and dissimilation (rather than the overly simplistic separationist focus of sectarian typologies) should be imagined for the variety of synagogues and congregations (or individuals) within the polis of the Greek East. While particular groups (or individual members or leaders) might firmly reject certain aspects of the values, symbols, conventions, and institutions of Greco-Roman culture and society, they might also maintain, accept, or adapt others, without necessarily undermining or losing their own distinctive way of life, worldview, or group identity (monotheism being the key). There would be a range of possibilities for interactions between a given group and society without losing group boundaries. We shall see some of these complexities in group-society relations and in levels of assimilation presently in connection with many synagogues in Asia and, in the following chapter, with respect to imperial honors among both synagogues and congregations.

A Revised View of Jewish Synagogues in the Diaspora

Until recently, it was common for scholars to depict Jewish groups of the diaspora as isolated and introverted communities living in hostile environments, largely alien to the institutions, conventions, and values of society in the Roman Empire. This exclusivity ensured their identity over against "syncretism," serving as a "barrier against the influence of the alien environment," as Victor Tcherikover puts it (Tcherikover 1966:29; cf. Smallwood 1981:123; also see Trebilco 1991:186, 263 nn.1–3). This depiction of Jewish groups as sectarian has continued to influence discussions of congregations in the same setting, including those of Meeks and Elliott.

However, other studies have challenged this view. The emergent picture shows a variety of Jewish groups, many of which could be at home as participants in the polis despite their distinctive self-understandings and identities (cf. Kraabel 1968; Blanchetière 1974, 1984; Rajak 1985; Trebilco 1991:167–85; S. Cohen 1993; Gruen 1998). Thus John J. Collins (1983: 129) states that "the dominant tendency of Diaspora Jewry was to live as loyal subjects of their gentile masters and participate in the culture and society as fully as possible within the constraints of their religious tradition." Paul R. Trebilco's (1991:187) study of Jews in Asia Minor specifically finds that "the Hellenistic polis accommodated considerable diversity of population without demanding uniformity," and that "a degree of integration did not mean the abandonment of an active attention to Jewish tradition or of Jewish distinctiveness."

Along similar lines, John M. G. Barclay's study of Jews in the diaspora and in Asia specifically proposes a range of possibilities in levels of assimilation. There could be high assimilation among Jewish individuals like Niketas at Iasos, who in the second century B.C.E. made financial contributions to a Dionysiac festival (*CIJ* 749; cf. *CIJ* 82 [Oropos, Greece]); medium assimilation among many Jews in Asia who maintained their distinctive identities while also being integrated within civic life; and low as-similation among others, especially at times and places where conflicts with outsiders were more prevalent (Barclay 1996:259–81, 320–35). These revised understandings of synagogues and the polis (along with evidence concerning other associations) provide instructive analogies concerning the spectrum of possibilities in group-society interactions among some congregations within the context of cities in Roman Asia.

Participation of Jews in civic life is attested in several ways, some of which seriously undermine scholars' contentions that most Jewish groups, like Christian ones, were fundamentally sectarian or utterly exclusive in terms of membership, "supplanting all other loyalties," as Meeks (1983:78) puts it. There is clear evidence from Roman Asia (esp. epigraphic evidence) that being a member in a Jewish group did not mean the dissolution of all participation in conventions, institutions, and constituent groups of the polis. Some synagogues' practices and relations were akin to those of various other associations.

Here I focus as much as possible on the first two centuries but enter into the third where helpful, and briefly discuss as examples three main features or areas of participation in civic life: sociocultural institutions, social networks of benefaction, and other subgroups, including guilds or associations. The following chapter discusses at length another area of potential participation in or rejection of conventions of society among both synagogues and assemblies, focusing on imperial dimensions of civic life. Evidence along these lines attests to some of the dynamics of cultural and structural assimilation among Jewish groups or individuals, but it does not tell of the disappearance of boundaries between group and society, nor of the disintegration of the specific identities, worldviews, and cultural practices of these groups and their members.

First, like many other associations (or their members), Jews could be present as participants within the central sociocultural institutions of the polis. The theater was among the focal points of the polis, since this is where various celebrations and performances were held and where the assembly of the people met. At the theater of Miletos there was reserved seating for the "Jews and God-fearers" alongside other guilds such as the "emperor-loving goldsmiths" (see fig. 21a, p. 110; Kleiner 1970:18–20; 2d century C.E.). Some Jews could also participate in the activities of the gymnasium, even forming age-group associations or joining those that already existed. Thus we find a reserved place for the association of Judean youths (*Iouda[i]ōn neōterōn*) at Hypaipa (between Ephesus and Sardis); Jews among the young-men's organization (*ephēbes*) at Iasos (southeast of Miletos); and

Jews (or perhaps Christians) as members of the local elders' organization at Eumeneia (south of Akmoneia), all dating to the second or third century.[14] Such evidence may also suggest citizenship in the polis.

Second, some Jewish groups actively participated within civic networks of benefaction in a manner comparable to other associations, which could also involve interaction with the principal institutions. For example, a lengthy inscription from Smyrna in the reign of Hadrian lists the donations to the polis by several individuals and groups including an imperial cult high priest, theologians, hymn singers, and *hoi pote Ioudaioi* (*ISmyrna* 697 = *CIJ* 742 = *IGR* IV 1431 = *CIG* 3148). Identifying the precise meaning of the last phrase is difficult, since it is otherwise unattested. The traditional interpretation of this phrase in religious terms as "the former Jews," namely apostate Jews who had repudiated their faith, is problematic, however.[15] A lengthy inscription recording various benefactions to the polis would, as Kraabel also notes, be an unlikely place to make a public statement of apostasy. The announcement of one's *former religious status* not only as an individual but as a group would also be peculiar; however, the clear proclamation of one's geographical origins (with its obvious accompanying religio-cultural implications) is common in inscriptions. Moreover, it seems more plausible that the term *Ioudaioi* should be understood in a geographical sense, referring to "the former Judeans" (an immigrant association of Judeans).

Even though it is clear that *Ioudaioi* had geographical (alongside cultural) connotations to the ancient hearer, the difficulty here is that we have no other exact parallels to this specific usage of *pote* in the known cases of ethnic- or geographic-based associations of foreigners specifically. It is important to point out, however, that there is no consistently employed form of self-designation by such associations in Asia anyway, such that we cannot speak of deviations. Often groups simply designate themselves "the Alexandrians," "the Phrygians," "the settlement of Romans," "the association of Asians," "the Samothracians," without any further clarification or use of a preposition, for instance. Perhaps more importantly, there is a similar phrase used on inscriptions to designate former geographical origins that parallels closely the case at Smyrna: namely, the use of *prin* (instead of *pote*), as in the phrase "when Aurelius, son of Theophilos, *formerly* of Pieria, was secretary (*grammateōs Aureliou Theophilou tou prin Pierionos*)."[16]

There is evidence of similar interactions by synagogues within networks at Sardis. In a decree from an earlier era recorded by Josephus, the civic institutions there provided the Jewish group (which is elsewhere called a *syn-*

odos) with a place to meet (*Ant.* 14.259-61; cf. *Ant.* 14.235 [48 B.C.E.]). By the late third century, the synagogue in Sardis was contained within the bath-gymnasium complex, a central cultural institution of the polis.[17]

Although dating to a later period, this synagogue illustrates well the ways in which a Jewish group could, quite literally, find a place for themselves within the polis. As an institution common to many cities in Asia Minor, the bath-gymnasium was a place of education and athletics, as well as a place to gather, socialize, honor the gods, exercise, and, of course, bathe. Construction began on the complex at Sardis in the first century, and the main structure of the buildings was most likely dedicated to the emperor Lucius Verus about 166 C.E., with the addition of the "Marble Court" (devoted to the emperors as gods) in the central area about 212 C.E. When completed, the complex measured about 120 by 170 meters and consisted of a large colonnaded exercise area (palaestra) with smaller rooms on either side (eastern portion), the central imperial cult hall ("Marble Hall"), and the baths (central and western portion).

Some time in the late third or early fourth century, the Jewish group in Sardis acquired the rooms to the south of the exercise area (which had already been remodeled into a long basilica-style hall), and this would have required approval from the civic council. In its final stage, the synagogue section consisted of a forecourt (with mosaic floors, columns and a central fountain) and the main meeting hall (with mosaic floors, a reading desk with lions on either side, a torah shrine, and a small *odeion*-style seating area; see the photo in fig. 28). The Jews' sense of belonging within Sardis is clearly demonstrated by the presence of the synagogue here, and yet there are also signs of religious distinctiveness that are expressed architecturally. The synagogue was right next door to the imperial cult hall of the complex, where the emperors would be regularly honored as gods. However, the Jews had the entranceway from the synagogue into that sanctuary completely blocked off, most likely to avoid any idolatrous implications (see photos in figs. 29–30). It was also in this same era that some donors to the synagogue, including goldsmiths, were members of the civic council (*bouleutai*; Kroll 2001:10, 28, 34–35, nos. 25, 36–37 [goldsmiths]). The group also had connections with civic or imperial functionaries in the fourth century, including a "count" (*comes*) and a former procurator (*epitropōn*), who each made donations to beautify the synagogue (see Kroll 2001:18–19, 44–45, nos. 5 and 70).

Such evidence of positive relations does not, of course, preclude incidents when Jewish groups' relations with civic inhabitants or institutions or even Roman officials was rocky, especially in the unstable closing years

FIGURE 28: Main hall of synagogue (taken from the northeast corner) showing the mosaics, table, two lions, and the seating area for the leaders.

FIGURE 29: The imperial cult hall within the bath-gymnasium, located next door to the synagogue.

FIGURE 30: The doorway between the synagogue and the imperial cult hall that was blocked off.

of the republic (the decades leading up to 31 B.C.E.).[18] Yet, though sporadic conflicts could certainly arise in later years, the more stable conditions in Asia that followed the establishment of the "peace of Rome" (*pax Romana*) would lessen some of the tensions between synagogues and other inhabitants of the cities (cf. Barclay 1996:279–81).

A third illustration of the involvements of Jews in the life of the cities pertains to connections with other subgroups. Despite the partial nature of epigraphic evidence, there are indications that members of synagogues could continue to maintain important connections—for social, business or other purposes—with individuals and groups in the polis, including affiliations with other associations. We can better understand the following evidence of multiple affiliations among Jews within the context of association life generally. The most general, yet instructive, evidence we have regarding the potential for multiple memberships among associations generally comes from Roman imperial legislation. In the late second century, Marcus Aurelius and Lucius Verus reenacted a law to the effect that it was not lawful to belong to more than one guild or association ("*non licet autem amplius quam unum collegium legitimum habere*"; *Digest* 47.22.1.2). Regardless of the rationale behind or (in)effectiveness of such imperial legislation,[19] what is clear from such actions is the commonality of one person belonging to more than one association.

The evidence we do have for the occupational status of Jews (as with Christians) represents an array of activity comparable to the known guilds, and the fact that occupations are mentioned at all on Jewish grave and other inscriptions suggests that this was an important component in their identities (cf. Horst 1991:99–101; S. Cohen 1993:10; Reynolds and Tannenbaum 1987:116–23). Thus it is not too surprising (despite neglect of the subject in scholarship) to find indications that Jews could also affiliate with their fellow workers within occupational networks and associations. Julius was the chief physician at Ephesus, and hence leader of the sanhedrin (*synedrion*) of physicians, but he had the Jewish group there take care of his family grave (*IEph* 1677 = *CIJ* 745).[20] In a later era we find Moses' namesake as the head of the goldsmiths' guild at Korykos in Cilicia (*CIJ* 793; perhaps early Byzantine times; cf. M. Williams 1994).

Though moving out of the geographical bounds of our present focus, evidence in Philo (the Jewish philosopher) indicates that Jews in first-century Alexandria were commonly involved in trade as shippers, merchants, and artisans (Philo, *Against Flaccus* 57). Torrey Seland's recent study shows that some Jews also joined local guilds or associations in the cities. Philo "does not strictly and totally forbid participation, but he is very critical of the associations, and skeptical of joining them" (Seland 1996:110; see *On Drunkenness* 20–26; *Embassy to Gaius* 3.155–59). In light of these indications, it would be reasonable to suggest that similar multiple affiliations or memberships could exist among other Jews (as well as Christians),[21] and, it turns out, this may help us to understanding some of the practices among certain Christians or Jewish-Christians addressed by the Apocalypse.

A recently reedited inscription from Hierapolis in the Lycus Valley pertaining to such multiple affiliations will serve as an appropriate conclusion to this section (Ritti 1992–93 = *AE* [1994] 510, no. 1660 = Miranda 1999:131–32, no. 23, revising *CIJ* 777). It dates to the late second or early third century of our era (probably c. 190–220 C.E.), but it illustrates the sorts of connections that could exist between Jews (or Christians) and guilds at other times and places. It is worth quoting in full, for it also reveals other aspects of cultural and structural assimilation:

> This grave and the burial ground beneath it together with the surrounding place belong to Publius Aelius Glykon Zeuxianos Aelianus and to Aurelia Amia, daughter of Amianos Seleukos. In it he will bury himself, his wife and his children, but no one else is permitted to be buried here. He left behind 200 denaria for the grave-crowning ceremony to the most holy presidency of the purple-dyers (*tē semnotatē proedria tōn porphyrabaphōn stephanotiko[u]*), so that it would produce from the interest enough for each to take a share on the sixth day of the month during the Festival of Unleavened Bread (*tē heortē tōn azymōn*). Likewise he also left behind 150 denaria for the grave-crowning ceremony to the association of carpet weavers (*tō synedriō tōn akairodapistōn stephanōtikou*), so that the revenues from the interest should be distributed, half during the Festival of Kalends (*en tē heortē tōn kalandōn*) [i.e., Roman New Year] on the fourth and seventh of the month and half during the Festival of Pentecost (*tē heortē tēs pentēkostēs*). A copy of this inscription was put into the archives (*tois archeiois*).

The inscription reveals that Glykon, a Roman citizen, prepared a grave for himself and his wife and children. As most commentators agree, Glykon's request that a customary grave ceremony be held on two of the most important Jewish holidays–Passover and Pentecost (alongside the third non-Jewish festival of the Roman New Year)–points to his family's identity as practicing Jews (or perhaps God-fearers or proselytes). In light of this clear Jewish identity, it is reasonable to assume that this family also affiliated with the synagogue, which is otherwise attested in inscriptions from Hierapolis around this period. But unlike some other Jews there, this family chose to include local guilds, not the Jewish association, in these funerary provisions (contrast *IHierapJ* 212 = *CIJ* 775; *IHierapJ* 69 = *CIJ* 776; see *SEG* 44 [1994] 828).

What interests us most here are this Jew's interactions with occupational associations at Hierapolis. Glykon definitely makes financial provisions for both the purple-dyers and the carpet weavers to regularly perform the grave ceremonies. Most of the debate concerning the inscription centers on the identity of these guilds and their composition: whether they were (1) solely Jewish, (2) solely "pagan" (Gentile), or (3) a mixture of both. Erich Ziebarth (1896:129) was among the first to assume that these two guilds were solely Jewish in membership, and other scholars have followed suit (cf. Ramsay 1902:98–101; Applebaum 1974b:480). In contrast, Walther Judeich holds the view that Glykon was simply following common custom in asking a guild with whom he had business or other contacts to take care of the grave ceremony; that is, the guilds were not Jewish but Gentile, as were most other known guilds in Hierapolis (Humann, Cichorius, and Judeich 1898:46, 51, 174). The new edition of Emil Schürer's work does not engage the issue but states that "the members of the guilds must also have been influenced by Judaism," implying that they were Gentile sympathizers or God-fearers (Schürer 1973–87, 3:27). Most recently, Trebilco (1991:178–79) addresses these possibilities and adds another, namely that the guilds included a mixture of both Jews and Gentiles (cf. Seager and Kraabel 1983:181), but he is hesitant to take a stand on which possibilities seem most or least likely.

I would suggest that the first option is quite unlikely, the second is plausible, and the third is most likely. My argument is based on the consonance of this view with other epigraphic sources from Hierapolis; it is also most compatible with the evidence for the involvement of Jews in occupational networks and with other signs of assimilation in the Glykon inscription. First, other inscriptions concerning guilds in Hierapolis and the purple-dyers speak specifically against the solely Jewish hypothesis. This inscription does not give any indication that these guilds were distinctively Jewish, nor that they stood out from other such groups in Hierapolis. More importantly, seven other second- and third-century inscriptions concerning the same guild of purple-dyers suggest that, rather than being distinctively Jewish, this guild consisted principally of Gentiles and was viewed as a typical guild.[22] (Unfortunately, we have no other evidence for the carpet weavers.) So, although we cannot necessarily assume that the purple-dyers were solely Gentile, we do know that they were not solely Jewish during the era of the Glykon inscription, contrary to the assumptions of Ziebarth, W. M. Ramsay and S. Applebaum.

In light of this, there remain two possibilities regarding the composition of the guilds in question. In either case we have evidence not only of the participation and integration of Jews in civic life but also of Jews' affiliations with or even memberships in the local occupational associations of Hierapolis. On the one hand, if the guild was composed exclusively of Gentiles, we have a Jew following the usual burial customs of non-Jews in Hierapolis (and Asia generally) by including guilds in funerary provisions (see *SEG* 44 [1994] 828). If this is the case, the reason for Glykon's asking these guilds (instead of other Jewish groups) to perform the grave rituals would presumably relate to the fact that he had contacts with purple-dyers and carpet weavers in the context of business or commercial networks, perhaps as a regular customer or benefactor of the groups.[23] On the other hand, what seems even more plausible is that, although consisting principally of Gentiles, at Glykon's time these two guilds included Jewish individuals (or perhaps God-fearers or proselytes) who happened to be purple-dyers or carpet weavers. Suggesting the presence of Jews (or God-fearers) in the guilds would have the advantage of better accounting for Glykon's request that apparently "pagan" guilds perform the customary grave ceremony on Jewish holidays, and we know that Jews (and Christians like Lydia the purple-dyer) sometimes did engage in clothing and other related occupations (cf. *CIJ* 787, 873, 929, 931; Reynolds and Tannenbaum 1987; Acts 16:14–15; 18:2–3). If this is the case, his reasons for choosing these guilds (rather than others) would include a combination of factors: commercial contacts with both Jews and Gentiles *and* ethnocultural affiliations with fellow Jews in Hierapolis.

Both Glykon and the Jews who belonged to these guilds illustrate the potential for multiple affiliations or even memberships in subgroups of local society,[24] which is one of the factors involved in the process of informal structural assimilation. This understanding of the inscription also fits well with the fact that Glykon and his wife, like other Jews in Roman Asia who maintained a distinctive sense of Jewish identity, show other signs of some cultural and structural assimilation: acculturation to local funerary practices including the form of the epitaph and the grave-crowning ceremony; concern with celebration of the Roman New Year (see Ritti 1992–93:58) alongside the more traditional Jewish festivals; and the structural assimilation implied in the provisions for depositing a copy of the inscription in the civic archives, indicative of the legal procedures to be followed within civic institutions should anyone violate what was stipulated on the epitaph (cf. Strubbe 1994, 1997).

Evidently, Jewish groups and their members were often integrated within civic life in numerous ways, and this sometimes involved memberships in or affiliations with subgroups within the polis, including occupa-

tional associations. This sort of evidence throws into question many scholars' overemphasis on the exclusivity of membership in synagogues (and,
often by implication, congregations), but it does not necessarily involve a
lack of some distinctive cultural characteristics on the part of Jews in relation to society at large, or the disintegration of group boundaries.

Conclusion

When Meeks sets about looking for models or analogies in the ancient
context with which to compare Christian groups, including the household, association, philosophical school, and synagogue, he finds that although the synagogue provides the "nearest and most natural model,"
"none of these categories quite fits" (Meeks 1983:80, 74). In each case he
suggests that the differences between congregations and a given model
outweigh the similarities in a way that makes further comparison less than
fruitful. One begins to get the impression that Meeks views Christian
groups not only as distinctive but as unique in the sense that they are incomparable. The supposed substantive differences that Meeks perceives,
when investigated further, need considerable qualification or rejection.

Meeks assumes that the sociological model of the "sect" is useful for
comparison to Christian groups. Not surprisingly, this model is used in a
way that stresses features of congregations that set them apart from their
environment, further affirming the uniqueness and incomparability of
Christian (but also Jewish) groups. These two features of the approach—
one concerning the incomparability of most ancient models and the other
concerning sectarianism—may be partially understood in terms of a
broader scholarly tradition (sometimes with apologetic overtones) that
avoids comparison because of a concern to insulate Christianity, but also
Judaism, from the possibility of "influences" or "borrowings" from the
cultural environment.

Jonathan Z. Smith's *Drudgery Divine* (1990) thoroughly traces this
scholarly tradition as it manifests itself in discussions of the mysteries and
early Christianity (cf. Gasparro 1985:xiii–xx). Several of his main observations are worth mentioning here, since they also apply to the question at
hand. According to Smith, the Christian evidence has detrimentally
shaped scholars' approaches to the collection and assessment of evidence
for the mysteries. Issues of genealogy (e.g., "borrowings," "influences")
rather than analogy have predominated in studies of Christianity in relation to Greco-Roman religions. Furthermore, Judaism has often been used

as a device to insulate Christianity from the influences of the "pagan" environment. Finally, religions of the ancient Mediterranean are often spoken of as, in a broad sense, the "same," while Christianity is viewed as "different" or "unique," and hence incomparable. As Smith argues, the genealogical approach to the question of comparison misunderstands the character, purpose, and value of analogical comparison as I employ it here.[25]

The appropriateness of comparing such socioreligious groups has become increasingly evident in the present study. There are significant similarities apparent between associations and both congregations and synagogues at various levels; this is not surprising, considering that these groups lived and developed within similar civic settings. In broad terms, associations, synagogues, and congregations were small, noncompulsory groups that could draw their membership from several possible social network connections within the polis. All could be either relatively homogeneous or heterogeneous with regard to social and gender composition; all engaged in regular meetings that involved a variety of interconnected social, religious, and other purposes, one group differing from the next in the specifics of activities; all depended in various ways on commonly accepted social conventions such as benefaction for financial support (e.g., a meeting place) and the development of leadership structures; and all could engage in at least some degree of external contacts, both positive and negative, with other individuals, benefactors, groups, or institutions in the civic context.

Perhaps most striking is that in antiquity Christian, Jewish and Greco-Roman authors alike *did* compare the groups. Despite their peculiarities, both synagogues and congregations could be viewed by contemporaries as associations in the usual sense, and there are clear indications that these groups could also understand themselves as such. In one of the earliest Roman descriptions of Christians, for instance, Pliny the Younger (governor of Bithynia-Pontus) writes to the emperor Trajan concerning the Christ devotees who had been brought before him, describing their gatherings in terms familiar from religious activities of associations and confirms that they had obeyed his edict regarding meetings of associations (*hetaeriae*, sometimes a synonym for *collegia*; *Epistles* 10.96.7–8). In the midst of his ridiculing satire on the (once) Christian Peregrinus, Lucian of Samosata characterizes him as a leader of a "cult society" (*thiasiarch*); he also speaks of Christianity as a "new initiation rite" (*kainēn tautēn teletēn; Passing of Peregrinus* 11). Similarly, the critic Celsus characterizes the followers of Jesus as "members of a cult society" (*thiasōtai*), though he specifically complains about the Christians' strange avoidance of "setting up altars, images, and temples," which he interprets as a "sure token of an obscure and secret association [*koinōnias*]"—but an "association" nonetheless (in Origen, *Against Celsus* 3.23; 8.17; cf. 1.1). We have seen that both Jews and Christians, too, identified their groups using common terminology for associations, and that several authors, including Philo and Tertullian, explicitly compare the activities of Jewish or Christian associations with their "inferior," "pagan" counterparts.[26]

The shared language of identity and the comparison between such groups is not surprising since congregations and synagogues were, like the local devotees of Zeus or Dionysos or the guild of purple-dyers, relatively small, unofficial groups that assembled regularly to socialize, share communal meals, and honor both their earthly and their divine benefactors. From an outsider's perspective, this general similarity might help to make sense of what was in other respects quite strange: a group of "atheists" (a common derogatory term) that insisted that only their god and no one else's was deserving of recognition or honor (a sentiment evident in Celsus's comments). From an (ancient) Jewish or Christian perspective, describing oneself in terms drawn from the world of associations might simultaneously establish a sense of place within local culture or society while also forming a basis from which to assert distinctiveness and even preeminence (for the group or its God).

Attention to similarities among associations, synagogues, and congregations, then, is not meant to underplay variations among each of these three types of groups, as well the variance of individual self-understandings of specific groups. Nor is this meant to ignore the culturally distinctive elements in the worldviews, values, and practices of both synagogues and congregations (as well as some other ethnic-geographic associations like Samaritans) that could distinguish them as minority cultural groups. Attention to both similarities and differences among associations with regard to imperial aspects of civic life will now further our understanding of the numerous and individual ways in which such groups and their members found places for themselves (or failed to do so) within the social and cultural landscape of the polis under Roman rule.

8

Positive Interaction

Jews, Christians, and Imperial Honors in the Greek City

Introduction

Our discussion of associations has shown that groups of various types maintained relations with the polis and that imperial cults and connections played a significant role. Associations could be integrated in varying ways and to different degrees within the polis and empire. Moreover, I have argued that Christian congregations and Jewish synagogues are comparable to associations in some important respects, casting doubt on common wholesale categorizations of these groups as "sects" that were separated from virtually all aspects of life within the polis. Instead, I suggested a more complex scenario for group-society relations entailing a range of possibilities with regard to participation in or separation from particular social and cultural facets of the polis under Roman rule. The case of Jewish groups in Roman Asia showed that some synagogues, like associations, were active participants within certain areas of life in the polis.

The purpose of this chapter is to reassess the evidence regarding imperial honors and connections among both synagogues and congregations through a comparison with the pattern previously outlined in the case of associations (chapters 4 and 5). This roots us in the realities of life for actual groups in Roman Asia, rather than merely theorizing in a vacuum concerning group-society interaction. This comparative case study allows us to see both similarities and differences among associations, on the one hand, and synagogues and congregations, on the other, pointing to areas of both participation and nonparticipation, positive interaction and tension. It also draws attention to a range of possibilities in group-society relations among diverse synagogues and assemblies within the same geographical region. There were, as we shall see, different grades of participation in these areas of society.

With regard to positive interaction, some Jewish synagogues and Christian assemblies, like associations, could be involved in conventions of civic life relating to honors for emperors and imperial representatives, participating within relations that linked the polis to province and empire. Furthermore, the emperors were significant for the internal religious life of some synagogues and assemblies, in the form of prayers for the emperors and empire, for instance. This is a trajectory visible in 1 Peter, the Pastoral Epistles, Polycarp (bishop of Smyrna), and Melito (bishop of Sardis), representing what I call a *moderate position*. This position can be placed within the broader context of early Christianity with reference to Paul's letter to the Romans, *1 Clement*, and Luke–Acts. This is the political posture against which we can begin to understand the alternate stance and strategy of John's Apocalypse, which promoted strict sectarian boundaries and a much lower participation level in the life of the polis.

Alongside positive interaction, there were also areas of nonparticipation and tension that I put into proper perspective in the following chapter. For, unlike some associations, virtually all Jews and Christians, at least as groups, refrained from active involvement in rituals (such as sacrifices and mysteries) that implied recognition of the emperors as gods. This had implications regarding tensions between these groups and society, but we should not exaggerate the importance of nonparticipation in imperial cults specifically, since these cults were embedded within religious life in the polis. The significance of nonparticipation in imperial cults for our comprehension of group-society relations should be understood within the broader context of Jews' and Christians' monotheism ("atheism" in the eyes of some Greeks and Romans), their failure to honor any gods other than their own (through sacrificial and other offerings), which could occasionally lead to tensions in relation to others in the civic context. Attention to these areas of both involvement and avoidance furthers our understanding of how some synagogues and congregations found a place for themselves within the sociocultural matrix of the polis under Roman rule, despite areas of tension. It clarifies the ways in which they simultaneously maintained their distinctive identities.

Discussion of neglected areas of positive interaction as well as areas of tension provides a context in which to reassess specific aspects of the Apocalypse of John in the following chapter. Clearly, John disapproved of

Christians participating in social, religious, and economic practices of civic life, especially its imperial dimensions, and he advocated a sectarian perspective, drawing sharp boundaries between the congregations and society. Yet this is only one side of a conversation, for a significant number of Jews and Christians in the cities of Asia, it seems, were more open toward participating in some aspects of the polis. After briefly discussing attitudes toward the Roman Empire in Jewish apocalyptic literature, I go on to evidence concerning Jewish and then Christian participation in imperial aspects of civic life, which further challenges the common sectarian reading of these groups.

Jewish Literature, Roman Imperialism, and Group Practice

In light of the diversity within ancient Judaism, it is not surprising to find varying viewpoints with regard to the Romans and their empire within Jewish literature (cf. Bruce 1978; Alexander 1991). Strong criticisms of Rome and its rulers come to the fore precisely in writings that are, by nature of genre, concerned with political powers, national calamities, and their relation to the unfolding of God's cosmological plan, especially apocalyptic and oracular writings.

Yet the relation between rhetoric and the reality of Jewish group life is not easy to discern (cf. Momigliano 1987b:141; Goodman 1991:222–24). In the biblical commentaries associated with the Qumran community, for instance, we find references to the Romans (*Kittim*) both as objects of God's vengeance and as tools by which God brings about his eschatological plan (cf. 4QpNah 1–2; 4QpIsa 7–10; 1QpPs 9; 1QpHab 2–4, 6). As George J. Brooke's (1991:159) study cautions, the "image of empire" that emerges is most often controlled by the motifs of Scripture, telling us more about methods of biblical interpretation than it does of actual events or perceptions of the Romans or their empire among these Palestinian Jews specifically.

Understandably, the Romans' destruction of the temple in Jerusalem was among the focal points of expressions of hostility in literature. Both *4 Ezra* and *2 Baruch* relate the second destruction of the temple (70 C.E.) in the code of the first (586 B.C.E.), presenting the destruction as God's punishment for Israel's disobedience in which ruling powers (Babylon/Rome) are functionaries in bringing about God's ultimate plan (cf. *4 Ezra* 11.39; Kirschner 1985; J. J. Collins 1998:194–232). Within this framework we find *4 Ezra* nonetheless harshly condemning the Roman Empire in a manner comparable to John's Apocalypse: "you will surely disappear, you eagle, and your terrifying wings, and your most evil little wings, and your malicious heads, and your most evil talons, and your whole worthless body, so that the whole earth, freed from your violence, may be refreshed and relieved, and may hope for the judgement and mercy of him who made it" (*4 Ezra* 11.45–46; trans. B. M. Metzger, *OTP* 1:549; cf. *2 Bar.* 36–40; *Sib. Or.* 5.398–413). Further on, the same author denounces Asia (Asia Minor), along with Egypt and Syria, for its affiliations with Babylon/Rome: "And you, O Asia, who share in the glamour of Babylon and the glory of her person—woe to you, miserable wretch! For you have made yourself like her; you have decked out your daughters in harlotry to please and glory in your lovers, who have always lusted after you. You have imitated that hateful harlot in all her deeds and devices" (*4 Ezra* 15.46–49; trans. *OTP* 1:557). It is unlikely that we would find the (probably Palestinian) Jewish circles in which such literature was produced or read devoting time to honoring the Roman emperors, but we cannot generalize from this regarding the actual practice of Jewish groups at other times and places.

Similar rhetoric against the Roman Empire appears within oracles attributed to the Jewish Sibyl (a prophetess known as Sabbe or Sambathe), some of which refer to Asia Minor specifically. In particular, one oracle incorporated within the third book, whose initial context of circulation may very well have been Roman Asia in the first century B.C.E. (see Bauckham 1991:86–90),[1] focuses on economic exploitation in railing against the Roman imperial presence in Asia: "However much wealth Rome received from tribute-bearing Asia, Asia will receive three times that much again from Rome and will repay her deadly arrogance to her. Whatever number from Asia served the house of Italians, twenty times that number of Italians will be serfs in Asia. . . . O luxurious golden offspring of Latium, Rome, virgin, often drunken with your weddings with many suitors" (*Sib. Or.* 3.350–57; trans. J. J. Collins, *OTP* 1:370). Similar sentiments regarding Roman imperial extortion of Asia and other regions continue to be echoed in other oracles as well, some of them written in light of the destruction of the temple in 70 C.E. (cf. *Sib. Or.* 4.145–50 [c. 80 C.E.]; 5.155–78 [c. 80–131 C.E.]; 8.68–130 [c. 175 C.E.]). On the other hand, later oracles of the Jewish Sibyl actually demonstrate positive attitudes toward Rome and its emperors (*Sib. Or.* 11–13 [3d century C.E.]).

For several reasons, there are difficulties in extracting general attitudes or practices of Jewish groups with respect to the Roman Empire or emperors from such literature, especially regarding the diaspora (cf.

Momigliano 1987b; Goodman 1991:222–24). First, by nature of genre, sibylline oracles (whether Jewish or not) and apocalyptic writings were concerned with prophetic doom and, especially, with critique of political powers or nations generally. The Romans, though often at the top of the list, were by no means the only ruling power or nation railed against within Jewish sibylline oracles or apocalyptic literature of the Roman era. Second, these writings were quite frequently specific to an occasion, reacting to particular circumstances or cataclysmic events and placing them within a broader cosmic or eschatological framework characterized by dualistic conflict, utilizing imagery and language from earlier Hebrew prophetic literature. Third, as Lester L. Grabbe (1989) and others caution, we should not so readily assume that an apocalyptic writing necessarily reflects an actual millennial movement (cf. P. Davies 1989; J. J. Collins 1998:12–14, 37–38, 280–81; Thompson 1990:25–34). The relationship between apocalyptic literature and social realities could be far more complex, as we shall also find with John's Apocalypse. Moreover, in light of the evidence that I am about to discuss, we are better off taking the anti-Roman rhetoric of this literature as representing one end of a range of perspectives that may or may not have been replicated in the ongoing practices of some synagogues.

There is, however, other literary evidence concerning the actual activities of synagogues in the diaspora that provides helpful background to the situation in Roman Asia. Despite their apologetic purposes and somewhat philo-Roman tendencies, Josephus and Philo provide evidence of diaspora Jewish attitudes and practices in the first century (on Philo's and Josephus's views of empire see Barraclough 1984; Stern 1987; Goodman 1994). Both suggest that granting special honors to emperors and members of the imperial family was common among many Jewish groups in the Roman Empire, though this clearly and understandably stopped short of cultic honors or the dedication of images or statues, which would be considered idolatry or "fornication" by virtually all Jews (cf. Wis 14).

Thus when Josephus responds to the accusations of Apion of Alexandria concerning the failure of the Jews to "erect statues (*imagines*) of the emperors," he points out that this stemmed not from intentions to foster sedition or dishonor these figures, but from obedience to the Jewish God's law forbidding the making of images of any kind.[2] Furthermore, Josephus suggests, Jews did grant other distinctive honors for emperors and members of the imperial family, among them the sacrifices performed in the temple at Jerusalem *on behalf of* the rulers (*Ag. Ap.* 2.68–78; cf. *J.W.* 2.195–98, 409–16).

In important respects we should not assume that the sociopolitical circumstances of Jews in Alexandria or Egypt are representative of situations
in areas like Asia Minor. Most notably the conflicts between Egyptians,
Greeks, and Jews that undergirded the disturbances during and following
the time of Gaius Caligula reflect a historical situation specific to Egypt.
Alexandria was in certain respects a focal point of anti-Jewish feelings and
actions, as well as anti-Roman sentiment, in a way that other regions were
not.[3] Nonetheless, there are some ways in which Judaism in Alexandria
does evince common diaspora practices. Most importantly here, in discussing the riots of 38 C.E. (in which the Jews were attacked by others),
Philo refers to the fact that it was common for synagogues to follow the
convention of setting up honorary monuments for emperors. He mentions several different forms that the honors could take including "shields,
golden crowns, plaques, and inscriptions" (*aspidōn kai stephanōn epichrysōn
kai stēlōn kai epigraphōn*), but not images (*Embassy to Gaius* 133).

Furthermore, before both the Alexandrian riots and Gaius's attempt to
set up his image in Jerusalem (c. 40–41 C.E.), Jewish groups of Alexandria
had followed their usual custom in passing a decree granting honors
(*timas*) to Gaius specifically, most likely in connection with his accession
in 37 C.E. Word of the Jews' decree, which was supposed to be delivered to
the emperor by Flaccus, the Roman prefect, was suppressed (according to
Philo) until the visit by King Agrippa I just before the riots. Agrippa
praised the Jews for their "piety toward the house of our benefactors" (*eu-
sebein eis ton euergetēn oikon*) and promised to relay the message to Gaius
(*Against Flaccus* 97–104).

Moreover, Philo contrasts the demonstrative Jewish respect for imperial authorities to the dishonor shown by the Alexandrians involved in the
riots. Ironically, he suggests, these Alexandrians (including associations
under the patronage of Isodoros)[4] were dishonoring imperial figures by
tearing down the Jews' monumental honors and, at the same time, falsely
claiming to honor the emperor by setting up statues (*eikones*) of Gaius in
the synagogues, thereby deeply offending Jews and dishonoring God (*Embassy to Gaius* 132–40; cf. *Against Flaccus* 51–52).[5] Philo imagines what ra-
tional Jews might have said to their attackers: "You have failed to see that
you are not adding to but taking from the honor given to our masters (*tois
kyriois timēn*), and you do not understand that everywhere in the world the
piety of the Jews toward the revered household (*tēs eis ton Sebaston oikon ho-
siotētos*) clearly has its basis in the prayer houses, and if these are destroyed
no place, no method, is left to us for paying this honor" (*Against Flaccus*
49; trans. Colson 1941–62 [LCL], with adaptations).

Due to the accidental nature of archeological finds, we simply do not have any concrete examples of these Jewish honorary monuments and dedications for the emperors from Roman Alexandria specifically. Epigraphic finds from elsewhere in Egypt do show that Jewish prayer houses, like the meeting places of other associations, were frequently dedicated on behalf of current rulers in the Hellenistic era (e.g., *IEgJud* 13 [37 B.C.E.], 24 [140–116 B.C.E.], 27–28 [2d–1st century B.C.E.], 125 [47–31 B.C.E.]). Philo's comments confirm that similar monumental practices, comparable to those of associations we have discussed, continued under Roman rule as well. That Josephus's and Philo's statements regarding Jewish practice in the diaspora are not merely apologetic, or totally removed from reality within some circles, we shall see presently with respect to the situation in Roman Asia.

Jewish Synagogues in Roman Asia

Earlier we found that granting special honors for the emperors or imperial officials in the form of inscriptions, dedications, or other monuments was common convention among associations in Roman Asia. Such actions were one of the means by which a given group staked a claim, I argued, within the civic context, making a statement regarding its place within the networks and hierarchies of polis, empire, and cosmos. This was the case despite the potential intermittent involvements of associations in civic disturbances or other areas of tension within society. There is further evidence that some groups of Jews in Asia, like associations, could take part in similar civic conventions associated with both the emperors and other imperial-connected individuals. These links suggest that synagogues were in some ways participants within civic life and could be among those associations and communities that helped to cement relations between polis and empire.

With regard to honoring the emperors, a decree of Augustus preserved by Josephus will serve as a point of departure for our discussion of synagogues in Asia. In keeping with Josephus's apologetic purposes, this decree confirms the rights of Jews in Asia "to follow their own customs," including the transportation of sacred funds to Jerusalem and Sabbath observance (*Ant.* 16.162–65 [c. 12 B.C.E.]; cf. Philo, *Embassy to Gaius* 311–13). More importantly for our present purposes, Augustus happens to refer to an earlier "decree which was offered by [the Jews of Asia] in my honor concerning the piety (*eusebeias*) which I show to all men, and on behalf of

Gaius Marcius Censorinus" (16.165). One or more synagogues in Asia had apparently followed common custom among communities and associations by passing an honorary decree for the emperor, as well as for a Roman official. Word of the decree was subsequently forwarded to Augustus himself. Augustus ordered that copies of both his own and the Jews' honorary decree be placed in a prominent spot in the imperial cult temple of the provincial assembly or council (*koinon*) of Asia, which was located at Pergamum.[6]

In connection with this incident, several points merit discussion that shed light on the nature of synagogues' potential involvements in civic conventions associated with the emperors. First, besides their act of honoring the emperor by way of a decree (probably setting up an inscription in a meeting place), these Jews in Asia involved themselves in common conventions of diplomacy by subsequently communicating word of the decree directly to Augustus. As we saw in the case of the Dionysiac initiates at Smyrna, who sent word of their celebrations at the birth of a son within the imperial family, associations could sometimes forward such honors directly to the recipients by way of an embassy or ambassador and could receive a letter or rescript in return (*ISmyrna* 600–601). Similarly, the hymn singers of Pergamum had sent a copy of their honorary decree to Emperor Claudius; only the opening of his positive letter of response survives (*IEph* 3801.15–20). Sometimes a provincial governor or some other important ruling official who had direct contacts with the emperor could be asked to convey the message, as was the case when the Jews of Alexandria decreed honors for Gaius.

Yet communicating honors was just one part of a larger set of diplomatic practices in which synagogues, like some other associations, could be involved. In some respects these groups were replicating the activities of civic and provincial communities. Fergus Millar's study of *The Emperor in the Roman World* (1977) clearly demonstrates the request-response character of Roman rule and the importance of such diplomatic ties in maintaining links between the central imperial power and communities and groups in the provinces. This interaction was part of the glue that held the empire together, and associations could participate in it.

Quite often, links with an emperor or some other imperial official were a means of furthering the interests of the group in question, gaining favors or benefactions in return. Thus we found that the Demetriasts at Ephesus, like Jewish groups in Asia, had on numerous occasions successfully gained special recognition of their religious practices from both emperors and proconsuls, which they publicized in the form of a monument (*IEph* 213 [under Domitian]). Such diplomatic activities were also of key importance for the settlement of disputes and judicial administration under Roman rule. The Dionysiac worshipers at Kyme who sent an ambassador to the Roman proconsul did so in the hopes of gaining a favorable decision in a case regarding the reacquisition of their meeting place, and they were successful (*IKyme* 17 [under Augustus and Agrippa]).

It is within this context of diplomatic practices among communities and associations under Roman rule, I would suggest, that we can partially understand the activities of Jewish groups in Asia and the favorable decisions they sometimes gained as a result, some of which we find in Josephus's *Antiquities*.[7] Josephus records several occasions when Roman authorities (emperors, consuls, proconsuls, and others) granted Jewish groups in cities such as Ephesus, Sardis, and Miletos various privileges, including exemption from military service, freedom to practice native customs, and freedom to transport the temple tax to Jerusalem. Thus, according to one document, when the proconsul Jullus Antonius was at Ephesus (c. 9–6 B.C.E.), an embassy of Jews requested that he reacknowledge the earlier privileges of Augustus and Agrippa that permitted them to deliver the temple tax and "to live and act in accordance with their ancestral customs without interference" (*Ant.* 16.172–73). Josephus explicitly states his apologetic purposes in presenting such documents: to show the Romans' benefactions to the Jews in the hopes that the Greek inhabitants would follow suit in not hindering the Jews from following their customs (*Ant.* 14.186–89, 265–67; 16.174–78). Josephus includes some examples when cities did indeed follow this pattern (e.g., *Ant.* 14.156–61 [Halicarnassus and Sardis]). In keeping with his apologetic purposes, though, Josephus tends toward generalizing or universalizing what were originally more modest or limited actions and statements (cf. Barclay 1996:262–63).

In contrast to the perspective presented here, the traditional scholarly approach to these documents in Josephus and to Roman "policy" concerning diaspora Judaism more generally has been dominated by a legalistic focus. Jean Juster's discussion of the documents as juridical sources, depicting the actions of Roman authorities as a series of legal proclamations along the lines of a "Jewish Magna Carta," reflects common approaches among other scholars (Juster 1914:1.217, 132–58; cf. Rabello 1980). Thus E. Mary Smallwood speaks of the actions of Roman authorities after Julius Caesar as "comprehensive permanent legislation giving positive rights to legalize the practice of Judaism in all its aspects" (Smallwood 1981:128). This was a "charter of Jewish rights," then, which made Judaism a "legal religion" (*religio licita*), unlike the many other supposedly illicit religious groups or associations throughout the empire. Like those scholars who look at the occasional interventions of authorities in the life of associations and interpret them in terms of the establishment and enforcement of permanent legislation, these scholars have taken a similar approach to Roman-Jewish relations of the diaspora. The Jewish Magna Carta theory also depends, in part, on another assumption within scholarship that needs considerable qualification: the notion that Jews needed special legal protection because the relationship between synagogues and their polis of residence was by nature conflictual in an ongoing and consistent manner, an assumption I have begun to qualify in this study.

As Tessa Rajak and others argue, the traditional approach to Roman "policy" regarding diaspora Judaism is inadequate (Rajak 1984; cf. Trebilco 1991:8–12). The privileges found in the decrees that Josephus records do not represent some sort of legally defined Magna Carta protecting the Jews, nor an acknowledgment of their official status as a legally recognized religion (*religio licita*). Rather, these were ad hoc responses to requests or complaints that were standard procedure under Roman rule. Indeed, as Millar (1973:145) points out, the notion that "each cult in the Empire was either a *religio licita* or a *religio illicita*" is not supported by any ancient source. The benefits granted were part of the exchanges involved in conventions of friendship and patronage, part of the benefactor-beneficiary relationships in which, as I have pointed out, many other associations of Asia were also participants.[8] As such, they were, in Rajak's (1984:116) words, "things of the moment" with an impermanence that required the continued activity of Jewish groups in regaining from Roman authorities confirmation of earlier acknowledgments and benefits.[9]

Returning to the Asian Jews' honorary decree for Augustus, a second point worthy of note concerns the placement of the monument. The Jews gained something other than just recognition of the honors for the emperor and the right to perform their religious customs from this action. If we can understand monumentalizing as, in part, an expression of a group's place within society, as I have argued, then this particularly public placement of the Jews honorary decree within the imperial cult temple of Asia is significant. This tells us something about how the Jewish groups in question might have been perceived by those who frequented the temple and about the feelings of prestige and importance that the Jews would have felt as a result. Certainly the Jews' honorary decree for an emperor and imperial official could be interpreted by those who saw it as an indication that synagogues, like other associations, were participants within customary civic and imperial practices. They, like others such as the hymn singers at

Pergamum (*IEph* 3801, part 2), had granted appropriate honors to important benefactors of the provincial communities, and this was recognized within the context of a provincial institution. In this sense, the Jews could be viewed as participants in maintaining the connections between Rome and the province that ensured the well-being and prosperity of the Asian communities.

There would be prestige for the Jews associated with this placement of a monument in such an important location, then, but there is another side to this that pertains to the competitive cultural framework. Other communities, groups, and associations would certainly seek to gain imperial recognition of their practices and to have their monuments set up in such a desirable location, but not all could hope to achieve this. In some respects, synagogues could be competitors alongside other associations for visibility or prestige not only at the local civic level but also within the broader provincial context. Presumably, there were times when this competitive element could be a source of tensions with other communities or groups.

Before going on to discuss Jewish connections with other Roman functionaries, like Censorinus, it is important to note that the honors granted to emperors specifically find parallels among other Jewish groups as well. Like their counterparts in Asia and in Alexandria, it seems that some synagogues at Rome and Ostia visibly demonstrated their respect for imperial authorities and emperors. One synagogue at Rome called itself the "Augustesians" in honor of their patron, Augustus, and another named itself the "Agrippesians" (after Marcus Agrippa), reminiscent of the "friends-of-Agrippa" association we have already encountered at Smyrna and a similar association at Sparta.[10] An inscription from the synagogue at Ostia (a port city of Rome) involves a benefactor, Mindius Faustus, dedicating a structure and a Torah "ark" for the group. What is especially noteworthy here is the use of a customary Latin invocation: *pro salute Augusti*, "For the well-being of the emperor" (*IEurJud* I 13; cf. L. White 1998b:53–57; probably 2d century c.e.). L. Michael White (1998b:57) aptly states that imperial ties such as these "would inevitably link Jewish residents of Rome or Ostia directly to the non-Jewish population in important social and economic ways." The formula, which would not traditionally be expected in connection with Jews, is used in a similar way in building dedications by Mithraic associations at both Ostia and Rome (*CIMRM* 273, 510).

We have already encountered considerable evidence that associations of various kinds could proclaim honors for and maintain positive links with influential figures besides the emperors themselves, including Roman provincial officials of senatorial or equestrian status. Returning to the

Asian Jews' honorary decree (recorded by Josephus), the second honoree, C. Marcius Censorinus, was an important imperial official of the senatorial order with considerable experience in the Greek East (see *PIR*[1] M 163; Bowersock 1964; 1965:18–19; Sherk 1980:1036–37; *IPergamon* 292 = *OGIS* 466; *IMilet* 255). Among his services in Asia Minor, Censorinus was a legate of Augustus at Sinope in Bithynia-Pontus, probably in the wake of a Bosporan rebellion around 13–12 B.C.E. (Bowersock 1964:208–9). Several years after attaining the consulate at Rome in 8 B.C.E., he became proconsul of the province of Asia, perhaps in 2 or 3 C.E., and shortly thereafter he died (Velleius Paterculus, *Roman Histories* 2.102.1). Censorinus's popularity among other inhabitants of Asia Minor, besides the Jews, is suggested both by a Pergamene honorary decree for him and by the cult (including games) established in honor of this "savior and benefactor" at Mylasa, which happens to represent the latest evidence we have from the Greek East concerning cults for Roman governors (*IPergamon* 422; *SEG* 2 (1924) 549; Sahin and Engelmann 1979; cf. Bowersock 1965:150–51; Price 1984:42–43, 46–47). Like other associations that maintained such positive contacts with provincial officials, the Jewish groups' early ties with Censorinus (probably beginning around or before 12 B.C.E.) could in subsequent years be translated into other favors or benefactions.

Although we happen to lack further concrete examples of honorary monuments set up by Jewish gatherings for provincial functionaries in Asia specifically, we do encounter similar evidence elsewhere, as at Berenike in Cyrenaica (north-central Africa).[11] Three inscriptions have been found relating to Jewish groups at this location, each of them suggesting some degree of integration of the Jews with their Greek neighbors, as Joyce Reynolds also points out.[12] The inscription that interests us most here concerns a monument erected by a Jewish community (probably c. 24 C.E.) in honor of a Roman provincial official named Marcus Tittius, son of Sextus, of the Aemilia tribe.[13] This gathering of Jews, like other associations we have encountered, called itself a "corporate body" (*politeuma*), and was led by several leaders called "archons" (a term also used of leaders of the polis), one of whom possessed Roman citizenship.[14] The inscription reads as follows:

> In the fifty-fifth year, on the twenty-fifth of Phaoph, at the assembly of the Feast of Tabernacles, during the archonships of Kleandros son of Stratonikos, Euphranor son of Ariston, Sosigenes son of Sosippos, Andromachos son of Andromachos, Marcus Laeilius Onasion son of Apollonios, Philonides son of Hagemon, Autokles son of Zenon, Sonikos son of

Theodotos, Josepos son of Straton:

Whereas Marcus Tittius son of Sextus, member of the Aimilia tribe, an excellent man has, since he arrived in the province over public affairs, performed his governorship over these affairs in a good and humane manner (*paragenētheis eis tēn eparcheian epi dēmosiōn pragmatōn tēn te prostasian autōn epoiēsato philanthrōpōs kai kalōs*) and has always displayed a calm disposition in his behavior. He has shown himself to be nonburdensome not only in these affairs but also with the citizens (*tōn politōn*) who meet with him individually. Furthermore, in performing his governorship in a useful way for the Judeans of our politeuma, both individually and as a group (*kai tois ek tou politeumatos hēmōn Ioudaiois kai koinē kai kat idian*), he never fails to live up to his own noble rank.

For these reasons, the leaders (*tois archousi*) and the politeuma of Judeans in Berenike decided to praise (*epainesai*) him, to crown him by name at each gathering and new moon with a crown of olive branches and ribbon, and to have the leaders engrave the decree on a plaque of Parian stone which is to be set up in the most prominent place in the amphitheater. All pebbles white [results of the vote].

The language of the inscription is most compatible with the suggestion that Tittius was proconsul of Cyrenaica and Crete,[15] but the provincial positions of quaestor or proconsular legate are not out of the question (cf. Reynolds 1977:245; Bowsky 1987:498–501). So Tittius was probably of the senatorial order but possibly an equestrian. If the name is misspelled here with an extra "t," and the honorand is in fact a son or grandson of Sextus Tittius, a quaestor to Antony in 43 B.C.E., then it is even more likely that Marcus would have reached the senatorial order by this generation (cf. Münzer 1937).

The Jewish association's decree, which was passed during its celebration of the Feast of Tabernacles, is saturated with the conventional honorary language of benefaction. It also shows the group's common concern for the well-being of the civic community at large. They praise Tittius as an excellent man and administrator who had exercised his governorship over the province's public affairs in a humane manner, benefiting the Judeans, both as a group and as individuals, but also other citizens of Berenike. In response to his beneficent behavior, the leaders and members of the Jewish association voted that he be commended and granted an honorary crown at each monthly gathering of the group.

Furthermore, the decree was to be inscribed on a plaque and set up in a prominent spot within the amphitheater (*amphitheatron*). Several years earlier (c. 8–6 B.C.E.) the same Jewish group had placed another monument in the "amphitheater," honoring the Roman citizen D. Valerius Dionysios (likely a member) for plastering and painting the structure or a room therein (Reynolds 1977:245–47, no. 18 = *NewDocs* IV 111).[16] Regardless of where the monuments were erected–in the Jews' meeting place or in the civic amphitheater–here we have a Jewish group clearly participating in common conventions of honors in return for benefactions, maintaining links with a provincial official, most likely a proconsul.

There has been some debate as to whether "amphitheater" is a non-technical designation of the Jewish group's meeting place or if it is in fact a reference to an actual civic structure. Those who argue against the possibility of it being a civic structure, such as Gert Lüderitz, base their assessment on the unlikelihood that the floors of a civic amphitheater would have been plastered, and that it would be "improbable that the Jewish politeuma had a right to put up inscriptions in a public place" (Lüderitz 1994:213; cf. Applebaum 1979:161, 164–67). S. Applebaum (1979:165) questions the possibility that a Jewish group would have frequented such a building, also expressing an important assumption behind the view: "it is hardly to be imagined that the community (however assimilated to Greek habits) would have met to pray in a building contaminated by gentile idolatry."

There is much evidence, however, to challenge Lüderitz's view, as the following discussion will indicate. Monumentalizing did not make much sense unless at least some degree of public visibility was expected, and associations would naturally seek, though not always receive, permission to set up a monument in or near more significant civic or provincial structures. Furthermore, as the evidence for Jews in the theater at Miletos and in the bath-gymnasium complex at Sardis suggests, it would not be odd to imagine the Jews of Berenike at least seeking a place in some sense within a sociocultural institution of the polis (such as the amphitheater), possibly even attending as a group. Both monuments in the amphitheater, although set up by the Jewish association, also refer clearly to the civic inhabitants of Berenike as mutual beneficiaries of Dionysius's and Tittius's actions. Like Reynolds, I believe we should be more inclined to the view that this structure is in fact what its name suggests: a civic amphitheater (Reynolds 1977:247; cf. Zuckerman 1985/88:179; *NewDocs* IV 111). If so, this makes quite a statement regarding the integration of this Jewish group within local society. The monument clearly communicated the Jews' contribution to the life of the polis, indicating the group's important role in maintaining fitting relations within the webs of power that ensured the well-being of civic communities under Roman rule. Such participation in social networks is further confirmed on a more local basis within Asia specifically.

When we looked at the evidence for associations, we found that contacts with imperial-connected individuals were certainly not limited to emperors or provincial officials like Censorinus or Tittius, but also involved links with other religious functionaries and civic officials. Thus at Akmoneia, for instance, we found the guild of clothing cleaners honoring T. Flavius Montanus, a local aristocrat who had assumed the high priesthood at the Ephesian temple for the imperial gods for a time (*IGR* IV 643). Such aristocratic families were an important link between the polis and both province and empire. Solicitation and offer of support from a patron did not necessarily mean that she or he was a member or adherent of the cult or group supported. "In parts of Phrygia, Judaism had a high religious profile, and we need not be surprised to see this echoed in social contacts and mutual esteem" (Rajak and Noy 1993:88; cf. Sheppard 1979; Trebilco 1991). The case of Julia Severa at Akmoneia is illustrative.

Julia Severa was a member of a prominent family descending from Galatian royalty, a family that came to play a key role within the webs of imperial power in Asia Minor, as we have found (see fig. 23, p. 141). Together with her Italian husband, L. Servenius Capito, she had a son, L. Servenius Cornutus, who became a senator under Nero, assuming positions including quaestor in the province of Cyprus and legate of the proconsul of Asia around 73–77 c.e. (Halfmann 1979, no. 5). Two of her kinsmen (perhaps second or third cousins), C. A. A. Julius Quadratus of Pergamum and C. Julius Severus of Ankyra, were members of the consular order who also assumed the office of proconsul of Asia at one point in their careers (109–110 c.e. and 152–153 c.e., respectively).[17]

Julia Severa herself was a noteworthy benefactor and civic leader within Akmoneia in the decades of the mid- to late first century, but she was not a Jew, as some had suggested (e.g., Ramsay 1895–97:639, 650–51, 673; see Trebilco 1991:57–60). On one occasion, the local elders' organization honored her with a monument, also mentioning her role as high priestess and director of games for the civic cult devoted to the *Sebastoi* gods (*MAMA* VI 263; cf. *MAMA* VI 153* = *IGR* IV 656; Ramsay 1895–1900:649). An inscription from the late first or early second century (which represents our earliest epigraphic attestation of a synagogue in Asia) reveals that the Jews of Akmoneia also apparently had ties with this influential woman who was an imperial cult high priestess at one point (*MAMA* VI 264 = *CIJ* 766 = L. White 1996:307–10, no. 65):

The meeting place, which was built (*ton kataskeuasthe[n]ta o[i]kon*) by Julia Severa, was renovated by P. Tyrronius Klados, head of the synagogue (*archisynagogos*) for life, Lucius son of Lucius, also head of the synagogue, and Publius Zotikos, leader (*archōn*) from their own resources and from the common deposit. They decorated the walls and ceiling, made the windows secure, and took care of all the rest of the decoration. The synagogue honored them with a golden shield (*eteimēsen hoplō epichrysō*) because of their virtuous disposition, goodwill (*eunoian*), and diligence (*s[pou]dēn*) in relation to the synagogue.

Severa had apparently shown her beneficence by contributing the building in which the Jewish group met sometime around the period 60–80 C.E. (cf. Luke 7:1–5, regarding the story of a Roman centurion who built a synagogue for the Jews at Capernaum). Along with others who later renovated the building, Severa was honored by the synagogue with a golden shield and this monument. This positive connection with a high priestess is not the only sign of linkages with the local elites in this inscription. It seems likely that P. Tyrronius Klados, the head of the synagogue, was associated with the Tyrronius family as a relative, freedman, or client (cf. L. White 1996:309–10 n.48), and the suggestion that he too is not even Jewish is within the realm of possibility in light of typical values and practices among associations.[18] Members of the Tyrronius family held important civic positions at Akmoneia; C. Tyrronius Rapon served alongside Severa at one point, most likely as civic high priest (*MAMA* VI 265 = *IGR* IV 654; c. 70–80 C.E.). Thus, like other associations, Jewish groups could be among the competitors for benefactions from influential figures within the civic and provincial context.

Christian Assemblies in Roman Asia Minor

Unfortunately, unlike synagogues for which we have some epigraphic remains, concrete material evidence of Christian group life in Roman Asia is wanting concerning our period of focus (up to the time of Antoninus Pius). In fact, material remains identifiable as Christian (including grave inscriptions) do not even come into the picture until the mid- to late second century. The lack of surviving archeological evidence concerning Christian participation in imperial facets of civic life specifically is relatively unsurprising in light of the generally partial nature of survival and discovery, as well as the limitations of archeological digs in some areas of Asia Minor.

Added to this is the fact that Christians were a numerically insignificant portion of the population in our period of focus (cf. Hopkins 1998; Snyder 1985). The case of the Jews at Alexandria in the first century (considered a central locus of the Jewish diaspora population) is illustrative of the vagaries of archeological remains: although we know that Jewish groups there did conventionally erect honorary inscriptions and monuments for imperial figures (from Philo), none has survived (see *IAlexandriaK* for inscriptions from the area). So the absence of inscriptions relating to early Christians comes as no surprise, and one should not assume that the silence of material evidence means that Christians did not engage in such honorary practices within local civic contexts, as we shall see.

Even when we turn to literary evidence of Christianity in Asia, it is unfortunate that some authors simply did not have occasion to refer to the emperors or to common Christian attitudes and practices in regard to imperial facets of civic life. For example, there are no clear references to such things in Ephesians, Colossians, the epistles of John, and (in spite of attempts to read anti-imperial attitudes into them) the epistles of Ignatius.[19]

Despite these shortcomings, there is important and neglected literary evidence that Christian assemblies in Asia Minor could in significant ways also participate in certain imperial practices. This provides us with clear signs of positive interaction within civic life. Some Christian groups did so in a manner comparable to the involvements of other associations and synagogues. This participation was one of the means by which congregations, like both associations and synagogues, could find a place for themselves within the sociocultural framework of the polis and empire, despite distinctive identities and some areas of tension. Yet, as with many synagogues or individual Jews, involvements stopped short of cultic honors specifically, a point I will return to concerning areas of nonparticipation. It seems that the distinction between cultic (religious) and noncultic forms of honors for the emperors was an important one within many Jewish and Christian circles, even though the distinction could be blurry or nonexistent for some other inhabitants in the cities of Asia. Yet not all Jews or Christians would necessarily consider the same activities within their definition of active participation in cultic honors or "idolatry," as we will see when we turn to the Apocalypse and its opponents. So there was ambiguity and variety in what Jews and Christians considered acceptable practice in relation to this and other dimensions of life in the polis.

In contrast to the perspective of the Apocalypse, many Christian leaders in Asia, including the author of the Pastorals, the author of 1 Peter, Polycarp, and Melito held a relatively positive view of empire and, on occasion, encouraged their followers to adopt the common conventions of praying for and/or honoring civic or imperial authorities and emperors. A brief discussion of Melito (bishop of Sardis) and Polycarp (bishop of Smyrna) will set the stage for a fuller discussion of 1 Peter and the Pastorals.

Although not dealing with Christian practice per se, Melito of Sardis's positive view of empire and Christianity's place within it reflects a particular trajectory of Christianity in Roman Asia. In writing his apology to Marcus Aurelius (161–180 C.E.), Melito states the following with some hyperbole:

> [Christianity's] full flower came among your nation in the great reign of your ancestor Augustus, and became an omen of good to your empire, for from that time the power of the Romans became great and splendid. You are now his happy successor. . . . Your ancestors nourished it together with the other cults, and the greatest proof that our doctrine flourished for good along with the empire in its noble beginning is the fact that it met no evil in the reign of Augustus, but on the contrary everything splendid and glorious according to the wishes of everyone. The only emperors who were ever persuaded by malicious men to slander our teaching were Nero and Domitian, and from them arose the lie, and the unreasonable custom of falsely accusing Christians. (Melito in Eusebius, *H.E.* 4.26.7–9; trans. Oulten and Lawlor 1964 [LCL])

Speaking against a recent incident of mistreatment of Christians in Asia, Melito evidently believes that empire and Christianity are not incompatible and he even suggests that the success of empire is dependent on Christianity. Such views could work themselves out in the actual practices of Christian groups in Asia.

For instance, when faced with martyrdom, Polycarp of Smyrna refers to the common Christian teaching "to render honor (*timēn*), as is fitting, if it does not hurt us, to princes and authorities appointed by God" (*Mart. Pol.* 10.2 [LCL, with adaptations]). He also exhorts the Christians at Philippi to pray for the emperors and other authorities (Pol. *Phil.* 12.3). This trajectory of Christianity is also evident in writings from an earlier era.

Moreover, as the following discussion of the Pastoral Epistles and 1 Peter illustrates, for many congregations in Asia (around the end of the 1st century) participation in at least some imperial-related activities within the polis was considered normal. In this respect, there are important analogies between congregations and other associations in the same civic contexts.

Scholars are in general agreement that the Pastoral Epistles (1–2 Timothy and Titus) represent one important strand of Christianity in western Asia Minor, likely centered at Ephesus, in the late first or early second century. Among the principal aims of these letters, written in Paul's name, are concern for "sound teaching" over against "godless and silly myths" and the proper management of both Christian households and the Christian assembly, the "household of God" (1 Tim 3:15). In the process, the attitudes, values, and practices advocated by the Pastorals reflect considerable crossovers with Greco-Roman values and conceptions of good citizenship, as scholars since Dibelius (1931) suggest. Furthermore, as in 1 Peter, there is a clear concern with the appearance of the Christian assemblies in the eyes of other civic inhabitants. Thus the Pastorals are, in some respects, an attempt to find a place for these Christian assemblies within society.

In this framework, positive viewpoints and practices pertaining to Roman emperors and other authorities play a significant role in the Pastorals' vision of Christian group life and the relation of these assemblies to surrounding society. The evidence we have discussed with regard to imperial-related practices of associations, both internal and external, provides a context for this. The author of 1 Timothy gives a prominent position to the following exhortation: "First of all, then, I urge that supplications, prayers, intercessions, and thanksgivings be made on behalf of all people, for emperors and all who are in high positions, that we may lead a quiet and peaceable life, godly and respectful in every way" (1 Tim 2:1–2). Again, in the letter to Titus we find a less specific admonition for leaders to remind Christians "to be submissive to rulers and authorities," along with other guidelines as to fitting behavior in relation to others (Titus 3:1–2).

Although these passages reflect traditional material common within the Greco-Roman world and present within Paul's letters themselves (Rom 13:1–7; cf. Dibelius and Conzelmann 1972:36–39), they nonetheless show this author's concern for and knowledge of actual practices within the Christian assemblies in the cities of Asia. They suggest that emperors and other authorities were singled out as deserving of special respect, and that this was expressed within the ongoing religious life of the group, in this case within the context of prayers. Tertullian also refers to this common Christian practice of "praying for the emperors, and for the whole estate of the empire and the interests of Rome" (*Apology* 32.1; cf. 30.4–5). The letter of the Roman Christians to the Corinthians (c. 90 C.E.) provides an example of just how such a prayer might go, calling for Christians' obedience "to rulers and governors" who are put in a position of power by God and asking for the "health, peace, and concord" of the empire (*1 Clem.* 60.4–61.3). As in 1 Peter, the Pastoral Epistles' reference to actual concrete behaviors on the part of Christians with regard to imperial or other figures of authority is closely linked with how the author imagines Christians will "lead a quiet and peaceable life" within the polis.

We do indeed find such prayers and rituals as common practices within the cities of Asia and elsewhere, sometimes in connection with other associations.[20] Thus, for instance, a man from Philadelphia thanks the "great and holy god Sabathikos" for answering his earlier prayer for Roman citizenship; he then prays for the continued increase of both the imperial Julian household and the association (*oikos*) of which he was evidently a member (*TAM* V 225 = *ILydiaKP* II 224; late 1st century B.C.E.–early 1st century C.E.).[21] A passage in Apuleius of Madaura's novel provides us with a glimpse of just such a group ritual performed at a gathering of Isis initiates (set in Cenchreae, Greece): "[a cultic functionary] went up into a high pulpit and read out of a book blessings upon 'the mighty emperor, upon the senate, upon the equestrian order, and upon the whole people of Rome, and upon all sailors and all ships who owe obedience to our empire'" (*Metamorphoses* 11.17; trans. Graves 1990, with adaptations).[22] That the Christian assemblies addressed by the Pastorals could share such practices in common with other associations also suggests at least some similarities in worldviews. The emperors and imperial officials were very important and powerful figures within the cosmic order of things, deserving of distinctive attention and positive expressions of goodwill within the religious life of the group.

Before I go on to the evidence of 1 Peter, a few words are in order about what is often considered an alternative trajectory of Christianity in Asia Minor to be contrasted to that of the Pastorals specifically. In certain respects, the views preserved within the second-century apocryphal *Acts of Paul* reflect alternative perspectives and practices concerning various aspects of society, especially marriage and the household, but also imperial dimensions. To some extent, these countercultural traditions also found social expression in the so-called Phrygian (or Montanist) movement of the mid-late second century, at least with regard to women's leadership (cf. Trevett 1996). However, Dennis Ronald MacDonald (1983:66, 40–42) overstates the contrast with the Pastorals in proposing that the *Acts of Paul* "bristles with anti-Roman hostility" and exudes the conflict between the cult of Christ and that of Caesar. MacDonald is not alone in this tendency to read into Christian sources references to imperial cults or to exaggerate anti-Roman sentiments, as Allen Brent's study of Ignatius and the imperial cult (1998) and Richard A. Horsley's book on *Paul and Empire* (1997) further illustrate.[23] Unlike their role in the Apocalypse, imperial cults specifically do not expressly play a role in any stories in the *Acts of Paul;* and, if the Armenian version of Thecla's removal of Alexander's crown (which refers to a "figure of Caesar") is taken as secondary, the *Acts of Paul* do not refer to these cults at all.[24] Furthermore, as in the Acts of the Apostles, the portrayal of other imperial authorities is neutral or relatively positive, even in the story of Paul's martyrdom.[25]

It is in this same martyrdom story, though, that traditions reflecting tensions between Christianity and the imperial power in connection with Emperor Nero come to the fore. Along with others from the imperial household who came to hear Paul speak in a rented barn outside Rome was Nero's cupbearer, Patroclus, who (in a Eutychus-like manner) had fallen from a window, died, and subsequently been raised (*Acts of Paul* 11.1; cf. Acts 20:9). When asked by Nero who made him alive, Patroclus answers that it was "Christ Jesus, king of the ages," who, it is added, "destroys all kingdoms under heaven" and for whom Patroclus was a "soldier" (trans. J. K. Elliott 1993).[26] Indignant at the existence of this alternative army of Christ, Nero issues his "edict that all Christians and soldiers of Christ that were found should be executed" (11.2–3). It is only later in the story that Paul's anti-imperial speech before Nero is softened somewhat when he states that the Christian "soldiers" "fight not, as you suppose, for a king who is from the earth but for one who is from heaven" (11.4; cf. Eusebius, *H.E.* 20 [Hegesippus on Christians before Domitian]). Although the apparent link with Nero's infamous slaughter of Christians following the fire at Rome (cf. Tacitus, *Annals* 15.43–44; Rordorf 1982) should caution us in assuming that this story is a general statement regarding perceptions of and practices in relation to all emperors or imperial power, it does contain anti-imperial attitudes that can be contrasted to those advocated by the Pastorals and 1 Peter.

Written in the form of a diaspora letter to the provinces of Asia Minor sometime in the closing decades of the first century, 1 Peter is particularly relevant to our understanding of Christian groups in regions like Asia, Bithynia, and Pontus and to the issue of imperial practices specifically. The addressees were primarily Gentile converts who had turned from their previous life of "idolatry" to become, in the author's words, "a chosen race, a royal priesthood, a holy nation, God's own people" (1 Pet 1:13–2:11). As a result, they faced "suffering" in the form of social harassment and verbal abuse from fellow inhabitants, which was similar to that faced by the "brotherhood throughout the world" (1:14–19; 4:3–5;

5:9). The author wrote to these "exiles" or "aliens" in order to comfort, encourage, and exhort them to continue in their new lives as the elect people of God, members of his "household."[27] There are apocalyptic elements in the letter with respect to the expectation of Christ's return, and the author is emphatic about the distinctive identity of the Christians who are in some respects living as "exiles in the diaspora."[28] At the same time, 1 Peter is clearly concerned with the practicalities of how Christian individuals and groups were to live *within* society alongside others in the polis or village, limiting tensions as much as possible.

One of the more important sections of 1 Peter contains a series of practical guidelines regarding how these Christians were to "maintain good conduct among the Gentiles, so that in case they speak against you as wrongdoers, they may see your good works (*tōn kalōn ergōn*) and glorify God on the day of visitation" (2:12). Here imperial dimensions of group life immediately come into the picture: "Be subject for the Lord's sake to every human creature, whether it be to the emperor (*basilei*) as supreme, or to governors (*hēgemosin*) as sent by him to punish those who do wrong (*kakopoiōn*) and to praise those who do good (*epainon de agathopoiōn*). For it is God's will that by doing good (*agathopoiountes*) you should put to silence the ignorance of foolish men. . . . Honor all men. Love the brotherhood. Fear God. Honor the emperor (*ton basilea timate*)" (1 Pet 2:13–17 [RSV, with adaptations]).

Like the Pastoral Epistles, 1 Peter is here reflecting a clearly positive view regarding the position of the emperor and other imperial officials within God's ordained order of existence (as that author understood it). Both of these authors are also reflecting widespread Greco-Roman traditions concerning respect for authorities along the lines of what we also find in literature concerning Christianity in other regions (cf. Rom 13:1–7). Nonetheless, as with the Pastorals, these are not just empty words or merely a "stock phrase taken over from some current formula of instruction in civic duty" (Beare 1958:117; cf. Légasse 1988). Rather, they are practical exhortations with direct implications regarding the concrete behaviors of congregations and their members.

First Peter explicitly encourages Christians to "honor the emperor" and to engage in activities that may be perceived by rulers and other outsiders as good and worthy of praise (1 Pet 2:11–17). The author apparently maintains a distinction, however, between honors, on the one hand, and cultic rituals, on the other, the latter being idolatry in his view (cf. 1:14–19; 4:3–5). This exhortation for Christians to honor the emperor has not been sufficiently explained or contextualized by scholars, who often speak as

though 1 Peter is merely referring to inner attitudes rather than actual behaviors (cf. Beare 1958:113–19; Goppelt 1993:189–90; Michaels
1988:121–32). Such vague interpretations do not seem compatible with
the context of the passage regarding the call for Christians to do "good
works" in the eyes of outsiders, among them being subject to and honoring the emperor (2:12). As Bruce J. Malina (1981:51–93) and others have
begun to show, the ancient Mediterranean personality was a dyadic one
embedded within social groupings; what mattered most was what, concretely, others perceived one to be doing, not what one thought internally,
though certainly one's actions might reflect inner attitudes.

Moreover, the honor for the emperor that 1 Peter proposes seems to
have a more concrete basis that finds analogies in some of the practices of
other associations and synagogues within the polis. That the author links
his advice with lessening tensions in relation to outsiders suggests that it is
actual demonstrations of honor for the emperors that are encompassed by
his exhortation. The possibilities for such honors were well illustrated
above, including setting up an honorary inscription, dedicating a structure
or building, and engaging in rituals or prayers that encompassed the emperor or other authorities in the setting of group worship. This practical
understanding of the exhortation fits well with what scholars such as W. C.
van Unnik, David L. Balch, and Bruce W. Winter observe concerning
1Peter's social strategy: he exhorts Christians to adopt and/or adapt some
civic values and practices, including "good works" or benefaction and
good household management, which will receive "praise" (*epainos*) from
outsiders and authorities while also lessening group-society tensions.[29] As
we saw clearly in the case of both associations and synagogues, participation in such honorary activities was indeed commonly viewed among the
"good works" that helped to maintain fitting relations within the social
and cosmic order of things.

The evidence of the Pastorals, 1 Peter, Melito, Polycarp, and others
represents a particular trajectory of Christianity in Asia Minor that reflects
what we could call a "moderate stance" with regard to attitudes toward empire and at least some participation or positive interaction in certain imperial dimensions of society, in contrast to the perspective of John's
Apocalypse. Although the focus of this study is on Roman Asia, it is important at least to note the context of similar traditions within Christianity more broadly. Attitudes toward empire or the emperor, whether
positive or negative, are noticeably absent from most of Paul's letters, so it
is worth quoting the famous passage from Paul's letter to the Christians in
Rome that does deal explicitly with such issues:

Let every person be subject to the governing authorities. For there is no authority except from God, and those that exist have been instituted by God. Therefore he who resists the authorities resists what God has appointed, and those who resist will incur judgment. For rulers are not a terror to good conduct, but to bad. Would you have no fear of him who is in authority? Then do what is good, and you will receive his praise (*to agathon poiei, kai hexeis epainon ex autēs*), for he is God's servant for your good. But if you do wrong, be afraid, for he does not bear the sword in vain; he is the servant of God to execute his wrath on the wrongdoer. Therefore one must be subject, not only to avoid God's wrath but also for the sake of conscience. For the same reason you also pay taxes, for the authorities are ministers of God, attending to this very thing. Pay all of them their dues, taxes to whom taxes are due, reverence (*phobon*) to whom reverence is due, respect to whom respect is due, honor (*timēn*) to whom honor is due. (Rom 13:1–7 [RSV, with adaptations])

This is not the place to engage in a full exegesis of the passage.[30] It is sufficient here to note that, as with 1 Peter, this passage clearly states that the attitude and actions of Christians toward emperors and others in authority was to demonstrate respect and honor. As Justin Martyr's discussion of a similar tradition shows, Jesus' teaching to give "to the emperor the things that are the emperor's and to God the things that are God's" could be invoked as support for similar calls to respect authorities and pay taxes (Justin Martyr, *Apology* 1.17; Matt 22:15–22; cf. Mark 12:13–17; Luke 20:20–25). Akin to this is the political posture communicated when the Christians at Rome wrote to those at Corinth, encouraging them to pray for the well-being of the empire and its rulers (*1 Clem.* 60.4–61.3; cf. Tertullian, *Apology* 30.4–5; 32.1).

Finally, there is Luke–Acts' portrayal of earliest Christianity in a way that posits its valid place within, not opposition to, the Roman Empire (cf. Walaskay 1983; Robbins 1991; D. Edwards 1996). The presumed symbiotic relationship between Christianity and empire that was so strongly stated by Melito also finds similar (though less direct) expression within Luke–Acts. The author often portrays Roman functionaries in a neutral or positive light. The Roman centurion at Capernaum (Luke 7:1–10; cf. Acts 10) had, like Julia Severa at Akmoneia, built a synagogue for the local Jews: "for he loves our people, and it is he who built our synagogue for us" (v. 5 RSV). When he sends for Jesus to heal his slave, the centurion clearly acknowledges how his power within Roman imperial structures parallels Jesus' own authority; Jesus expresses amazement at the centurion's faith (vv. 6–10).

The author of Acts also frequently emphasizes the status of Paul as Roman citizen and relates incidents concerning Paul's positive contacts with Roman officials. When Paul and Silas are accused of advocating "customs which it is not lawful for us Romans to accept or practice" at the Roman colony of Philippi, it turns out that the accusers have engaged in unlawful activity by beating and imprisoning Roman citizens (Acts 16:19–40). The proconsul of Cyprus, Sergius Paulus, summons Paul and Barnabas "to hear the word of God," and he ultimately believes (13:7–12). Also, the proconsul of Achaia, Gallio, questions the validity of bringing accusations against Paul before him, since there is no evidence that Roman laws have been broken (18:12–17). It is evidence such as this that leads Vernon K. Robbins (1991:202) to argue that Luke–Acts reflects "a narrative map grounded in an ideology that supported Christians who were building alliances with local leaders throughout the eastern Roman empire." The prominence of this trajectory of early Christianity both in Asia Minor and elsewhere will be especially relevant when we come to consider the alternative stances toward empire and imperial facets of civic life reflected in John's Apocalypse.

Conclusion

Returning to our main focus on actual group practice, the participation of some synagogues and congregations in imperial facets of civic life in Roman Asia demonstrates one of the ways in which they could claim a place within society, tending toward some degree of positive interaction and integration along with other associations in that context. This illustrates one aspect of group-society relations that is not adequately addressed by those who propose a sectarian reading of Christian groups in Asia Minor. These group practices suggest that, like their fellow civic inhabitants, many Jews and Christians viewed the emperors as important figures within the cosmic order of things, figures deserving of special respect and honors. Unlike others, however, both Jews and Christians clearly did not place the emperor alongside God, which leads us back to the issue of religious rites for the imperial gods, or imperial cults. This is an area of tension that needs to be put into proper perspective.

Tensions in Perspective

Imperial Cults, Persecution, and the Apocalypse of John

Introduction

The evidence I have discussed thus far points to positive dimensions of group-society interactions among some synagogues and some congregations in Roman Asia, drawing attention to similarities between these groups and other associations in the same context. This neglected evidence throws into doubt common sectarian readings of these groups, which do not adequately address this potential for positive interaction in the social and cultural conventions of civic life under Roman rule. But we must not forget to consider the nature of negative dimensions of relations and some of the differences between associations, on the one hand, and synagogues and congregations, on the other.

The discussion thus far shows that there were grades of participation in imperial-related practices within the context of the polis. While some Christians and Jews might pray for the emperors, dedicate a monument or building on their behalf, or honor Roman officials, others such as the author of the Apocalypse might reject any of these sorts of imperial-related activities. Yet virtually all Jews and Christians seem to have avoided participation in rituals aimed at worshiping the emperors as gods. What was the significance of this difference in participation? To what degree was this lack of participation in imperial cults a factor in tensions between these groups and society (civic inhabitants and civic or imperial authorities)?

In reassessing this subject, I argue that scholars have often overplayed the significance of imperial cults for early Christianity (as well as Judaism) without recognizing the broader framework within which these cults were embedded. Scholars tend to exaggerate the importance of emperor worship with respect to the persecutions in particular. In this regard, it is common for some to assume that hostilities toward empire as evidenced in John's Apocalypse were naturally widespread since imperial rituals were at the center of conflict. I argue, however, that imperial cults were an issue for group-society tensions only insofar as they were part and parcel of religious life in the cities generally. Failure to honor imperial gods should be understood in relation to the broader issue of Jews' and Christians' monotheism or "atheism" (in the eyes of some outsiders). This was at the root of dislike of Christians among some inhabitants that could occasionally lead to more significant incidents of persecution, now and then reaching the attention of Roman authorities.

This provides a context in which to explain further the sporadic character of persecution in Asia Minor (in the first two centuries) and the reasons for it. Three main incidents illustrate the actual character of persecution and the relative significance of imperial cults: (1) accusations before Pliny in Pontus, (2) the rescript of Hadrian concerning Christians in Asia, and (3) the martyrdom of Polycarp. I argue that disloyalty to empire (which many see as corresponding to nonparticipation in imperial cults) was neither the basis of persecutions against Christians by inhabitants, nor the reason for convictions on those few occasions when such things reached the attention of the Roman authorities. Overall, we should not exaggerate this potential source of tensions or the frequency of such persecutions, as though Christians were in a constant state of conflict with others in their daily lives.

This sets the stage for a reconsideration of the Apocalypse on three key points. First, John's strategy and his anti-imperial stance can be better understood in opposition to both the moderate position of other Christian authors (e.g., Paul, Acts, 1 Peter, Pastorals, Polycarp) and the actual practices among some congregations and synagogues. By contrast, John views Roman imperialism as an evil force and he calls on Christians to change the patterns of their participation within the polis. Second, John's focus on the problem of imperial cults specifically arises less from their prominence in actual conflicts between Christians and society than it does from his attempt to point out the blasphemous character of imperial rule. Imperial cults take on a prominent role in the Apocalypse as part of John's attempt to convince Christians of his particular view of empire. Finally, the evidence discussed throughout the study sheds light on John's opponents ("Jezebel," Nicolaitans), whose level of participation in occupational, imperial, and other aspects of life in the polis was among the main reasons for his opposition to them. These opponents provide further evidence for the participation of some Christian groups or individuals in the life of the polis under Roman rule.

How Significant Were Imperial Cults for Judaism and Christianity?

Scholars tend to overplay the significance of imperial cults–distinguished from religious life generally–in connection with diaspora Judaism and, even more so, early Christianity. According to E. Mary Smallwood (1981: 137, 147), whose views are frequently repeated, the charter of Jewish rights granted by the Romans made Judaism a legally recognized religion (*religio licita*), and this "automatically" included "the Jews' exemption from participation in the imperial cult," an exemption that was "established universally" (cf. Applebaum 1974a:458; Hemer 1986:8–10; Thompson 1990:144; Winter 1994:124–43; Kraybill 1996:192–95). This meant that Jews, unlike others, could not be "forced" to participate in cultic honors for the emperors, though a ruler such as Gaius might temporarily waver from Roman policy (Smallwood 1981:244–45, 344–45, 348, 379–81). A corollary of this view is that as the Jesus movement was increasingly recognized as separate from Judaism in the decades around the turn of the second century, it no longer enjoyed protection and was susceptible to the "enforcement" of imperial cults.

Flowing from this line of thought is the common emphasis on the centrality of imperial cults per se for our understanding of Christian assemblies' relations to society, particularly with regard to persecutions. Thus we find frequent references within scholarship to the antagonism or "clash" between the cult of Christ and the cult of Caesar, the latter being singled out from religious life generally (cf. Deissmann 1995:338–78; Cuss 1974:35). For instance, Donald L. Jones (1980:1023) can begin his paper on Christianity and the imperial cult with the statement: "From the perspective of early Christianity, the worst abuse in the Roman Empire was the imperial cult." Similarly, Paul Keresztes (1979:271) claims that "Christianity was engaged in a death battle with Imperial Rome." An important basis of this view is the assumption that we can take the hostile viewpoints and futuristic scenarios of John's Apocalypse as representative of the real situations and perspectives of most Christians, or even as a reliable commentary on the nature of imperial cults.

Along with such views comes a common, but highly questionable, depiction of imperial cults. One often reads of how emperor worship (particularly though not solely under emperors like Domitian) was "enforced" by Roman authorities, or that there was considerable "pressure" or "demand" on Christians in their daily lives to conform to the practices of imperial cults specifically (cf. Cuss 1974; Schüssler Fiorenza 1985:192-99; Hemer 1986:7–12; Winter 1994:124–43; Kraybill 1996; Slater 1998; Beale 1999:5–15, 712–14). Moreover, in this perspective, Rome took an active role in promoting such cults in the provinces. Neglecting to participate could be taken as the equivalent of political disloyalty or treason, especially since imperial cults were merely political. Imperial cults stood out as a central factor leading to the persecution of Christians both by the inhabitants in the cities and by the imperial regime itself, especially in the time of Domitian when Christians were faced with death if they did not participate in such cults and acknowledge him as "lord and god." Earlier I addressed the problems with a Domitianic persecution and the highly questionable portrait of Domitian after his *damnatio* (see chapter 7; cf. Southern 1997:45–46, 114–18; Pleket 1961). For now it is important to note some of the problematic assumptions concerning imperial cults that inform this view.

This traditional view regarding the significance of imperial cults for Judaism and Christianity falters on several interrelated points concerning the actual character of these cults in Asia Minor. Although imperial cults were among the issues facing Christians and diaspora Jews, these cults were not in and of themselves a key issue behind group-society tensions, nor a pivotal causal factor in the persecution of Christians (cf. de Ste. Croix 1963:10; Millar 1973; S. Price 1984:15, 220–22). First, we found that cultic honors for the emperors were not an imposed feature of cultural life in Roman Asia. Rather, they were a natural outgrowth and spontaneous response on the part of civic communities and inhabitants in relation to imperial power. The local, grassroots nature of such worship of the emperors, which was well illustrated in our study of associations, suggests that there was no need for emperors to take an active stance in enforcing imperial cults. Most emperors and officials were not concerned whether the living emperor was worshiped so long as they were shown respect and honor (in whatever form) indicative of a situation in which order and peace could be maintained in the provinces. Indeed, quite often these religious honors exceeded what the emperors themselves would expect or desire, at least in the case of emperors who wanted to keep in line with some republican and Augustan traditions (cf. Suetonius, *Divine Augustus* 52).

Second, in contrast to a popular tradition within scholarship, we found that imperial cults in Roman Asia were not solely political phenomena devoid of religious dimensions. If imperial cults were indeed merely political then we could understand the Christians' nonparticipation as the equivalent of disloyalty or treason, in which case this would be a central cause of the persecution of Christians. However, G. E. M. de Ste. Croix, Fergus Millar, and others show the inadequacies of such political explanations of the persecutions, which had more to do with broader though interconnected religious and social issues. That is, persecution was often linked to the failure of Christians to participate fully in religious activities (esp. sacrifice) in honor of the Greco-Roman gods generally.

Third, far from being totally distinct phenomena in the eyes of most inhabitants in Asia, imperial cults were thoroughly integrated within religious life at various levels of civic and provincial society. We found that groups and communities reflecting various social strata integrated the emperors and imperial power within their cultural framework. The forms of honors or rituals addressed to "the revered gods" (*Sebastoi*) were not fundamentally different from those offered to traditional deities. This integration is a key to understanding the actual significance of the imperial cults for both Judaism and Christianity.

The imperial cults and the gods they honored were an issue for group-society relations only insofar as they were part and parcel of religious life in the cities. Failure to participate fully in appropriately honoring the gods (imperial deities included) in cultic contexts was one of the sources of negative attitudes toward both Jews and Christians among some civic inhabitants. Jewish and Christian "atheism" could then be perceived by some as lack of concern for others ("misanthropy") and, potentially, as a cause of those natural disasters and other circumstances by which the gods punished individuals, groups, and communities that failed to give them their due (cf. Tertullian, *Apology* 40.1–5). This is why we find inhabitants of western Asia Minor, on one occasion, protesting that "if the Jews were to be their fellows, they should worship the Ionians' gods" (Josephus, *Ant.* 12.126; c. 16–13 B.C.E.; cf. *Ag. Ap.* 2.65–67; Apollonios Molon of Rhodes in Stern 1976, 1:148–56). This issue, which is broader than, though inclusive of, imperial cults, is also a key to understanding sporadic outbreaks of persecution against Christians in Asia Minor.

Persecution and Imperial Cults: Pliny, Hadrian, and Polycarp

Three particular incidents will help to clarify both the modest role of imperial cults and the actual nature of persecution in Asia Minor: the trials of Christians by Pliny in Pontus (c. 110 c.e.), Hadrian's rescript to the proconsul of Asia concerning accusations against Christians (c. 123 c.e.), and the martyrdom of Polycarp at Smyrna (c. 160s c.e.). These episodes show that the reasons for accusations by inhabitants and convictions by Roman authorities are to be sought somewhere other than in the realm of disloyalty to empire or failure to participate in imperial cults specifically. In effect, Christians were not martyred for refusing to worship the emperor.

The reasons for Christians being accused in the first place and the reasons for convictions by authorities were often different. Intermittent accusations by some inhabitants were rooted in dislike of Christians due to their failure to participate fully in religious life (their "atheism"), which could be perceived as a threat to the well-being of the civic community, particularly when natural disasters, famines, or plagues struck.

The rationale for Roman officials' convictions of Christians brought before them, although not always clear, seems to pertain primarily to the maintenance of order and the prevention of further civic unrest. Christians could be perceived as causing trouble, and officials felt a need to satisfy the crowds. Appeasement was more of an issue than disloyalty to empire. Imperial cult rituals along with rituals for other gods were brought in to trials by Roman officials only as a test to determine whether someone was indeed a Christian, not to establish loyalty to Rome.

The reason for discussing these incidents of the second century before addressing John's Apocalypse, written in the late first century, is that they set the stage for a reassessment of his critique of imperial cults as worship of the beast. This is especially important because the Apocalypse's emphasis on imperial cults has often been taken as a general indication that these cults (more so than others) were a central factor in a confrontation between Christianity and Roman society. On to the first episode.

Pliny the Younger's Letter to Trajan

In governing the province of Bithynia-Pontus as a specially appointed legate in the years around 110–112 c.e., Pliny regularly consulted the emperor, Trajan, regarding his approach to the problems in this region. We have already come across some of this correspondence in connection with associations and imperial authorities. While visiting the coastal region of Pontus (c. 112 C.E.), perhaps at Amisos or Amastris, Pliny wrote to Trajan regarding accusations (one of them anonymous) against so-called Christians "of every age and class, both men and women" who were being brought to trial by local inhabitants of the region (*Epistles* 10.96–97 [LCL]).[1]

The actual reasons for the accusations in Pontus are not clearly stated. Still, it seems likely that, as in the martyrdom of Polycarp, it is the Christians' failure to honor the gods or participate in religious life ("atheism"), not imperial cults specifically, that is a key issue in the perception of the accusers. This central factor seems to have interconnected social, religious, and economic dimensions in this case. That it is the accusers' dislike of Christians because they do not fully participate in religious life generally is suggested by Pliny's allusion to rumors concerning the Christians' "crimes" (*flagitia*), which he ultimately finds to be untrue (e.g., "food of an ordinary and harmless kind," 96.7–8).[2] It is worth mentioning that Tacitus alludes to similar rumors when he suggests that Nero chose to blame the fire on the Christians at Rome because they were "hated for their crimes (*flagitia*)" (*Annals* 15.44). The alleged crimes in the Pliny case may well have been similar to those attributed to Christians in later years, such as those aimed at the Christians at Lugdunum in Gaul who were accused of engaging in "Thyestean feasts" or cannibalism (Eusebius, *H.E.* 5.1; cf. Henrichs 1970:19–20; Wilken 1984:17–21).

As M. J. Edwards (1992) argues, rumors along the lines of human sacrifice and cannibalism apparently derive less from a misinterpretation of what Christians *did* (e.g., a distortion of the Lord's Supper or attribution of supposed Gnostic practices to all Christians) than from what Christians (and their Jewish counterparts) *did not do*.[3] They abstained from sacrifices to the gods and goddesses, the central religious rite of antiquity. This failure to honor the gods together with its implications with respect to disregarding fellow human beings could lead some outsiders to fill in the gap with alternative, stereotyped rituals which inverted all that was "good" and "holy," such as human sacrifice or infanticide. This general situation underlying the accusations before Pliny, but not necessarily actual court trials, seems to coincide with what we find in 1 Peter. These Christian addressees were faced with verbal abuse (*katalalein, blasphēmein, oneidizein, epēreazō, loidoria*) and viewed by others as wrongdoers (*kakopoioi*) primarily due to the fact that they no longer engaged fully in religious life or, as the author puts it, "lawless idolatry" (see 1 Pet 2:12; 3:9, 13–17; 4:3–5, 14–16).

Another clue as to the accusers' motivations comes toward the end of Pliny's letter. In an exaggerated fashion, he refers to increased activity in the sale of sacrificial meat and in the attendance at temples "which had been almost entirely deserted for a long time." As A. N. Sherwin-White (1966:709) notes, this seems to imply a connection between the accusations against Christians and the sale of sacrificial meat, perhaps alluding to the fact that some merchants or temple functionaries were among the main accusers in these cases (cf. Henrichs 1970:21; Wilken 1984:15; Acts 19:23–41).

Now that we have some idea of the background leading to the accusations before Pliny, we can go on to look at the modest place of imperial cults in the trials. Pliny's letter begins with the following statement regarding his unfamiliarity with what procedure to follow in the case of Christians: "I have never been present at an examination of Christians. Consequently, I do not know the nature or the extent of the punishments usually meted out to them, nor the grounds for starting an investigation and how far it should be pressed. Nor am I at all sure . . . whether it is the mere name of Christian which is punishable, even if innocent of crime, or rather the crimes associated with the name" (*Epistles* 10.96.2; trans. Radice 1969 [LCL]). That Pliny had not been present at an examination of Christians at any time before these incidents is probably because so few, if any, such trials had been held previously in Asia Minor (cf. Downing 1988). When one considers that Pliny spent most of his career at Rome as quaestor (c. 90 C.E.), tribune of the people (c. 92 C.E.), praetor (c. 93 C.E.), and consul (100 C.E.), before being sent to the province as legate (c. 110 C.E.; see Sherwin-White 1966:72–82), it is also very unlikely that any substantial, official trials of Christians took place at Rome in this period, namely, during and following the principate of Domitian.

Lacking any precedents to follow, Pliny adjudicated differently depending on the response of the accused, and convicted based not on crimes (*flagitia*) but simply on whether one was a Christian (*nomen*), even though he expressed some doubt on this method. First, those "stubborn" and "obstinate" persons who were asked repeatedly and admitted to being Christians were either led off to execution or, if Roman citizens, sent to Rome for trial, without any need for a test involving the gods. The second category were those who denied the charge, and the third were those who had been, but were no longer, Christians. In both of these cases, rituals associated with images of the gods, but also of emperors, became the test simply to determine whether one was really a Christian. Those who denied the charge, Pliny states, "repeated after me a formula of invocation to the gods and had made offerings of wine and incense to your statue (which I had ordered to be brought into the court for this purpose along with the images of the gods), and furthermore had reviled the name of Christ: none of which things, I understand, any genuine Christian can be induced to do" (10.96.5). At no point is the issue of political disloyalty brought up, and imperial cult rituals appear not as the reason why Christians were accused by inhabitants or condemned by the Roman official, but simply as part of a test along with rituals addressed to the gods more generally.

Trajan's response approves of testing whether the accused is a Christian by simply having him or her offer "prayers to our gods" (10.97). He also cautions that Christians "must not be hunted" down and that anonymous accusations must not be permitted, sentiments similar to those repeated in Hadrian's rescript about ten years later (c. 123 C.E.).

Hadrian's Letter to the Proconsul of Asia

Emperor Hadrian's letter to the proconsul of Asia concerning accusations against Christians was recorded by Justin Martyr and subsequently copied and translated into Greek by Eusebius.[4] This rescript is not nearly as informative regarding the nature of accusations, the procedure of trials, and the role (if any) of imperial cult rituals as is the Pliny correspondence. Still, it is at least worth quoting here in order to make a few observations.

> Hadrian to Fundanus. I have received a letter addressed to me by your illustrious predecessor, Serenus Granianus, and his report, I think, ought not to be passed over in silence, lest innocent people be molested and an opportunity for hostile action be given to malicious accusers. If the provincials plainly wish to support this petition of theirs against the Christians by bringing some definite charge against them before the court, let them confine themselves to this action and refrain from mere appeals and outcries. For it is much more than just that, if anyone wishes to bring an accusation, you should examine the allegations. If then anyone accuses them and proves that they are doing anything unlawful, you must impose a penalty in accordance with the gravity of the crime; but if anyone brings such accusations simply by way of blackmail, you must sentence him to a more severe penalty in proportion to his wickedness. (trans. Bruce 1971:429)

Once again, in this case it is clearly on the initiative of inhabitants in the province that accusations were brought against Christians. The letter gives no details as to why these inhabitants had petitioned the proconsul of Asia (Granianus), but it is plausible that similar factors to those involving Christians in Pontus and Polycarp at Smyrna were at work. Like Pliny, Granianus wrote the emperor to ask his opinion on how to deal with the accusations, but by the time Hadrian responded, Granianus had been succeeded by Fundanus, who is the addressee. Hadrian's concern is not with protecting Christians per se, but with ensuring proper legal procedure: accusations lacking sufficient evidence are not to be accepted and persons bringing false accusations are to be punished. Christians found guilty of doing something unlawful are still to be punished, but little more is said with respect to whether the punishment is for the name or for crimes. Hadrian, though, says nothing to suggest that disloyalty to empire or failure to engage in the imperial cults were the principal issues here.

The Martyrdom of Polycarp

This brings me to a third episode indicative of the character of persecution and the modest role of imperial cults: the martyrdom of Polycarp at Smyrna (under Antoninus Pius or Marcus Aurelius; c. 155–167 c.e.). Many aspects of this story—preserved as a letter from the Christian assembly at Smyrna to that in Philomelion in Phrygia—can cautiously be taken as historical, keeping in mind its author(s)' imposition of the pattern of Christ's arrest and trial onto Polycarp's situation, including a key role for "the Jews" (see Schoedel 1993:349–58).

The temporary nature of this persecution is clearly indicated when the senders of the letter state that Polycarp "put an end to the persecution by his martyrdom as though adding the seal" (*Mart. Pol.* 1.1 [LCL]). Indeed, to the time of Polycarp (about one hundred years after the beginnings of Christianity in Roman Asia and seventy or so years after the writing of the Apocalypse), it seems that there had been only a total of twelve Christian "witnesses" (some from Philadelphia) killed in Smyrna, including those in this particular outburst (*Mart. Pol.* 19.1; *Polykarpon, hos syn tois apo Philadelphias dōdekatos en Smyrnē martyrēsas*; cf. Origen, *Against Celsus* 3.8). Although praising Polycarp as a "witness" par excellence, Smyrna's letter is written, in part, actually to discourage others (like the dropout "Phrygian," Quintus) from "voluntarily" presenting themselves to authorities in order to seek martyrdom (*Mart. Pol.* 4).[5] This may be a response to the Phrygian (or Montanist) movement that was known for its emphasis on being a "witness." As with the Pliny incident, the prime instigators of the persecution are not civic or imperial officials but inhabitants.

The account does not reveal the precise circumstances that transformed dislike of Christians into mob violence in this case, but recent natural disasters, plagues, or famines sent by the gods as punishment may have played a role. There was a failure of harvests and ensuing famine around this time (160s C.E.); furthermore, Roman troops returning from the victory over the Parthians brought with them a disease that resulted in epidemics in several regions, including Asia (Gilliam 1961; cf. Magie 1950:663, 1533–34 nn.8–9). Several oracular responses from Apollo at Klaros to cities of Asia pertain to a "deadly plague" that may well relate to this same period (see Parke 1985:150–54). Apollo's response to Hierapolis states: "you are not alone in being injured by the destructive miseries of a deadly plague, but many are the cities and peoples which are grieved at the wrathful displeasures of the gods" (trans. Parke 1985:153–54). Unpredictable events like this might well spark off violence against Christians, who failed to honor these same deities.

The story of Polycarp's martyrdom clearly indicates one of the most important motivating factors for the crowds' actions: the Christians did not join others in honoring the gods, they were "atheists" (3.2; 9.2; cf. Eusebius, *H.E.* 5 = Musurillo 1972:64–65). This is most evident when, at a climactic point after the proconsul's hearing and Polycarp's proclamation that he was indeed a Christian, the crowds "cried out with uncontrollable wrath and a loud shout: 'This is the teacher of Asia, the father of the Christians, the destroyer of our gods, who teaches many neither to offer sacrifice nor to worship'" (12.2).

As in the Pliny incident, imperial cult practices come into the picture only as a test by the authorities, though they are certainly more visible in this account than they are in Pliny's letter. (In fact, of the earliest martyr acts, imperial cult practices play the most evident role in that of Polycarp, albeit still a modest one.)[6] After acquiescing to the demand of the crowds to arrest Polycarp, the civic police chief (*eirēnarchos*), Herod, and his father attempt to persuade the bishop: "what harm is it to say, 'Caesar is lord (*kyrios kaisar*),' and to make an offering, and so forth, and to be saved?" (*Mart. Pol.* 8.2). Again, when Polycarp is brought to the stadium, the Roman proconsul attempts to persuade him to perform a more specific test as to whether he was a Christian, and thereby save his life: "Swear by the genius (*tychēn*) of Caesar, repent, say: 'Away with the atheists' . . . and . . . 'revile Christ'" (9.2–3). The practice of taking an oath on the genius (guardian spirit) of the emperor became common, especially by the time of Antoninus Pius (138–161 C.E.), but Polycarp refused to take the oath. Most Christians considered such oaths unacceptable for two apparent reasons: Jesus' teaching against taking oaths (Matt 5:34–37) and, perhaps more importantly, the religious implications associated with the emperor's guardian spirit (see Grant 1970:15–17; cf. Origen, *Against Celsus* 8.65).

It becomes clear that the purpose of swearing on the genius of Caesar, which is also accompanied in the narrative by accusations of "atheism," is simply to confirm that the accused is a Christian, not to assert treason as the basis of the judgment. Thus when Polycarp becomes fed up with the officials' offers he states: "If you vainly suppose that I will swear by the genius of Caesar, as you say, and pretend that you are ignorant who I am, listen plainly: I am a Christian" (*Mart. Pol.* 10.1). It is after this clear identification and final refusal that the proconsul tells Polycarp to persuade the people to change their minds. The bishop then actually refers to the usual Christian approach to authorities: "You I should have held worthy of discussion, for we have been taught to render honor (*timēn*) in a fitting manner, if it does not harm us, to officials (*archais*) and authorities (*exousiais*) who are appointed by God" (10.2 [LCL, with adaptations]; cf. Pol. *Phil.* 12.3). In this instance, as in the cases held by Pliny, it is simply the fact of being a Christian that is enough for a negative verdict, not an accusation of treason or disloyalty (cf. de Ste. Croix 1963; Bickerman 1968:294–95; Grant 1970).

Evidently, failure to honor the gods set Jews and Christians apart in some respects from other inhabitants, including the members of other associations, even though they could be integrated in other respects. On occasion differences along these lines, together with other specific circumstances (e.g., natural disasters), increased the potential for disturbances or persecutions, which might result in intervention by civic and, less often, imperial authorities. Even so, one can argue that Christian martyrdom itself was in some respects "solidly anchored in the civic life of the Graeco-Roman world" and can actually be viewed as *participation* in that society (Bowersock 1995:54; pp. 41–57 generally; C. A. Barton 1994). G. W. Bowersock (1995) shows how Christian martyrdoms, as public spectacles, were rooted both in sophistic traditions of public critique (e.g., the critique of the crowds by the "distinguished teacher," Polycarp) and in notions of gaining honor (and fame) through participation in public spectacle or competition. Within this context, the martyr's fame "was far closer to that of the great athletes and gladiators" (Bowersock 1995:52). Those exceptional persons who endured to the point of death for Christ's sake were especially honored and "spoken of by 'pagans' everywhere (*hypo tōn ethnōn en panti topō laleisthai*)" (*Mart. Pol.* 19.1).

Yet it is important to put such tensions in perspective. We should not overplay these intermittent conflicts, imagining that all Christians were in a constant state of tension with their fellow civic inhabitants in everyday life. In many respects, both Christians and Jews in Asia Minor could live and work peaceably alongside others in the civic context despite their distinctive practices and worldviews. This was something that some Christian intellectuals ("apologists") were sure to point out in their literary attempts to claim a place for Christianity within the empire (esp. from the mid-2d century on). For instance, the author of the *Epistle of Diognetus* (c. 150–225 c.e.) states the following:

> Christians are not distinguished from the rest of humanity by country, language, or custom. For nowhere do they live in cities (*poleis*) of their own, nor do they speak some unusual dialect, nor do they practice an eccentric lifestyle (*oute bion parasēmon askousin*). This teaching of theirs has not been discovered by the thought and reflection of ingenious men, nor do they promote any human doctrine, as some do. But while they live in both Greek and barbarian cities, as each one's lot was cast, and follow the local customs in dress and food and other aspects of life, at the same time they demonstrate the remarkable and admittedly unusual character of their own citizenship (*politeias*). They live in their own homelands (*patridas*), but only as aliens (*paroikoi*) [cf. 1 Pet 2:11–12]; they participate in everything as citizens (*politai*), and endure everything as foreigners (*xenoi*). Every foreign country is their homeland, and every homeland is foreign. (*Diognetus* 5.1–5; trans. Holmes 1992, with adaptations)

This expression of Christian identity in terms of being at home yet distinctive in the Greco-Roman world was often accompanied by a critique of polytheism (the worship of "ordinary utensils") and praise of monotheism ("Christians are not enslaved to such gods"; *Diognetus* 2).

New Perspectives on John's Apocalypse

The evidence I have discussed in this study provides a new vantage point from which to view and understand several aspects of the Apocalypse and the situation it addresses concerning John's strategy, imperial cults, and the opponents. Before I look at these three issues, it is important to outline briefly evidence from the Apocalypse that demonstrates just how pervasive anti-imperial sentiment is in this writing. For it is over against this particular stance that we can begin to map out the range of other Jewish and Christian perspectives and practices as discussed earlier, including those of 1 Peter and the Pastorals. The Apocalypse provides a very different Christian stance toward empire to those we have already discussed, and this has implications regarding actual practices within congregations. Yet there are also affinities here with the sentiments of some other Jewish apocalyptic writers discussed earlier.

Although the implied contrast between honoring God (and the Lamb) and honoring Satan (and the beast from the sea) is an element throughout the work, the main anti-imperial viewpoints come to the fore in chapters 13 and 17–18. John relates futuristic visions that presuppose antagonism between Christians and an evil empire. As in the Jewish oracular and apocalyptic literature, there are religious, military, and economic aspects to the anti-imperialism of the Apocalypse.

Chapter 13 focuses on the interconnected religious and military pretensions of Rome. John characterizes the Roman emperor or imperial power as a beast rising from the sea with seven heads, and this beast derives its authority from the great red dragon, the devil or Satan himself (Rev 12). In light of the mention of the mortal wound previously suffered by the beast (13:3) and the references to his death and subsequent return (17:8–11), which I discuss below, John probably has the resurrected Nero in mind here. The beast utters "haughty and blasphemous words" and it makes "war on the saints." "And authority was given it over every tribe and people and tongue and nation, and all who dwell on the earth will worship it, every one whose name has not been written before the foundation of the world in the book of life of the Lamb that was slain" (13:5, 7–8 RSV).

A second beast, this one from the earth, "exercises all the authority of the first beast in its presence, and makes the earth and its inhabitants worship the first beast" (13:12). Using miraculous signs, it deceives the inhabitants into worshiping the first beast and causes "those who would not worship the image of the beast to be slain" (13:15). It also marks everyone with its number, without which it is impossible to buy or sell. Ultimately, "if any one worships the beast and its image . . . he also shall drink the wine of God's wrath . . . and he shall be tormented with fire and sulphur in the presence of the holy angels and in the presence of the Lamb" (14:9–10). The Roman Empire and its leaders in this way are portrayed as hostile to Christianity and vice versa.

In chapters 17–18, John's condemnation of the Roman Empire turns to related economic aspects. Here he brings in the image of "Babylon the great, mother of harlots and of earth's abominations," perhaps a play on the goddess Roma, who rides upon the first beast. This is the great harlot, the city of Rome, whose attire in purple, scarlet, gold, and jewels speaks of great wealth (17:4). She is "drunk with the blood of the saints and the blood of the witnesses of Jesus" (17:6). John then goes on to portray the forthcoming fall of Babylon/Rome, relating the angel's condemnation of those who associated with this harlot: "Fallen, fallen is Babylon the great! . . . For all nations have drunk the wine of her impure passion, and the kings of the earth have committed fornication with her, and the merchants of the earth have grown rich with the wealth of her wantonness" (18:2–3). Another voice within the vision calls from heaven "Come out of her, my people, lest you take part in her sins, lest you share in her plagues; for her sins are heaped high as heaven, and God has remembered her iniquities" (18:4–5). John then goes on to portray the great mourning of those kings, merchants, and others who associated with the Roman imperial power.

Rhetorical Situation and Strategy

The findings of this study help to put the Apocalypse's strongly sectarian stance and especially its anti-imperial dimensions in proper perspective as a minority opinion within a spectrum of other viewpoints among Jewish and Christian circles in the cities of Asia (cf. Thompson 1990:120, 132, 186–97; Friesen 1995a:250). Using the imagery of harlots and beasts, John, like some other Jewish authors of his time, draws on the Hebrew prophetic tradition to criticize the social, political, economic, and religious manifestations of the Roman imperial presence in the cities (cf. Isa 13; 34; Jer 51; Ezek 26–27; also see chapter 8 on the Jewish *Sibylline Oracles* and apocalyptic literature). For him, contacts with or honors for emperors and imperial representatives in any form are intertwined and dichotomous to honoring and worshiping God and the Lamb. Hence involvement in such things is "fornication" or idolatry in its most blatant form (cf. Rev 4:11; 5:12–13; 7:11–12; 13:4–8; 14:7; 14:9–11; 20:4–6; 22:8–9). Yet John's hostile perspective and its practical implications for the actual lives of the groups it addresses is only one side of a conversation.

To clarify the rhetorical situation of the Apocalypse it is important to ask who were the general recipients of the Apocalypse and at whom was this anti-imperial "propaganda" aimed. There was certainly variety in the situations of congregations in Asia. Overall it seems that the congregations drew their membership from both Jewish and Gentile backgrounds; some of the Gentiles may also have been previously associated with synagogues (as God-fearers).[7] Some of these might have been or still were members in other subgroups, guilds, or synagogues within the civic context.

When we remember this, the evidence discussed earlier with regard to the typical activities of numerous associations, synagogues, and congregations takes on added significance. For in many, perhaps most, of these groups, honoring the emperors or other officials in some form was a normal and acceptable part of group life, and this included cultic honors and related commensal activities in the case of associations. We found that some synagogues in Asia and elsewhere engaged in monumental honors for emperors, as well as participating within social networks of benefaction that by nature entailed affiliations with imperial-connected individuals. Likewise within other Christian circles in Asia Minor, honoring the emperors (in a nonreligious sense) was not only acceptable but advocated, as we saw with 1 Peter and the Pastorals. Some degree of participation in this aspect of group practice in the cities was one way in which such assemblies and synagogues could resemble other associations within the polis, thereby helping to diminish tensions between group and society.

There are some similarities between the worldviews evident in these Jewish and Christian circles and the worldview of the Apocalypse, but there are more significant differences. John shares in common with others a rejection of active participation in rituals for the gods, including imperial gods (i.e., rituals that entailed acknowledgment of the emperors as gods), which most Jews and Christians also considered "idolatry." However, John's definition of this "fornication" expands to include many activities that others (including the Nicolaitans and followers of "Jezebel" and of "Balaam") would deem acceptable. John does not accept the distinction evident among many Jews and Christians between noncultic forms of honor, on the one hand, and conscious or active participation in imperial cults, on the other. For many Jews and Christians the emperor held a prominent and, most often, positive position within the cosmic order of things, deserving of honor and respect. In John's symbolic universe the emperor's position was also quite high, but at the height of evil. These differences in practices and worldviews also correspond to varying notions on where and how strongly the lines between group and society were to be drawn, and they help to elucidate John's rhetorical strategy.

Scholars increasingly recognize the functional characteristics of apocalyptic literature and the deliberative character of John's rhetoric specifically.[8] Addressing the Christian assemblies and using a visionary framework, John seeks to persuade others to adopt or reject particular viewpoints and practices in the present, not only in the letters to the seven congregations but also throughout the work. Among John's purposes is to convince his recipients that it is his more radical perspective involving separation from various aspects of civic life and complete avoidance of honoring imperial figures that they should follow, not the normative practice within many associations, synagogues, and assemblies. John tries to persuade his readers that what at first appears to be normal practice is, at a more profound, cosmic level, an utterly unacceptable compromise with evil. He does so by expounding a symbolic universe in which any form of honors for the emperors and even social, economic, or religious affiliation with imperial aspects of society were inextricably bound up in the evils of Satan (cf. Thompson 1990; A. Collins 1984:111). John also makes practical exhortations to the Christians in Asia concerning withdrawal from such contacts (cf. Klauck 1992:176–80; Harrington 1993:178–79). Thus we find the angel's concrete call for Christians to remove themselves from contact with Rome, the harlot, echoing Jeremiah's exhortation to the Israelites in Babylon (Jer 51:6, 45; cf. Isa 48:20; 52:11): "Come out of her, my people, lest you take part in her sins, lest you share in her plagues; for her sins are heaped high as heaven, and God has remembered her iniquities" (Rev 18:4).

Practically speaking, John's call to withdrawal from Babylon means that Christians living in the cities of Asia should distance themselves from any direct or indirect support of an evil empire whose demise is near. It means the rejection of the politically moderate position that characterized a more prominent trajectory of Christianity in the region and has implications regarding participation in economic life in the cities. While many Christians in Asia Minor did not perceive a problem with such participation in imperial aspects of civic life, John did, and it seems that his was a minority opinion.[9]

To say that John's is a minority opinion within Christianity is not to say that his views of empire, though extreme, are totally without reason. When we consider the reasons why John condemns the empire it becomes clearer how participation in imperial dimensions of civic life by Christian assemblies (i.e., association-like behavior) could be viewed as a threat. John, like some other Jewish authors discussed earlier (e.g., *Sibylline Oracles*), chooses to focus on the negative characteristics of imperialism and criticizes the empire based on interrelated military, economic, and religious factors. These factors, though selective, do have some basis in the reality of Roman rule.

Several reasons for John's negative posture in relation to the Roman Empire are discernible. Although not explicitly stated in the Apocalypse, it is the power of Rome and the emperor that recently manifested itself in the slaughter of Christians following the fire at Rome (under Nero) and in the destruction of God's temple at Jerusalem (Tacitus, *Annals* 15.43–44; Josephus, *J.W.;* cf. Marshall 2001). In John's visions, it is the military might of Rome and its apparent indestructibility that mislead people into treating Rome and its emperors as though they deserve honors on a par with God himself. "Men worshiped the dragon, for he had given his authority to the beast, and they worshiped the beast, saying 'Who is like the beast, and who can fight against it'" (Rev 13:4). It is this power that allows Rome, the harlot, to hold sway over all the kings of the earth and to profit economically from its exploitation of the provinces, even with the help of provincials who are portrayed as ignorant of this overall system of exploitation (Revelation 17–18; cf. *Sib. Or.* 3.350–57). In light of the abusive and blasphemous actions of the Roman power that are often disguised (according to John), the practice of Christians honoring the emperor could be viewed as unconscious participation in an evil system. It is the potential for deception of Christians that John is worried about. They are in danger of buying into what is, in his view, a false imperial ideology. Moreover, Christians living within a context where inhabitants regularly honored the emperors as gods and where the benefits of imperialism were praised could be misled into accepting similar ways of perceiving and acting. The potential threat to Christian groups, then, is that they would become indistinguishable from others who were deceived by the false pretensions of Roman imperial power in the cities of Asia.

In this context it is possible to see association-like behavior among congregations as a problem, as did John. Yet many others did not; other Christians and Christian leaders living in Asia Minor and elsewhere did not focus on these same factors regarding imperialism. Instead, they sought to find ways in which Christians could claim a place for themselves within polis and empire without engaging fully in religious honors for the emperors or other gods and goddesses.

Imperial Cults: Rhetoric and Reality

In the process of persuading his readers that they need to remove themselves from such involvements in civic life, John also speaks, in chapter 13, of "worshiping the beast" or its image (*eikōn*) (drawing much symbolism from the book of Daniel). According to John's vision of the future, the great red dragon, Satan, gave the first beast from the sea "his power and his throne and great authority" and people "worshiped the beast, saying,

'Who is like the beast, and who can fight against it?'" (Rev 13:1–4 RSV). The second beast, who is also a "false prophet," promoted the worship of the first beast, causing "those who would not worship the image of the beast to be slain" and marking those who did with the number of the beast, which was required to engage in buying and selling (13:11–18). Those who worship the beast and receive the mark, John emphasizes, will ultimately "drink the wine of God's wrath," being tormented forever (14:9–11). To the contrary, those who refuse to do so and face death will have their names written in the book of life.

Scholars most often recognize John's depiction of the beasts as some kind of allusion to worship of the emperor or imperial cults. Yet they differ on how they would evaluate the relation between rhetoric and reality, between John's apocalyptic imagery here and the actual characteristics of imperial cults in Roman Asia and their importance with respect to the contemporary situation of Christians. In light of what we found earlier, the traditional approach that gives priority to the Apocalypse and reads imperial cults and persecution in light of the book (cf. Scherrer 1979) is not plausible, even for the time of Domitian. Furthermore, the influences of Jewish Scripture on the details of John's futuristic scenarios, especially episodes such as Nebuchadnezzar's command that all should "fall down and worship the gold statue" or else be "thrown into a furnace of blazing fire" (Daniel 3), should also caution us in assuming a direct relation between what John describes in Revelation 13 and the realities of imperial cults or persecution as faced by Christians in Asia.[10]

Instead of asking what chapter 13 of the Apocalypse tells us about imperial cults, then, we need to ask, In light of what we know about imperial cults and the actual persecution of Christians, how does John's futuristic, apocalyptic scenario relate to them? There are indeed aspects of imperial cults or other historical events around John's time that did inform his depiction of the future (cf. Bauckham 1993:445–48). In some ways, John's cult of the beast *is* modeled on aspects of imperial cults. The first beast from the sea is the emperor. It seems probable, though, that John has the myth of Nero returned from the dead (*redivivus*) in mind when he speaks of this first beast. This suggestion is based, in part, on the reference to the beast's "mortal wound" that was healed (13:3) and, more importantly, the interpretation of phrases in 17:9–11: "The beast that you saw *was, and is not, and is to ascend* from the bottomless pit and go to perdition. . . . This calls for a mind with wisdom: the seven heads are seven mountains on which the woman is seated; they are also seven kings, five of whom have fallen, one is, the other has not yet come, and when he comes he must remain only a little while. As for the *beast that was and is not*, it is an eighth but it belongs to the seven, and it goes to perdition." This is not the place to engage in a full discussion concerning the identification of the heads with specific emperors, or to explain related passages in chapter 13 (including the meaning of the number 666; see Court 1979:122–53; Bauckham 1993:384–452; Beale 1999:872–75). Here it is sufficient to point out that the phrases emphasized above would suggest that, when he records his visions, John has in mind the widespread myth (among Jews, Christians, and others) that the emperor Nero would return from the dead.[11]

Considering the futuristic element in the depiction of the first beast, John may or may not have a particular contemporary figure in mind as a model when he speaks of the second beast. But since the second beast "exercises all the authority of the first beast" and plays a key role in promoting the worship of the image of the first beast (13:12–18), some scholars suggest that John may be thinking of provincial figures associated with imperial cults, such as high priests or the council of Asia (cf. S. Price 1984:197; Friesen 1996). Yet these identifications are not certain.

There are further possible connections between John's rhetoric and contemporary realities. John's references to the attractiveness of worshiping the emperor (e.g., Rev 13:4) do reflect the nature of imperial cults as a spontaneous response on the part of civic inhabitants to the power of the emperor and Rome. But he also envisions that worship of the emperor will be enforced in the future with the threat of death. Regarding the latter, it is possible (though not likely) that John was familiar with the test that some Christians faced when brought to trial (cf. Downing 1988:119; Klauck 1992:161–63), namely, ritual acts in honor of the emperor alongside other gods. If so, John has clearly magnified the role of imperial cults specifically, for we found that these cults played only a modest role in actual persecutions by and beyond the time of Trajan, and there is no evidence of such tests before Pliny's time (c. 110 C.E.). The worship-or-die aspect of John's portrait may well have been influenced by biblical sources (see esp. Dan 3).

Regarding John's depiction of the slaughter of Christians, Nero's brutal execution of Jesus' followers after the fire in Rome may also have been fresh in John's memory, but the mass slaughter envisioned in the book certainly does not (nor does it claim to) reflect actual persecution in Asia Minor in the late first century. If John was in fact writing after the Romans' destruction of Jerusalem, we can better understand why he, like the Jewish authors of *4 Ezra* and *2 Baruch*, might tend to portray the imperial power taking brutal actions against God's people.

Despite these possible connections between rhetoric and reality, we need to realize that the Apocalypse is not, nor does it claim to be, a historical commentary on the actual situation in Roman Asia, nor is it a response to imperial cults of the time specifically. Scholars such as Adela Yarbro Collins and Leonard L. Thompson make similar observations.[12] Rather than history, it is an apocalyptic portrayal of the forthcoming final confrontation between the forces of good (God, the Lamb, those in the book of life) and the forces of evil (Satan, the beast, those who worship the beast) whose purpose is, in part, to persuade Christians in the seven cities of Asia to take certain oppositional stances toward society in the present, especially its imperial dimensions. This does not mean that the Apocalypse was out of touch with reality, for as I discussed earlier, John chooses to portray the futuristic confrontation of Christianity and empire in this manner for several reasons. Writing in an apocalyptic tradition, John employs common biblical imagery used in criticism of ruling powers, placing the Roman imperial power, with its claims to be god,[13] on the side of evil in the final eschatological battle. Within this framework, involvements in imperial facets of civic life, which John epitomizes as worshiping the beast (Rev 13) or fornicating with the harlot (chaps. 17–18), are among the most dangerous forms of idolatry. These two themes, idolatry and fornication, are also prominent in the opening letters of the Apocalypse.

John's Opponents in the Letters: Nicolaitans and Others

A third way in which the evidence discussed throughout this study sheds light on the Apocalypse concerns John's explicit opponents. Once again drawing on biblical language and imagery, John accuses the Nicolaitans and the followers of "Jezebel" and "Balaam" of eating idol food and of committing "fornication," a traditional metaphorical reference to involvement in specific aspects of society.[14] These adversaries are noteworthy at Ephesus, but their influence on the congregations is most threatening, in John's view, at Pergamum and Thyatira (Rev 2:6, 14–17, 19–23). As several scholars note, the activities of these opponents most likely included imperial dimensions, which is further indicated in the prominence of anti-imperial themes throughout the rest of the book.[15] What, concretely, were these opponents doing and in what contexts were they engaging in what John considers idolatry?

The largely neglected epigraphic evidence concerning associations in the seven cities provides some answers to this in two interrelated ways. First, the analogy of associations suggests a range of typical activities and practices, including honors for and dedications to the emperors, in which small groups in the civic setting did engage, including synagogues and assemblies. Honoring the emperors is a norm that John clearly opposes. It seems quite possible that John singles out the opponents for special castigation because their "fornication," that is, their participation in such aspects of society, is more pronounced or explicit than in other Christian or Jewish circles. Perhaps "Jezebel," as a leader or benefactor of a Nicolaitan group, was a woman of relatively high standing in Thyatira (possibly a Julia Severa-type figure) who took honoring the emperors and other imperial representatives, as well as full participation in the economic life of the city, as appropriate activities for members of the Christian groups with whom she affiliated.[16]

Second, one of the opponents' compromises with society (according to John's accusations) involved eating idol food (*eidōlothyta*), a hotly debated group-society issue among early Christians (cf. Acts 15; 21:25; *Did.* 6.3; Borgen 1988; J. Brunt 1985; Aune 1997–98, 1:191–94). Mary Douglas's (1973) anthropological studies demonstrate clearly that boundaries between the physical body and things in the external world are often symbolic of boundaries between a given cultural group and society. Thus the issue of what food one eats or does not eat can be indicative of group-society relations. As Paul's first letter to the Corinthian Christians indicates, a person might encounter idol food or sacrificial meat (that had previously been offered to the gods) in a number of settings in cities of the empire, from the marketplaces, to temple dining halls, to the private dinners held in the home of a friend (cf. Gooch 1993; Willis 1985). Perhaps the most widespread social contexts for banquets involving the consumption of food that had been sacrificed to the gods or emperors in Asia were the communal meals of associations and guilds.

We have seen that occupational and other associations were a widespread aspect of life throughout Asia. In cities like Thyatira we found guilds of merchants, coppersmiths, bakers, linen workers, dyers, clothing cleaners, tanners, and leather workers, among others. Furthermore, being a member in such groups was less than "voluntary" in the sense that, if one was a dyer or merchant, one naturally belonged to or associated with one's fellow workers in the guild of dyers or merchants. One's occupation was in many ways a determining factor in social and economic affiliations. Both Jews and Christians engaged in occupations reflecting the spectrum of known guilds, and we have encountered multiple memberships or affiliations among some Jews in chapter 7. In a sense we should be surprised if a person were to cut off contacts with fellow workers once affiliated with another group such as the Christians or the local synagogue. For removing oneself would sever the network connections necessary for business activity, thereby threatening one's means of livelihood. Paul himself, who seems to have considered his occupation as a craftsman an important component of his identity, found the workshop or guild hall a key setting for his missionary activity (cf. 1 Thess 2:9; 4:9–12; 1 Cor 2:12; 4:8–13; 9:12–15, 19; 2 Cor 11–13; Hock 1980; Malherbe 1983:89–90).

In this light, it is quite plausible to suggest that some of the opponents of John were continuing in their occupational affiliations and sustaining memberships in other local guilds, where they encountered sacrificial food.[17] Several scholars, following the lead of W. M. Ramsay, also make the suggestion that some of these Christians were participating within local guilds, especially at Thyatira.[18] Still, these scholars do not fully discuss the extensive epigraphic evidence outlined throughout this study specifically concerning imperial and other dimensions of association life.

The suggestion that John is objecting, in part, to Christians joining in the activities of guilds and taking part in commercial networks associated with the imperial presence corresponds well with other economic dimensions of his book. We find John criticizing the Christians at Laodicea who are wealthy, probably due to involvement in mercantile activities: "I know your works: you are neither cold nor hot. . . . For you say, I am rich, I have prospered, and I need nothing; not knowing that you are wretched, pitiable, poor, blind, and naked" (Rev 3:15–18). John also links involvement in trade with worship of the beast in his futuristic portrayal of society. For only those who have the mark of the beast, that is, those who associate with Rome or "worship the beast," will be able to "buy and sell" (13:16–18).

Perhaps most telling is John's condemnation of those merchants (*emporoi*), shippers (*nautai*), and craftsmen (*technitai*) who "fornicate" with the harlot, Babylon/Rome, and mourn at her ultimate demise (Rev 18):

> The merchants . . . who gained wealth from her will stand far off, in fear of her torment, weeping and mourning aloud, "Alas, alas, for the great city that was clothed in fine linen, in purple and scarlet, bedecked with gold, with jewels, and with pearls! In one hour all this wealth has been laid waste." And all the shipmasters and seafaring men, sailors and all whose trade is on the sea, stood far off and cried out as they saw the smoke of her burning, "What city was like the great city?" And they threw dust on their heads, as they wept and mourned. (18:15–19 RSV)

As both Richard Bauckham (1991:84) and J. Nelson Kraybill (1996: 100–101) suggest, it seems probable that these merchants included at least some Christians in their number. Groups of merchants and shippers, Italian or otherwise, played a key role in the local economic life of the cities in Asia, also actively participating in honors for emperors and officials within civic networks. Thus, for example, in the mid-first century the "merchants (*emporoi*) who are engaged in business in Ephesus" set up a monument in honor of "their savior and benefactor, the proconsul, Gaius Pompeius Longinus Gallus, son of Publius" (*AE* [1968] 153, no. 485, revising *IEph* 800; cf. *IGR* IV 860 from Laodicea). The association of Roman businessmen at Apameia (east of Laodicea) joined with the civic institutions and a guild of workers to honor P. Manneius Rhuso (of Italian descent), the polis's benefactor and ambassador to the emperors (*IGR* IV 791; 1st century C.E.; cf. *IGR* IV 785–86, 788–96; *MAMA* VI 183–84).

John calls on Christians to distance themselves from such aspects of civic life, but it is not always clear what, practically speaking, John expected these people living in the cities of Asia to do. He certainly wanted them to avoid sacrificial food that had been offered to imperial and other gods within any social context, including the communal meals of guilds. He also would want them to avoid the guilds altogether since imperial rituals and other practices he considered idolatrous took place in them. This would require that Christians limit social and business contacts with fellow workers and other merchants and traders. He also certainly did not approve of involvement in the production and trade of goods that contributed, in his view, to the well-being of an evil empire whose ultimate demise was imminent. How, then, did John expect Christians to make a living? Were they to live in isolation from others? What occupations were acceptable? How would a local Christian merchant or dyer continue in his or her occupation without maintaining at least some friendly contacts with both fellow workers and with wealthier customers or patrons? How was one to avoid all contact with an imperialism that was embedded within virtually all dimensions of the polis? The Apocalypse does not provide clear answers to such questions, and we are left wondering.

The Christian opponents of John who participated in such contexts and practices were not likely to perceive their own behaviors as unsuitable compromise or idolatry, as did John. Instead, they would view this as a normal or necessary part of living and working within the polis. Perhaps one of the Nicolaitans or followers of "Jezebel" might have offered, if questioned, an (ideological or theological) justification of such participation in the communal meals of associations in a manner similar to those of the Corinthian Christians who knew that "an idol has no real existence" and that "there is no God but one" (1 Cor 8:4; cf. Schüssler Fiorenza 1985:117–20; Räisänen 1995:1633–37). The average Nicolaitan Christian would not likely have understood the question, however, since participation in such social and economic contexts had been and apparently continued to be a normal and significant part of their lives. Total separation and exclusivity in relation to all such facets of civic life would not have entered their minds. John, whose apocalyptic and sectarian outlook led him to perceive things differently, tried to convince them otherwise. Between these views and practices of John and the Nicolaitans lies a spectrum of possibilities regarding interaction with, involvement in, or separation from imperial, occupational, and other aspects of society.

Conclusion

As this case study shows, an oversimplified categorization of synagogues and congregations as sects in the modern sociological sense does less to illuminate group-society interactions than does a comparison with other models or social groupings from the ancient context, chief among them associations and guilds. A comparison of imperial dimensions of association life in Roman Asia specifically, with attention to both similarities and differences, furthers our understanding in several respects. Some synagogues and congregations did involve themselves in imperial honorary activities that have parallels within many associations, including special honors for Roman authorities. In some respects Jews and Christians could also incorporate the emperors or imperial officials within the internal religious life of the group, at least in the form of prayers (though not worship) for these figures. Such similarities draw attention to one of the neglected ways in which these groups, like other associations, found places for themselves within the sociocultural framework of the polis, simultaneously lessening the potential for tensions between the group and society. This crossover in practice also suggests at least some commonalities in the relative position of the emperors within the worldviews of some Jews, Christians, and other civic inhabitants.

Yet there was also a range of opinions on the matter within both Jewish and Christian circles, reflecting differing notions on where and how starkly the lines between group and society were to be drawn. In contrast to many others, the Apocalypse clearly opposed any form of honoring the emperor (the "beast" in his view) or affiliating with the imperial presence.

John sought to persuade others who were more involved in imperial and other dimensions of civic life to adopt his sectarian stance.

Unlike other associations, participation among Jews and Christians stopped short of conscious or active involvement in religious rituals for the emperors as gods. This notwithstanding that some Christians or Jews could find themselves within social settings, such as associations, where these rituals did take place and where sacrificial food was consumed in the context of communal meals. Yet the failure to engage in imperial religious ceremonies should be understood within the broader context of Christians' and Jews' avoidance of full participation in worship of the gods and goddesses generally (their monotheism), since rituals for the imperial gods were embedded within the broader religious life of the polis in Roman Asia.

Following from the latter point is that imperial cults in and of themselves were not a principal causal factor of occasional conflicts between civic inhabitants and either Jews or Christians, nor of the intermittent persecution of Christians specifically. Instead, the principal source of sporadic tensions between these groups and others in the civic context most often pertained to Jewish and Christian "atheistic" practices and worldviews. Yet acknowledgment of this potential source of tensions should not lead us to exaggerate its effects on the everyday lives of Jews and Christians in Asia, who could in many respects live and work peaceably alongside others within the civic context and, as groups, participate in some aspects of life in the polis under Roman rule.

Conclusion

Our visit to the cities of Roman Asia has brought us into the world of early Christians and Jews and has shed new light on life within a variety of associations, synagogues, and congregations in antiquity. We have seen some important features of cultural life in the Roman Empire. The visit has also begun to point us in new directions for fruitful research on social and religious life among these groups. Rather than merely reiterating conclusions, here I sketch out some prospects for research in this area, particularly with respect to the value in comparing associations with synagogues and congregations.

This study barely scratched the surface of the abundant archeological evidence available concerning social and religious history in Roman Asia, let alone other regions. Despite the shortcomings of such evidence, it provides glimpses into the everyday lives of persons, groups, and communities of specific localities in a way that other evidence does not. However, monuments and inscriptions should not be used merely as a supplement to what we can know of the realities of ancient life from (often elite-produced) legal or literary sources, whether Greco-Roman, Jewish or Christian. Rather, artifacts provide an alternative window into life in the ancient world that can actually change our understanding of society and religion within it. Thus, for instance, our assessment of the relation between Roman imperialism and associations in the provinces radically changed when we looked at the ongoing lives of these groups from the perspective of epigraphic and archeological remains.

When it comes to the use of artifactual evidence in the study of Christianity and Judaism or their "backgrounds," gone should be the days of picking and choosing bits of evidence from the Greco-Roman world based on questions dictated by Christian or Jewish literary evidence. We need to approach the study of phenomena in the ancient world on their own terms with attention to regional factors, placing evidence within as broad a context as possible; only then should we turn to the question of how this might shed light on Christianity or Judaism. Inscriptions and other material remains can significantly modify or even transform our understanding of various synagogues and congregations that lived and developed within the Roman Empire.

This study contributed in this area by looking at associations within civic communities in a specific region of the Roman Empire, the province of Asia. Moreover, associations deserve study in their own right. Here I have nowhere near exhausted the evidence for social, religious, and other dimensions of association life in Asia Minor, let alone other regions of the empire. Attention to group-society and other sociohistorical issues will help us to plot these groups on the cultural map of the ancient Mediterranean world.

Concentrating on imperial dimensions of association life specifically allowed me to elucidate one important aspect of the lives of these groups, challenging the tension-centered approaches of many scholars. Both associations' external relations within social networks and internal socioreligious activities suggest that the emperors and other imperial aspects were important and integrated elements within group life. Participation in monumental and ritual honors associated with imperial figures was among the means by which associations could tend toward integration within society (polis, province, and empire), also staking a claim regarding their place within the cosmos as they understood it. Most associations were not, as often assumed, subversive or anti-Roman groups, even though on occasion some could be involved in local civic unrest.

Attention to these groups that reflect various strata of the population illuminated broader issues concerning religion, culture, and society in Roman Asia. Some scholars approach the study of antiquity with inadequate and, often, modernizing definitions of religion in terms of the personal feelings of the individual, leading them to discount the significance of various phenomena, including imperial cults. Further theoretical work concerning how we should approach the study of religion in antiquity may provide more adequate concepts and categories. Contrary to common scholarly depictions, the evidence of imperial rituals within associations suggested the genuine importance of the imperial gods within religious life at the local level. Far from being solely political with no religious significance for the populace, imperial cults and the gods they honored were thoroughly integrated at various levels within society. Further regional studies of both imperial cults and associations will allow us to better evaluate what is or is not distinctive about Roman Asia, or specific localities within it, in this regard.

Moreover, attention to local associations helped to elucidate the nature of imperial rule. By virtue of its passive-reactive approach, Roman rule depended on ongoing relations with provincial communities and inhabitants. We have begun to see ways in which civic inhabitants and groups, including associations, synagogues, and congregations, could be part of the webs of relations that linked the polis to province and empire. We have gained a glimpse into some of the mechanisms that perpetuated imperialism in society of the time, but there remains much more to do in this area.

Some of the most important contributions of this study pertain to early Christianity and diaspora Judaism. Moreover, we have seen the value in comparing associations with both synagogues and congregations on a regional basis. Such comparison provides a new angle of vision on the New Testament and other early Christian and Jewish literature. Challenging a widespread, sectarian or tension-centered approach, I suggested a more complex scenario for group-society interaction by drawing on both social-scientific insights regarding acculturation and the ancient analogy of associations. Most directly affected was our reading of documents pertaining to Asia Minor, including 1 Peter, John's Apocalypse, the Pastoral Epistles, Ignatius's epistles, the *Martyrdom of Polycarp*, and the *Acts of Paul*.

We began to better understand the social and cultural world in which many early Christians lived and breathed, as well as neglected areas of positive interaction alongside tension and sporadic persecution. First Peter, on the one hand, and John's Apocalypse, on the other, illustrated the variety in Christian perspectives regarding how one was to inhabit the Greco-Roman world: one advocating alleviation of tensions through positive interaction and the other pushing for strong or sectarian boundaries between Christians and society. Nonetheless, both were concerned with the maintenance of distinctive Christian identities. Areas of positive interaction within society on the part of Jews or Christians helped to alleviate other areas of tension, which were centered on the fact that synagogues and congregations were—in regard to their monotheism at least—minority cultural groups. The potential for intermittent conflicts should not blind us to areas of participation in civic life by these minority cultural groups.

Yet comparison had further repercussions for our view of early Christian social history that extended beyond the focus on Asia Minor. Inscriptions and archeology shed new light on Paul and his communities at various points in our study, including issues of identity in Pauline circles. Occupational identity and networks were an important basis of association in the ancient world. Paul often expressed his own identity in terms of his occupation as a handworker (tent maker), and we found that the workshop and its networks were a significant social context for early Christian preaching. These networks could apparently form the primary basis of some nascent Christian groups, or guilds, like the one at Thessalonica. Furthermore, the importance of fictive kin language within some associations, including the use of the term "brothers" for fellow members and "mother" or "father" for leaders, provided a new framework for understanding the use of this language within some Pauline groups as well.

The Pauline correspondence also evinces the ongoing negotiation of group-society relations and the definition of group boundaries. Interactions between congregations and surrounding society could be far more complex than common sectarian approaches often suggest. It is in the light of the banqueting purposes of associations and the potential for multiple affiliations that we can better grasp the issue of eating idol food at Corinth (1 Cor 8–10), for example. Christian leaders such as Paul would need to decide what they felt was acceptable practice in relation to the broader cultural world, and not all followers of Jesus would agree on a definition in this regard. Stances toward the empire and both civic and imperial functionaries were also part of this ongoing negotiation of group-society interaction. The moderate perspective on the Roman Empire advocated by Paul in his letter to the assemblies at Rome was paralleled in Christian literature from Asia; both found concrete analogies in the stances and practices of many other associations in the cities of the Greco-Roman world. Thus comparison is clearly a fruitful endeavor in many respects, extending beyond our regional focus.

Most importantly, though, our case study of imperial dimensions of civic life specifically helped us to comprehend the place of Jews and Christians within society in Roman Asia Minor. In this regard, associations provided instructive models for comparison with both synagogues and congregations. Such a comparison employing inscriptional evidence rooted this study firmly in the social and cultural realities of life in the world of polis and empire. The results problematized the widespread sectarian reading of these groups. There was a range of attitudes and practices among Jews and Christians with respect to imperial and other dimensions of the polis, reflecting variant opinions on where and how starkly the line between group and society was to be drawn. Further regional and comparative studies along these lines may help us not only to better understand synagogues and congregations, but also to plot various groups and communities (Greek, Roman, Jewish, Christian, and other) on the sociocultural map of the Roman Empire.

Appendix

Some Dionysiac Associations

Translation Key

bakchoi = "bacchants"; *boukoloi* = "cowherds"; *hymnōdoi* = "hymn singers"; *mystai* = "initiates"; *presbyteroi* = "presbyters"; *speira:* "company"; *thiasos, thiasōtai* = "cult society," "cult-society members"

Asia

Akmoneia
> *MAMA* VI 239 (initiates of the sacred cult society of Dionysos Kathegemon)

Dorylaion, Nakoleia, and surrounding villages:
> *IPhrygDB* III 1 (initiates); *IPhrygHaspels* 144 (initiates of Zeus Dionysos); *IPhrygHaspels* 139 (initiates of Zeus Dionysos)

Ephesus
> *IEph* 275 (c. 119 C.E.; initiates), 293 (c. 180–192 C.E.; initiates), 434 (Baccheion), 1595 (initiates of Dionysos Phleos), 1600 (late 2d century C.E.; mysteries), 1601 (initiates), 1602 (initiates)

Erythrai
> *IErythrai* 132 (c. 139–161 C.E.; priest of Dionysos and a "sacred house [*oikos*]"), 222 (3d century C.E.; company of *Brachyleitai*)

Halikarnassos
> Cole 1993:293 (bacchants)

271

Knidos
  IKnid 160 (c. 350–250 B.C.E.; bacchants)
Kos
  IRhodM 492 (1st century B.C.E.–1st century C.E.; cult society of Bac-
    chists)
Kyme
  IKyme 17 (c. 27–26 B.C.E.; cult-society members), 30 (cult-society mem-
    bers)
Kyzikos
  CIG 3679 (Bacchic bankers [?])
Magnesia on the Maeander
  IMagnMai 117 (early 2d century C.E.; initiates and a "sacred house
    [*oikos*]"), 215 (mid-2d century C.E.; cult societies)
Miletos and Didyma
  Henrichs 1978:148 (3d–2d century B.C.E.; female bacchants); *IDidyma*
    502 (friends of Dionysos, Baccheion)
Pergamum
  IPergamon 222 (cowherds of Dionysos Kathegemon), 319–20 (com-
    pany), 485–88 (1st–early 2d century C.E.; cowherds); Conze and
    Schuchhardt 1899:179, no.31 (c. 108–109 C.E.; dancing cowherds);
    von Prott 1902:94–95, no. 86 (c. 197–159 B.C.E.; bacchants of the
    euastic god), *SEG* 29 (1979) 1264 (late Hellenistic era; chief
    cowherd of Dionysos Kathegemon)
Philadelphia and Vicinity
  ILydiaKP I 42 (2d century C.E.; initiates of Kathegemon Dionysos);
    TAM V 297 (Kula; 255/266 C.E.; relief depicting a bacchant)
Rhodes
  IG XII.1 155 (1st century B.C.E.; *koinon* of Dionysiasts); *ILindos* 449 (c.
    100 C.E.; mysteries of Bacchos Dionysos)
Saittai and Vicinity
  TAM V 91 (167 C.E.; Dion[ysiasts]), 92 (168 C.E.; synod of young
    men); 127 (249/250 C.E.; relief depicting a bacchant), 477 (17-year-
    old fellow initiate; 240 C.E.)
Smyrna
  ISmyrna 600–601 (157–158 C.E. and 161–163 C.E.; synod of Breseus
    Dionysos), 622 (c. 129–131 C.E.; initiates of Breseus Dionysos), 639
    (mid-late 2d century C.E.; sacred synod of performers and initiates
    of Dionysos Breseus), 728 (2d–3d century C.E.; Dionysiac-Orphic
    cult regulation for the initiates in the sanctuary of Bromios), 729 (c.
    247–249 C.E.; initiates of Breseus Dionysos), 730 (2d century C.E.;

dedication in connection with "Dionysos before the city"), 731 (c. 80–83 C.E.; synod of initiates), 732 (late 1st century C.E. or mid-2d century C.E.; initiates), 733 (2d–3d century C.E.; Baccheion), 734 (initiates); *ISmyrna* (addenda), 3:352, no. III (late Hellenistic era; Dionysiasts)

Teos

IGLAM 106 (initiates of Setaneios god Dionysos)

Thera Island

OGIS 735 (c. 150 B.C.E.; *koinon* of Bacchists)

Thyatira and Vicinity

TAM V 744 (Julia Gordos; hierophant in the mysteries of Dionysos), 817 (Attaleia Agroeira; 165 C.E.; narthex-bearing company), 822 (198 C.E.; narthex-bearing company)

Other Provinces of Asia Minor

Amastris (Bithynia-Pontus)

SEG 35 (1985) 1327 = Jones 1990:53–63 (155 C.E.; epitaph of a 30-year-old athlete who had led the rites of Dionysos)

Daskyleion (Bithynia-Pontus)

IBithMendel I 20 (epitaph mentioning cult societies and the initiates of Dionysos Bromios)

Iconium (Galatia)

CIG 4000 (attendants of Dionysos)

Seleucia on the Calycadnos (Cilicia)

IKilikiaHW 183 (initiates)

Termessos (Pamphylia/Pisidia)

TAM III 922 (rites of Bacchus)

Dacia and Moesia

Callatis Area

SEG 27 (1977) 384 (reign of Tiberius; cult-society members)

Dionysopolis Area

IGBulg 22bis (241–244 C.E.; initiates?); *BE* (1952) 160–61, no. 100 (company of Asians)

Histria

IGLSkythia I 99 (218–222 C.E.; company of Dionysiasts, presbyters), 100 (hymn-singing presbyters of Dionysos), 167 (161–211 C.E.; hymn-singing presbyters of Dionysos), 199 (compnay of Dionysiasts): 208 (hymn singers of Dionysos), 221 (hymn singers of Dionysos)

Tomis
> *IGLSkythia* II 120 (Bacchic cult society)

Thracia

Apollonia
> *IGBulg* 401 (initiates and/or cowherds)

Bizye Area
> *IGBulg* 1864 (fellow initiates), 1865 (Baccheion, initiates)

Byzantion
> *IByzantion* 30–35 (initiates of Dionysos Kallon), 39 (early 2d century C.E.; cult-society members of Dionysos Parabolos, perhaps fishermen)

Cillae
> *IGBulg* 1517 (241–244 C.E.; company), 1518 (company)

Heraklea-Perinthos
> *IGR* I 787 (196–198 C.E.; Baccheion of Asians)

Greece and Macedonia

Athens
> *CIG* 956 (cult-society members); *IG* II.2 1368 (c. 177 C.E.; *Iobacchoi*, Baccheion)

Cenchreae
> *IG* IV 207 (cowherd)

Megara
> *CIG* 1059 (Baccheion)

Physkos
> *LSCG* 181 (2d C.E.; *koinon*, cowherds, maenads)

Thasos
> *IG* XII.8 387 (Baccheion)

Thessalonica
> *IG* X.2 259 (1st century C.E.; initiates, "house [*oikos*]"), 260 (3d century C.E.; initiates, cult society), 261 (2d–3d century C.E.; "house" [*oikos*]), 503 (132 C.E.; priest of Dionysos), 506 (209 C.E.; cult societies of Dionysos)

Italy

Rome and Vicinity

IGUR 156 (sacred company), 157 (hierophant of Kathegemon Dionysos), 160 (Torre Nova; 160 C.E.; initiates), 1169 (7-year-old boy priest and initiate of the mysteries of Dionysos Kathegemon, initiates, friends), 1228 (7-year-old boy participant in the "*orgia* for Dionysos"); Merkelbach 1971 (Tusculum; 10-year-old female dance leader of the cult society)

Abbreviations

Epigraphic, Papyrological, and Prosopographical Abbreviations Cited in the Text

(Compare the abbreviations in Horsley and Lee 1994 [for Greek epigraphic volumes] and Oates et al. 1992 [for papyrological volumes].)

AE	Cagnat, Merlin, and Gagé 1888–
BE	Haussoullier, Reinach, and Roussel 1888–
CCCA	Vermaseren 1987
CCIS	Vermaseren and Lane 1983–89
CIG	Boeckh 1828–77
CIJ	Frey 1936–52
CIL	Mommsen et al. 1893–
CIMRM	Vermaseren 1956–60
CMRDM	Lane 1971–76
CPJ	Tcherikover and Fuks 1957–64
DFSJ	Lifshitz 1967
GCRE	Oliver 1989
GIBM	Hicks, Newton, and Hirschfeld 1874–1916
IAdramytt	Stauber 1996
IAlexandriaK	Kayser 1994
IAlexTroas	Ricl 1997
IAnkyra	Bosch 1967
IApamBith	Corsten 1987
IAphrodSpect	Rouché 1993

IAsMinLyk I	Benndorf and Niemann 1884
IAsMinLyk II	Petersen and Luschan 1889
IAssos	Merkelbach 1976
IBithMendel	Mendel 1900, 1901
IBoiotRoesch	Roesch 1982
IByzantion	Lajtar 2000
ICarie	Robert and Robert 1954
IDelos	Roussel and Launey 1937
IDidyma	Rehm 1958
IEgJud	Horbury and Noy 1992
IEgPortes	Bernand 1984
IEph	Engelmann, Wankel, and Merkelbach 1979–84
IErythrai	Engelmann and Merkelbach 1972–74
IEurJud	Noy 1993–95
IG	Gaertringen, et al. 1873–
IGBulg	Mihailov 1958–70
IGLAM	Le Bas and Waddington 1972
IGLSkythia	Pippidi and Russu 1983–
IGLSyria	Sartre 1982
IGR	Cagnat, Toutain, and Jovgvet 1906–27
IGUR	Moretti 1968–91
IHadrianoi	Schwertheim 1987
IHerakleaPont	Jonnes and Ameling 1994
IHierapJ	Judeich 1898
IHierapPenn	Pennacchietti 1966–67
IIasos	Blümel 1985
IIlion	Frisch 1975
IKalchedon	Merkelbach 1980
IKilikiaBM	Bean and Mitford 1965, 1970
IKilikiaHW	Heberdey and Wilhelm 1894
IKios	Corsten 1985
IKlaudiop	Becker-Bertau 1986
IKnidos	Blümel 1992
IKosPH	Hicks and Paton 1891
IKyme	Engelmann 1976
IKyzikos	Schwertheim 1980–
ILaodikeia	Robert 1969
ILindos	Blinkenberg 1941
ILLRP	Degrassi 1963–65
ILydiaB	Buresch 1898

ILydiaH	Herrmann 1962
ILydiaKP I	Keil and Premerstein 1910
ILydiaKP II	Keil and Premerstein 1911
ILydiaKP III	Keil and Premerstein 1914
IMagnMai	Kern 1900
IMagnSip	Ihnken 1978
IMilet	Wiegend, Kawerau, and Rehm 1889–1997
IMoesiaTH	Tacheva-Hitova 1983
IMylasa	Blümel 1987–88
INikaia	Sahin 1979–87
IPergamon	Fränkel 1890–95
IPergamonAsklep	Habicht 1969
IPhrygDB	Drew-Bear 1978
IPhrygR	Ramsay 1895–97
IPontBithM	Marek 1993
IPontEux	Latyschev 1965
IPriene	Gaertringen 1906
IPrusaOlymp	Corsten 1991
IPrusiasHyp	Ameling 1985
IRhodBresson	Bresson 1991
ISaittai	Petzl 1978, 1979
ISardBR	Buckler and Robinson 1932
ISardH	Herrmann 1996
ISardRobert	Robert 1964
ISelge	Nollé and Schindler 1991
ISide	Nollé 1993
ISmyrna	Petzl 1982–90
IStratonikeia	Sahin 1982–90
ITralles	Poljakov 1989
IXanthos	Guéraud 1931
LGS	Prott and Ziehen 1988
LSAM	Sokolowski 1955
LSCG	Sokolowski 1962
LSCGSuppl	Sokolowski 1969
MAMA	Keil, Buckler, and Calder 1928–
NewDocs	Horsley 1981–
OGIS	Dittenberger 1903–1905
PAntinoopolis	Roberts, Barns, and Zilliacus 1950–67
PEnteuxeis	Balland 1981
PIR[1]	Klebs, de Rohden, and Dessau 1897–98

PIR²	Groag, Stein, and Petersen 1933–
PLond	Kenyon, Bell, and Skeat 1893–1974
POxy	Egypt Exploration Fund 1898–
PParis	Letronne, Brunet de Presle, and Egger 1865
PPetaus	Hagedorn, Hagedorn, and Youtie 1969
PRyl	Johnson, Martin, and Hunt 1911–52
PSI	Vitelli and Norsa, 1912–79
PTebtunis	Grenfell, Hunt, and Goodspeed 1902–76
SB	Preisigke, Bilabel, and Kiessling 1915–
SEG	Roussel, Salav, and Tod 1923–
SIRIS	Vidman 1969
SIG	Dittenberger 1915–24
TAM	Kalinka, Heberdey, and Dörner 1920–

Periodical and Series Abbreviations
for the Bibliography

AGJU	Arbeiten zur Geschichte des antiken Judentums und des Urchristentums
AJA	*American Journal of Archaeology*
AJP	*American Journal of Philology*
AncSoc	*Ancient Society*
ANRW	*Aufstieg und Niedergang der römischen Welt*
AnSt	*Anatolian Studies*
BCH	*Bulletin de correspondance hellénique*
BJRL	*Bulletin of the John Rylands University Library of Manchester*
BR	*Biblical Research*
BTB	*Biblical Theology Bulletin*
CAH	*Cambridge Ancient History*
CP	*Classical Philology*
CRAI	*Comptes rendus de l'Académie des inscriptions et belles-lettres*
CRINT	Compendia rerum iudaicarum ad Novum Testamentum
CSHJ	Chicago Studies in the History of Judaism
DAWW.PH	Denkschriften der kaiserlichen Akademie der Wissenschaften in Wien, philosophisch–historische Klasse
DÖAW.PH	Denkschriften der österreichischen Akademie der Wissenschaften in Wien, philosophisch-historische Klasse
EpAn	*Epigraphica Anatolica*
EPRO	Études préliminaires aux religions orientales dans l'empire romain

GRBS	*Greek, Roman, and Byzantine Studies*
HE	Historia Einzelschriften
HFM	Historisk-filosofiske Meddelelser
HSCP	*Harvard Studies in Classical Philology*
HTR	*Harvard Theological Review*
HTS	Harvard Theological Studies
IGSK	Inschriften griechischer Städte aus Kleinasien
JAC	*Jahrbuch für Antike und Christentum*
JBL	*Journal of Biblical Literature*
JdI	Jahrbuch des kaiserlich deutschen Archäologischen Instituts
JECS	*Journal of Early Christian Studies*
JHS	*Journal of Hellenic Studies*
JJS	*Journal of Jewish Studies*
JÖAI	*Jahreshefte des Österreichischen archäologischen Instituts*
JRS	*Journal of Roman Studies*
JSNT	*Journal for the Study of the New Testament*
JSNTSup	Journal for the Study of the New Testament Supplement Series
JSOTSup	Journal for the Study of the Old Testament Supplement Series
LCL	Loeb Classical Library
MDAI(A)	*Mitteilungen des Deutschen archäologischen Instituts (Athenische Abteilung)*
NICNT	New International Commentary on the New Testament
NovT	*Novum Testamentum*
NovTSup	Novum Testamentum Supplements
NTS	*New Testament Studies*
PW	*Paulys Realencyclopädie der classischen Altertumswissenschaft*
REA	*Revue des études anciennes*
REG	*Revue des études grecques*
RevPhil	*Revue de philology*
RFIC	*Rivista di filologia e di istruzione classica*
SBLDS	Society of Biblical Literature Dissertation Series
SBLMS	Society of Biblical Literature Monograph Series
SBLSP	Society of Biblical Literature Seminar Papers
SBLTT	Society of Biblical Literature Texts and Translations
SBS	Stuttgarter Bibelstudien
SHAW.PH	Sitzungsberichte der Heidelberger Akademie der Wissenschaften, philosophisch-historische Klasse
SJLA	Studies in Judaism in Late Antiquity
SPAW	*Sitzungsberichte der königlich preussischen Akademie der*

	Wissenschaften zu Berlin
SR	*Studies in Religion/Sciences religieuses*
Sup	Supplement
TAPA	*Transactions of the American Philological Association*
StPB	Studia post-biblica
TynBul	*Tyndale Bulletin*
VC	*Vigiliae christianae*
WBC	Word Biblical Commentary
WUNT	Wissenschaftliche Untersuchungen zum Neuen Testament
WZ(H)	*Wissenschaftliche Zeitschrift der Martin Luther Universität Halle-Wittenberg*
ZPE	*Zeitschrift für Papyrologie und Epigraphik*
ZWT	*Zeitschrift für wissenschaftliche Theologie*

Notes

Introduction

1. See Pliny the Younger, *Epistles* 10.97.7–8; Lucian of Samosata, *Passing of Peregrinus* 11; Celsus in Origen, *Against Celsus* 1.1; 3.23; 8.17; Ign. *Eph.* 12.2; 19.1; Tertullian, *Apology* 38–39; Eusebius, *H.E.* 10.1.8; Josephus, *Ant.* 14.215–16, 235; Philo, *Embassy to Gaius* 312, 316; *On Virtues* 33.178. All designate Christian or Jewish groups drawing on association terminology (and some explicitly compare them, e.g., Philo, Tertullian): "association" (*koinōnia, hetaeria, factio, corpus*), "cult society" (*thiasos*), "synod" (*synodos*), "fellow initiates" (*symmystai*). Jewish groups in inscriptions from Asia Minor use the following association terminology: "synagogue," "household" (*oikos*), "settlement" (*katoikountes*), "people" (*laos*), "nation" (*ethnos*), and "associates" (*hetairoi*). For associations that use "synagogue" see, e.g., the inscription of the "synagogue of Zeus" (*IApamBith* 35; discussed in chapter two). The term *synagogos* was common terminology for a leader among associations (*thiasoi*) in the Bosporus, especially at Tanais (Ustinova 1991–92:153–54); in this case Jewish influence is quite possible, however (cf. Levinskaya 1996:105–16). At least some associations in Asia Minor, like Christians, draw on civic language in using the self-designation "assembly" (*ekklēsia*; cf. *IGLAM* 1381–82 from Aspendos, Pamphylia; Foucart 1873:223–25, no. 43 = *CIG* 2271).

2. Theodor Mommsen (1843) focused on legislative matters, and several other scholars followed this path as well (Conrat 1873; Gierke 1881; Radin 1910; Carolsfeld 1933; Duff 1938). Foucart (1873) focused on the internal life and organization of associations, and others have pursued this further (cf. Liebenam 1890; Waltzing 1895–1900; Ziebarth 1896; Kornemann 1901; Oehler 1893, 1905;

Poland 1909; San Nicolò 1912–13; Calhoun 1913). The period from the 1920s to the 1960s was relatively subdued, though several articles and studies discussed associations (cf. Tod 1933; Roberts, Skeat, and Nock 1936; Ferguson and Nock 1944; Nilsson 1957). The renewed interest in social history since the 1960s has been accompanied by attention to associations among scholars of ancient history. See, e.g., MacMullen 1966, 1974b; Schulz–Falkenthal 1966, 1971, 1973; Cenival 1972; Ausbüttel 1982; Cazanove 1986; Fellmeth 1987, 1990; Royden 1988; Fisher 1988a, 1988b; Brashear 1993; Arnaoutoglou 1994; van Nijf 1997; N. Jones 1999.

3. On social aspects of 1 Peter see Schröger 1981; Balch 1981, 1984–85, 1986; Elliott 1990, 1986a; Senior 1982; Downing 1988; Feldmeier 1992; Winter 1994. On the Apocalypse see Ramsay 1904; Aune 1981; A. Collins 1984; Schüssler Fiorenza 1985; Hemer 1986; Thompson 1990; Bauckham 1993; Scobie 1993; Slater 1998. On the Pastorals see M. MacDonald 1988; Kidd 1990. On Colossians and Ephesians see Arnold 1992, 1996; van Broekhoven 1997. On Ignatius see Malina 1978; Schoedel 1980; Maier 1991.

4. For theoretical discussions of the social sciences in the study of antiquity or early Christianity see, e.g., Carney 1975; Malina 1981; Finley 1985b; J. H. Elliott 1993; Holmberg 1990; Neyrey 1991; L. M. White 1992a–b. For a more general discussion of history and the social sciences see Burke 1992.

5. On the nature and methods of epigraphy see, e.g., Roberts and Gardener 1887–1905; Levick 1971; MacMullen 1982, 1986; Millar 1983; Mann 1985; Harris 1989; Meier 1990. On Jewish epigraphy see Kant 1987; Kraemer 1989, 1991; van der Horst 1991.

6. This excludes from primary consideration groups such as: the official age-based organizations of the gymnasia (*paides, ephēboi, neoi, gerontes/gerousia*); boards of functionaries officially involved in the ongoing management of civic sanctuaries or institutions; and, guilds of professional athletes (devoted to Herakles) or Dionysiac performers (actors, musicians, dancers), which often played an ongoing official role in civic festivals and engaged in somewhat exceptional diplomatic relations.

Chapter 1

1. To give some sense of the magnitude of this wealth, it is worth noting that an average laborer made about 1,000 sesterces *per year*, and would, therefore, have to work a total of 1,000 years without spending a penny in order to approach senatorial wealth. Due to the nature of inflation and differences in the standards of living from ancient Rome to the modern world, it is very difficult to give reliable equivalents of value in modern dollars or euros (cf. Shelton 1988:459).

2. *IMoesiaTH* II 101 (c. 200 C.E.; cf. I 13 [Troesmis], 48 [Tomis]). The name of this association, "sacred *doumos*," is indicative of Phrygian or Asian influence (cf. *TAM* V 179, 449, 470a, 483a, 536 [Saittai]; *SEG* 42 [1992] 625 [Thessalonica]). For further examples of "father" of the association as a designation for a leader or benefactor see *IPontEux* II 437, 445 (Tanais; both early 2d century C.E.); *IPontEux* IV 207, 211 (Panticapaion); *IGLSkythia* I 99 (Histria; 218–222 C.E.); *SIG*³ 1111 (Piraeus; 200–211 C.E.); *IG* XIV 1084 (Rome; 146 C.E.). On a "son of the friends-of-the-*Sebastoi*" association see *IMagnMai* 119 and Pleket 1958:7–8, no. 2. On the use of *pater* or *meter collegii* in the West see Poland 1909:371–73 and Waltzing 1895–1900, 1:446–49.

3. *PParis* 5 col. 2,5 (114 B.C.E.; mummy keepers as "brothers"); *IG* X.2.1 824 (Thessalonica; see van Nijf 1997:46); *OGIS* 189 (Philai; either 89 or 57 B.C.E.); *PParis* 42. See Vettius Valens, *Anthology* 4.11.11 (c. 170 C.E.): "I entreat you, most honorable brother of mine, along with those who are initiated" (*orkizō se, adelphe mou timiōtate, kai tous mystagōgoumenous*). Cf. Nicolo 1912, 1:33–34 n.4.; Moulton and Milligan 1952:8–9 (*adelphos*). On the use of "brother" in connection with the mysteries at Eleusis see Burkert 1987:45, 149 n.77; he nonetheless discounts this evidence in arguing that there was not a *real* sense of community among those who were initiated in the mysteries (true "communities" of Christians are Burkert's measuring stick here).

4. *IGLAM* 798 (Kotiaion, Aezanatis Valley); *IIasos* 116; *IMagnMai* 321; *IDidyma* 502 (a Dionysiac group); *IMylasa* 571–75; *TAM* V 93 (Saittai; 225 C.E.); *ISmyrna* 720; *IPontBithM* 57 (= *SEG* 35 [1985] 1337; Amastris, Pontus); *IPrusaOlymp* 24 (1st century C.E.); Hicks 1891:228–29, no. 5 (Olba, Cilicia); *IAsMinLyk* I 69 (Xanthos, Lycia). Cf. *IG* II.2 1369 (Athens; 2d century C.E.); *IG* III 1081, 1089, 1102 (Athens; c. 120s C.E.; *ephēbes*); *IGUR* 1169 (Rome).

5. The most common self-designations for such groups are *hoi pragmateuomenoi Rōmaioi*, *hoi katoikountes Rōmaioi*, and *negotiatores*, as well as *conventus* (see Hatzfeld 1919; Broughton 1938:543–54; Magie 1950:162–63, 1051–52, nn. 6–8; cf. Rauh 1993:29–41 on Italians and other associations on Delos). For the province of Asia see *IAdramytt* 19, 21; *IAssos* 14, 19–21, 28; *IPhrygR* 474, 511, 533 (Akmoneia and Sebaste); *IGR* IV 785–94 (Apameia Kelainai); *IEph* 409, 646, 884, 738, 800, 2058, 3019, 3025; *IIasos* 90; *IGR* IV 903–5, 913, 916–19 (Kibyra); *SEG* 28 (1978) 953 = *NewDocs* IV 2 (Kyzikos); *IHierapJ* 32; *IGR* IV 860, *IPhrygR* 2 (Laodicea); *IGR* IV 294, 1169 (Pergamum and Attaleia); *IGR* IV 1644 (Philadelphia); *SEG* 46 (1996) 1521 (Sardis); *ISmyrna* 534; *TAM* V 924, 1002–3 (Thyatira); *ITrall* 77, 80, 83, 145. Cf. *IGR* III 137, 292 (Isaura and Neoclaudiopolis, Galatia); *IGR* IV 965 (Paphos, Cyprus); *IBoiotRoesch* 24–26 (Thespiae, Boeotia); *CIG* 1997d (Pella, Macedonia).

6. For example, *synagōgē, oikos, katoikountes, synodos, hetairoi, ethnos*; cf. Josephus, *Ant.* 14.215–16 (*thiasos*), 235 (*synodos*). On the Israelites (Samaritans) on Delos see Bruneau 1982 = *NewDocs* VIII 12 (250–50 B.C.E.). Samaritans are also attested in Neapolis, near Thessalonica, and may have formed an association; but this bilingual inscription (Greek and Samaritan/Hebrew), which quotes from Num 6:22–27, dates to a later period (4th–6th century) (cf. *NewDocs* I 69).

7. See van der Horst 1989 (Aphrodisias); *MAMA* VI 264 = *CIJ* 766 (Akmoneia; mid-late 1st century C.E.); *IEph* 1677 = *CIJ* 745, *IEph* 1676 = *CIJ* 746; *DFSJ* 32 (Hyllarima); *CIJ* 755 (Hypaipa; 2d–3d century C.E.); *CIJ* 775–76; Miranda 1999 (Hierapolis); *CIJ* 748 (Miletos; 2d–3d century C.E.); *DFSJ* 31 (Nysa); *CIJ* 754 = *DFSJ* 28 (Philadelphia); *CIJ* 738 = *DFSJ* 13 (Phokaia; 3d century C.E.); *CIJ* 750, *DFSJ* 17–27; Kroll 2001 (Sardis); *ISmyrna* 295 = *CIJ* 741 (2d century C.E.), *ISmyrna* 697 = *CIJ* 742 (c. 124 C.E.); *CIJ* 744 = *DFSJ* 16 (Teos; 3d century C.E.); *CIJ* 752 ("Sambatheion" at Thyatira; time of Trajan [see discussion of Sabbatists further below]). Cf. Josephus, *Ant.* 14.213–67; 16.160–73.

8. Attested professions of Jews in the diaspora (from *CIJ*) include: painter (no. 109), butcher (210), teacher (333, 594, 1158c, 1266, 1268, 1269), soldier (79), slave (556, 619e), wine seller (681b), physician (600, 745), purple-dyer (777), boot seller (787), silk manufacturer (873), baker (902, 940), seller of small wares (928), clothing cleaner (929), linen seller (931), and goldsmith (1006). See van der Horst 1991:99–101. The Aphrodisias inscription includes persons of the following occupations among the main membership of the Jewish group: goldsmith, greengrocer, bronzesmith, confectioner, poulterer, rag dealer (Reynolds and Tannenbaum 1987). Philo mentions that Jews in Alexandria were involved in trade as shippers, merchants, and artisans (*Against Flaccus* 57).

9. *BE* (1952) 160–61, no.100 (Dionysopolis); *IGBulg* 480 (Montana); *IGR* I 787 (Heraklea-Perinthos; 196–198 C.E.); cf. Saucine-Sâveanu 1924:126–44, nos. 1–2 (Callatis, Moesia); *IGLSkythia* I 99, 199 (Histria, Moesia); *IGBulg* 1517 (Cillae, Thracia; 241–244 C.E.; cf. Nilsson 1957:50–51).

10. At Prusa a benefactor set up a relief depicting Cybele seated on a throne as a "promise" of benefaction to "the neighborhood"; a similar association at Prusias dedicated monuments to Zeus Soter on more than one occasion (*IPrusaOlymp* 50; 2d century C.E.; *IPrusiasHyp* 63–64; cf. *IGR* III 50; c. 102–114 C.E.). A man made fines for violation of his grave payable to Zeus Solymeus and the civic treasury at Termessos in Pamphylia, but also to the "sacred neighborhood" of the goddess Leto (*TAM* III 765; cf. *TAM* III 348).

11. Cf. Herodotus, *Histories* 2.167–68; Xenophon, *On Household Management* 4.1–6.10; Aristotle, *On Household Management* 1.2.2–3; Lucian, *Dream* 9; Pseudo-Socrates, *Epistles* 8, 9, 12, 18.

12. Because of the partial nature of our evidence, it is sometimes difficult to know whether a particular group should be categorized here or under one of the other principal social network bases. It is quite possible that a group devoted to, say, Dionysos or Demeter, who expressed this explicitly in their name, may have drawn their membership primarily from familial or occupational connections, for instance, without leaving us hints (in the surviving inscriptions) as to these origins.

13. Apollo Pleurenos: *SEG* 46 (1996) 1519–20 (Sardis; 1st century B.C.E.). Aphrodite: *IEph* 1202; Mordtmann 1885:204–7, no. 30 (Kyzikos; 1st century B.C.E.); *ILindos* 252, 391–94 (c. 10 C.E.), *SEG* 41 (1991) 654 (Rhodes); *IRhodBresson* 471 (1st century B.C.E.–1st century C.E.). Cybele (Great Mother) and Attis: *ISardBR* 17. Zeus: *MAMA* X 304, *CIG* 3857l (Aizanoi); *SEG* 40 (1990) 1192 (Akmoneia); *IPhrygR* 30–31 (Thiunta village, near Hierapolis; 2d century C.E.); *IPhrygR* 127 (Ormeleis/Killania; 207 C.E.); *IG* XII.1 161–62 (Rhodes); *TAM* V 536–37 (Maionia, near Saittai; 171 C.E.); *ISardBR* 22 (c. 100 B.C.E.), *ISardH* 3 (late 1st–2d century C.E.), *ISardH* 4 (mid-2d century C.E.); *IApamBith* 116 (near Byzantion). Heroes: *IEph* 3334 (late 1st century C.E.); *TAM* V 1098 (Thyatira; 1st century C.E.). Messengers of the gods ("angels"): *NewDocs* VI 31 (Upper Tembris valley; 3d century C.E.); Sheppard 1980–81; S. Mitchell 1999:102–5 (who links some cases to quasi-monotheistic worship of the "Most High" [Hypsistos]). Also see Paul's letter to the Christians at Colossae (Col 2:8–23), some of whom are accused of following a "philosophy" that involves worship of angels.

14. See *CMRDM* I 16–17 (Rhodes), 34 and A3 (Collyda, near Saittai), 53–54 (Maionia, near Saittai), 57 (near Saittai), 87 (Sebaste), and 127 (Tymandos, near Phrygian Apollonia); Lane 1971–76, 3:109–13.

15. See *CCIS* II 28 (Teos), 43 (Ormeleis in Pisidia; 207–208 C.E.), 46 (Rhodes; c. 100 B.C.E.), 51 (Piraeus; c. 100 B.C.E.). The Sabaziasts at Rhodes, for example, worship the god in a "male clubhouse" (*andrōn*), and a similar association in the Piraeus consisted of 51 men, both Athenian citizens as well as immigrants from Antioch, Miletos, Macedonia, Laodicea, and elsewhere. There are only three known female dedicants of monuments for Sabazios in the Roman era (*CCIS* II 58, 63, 76), none from Asia Minor (cf. Lane 1989:7–8, 45).

16. See *SIRIS* 285 (Heraklea-Latmos), 295 (= *ITrall* 86; 2d century C.E.), 307 (= *IMagnSip* 15; 2d century B.C.E. and 2d century C.E.), 314 (= *IPergamon* 338), 318–19 (Kyzikos; 1st century C.E.), 324 (= *IKios* 22; 1st century C.E.), 326 (= *IPrusaOlymp* 48; 2d century C.E.); *IPrusaOlymp* 1028 (= *SEG* 28 [1978] 1585). An association devoted to Anubis (*Synanubiastai*) is attested at Smyrna in the early 3d century B.C.E. (*SIRIS* 305 = *ISmyrna* 765). For temples of Isis or Serapis and, therefore, possible meeting places of associations of worshipers see Wild 1984, esp. nos. 9, 12, 21, and 27. Most of the Isis or Serapis associations attested in Asia Minor

that list their membership consist principally of men (including those at Kyzikos, Magnesia opposite Sipylos, and Prusa). At Magnesia, at least one member was a Roman citizen, and the group at Prusa also included one Roman citizen among the six men who were gathered around their priest, Leonides (two of them apparently relatives, perhaps brothers, of the priest).

17. The mysteries in honor of Kore at Kyzikos appear to have gained official status within the polis (see *CIG* 3663, 2666; Hasluck 1910:210–13). Mysteries of Demeter are also attested in Bithynia at both Nikomedia and Prusias (*TAM* IV 262; *IPrusiasHyp* 69). On the initiates at Messenia in Greece see Pausanias, *Description of Greece* 4.1.6. At Pessinos in Galatia, an association of farmers dedicated a structure to Demeter, perhaps their patron deity (*CIG* 4082). Two inscriptions from Rome involve an imperial freedman dedicating a monument to the goddess Kore for the association of Sardians, who may have included her as a patron deity (*IGUR* 86–87).

18. See *IEph* 213, 1210 (temple, c. 120 c.e.), 1270, 1595, 4337; *IMagnMai* 158 (cf. Strabo, *Geography* 14.1.3; Oster 1990:1671–73). On the mysteries of Demeter and Men at the nearby village of Almoura see Pleket 1970:61–74, no. 4. In the mid-2d century the initiates of Demeter at Ephesus joined with those of Dionysos Phleos (*IEph* 1595), a combination of mysteries that is also attested in Larisa, Macedonia (*IG* IX.2 573; *BE* [1959] 201, no. 224).

19. See Hepding 1910:457–59, 476, nos. 40–42 (a female hymn singer and a male initiate), 63 (the civic board of *thesmothetai* honors a male initiate); Ippel 1912:286–87, 298–99, nos. 13 (Asklepiake sets up a monument for her own "company"), 16 (a male initiate and his daughter, a hymn singer), 24 (the *thesmothetai* honor a priestess), 25 (a daughter honors her mother, a priestess of Demeter and Kore).

20. The wealthy Servilius family was prominent in the leadership of the Ephesian group in the early 1st century (*IEph* 4337), and another (probably wealthy) woman, Juliana from Magnesia, was the priestess c. 38–42 c.e. (*IMagnMai* 158). A Roman citizen named Lucius Pompeius Apollonios was their advocate in the late 1st century (*IEph* 213). There appears to be a close link between Demeter and the meeting place of the presidents (*prytaneion*) at Ephesus (cf. *IEph* 10, 1058, 1060, 1067, 1070a, 1071), and at least one female president, Terentia Aeliane, was a benefactor of the association (see *IEph* 47.19, 720a, 1595).

21. The Orphics (which were often grouped by others with Pythagoreans) were initiates (usually of Dionysos) who connected their practices to a legendary singer named Orpheus; they were known for their peculiar dietary practices (primarily vegetarianism) and objection to animal sacrifice. An ancient collection of Orphic hymns with Dionysiac connections has survived (Athanassakis 1977).

22. Of the twenty-three members mentioned in *IPergamon* 485, five (21.7 percent) certainly possess Roman citizenship. Of the seventeen members legible in Conze and Schuchardt 1899:179–80, no. 31, one is a woman and six (35.3 percent) possess Roman citizenship. In no. 32 (revision of *IPergamon* 486) only one name is legible, a woman. One cowherd, L. Aninius Flaccus, also belonged to the hymn-singers' association, which sang hymns in honor of the emperors.

23. For other dedications to Dionysos Kathegemon by associations see *MAMA* VI 239 (Akmoneia); *IGUR* 157 (Rome).

24. See *TAM* V 477 (Saittai); *CIG* 400 (Iconium); *IGUR* 1169, 1228 (Rome); Merkelbach 1971 (Tusculum). Cf. Cole 1993:288–91.

25. Hicks 1891:233–36, nos. 16–17 = *OGIS* 573 = *LSAM* 80. Evidence often discussed in connection with this inscription includes *SB* 12 = *IGR* I 1106 (a "Sambathike *synodos*" at Naukratis, Egypt); *CIJ* 752 ("Sambatheion" = "Sabbatteion" at Thyatira); *TAM* V 225 and 355 (mentioning god "Sabathikos"). Also important in this connection are personal names in inscriptions that seem to derive either from Sabbath or the god of the Sabbath. For evaluations of the evidence see Tcherikover 1964; Schürer 1973–87, 3:622–26. The new edition of Schürer states that "there seems to be little doubt that the term [Sabbatists] denotes those who observe the Sabbath" (1973–87, 3:161 n.50). They were a "pagan fellowship of those who celebrated the Sabbath" (1973–87, 3:625 n.183).

26. Levinskaya 1996:83–116, 242–46; S. Mitchell 1999:116–17; cf. Schürer 1897; contrast Ustinova 1991–92; Gibson 2001 (who suggests that these *thiasoi* are Jews, not Gentiles). As S. Mitchell's (1999) study shows, we need not always assume Jewish influence when the title "Most High" is attributed to a deity. Dedications to Hypsistos or Theos Hypsistos outnumber those for *Zeus* Hypsistos 197 to 81 (see S. Mitchell 1999:101). Mitchell warns against the common tendency among scholars to focus on dividing up the Hypsistos evidence into Jewish and "pagan" camps and instead deals with the evidence for "Hypsistarian" worship together. He proposes a more complicated process of "cross-fertilization" between local "pagan" cults (such as those for Zeus Hypsistos) and judaized forms of Hypsistos worship (among Gentiles) in this regard (S. Mitchell 1999).

For dedications to Hypsistos, Theos Hypsistos, or Zeus Hypistos in connection with associations or craftsmen in Asia Minor see the following: In a village north of Akmoneia, a coppersmith (*chalkeos*) and his wife made a dedication to Theos Hypsistos (Drew-Bear 1976:248–49, no. 2). On the island of Kos, the "sack bearers," or porters (*sakkophoroi*), dedicated a monument to Zeus Hypsistos and several other gods (*IKosSegre* EV199). In a village near Kyzikos, a man dedicated a monument depicting Zeus, Artemis, and Apollo to Zeus Hypsistos (*GIBM* IV.2 100, discussed in chapter 2). Near Miletos, a guild of farmers and a fleet of fishermen honored Ulpius Karpos, "prophet and priest of the Most Holy and Most High god" (*OGIS* 755–56; 140s C.E.). In Malos (northeast of Ankyra), a benefactor made a dedication "to the great and Most High god of heaven (*megalos theos hypsistos kai epouranios*) and to his holy angels (*hagiois . . . angelois*)" for his "house of prayer" (*proseuchē*; see Sheppard 1980–81:94–95, no. 11; late 2d–3d century C.E.). Associations devoted to Hypsistos could also be found in Thracia (*IGBulg* 1924; Serdica) and Macedonia (*NewDocs* I 5; Pydna; 250 C.E.; *IG* X.2 68; Thessalonica; late 1st century C.E.).

Chapter 2

1. For other publications of the same inscription see Perdrizet 1899:592–93, no. 1, plate IV = Goodenough 1953–68, vol. 3, fig. 845. For reliefs depicting feasts see Mitropoulou 1990, 1996; van Straten 1993.

2. For other publications of this inscription see Perdrizet 1899:593, no. 2 = Robert 1949a:42, no. 1 = *CCCA* I 252 = Pfuhl and Möbius 1977–79, vol. 2, plate 332 (with photo).

3. Similar gestures of worship appear in another relief from Kyzikos that shows a procession of eight persons, probably members of an association, with upraised hands in adoration of Cybele, who is enthroned above them with lions on either side (Hasluck 1910:217, fig. 19 = *CCCA* I 289; 1st century B.C.E.).

4. Nilsson stresses that the Dionysiac-Orphic group at Smyrna (*ISmyrna* 728 = *LSAM* 84) was an exception in maintaining the truly "sacral" character of its meals and activities. The prescriptions in this inscription, he asserts, were designed to combat the widespread "desacralization" of the Dionysiac mysteries that he otherwise assumes (1957:133–43, esp. 135, 139).

5. From Asia see, e.g., *MAMA* IX 49, 66 (a guild of farmers in the Aezanatis Valley honor Zeus Bennios and another a guild honors Mother Kouaene); Mordtmann 1885:204–7, no. 30 (merchants at Kyzikos dedicate a monument to Poseidon and Aphrodite Pontia; 1st century B.C.E.); *IG* XII.2 109 (leather workers at Mytilene set up an image of Aphrodite); *ISmyrna* 721 (the guild of silversmiths and goldsmiths repair a statue of Athena; 14–37 C.E.).

6. See Bruneau and Ducat 1983:179–85, 206–8, nos. 76, 80; Bruneau 1982; *NewDocs* VIII 12; L. White 1987; 1996, 1:37–40; 2:332–42, nos. 70–71. Cf. Rauh 1993.

7. Buckler thought that the man's name was Ulpianus Heros, but as Louis Robert (1968:581 n.4) points out, followed by Joseph Fontenrose (1988:194), the name Heros is very uncommon and the term is commonly used in inscriptions of this period to mean "deceased." Here I follow the reading (*enegkous[in ē]*) suggested by Theodor Wiegend and followed by Fontenrose (1988:193; cf. Buck 1955:27),

which is a more convincing reconstruction than Buckler's (*enegkous[ēs*), which he understands as a reference to "native country" (*hē enegkousa*; see Buckler 1923:34 n.1; cf. Parke 1985:76–77).

8. Wiegend 1904:83 = Buckler 1923:34–36, no. 3 = Fontenrose 1988:193–94, no. 19; cf. Parke 1985:76–79. W. H. Buckler and others (e.g., de Ste. Croix 1981:273; MacMullen 1966:176) are stretching things a bit far in interpreting this as an example of an impending or actual "strike," though. Another association, the friends of Dionysos, also consulted the oracle at Didyma (see *IDidyma* 502–3).

9. Cf. *MAMA* IV 230 (Tymandos); *IGR* IV 548 (Orkistos); *IPhrygDB* III 1 (Dorylaion); *TAM* V 536–537 (Maionia); *SEG* 41 (1991) 1329 (Karain, Pamphylia). On votive offerings (i.e., gifts for the gods in return for answered prayer) see van Straten 1981.

10. See, e.g., *LSAM* 69 (Stratonikeia); *ICarie* 132–39, 192–96 (Heraklea-Salbake); *IEph* 18d (lines 4–24), 1145.

11. See the stories in Apuleius, *Metamorphoses* 4.22 and in *Leukippe and Kleitophon* 3. The last relates a tale of cannibalistic bandits in Egypt called "cowherds" (*boukoloi*).

12. For other uses of Baccheion for a meeting place see *IDidyma* 502; *ISmyrna* 733; *IGR* I 787.

13. For other publications of the inscription see Wide 1894 = Drerup 1899 = *SIG*³ 1109 = *LSCG* 51. For discussions see Tod 1932:85–93; Lane Fox 1986:85–88; Schmeller 1995.

Chapter 3

1. Cf. Ziebarth 1896:191–93; Poland 1909:516; Tod 1932:71–73; Guthrie 1950:265–68; Dill 1956:256; Herrmann, Waszink, and Kötting 1978:94; J. Smith 1978:187.

2. Some scholars claim to have some sort of additional knowledge beyond what the evidence of continued participation in traditional forms of religion suggests. For example, Festugière asserts that the decline of civic religions is an "undeniable fact." What it comes down to is that this undeniable fact is based on Festugière's claim to be able to distinguish between the "outer form" of the cults, which he admits continued to function largely unchanged (i.e., the only evidence we have), on the one hand, and the "feelings" and "attitudes" of those who participated, on the other, which he asserts were no longer attached to the civic cults, and correspondingly, to the polis (Festugière 1960:37–38; cf. Dodds 1959:243–44; Green 1990:587; Nilsson 1964:295).

3. On associations or "clubs" in the classical era also see Calhoun 1913; Ferguson and Nock 1944; Fisher 1988a; Arnaoutoglou 1994; N. Jones 1995, 1999.

4. What seems to underlie Festugière's notion of personal or genuine religion, for example, closely resembles William James's definition of religion as "the feelings, acts, and experiences of individual men in their solitude, so far as they apprehend themselves to stand in relation to whatever they may consider the divine" (James 1963:50; cf. Festugière 1954:1–4; Dodds 1959:243; 1965:2; Nilsson 1961:711–12; Green 1990:588).

5. Many scholars who hold similar views to this stop short of explicitly stating, as G. H. Box (1929:45) does, that "[the mysteries] and the religious brotherhoods which made purity of life a condition of membership are genuine manifestations of the religious spirit, and may be regarded as a *real preparation for Christianity*."

6. See Jonathan Barnes's (1986:365) comment that "life in Hellenistic Greece was no more upsetting, no more at the mercy of fickle fortune or malign foes, than it had been in an earlier era." Paul Veyne (1990:41) states that, "as Louis Robert has taught us, it must *not* be said that the Hellenistic epoch was the era of individualism or of universalism, and that its people felt lost within kingdoms that were too big."

7. This view of associations as a response to social deprivations has some affinities with previously common approaches to social and religious movements within the social sciences (esp. in connection with the concept of *relative deprivation*). In the past, some sociologists attempting to explain the emergence of new groups within modern society have suggested that there is a direct causal relation between preexisting feelings of deprivation (economic, social, or otherwise) and the formation and success of social or religious movements. Charles Y. Glock and Rodney Stark's earlier work, for instance, suggests that felt deprivation is a "necessary precondition for the rise of any organized social movement, whether it be religious or secular," and that the emergent group then acts to "compensate for feelings of deprivation" (Glock and Stark 1965:249; cf. Aberle 1970). In this view, new religious groups, like associations within the decline theory, "function to provide individuals with a source of gratification which they cannot find in the society-at-large" (Glock and Stark 1965:256).

Since the 1970s, however, many social scientists have offered important criticisms and qualifications regarding this theoretical framework. Joan Neff Gurney and Kathleen J. Tierney's (1982:33) survey of research suggests that "the relative deprivation perspective is itself affected by too many serious conceptual, theoretical, and empirical weaknesses to be useful in accounting for the emergence and development of social movements." For further critiques of relative deprivation as a sociological concept see Wallis 1975; Beckford 1975:153–59; Berquist 1995.

8. For discussions of benefaction see Veyne 1990; 1987:95–115; Gauthier 1985, 1993; Wallace-Hadrill 1990:150–54; Mitchell 1993:1.210; Sartre 1991:147–66.

9. Aristides of Smyrna, *Orations* 17.8; 18, 19, 20; Dio Chrysostom, *Orations* 44; Artemidorus of Daldis, *Dream Interpretations* 3.66; Strabo of Amaseia, *Geography* 12.3.39, 12.3.15.

10. Most studies of citizenship focus on classical Athens because our evidence is more extensive for that time and place: Thomas 1981:47–48; Sinclair 1988:24–34; Whitehead 1991; Hansen 1993b (cf. Aristotle, *On Politics* 3.1–5). On Hellenistic and Roman times see, e.g., A. H. M. Jones 1940:160–62, 172–73; Magie 1950; Sartre 1991:126–33.

11. For multiple citizenships see, e.g., *IGR* IV 160, 162, 1272, 1344, 1419, 1519; *TAM* II 585; Magie 1950:640, 1503–4 n.27. For multiple memberships in civic councils see *IGR* IV 1761; *MAMA* VIII 421.40–45; Pliny, *Epistles* 10.14.

12. The *deme* was a division of the citizen body at Rhodes.

13. C. P. Jones 1978:80–81, 183–84 n.77 does, however, correctly argue against the view that "linen workers" is a general term for the lower classes here (as suggested by Broughton 1938:844).

14. Attaleia (near Pergamum; *IGR* IV 1169: leather workers); Hierapolis (*IHierapJ* 40, 2d–3d century C.E.: wool cleaners); Miletos (*SEG* 36 [1986] 1051–55: linen workers and sack bearers devoted to Hermes); Temenothyrai (*AE* [1977], no. 802, late 1st century C.E.: clothing cleaners); Thyatira (*TAM* V 932, 933, 986, 989, 1098: slave merchants, linen workers, tanners, dyers, Juliasts); Tralles (*ITrall* 74, 3d century C.E.: initiates).

15. There is some scholarly debate regarding the office of Asiarch. Some have suggested that this was a provincial functionary, a synonym for the high priesthood of the provincial imperial cult. However, more recent scholarship argues convincingly that Asiarchs were most likely civic (not provincial) functionaries, despite what the name may imply (see Magie 1950:449–50; Kearsley 1986, 1988, 1990). According to Acts, some Asiarchs were friendly with Paul (Acts 19:31).

16. Cf. *IEph* 425 (c. 81–117 C.E.): Silversmiths honor T. Claudius Aristion, secretary of the people and imperial high priest. *TAM* IV 33 (late 1st–2d century C.E.): Shippers at Nikomedia (Bithynia) honor a leader of the polis and high priest. *TAM* V 955 (3d century C.E.): Hymn singers of the Mother of the gods honor a civic magistrate and liturgist.

17. Cf. *IAdramytt* 19, 21; *IPhrygR* 533 (Akmoneia); *IAssos* 13–14, 19–21, 28; *IGR* IV 785–86, 788–91 (Apameia); *IIasos* 90; *ITrall* 80.

18. Cf. *IEph* 3079 (guilds); *IGR* IV 788–91 (guilds at Apameia); *IGR* IV 907 (leather workers at Kibyra); Quandt 1913:177 (initiates at Sardis); *ITrall* 74 (initiates).

Chapter 4

1. For other publications of the inscription see *SIG*³ 820 = *NewDocs* IV 22 (with trans.). On Florus see *PIR*² M 531; *IEph* 234, 2048.

2. Cf. Nock 1935:481; Bowersock 1973:180, 206; Veyne 1990:307; Fishwick 1978:1251–53.

3. Cf. Santero 1983; S. Price 1984:117–21; Friesen 2001:116–21. A votive offering (*euchē*) for the "new god, Antinoos" (the favorite of Hadrian) was found at Claudiopolis in Asia Minor (*IKlaudiop* 56; cf. Robert 1980:133); two other Greek votive inscriptions from the mid-1st century—one from Ilion (*ILS* 2.8787) and the other from Aphrodisias (see Friesen 2001:117–20)—reflect thanks for the special protection or benefactions offered by imperial gods. On prayers to the emperors see Aristides, *Orations* 26 and *ISardBR* 8.13–14 (cf. S. Price 1984:232–33). Versnel (1981:36–37) points out that the term *epēkoos*, "one whose nature is to hear," which is often associated with prayer, could be attributed to emperors. As with statues of other gods, individuals could take refuge in times of trouble at the statues of emperors, and there are examples of persons leaving petitions at the feet of imperial statues (cf. *POxy* 2130 [267 c.e.]; *Corpus Papyrorum Raineri* I 20 [c. 250 c.e.]; *PLond* inv. no. 1589 [295 c.e.]; P. Alexander 1967:31–32). For the involvement of households in royal sacrifices and other "private" dimensions of ruler cult in Hellenistic times at Ilion and in Egypt see Robert 1966.

4. But see Pleket 1965; S. Price 1984:50 n.122, 85, 88, 90, 105, 118, 190–91.

5. On these provincial temples see, e.g., Dio Cassius, *Roman History* 51.20.6; Tacitus, *Annals* 4.37, 3.66–69; S. Price 1984. Friesen (1993) focuses on the temple for the *Sebastoi* and Domitian at Ephesus.

6. The procession established by Vibius Salutaris at Ephesus, for instance, involved the hymn singers, the elders' organization (*gerousia*), official boards connected with the Artemision, and, most importantly, the youths, who carried images of Artemis, the Ionian and Hellenistic founders, and the emperors (*IEph* 27; Rogers 1991). During the principate of Claudius, the responsibility of singing honors to the members of the imperial household at Ephesus's civic celebrations, which had previously been performed by an association of hymn singers there, was handed over to the youths (*IEph* 18d.4–24; cf. *IEph* 1145). We also have Josephus's reference to an official celebration of mysteries in honor of Caligula at Rome for which a choir of boys was brought in from Asia to sing (Josephus, *Ant.* 19.30, 104; cf. van Unnik 1979).

7. See the following: *IEph* 742, 921 (hymn singers of Hadrian); *IEph* 645, 3247 (hymn singers of Artemis); *IEph* 18d.4–24 (hymn singers and youths; 44 c.e.); *ISmyrna* 595 (hymn singers of Hadrian; c. 200 c.e.), 697 (c. 124 c.e.), 758; *ISmyrna* 644 (elders). Cf. Rogers 1991:55, 76; Halfmann 1990 (Kyzikos); *IGR* IV 657 (Ak-

moneia); *IDidyma* 50; *IGBulg* 666–68 ("friends-of-the-*Sebastoi* hymn singers" at Nikopolis in Moesia).

8. A member named T. Claudius Procillianus had been a galatarch at Ankyra in Galatia; a civic tribe there honored him as benefactor (*IAnkyraBosch* 142 = *OGIS* 542 = *IGR* III 194). His father, T. Claudius Bocchus (equestrian order), had served as a tribune in the army; he was also a high priest and "revealer of the *Sebastos*" (sebastophant) in the provincial imperial cult of Galatia, as well as a member in an elite association called the "sacrificial priests" (*hierourgoi*) at Ankyra (*IAnkyraBosch* 98).

9. *[epei de]on pros ton Sebaston oikon euse[beias k]ai pasēs hieroprepous epinoias [deixin phan]eran kat eniauton pareches[thai, hoi apo pa]sēs Asias hymnōdoi tēi hierō[tatēi tou Seba]stou Tiberiou Kaisaros [theou genethliō hē]mera synerchomenoi eis [Pergamon mega]loprepes ergon eis tēn [tēs synodou dox]an epitelousin kathy[mnountes ton Seba]ston oikon kai to[is Sebastois theois thysia]s epiteloun[tes kai heortas agontes kai es]tiaseis [kai. . .]pan[. . . .*

10. Pleket (1958:4–10) suggests that the donors of the imperial cult temple for Caligula at Miletos consisted of an association calling themselves the *philosebastoi* (*IDidyma* 148). See also *IMagnMai* 119, which refers to a benefactor as "the son of the friends of the *Sebastoi*," probably an association. Outside Asia Minor, we find a "company" called the Trajanians at Portu near Rome (*IGR* I 385). The descriptive term *philosebastoi* was used by some associations when they decided on a name for the group. See *IEph* 293 (initiates); *ITrall* 77, 93, 145 (young men); *IGBulg* 667–68 (hymn singers at Nikopolis in Moesia Inferior). There were similar associations in Hellenistic times as well, such as the association of Attalists (devoted to the Attalid rulers of Pergamum) that met near the theater at Teos in the mid-2d century B.C.E. (*OGIS* 325–26; cf. *IG* XII.3 443).

11. See, e.g., Burkert 1985:54–75; Detienne and Vernant 1989; S. Price 1984:207–33; Zaidman and Pantel 1992:27–45; Stowers 1995.

12. Cf. *IGR* IV 603 (near Aizanoi); *IEph* 1506; Radt 1999:199 (Pergamum); *AE* (1984) 250, no. 855 (Hierapolis); *IMylasa* 403 (neighborhood association; cf. Robert 1937:537).

13. Price's other suggestion (1984:146–56; cf. Nock 1972a) is that imperial images that appeared in temples of other traditional gods were always subordinate; this is also problematic, since even traditional gods did not share fully in the temples of other gods. Both of Price's reasons for suggesting that the emperors were not perceived as divine (as true gods) but rather as somewhere between human and divine can be viewed as problematic (cf. Friesen 1993:73–75).

14. Cf. Robert 1980:132–38; Lambert 1984. There was a cult for "god Antinoos" at Mantineia that involved sacrifices, games, and mystic rites (*teletē*; see Pausanias, *Description of Greece* 8.9.7–8; *IG* V.2 312, 281). Pausanias mentions that similar rituals were practiced elsewhere, which is confirmed by Origen's reference

to mysteries for Antinoos at Antinoopolis (Origen, *Against Celsus* 3.36). At Claudiopolis, a votive offering for the "new god, Antinoos," has been discovered, and a chief initiate appears to have led mysteries in this god's honor, perhaps involving a continuing association of initiates. See *IKlaudiop* 7 (bronze medallion dedicated to god Antinoos by the homeland), 56 (votive), 65 (*mystarchēs*); S. Price 1984:266, catalogue no. 95. There is further evidence of cultic honors for Antinoos, sometimes involving associations: the "Hadrianic association" (probably performers) honored Antinoos as "the new god Hermes" (*IG* XIV 978a), an association (*collegium*) at Lanuvium in Italy was devoted to both Diana and Antinoos (*CIL* XIV 2112; 136 c.e.), and a hymn has been found at Kurion on Cyprus that praises Antinoos as Adonis (see Lebek 1973).

15. For sebastophants in Asia see *IGR* IV 522 (Dorylaion); *IGR* IV 643 (Akmoneia), *IEph* 2037, 2061, 2063 (early 2d century c.e.); *ISardBR* 62 (an association honors a sebastophant and hierophant of the mysteries); *IGR* IV 1410 (Smyrna). In Bithynia and Galatia sebastophants were often functionaries in the provincial imperial cult: *IPrusiasHyp* 17, 46, 47 (Bithynia); *IGR* III 22 (Kios, Bithynia); *CCCA* I 59–60 (Pessinos, Galatia); *IGR* III 162, 173, 194, 204 (Ankyra, Galatia).

16. It is quite possible that similar royal rituals took place within the known associations devoted to Egyptian rulers, such as the associations of *Basilistai* at Thera (*IG* XII.3 443) and at Setis (*OGIS* 130; 2d century b.c.e.), and the *Eupatoristai* on Delos (*OGIS* 367).

17. The civic cult and mysteries of Dionysos Kathegemon ("the leader") at Pergamum had a history of close connections with the royal Attalid family and ruler cult (cf. von Prott 1902; Ohlemutz 1968:90–122; Burkert 1993:264–68). There is also evidence of close connections between the association of Dionysiac performers centered at Teos, the cult of Kathegemon at Pergamum, and Attalid rulers (see von Prott 1902; Allen 1983:145–58).

18. We do know that at least one member of the hymn singers, a group whose imperial rituals are clear, was also a member of the cowherds (L. Aninius Flaccus; *IPergamon* 374 A 11).

Chapter 5

1. Cf. J. Mitchell 1969, 1973, 1974; Whitten and Wolfe 1973; Boissevain and Mitchell 1973; Boissevain 1974; F. Price 1981; Wellman 1983; Wasserman and Faust 1994.

2. Alongside interactional dimensions are the morphological dimensions, regarding the overall shape of a web of connections. The morphology of ancient net-

works is very difficult to assess owing to the fragmentary nature of the evidence.

3. For the basis of this partial family tree see *IGR* III 373–75 (= *IAnkyraBosch* 105, 156–57), Halfmann 1979 (passim) and L. White 1998a:366–71. C. Julius Severus at Ankyra in Galatia is known to be an *anepsios* (often meaning "cousin") of C. A. A. Julius Quadratus of Pergamum, and C. Julius Severus's brother was definitely a man named Julius Amytianus (*IGR* III 373 = *OGIS* 544). Simone Follet (1976:133) argues convincingly for the probability that this is the same Julius Amytianus that we find at Tralles, if not a relative in some other way. Scholars are in general agreement that Julia Severa is most likely a relative of C. Julius Severus of Ankyra, and therefore of the others, though we lack an inscription that states it explicitly. The Attalid and Galatian royal ancestry includes Attalos II, Deiotaros, and Amyntas (*IGR* III 373). On the methods and nature of prosopography see, e.g., Birley 1953; Boer 1969; Carney 1973; Graham 1974.

4. Arignotus had been prefect and then tribune of several cohorts in his career, taking him to numerous areas of the empire including Alexandria in Egypt, Trajanopolis in Cilicia, and Kyzikos in Asia, where he had also served as a temple warden.

5. On Aristion see *PIR*[2] C 788 and Pliny, *Epistles* 6.31.

6. For other publications and discussions of this inscription see Pleket 1958:49–66, no. 57 = Sherk 1969:313–20, no.61. Cf. Atkinson 1960; Oliver 1963; Millar 1977:317–18.

7. See Pleket 1958:61–62 and Sherk 1969:319–20 on the identity of the proconsul, probably [L.] Vinicius, consul suffect in 33 B.C.E.

8. Domesticus, a Roman citizen, could also boast of citizenship at Ephesus, Antinoopolis, and Athens (*IG* V.1 669 [Sparta]); he was the high priest and ambassador to the emperors for the athletic association devoted to Herakles (see *IGUR* 235–38; *IEph* 1089). The first two of these inscriptions (also see *GCRE* 86, 128), which Domesticus himself dedicated, refer to Hadrian's and Antoninus Pius's grant or reconfirmation of a place for the association to meet in Rome among other privileges. As William C. West (1990) points out, it seems that the original headquarters of the athletic association was in Asia, most likely at Ephesus (cf. *IEph* 1084, 1089, 1098).

9. *IAssos* 19 (Livia, Augustus's wife, as the "new Hera"); *IPhrygR* 474, 511 (Sebaste, Domitian); *MAMA* VI 177 (Akmoneia, Vespasian); *MAMA* VI 183 (Apameia); Conze and Schuchhardt 1899:173, no. 16 (Pergamum, time of Augustus).

10. Also see an inscription from Thera (*OGIS* 735) in which a royal official and his wife are similarly made honorary members of a cult society (*thiasōtai*).

Chapter 6

1. The secondary literature on control of associations and legal questions is vast, and cannot be dealt with fully here. See, e.g., Liebenam 1890; Waltzing 1895–1900; Kornemann 1901; Radin 1910; Carolsfeld 1969; Duff 1938; Cotter 1996. For a discussion of how legal questions have (often detrimentally) dominated the study of associations see Ausbüttel 1982:11–16.

2. Cf. Renan 1869:278–89; Reicke 1951: 320–38; Balch 1981:65–80; Stanley 1996:120. Contrast Judge 1960:43.

3. Contrary to a tradition in scholarship (cf. Waltzing 1895–1900, 1:123–27, who cites Mommsen), the senate's reply to the request of Kyzikos concerning recognition of the group (*corpus*) of young men (*neoi*) there (*CIL* III 7060; cf. *GCRE* 57–60) is best understood as "honorific, not constitutory" (Radin 1910:125; Forbes 1933:40–41). That is, without being required to do so, associations or other groups could seek the recognition of some institution or authority for the prestige and honor the display of such would attribute to them.

4. Also compare the incident of a later era (c. 382 c.e.) in Syrian Antioch related by Libanius, *Oration* 1.205–10. Libanius tells how he protected the guild (*ethnos*) of bakers (*sitopoioi*) from the Roman governor's punishment in connection with disturbances at a time of famine and rising bread prices.

5. Cf. *IBithMendel* II 184 (shippers at Amastris); *IApamBith* 33–35 (*thiasitai*), 103 (initiates), 116; *IKios* 20–22 (*thiasitai*); *INikaia* II.1 73 (coppersmiths); *TAM* IV 22, 33 (shippers at Nikomedia); *IBithMendel* I 3 (initiates at Prusa); *IPrusaOlymp* 48, 1028 (initiates), 1036 (sack weavers). All date to the 1st or 2d century. There was a synagogue of Jews/Judeans at Nikomedia as well (*TAM* IV 376–77).

Chapter 7

1. The literature in this area cannot be fully discussed here except to say that three main themes have dominated discussion of Christianity and Judaism with respect to associations: the relation (or lack thereof) of ideas associated with the mysteries to concepts and practices within Christianity (Reitzenstein 1978:76–81; see J. Smith 1990 for the history of scholarship); the internal organization of the group (see the discussion of Heinrici and Hatch below); and the relevance of imperial policy and laws concerning *collegia* for understanding the legal position of Christian or Jewish groups (Renan 1869:262–74; Ramsay 1901; Keating 1901:180–201; Hardy 1910:128–49; La Piana 1927; Guterman 1951:130–56; Reicke 1951).

2. Cf. Malherbe 1983:86–91; Kloppenborg 1993a. C. Holsten's theological concerns are evident when he accuses Heinrici of suggesting that Paul's organization of his communities actually "used the life forms of a cult association of demons (1 Cor 10:20)" (see Heinrici 1881:507). Adolf Harnack (1889:419) claimed that "the investigation of the organization of pagan associations had brought very little or no clarification." A few years later W. M. Ramsay (1901:98) acknowledged the importance of *collegia* but was careful to state: "no reconciliation was possible at that time between Christian principles and present social forms. . . . But . . . I must also confess that a strong inclination attracts me to the side of those who were trying . . . to combine Christian spirit with the existing institutions of society and civilization."

3. Studies of early Christianity that make substantial reference to associations or guilds focus on topics such as the social context of missionary activity (Hock 1980); the organization, hierarchy, and leadership structures of Christian groups (Countryman 1977; Barton and Horsley 1981; Maier 1991; Schmeller 1995; Kloppenborg 1996b); the influence of household structures on organization and internal life (Klauck 1981; L. White 1996; Maier 1991:15–28); the architecture of buildings or meeting places (L. White 1996); internal social and religious activities, esp. communal meals (D. Smith 1980; Barton and Horsley 1981; Klauck 1982:40–165); outsiders' perceptions and the self-understanding of Christian groups (Wilken 1972, 1984); the linguistic field of the NT (Danker 1982; Ascough 1996); and specific NT passages or documents including Paul's Corinthian, Thessalonian, and Philippian correspondence (Malherbe 1987; Kloppenborg 1993b; Schmeller 1995; Ascough 1997b). Similar studies with respect to Jewish groups include those on internal regulations and organization (Dombrowski 1966; Weinfeld 1986); the financial management of synagogues (Bonz 1993); and the architecture of synagogue buildings (Kraabel 1987; L. White 1987, 1996; Richardson 1996). Also see the studies by various scholars in Wilson and Kloppenborg 1996.

4. See Kloppenborg 1993a:231–34. On the use of *presbyteros* in connection with associations see, e.g., *IGLSkythia* I 99, 100, 167; *IGBulg* 666; *SEG* 42 (1992) 1312; *OGIS* 729; *SB* 996; *IGUR* 77. On the use of *diakonos* for cultic functionaries see, e.g., *IEph* 3416–18 (deacons alongside priests in cults for Zeus Krezimos, Hera, and Ares Tyrranos); *CCCA* I 289 (deacons among Cybele devotees at Kyzikos).

5. Louis Robert (1975; cf. *NewDocs* I 3) convincingly suggests the Persian character of this cult (in its 4th-century B.C.E. form), identifying Zeus with Ahura Mazda; this makes better sense of why the mysteries of native Phrygian deities, Sabazios (cf. *IPhrygR* 127 = *CCIS* II 6, 39, 43 [initiates of Zeus Sabazios near

Philomelion]) and Agdistis (cf. *ILydiaKP* III 18 = *LSAM* 20 = Barton and Horsley 1981), and the Cappadocian deity, Ma, were strongly discouraged. The situation and implications when the inscription was later republished in the Roman era, however, would be different.

6. Peter D. Gooch (1993:1–26) discusses some of the building remains of banqueting facilities associated with Asklepios and Demeter at Corinth, which may be among the contexts that Paul has in mind.

7. There are two other related incidents worth mentioning that involve Domitian. First, Dio Cassius (and subsequently Eusebius) relates the episode concerning Domitian's execution of his own nephew Flavius Clemens and the exile of Clemens's niece, Domitilla, on charges of "atheism" (*Roman History* 67.13.1–3). Dio does not explicitly link this with Christianity, but Eusebius does (*H.E.* 3.18.4). Whether Christians or Jews, the fact remains that Clemens and Domitilla were among the senatorial aristocracy and even members of the imperial family, which puts their case in a realm other than official persecution of ordinary Christians in the provinces. Second, Eusebius also records the "ancient story" that he derives from Hegesippus (c. 150 c.e.; *H.E.* 3.19–20). Domitian "gave orders for the execution of those of the family of David" and this included relatives of Christ (grandsons of Judas "who is said to have been the brother . . . of the Savior"). These peasants from Palestine, so the story goes, were brought before Domitian and interrogated, after which he released them and "decreed an end to the persecution" (*H.E.* 3.20.1–4). As Barnes also points out, various elements of the episode are less than believable and the story explicitly attempts to draw a parallel with the story of Herod and the birth of Jesus: "Domitian, . . . like Herod, was afraid of the coming of the Christ" (*H.E.* 3.20.1).

8. The six other types are: revolutionist (salvation through the supernaturally wrought destruction and transformation of the world), introversionist (salvation through withdrawal from the evil world), manipulationist (salvation through application of the proper means or methods), thaumaturgical (salvation through magic), reformist (salvation through reform of the world), utopian (salvation through the application of divinely given principles).

9. This despite the fact that Ignatius also emphasizes other respects in which there is a clear contrast between Christians and "the world," which come to the fore especially in the letter to the Romans (*Rom.* 2.2; 3.3; 6.2; 7; cf. *Magn.* 5 [two coinages, of God and of the world]). But quite often Ignatius seems to have in mind physical existence or the flesh (esp. his own life, which he expects to lose), wealth, and other such material things when he uses the term "the world" in such a negative way; usually it seems that he does not have outsiders in mind.

10. See Dibelius 1931 (cf. Conzelmann's more recent edition [1972] of the commentary); Spicq 1969. For further discussion see Kidd 1990 (cf. M. MacDon-

ald 1988:160–202). Aspects of Dibelius's influential view are based in part on notions that earliest Christianity was initially a "religion of the poor" that only in later years, as in the Pastorals, included wealthier members who brought with them Hellenistic values concerning wealth and good citizenship. This, together with the value-laden assessment of the Pastorals' viewpoint as a negative sign of accommodation to worldly ways and a fall from an ethically superior earlier Christianity, is also problematic; this also corresponds to value judgments concerning a shift from a superior eschatological earliest Christianity to an inferior ecclesiastical, catholic form of existence from the 2d century. Others who refer to the Pastorals as bourgeois or middle-class, such as Spicq, do not see the acceptance of some Hellenistic values or ethics in the Pastorals as a negative development, however; indeed, Spicq suggests, it was in significant ways in continuity with Paul himself (see Kidd 1990).

11. Elliott (1990:93, 160) largely ignores van Unnik's studies on 1 Peter, mentioning him only in two endnotes without discussion.

12. These paragraphs depend primarily on the following anthropological and sociological studies: Redfield, Linton, and Herskovits 1936; Barnett et al. 1954; Herskovits 1958; Berry 1980; Yinger 1981; Kim and Gudykunst 1988; Marger 1991:116–30; Elise 1995. I am indebted to Balch (1986) for sparking my interest in the subject; others have recently employed notions of assimilation or acculturation in studies of Christianity or Judaism in antiquity (cf. Barclay 1996; Snyder 1998). The processes of assimilation and acculturation are to be clearly distinguished from common value-laden terms such as "accommodation"; the former are not concerned with evaluating whether specific developments are "good" or "bad."

13. For another exception to polytheism see the discussion of the Sabbatists and other quasi-monotheistic associations of Gentiles (sometimes worshiping the Jewish God) in chapter one.

14. See *CIJ* 755; Robert 1946:100–101; Robert 1960a:436–39; cf. Lüderitz 1983:11–21, nos. 6–7, on Jews among the *ephēbes* at Cyrene in the late 1st century B.C.E.–early 1st century C.E.

15. Traditionally (following Jean-Baptiste Frey in *CIJ* 742), it has been understood as "former Jews" in the sense of apostates: "Jews who had acquired Greek citizenship at the price of repudiating their Jewish allegiance" (Feldman 1993:83, citing Smallwood 1981:507). Those who understand it as such cite no other inscriptional evidence for this interpretation. Moreover, it seems that broader assumptions concerning whether or not Jews could actually participate in such ways within the polis without losing their Jewish identity play a significant role in the decision to interpret the phrase as apostasy. A. T. Kraabel, followed by others, challenges this translation and suggests the possibility that the term means "people for-

merly of Judea" (cf. Lane Fox 1988:481; Trebilco 1991:175; *ISmyrna* 697 [notes to line 20]). He does not cite inscriptional evidence to back up this use of the term *pote* specifically to refer to a group of immigrants, however. Ross S. Kraemer (1989) builds on Kraabel's suggestion and pursues further evidence that suggests the term *Ioudaios* could indeed be used as a geographical indicator (i.e., "Judean"). Margaret H. Williams (1997:251–52) contests Kraabel's suggestion, arguing that conspicuous Jewish apostasy did occur and "foreign residents are *never* described as 'formerly of such and such a region'" (emphasis mine; she is incorrect, unless she is still focused on the *pote*). But she makes no positive arguments concerning how we should translate this phrase in the inscription (apparently resorting to the unfounded apostasy theory).

16. *NewDocs* I 5 = S. Mitchell 1999:131, no. 51 (Pydna, Macedonia). Cf. *IG* IV 783.b.4; *IG* X.2 564 (Thessalonica); *SEG* 27 (1977) 293 (Leukopatra). All date to the 3d and 4th centuries C.E.

17. On the bath-gymnasium complex as a whole see Yegül 1986. On the synagogue see Kraabel 1968; Seager 1974; Seager and Kraabel 1983; Hanfmann 1983; Bonz 1990, 1993. The Greek inscriptions from the synagogue are now published in Kroll 2001.

18. Cf. Josephus, *Ant.* 14.213–16 (Parion) and 14.244–46 (Miletos). Cf. Stanley 1996, though he overemphasizes anti-Roman sentiment among Gentiles in the cities of Asia Minor.

19. Russell Meiggs (1960:321–23) rightly doubts strict enforcement of such laws in the 2d century, citing plenty of evidence for multiple memberships in the guilds at Ostia. Imperial legislation along these lines did gradually develop toward the compulsory guilds of the late empire, when governmental control of *collegia* reached its peak. In the first two centuries, governmental involvement or interference in the life of associations was very limited and sporadic (see chapter six).

20. Julius was likely a Jew, but he may also have been a non-Jewish patron of the Jewish group.

21. Turning west, two inscriptions from Ostia seem to suggest that a Christian there was also a member in the shippers' guild (c. 192 C.E.); it is worth noting that Marcion (who was founder of a set of Christian groups and came from Sinope in Pontus) was himself a ship captain a couple of generations earlier (Lane Fox 1986:295; Tertullian, *Prescription Against Heresies* 30.1–2; Eusebius, *H.E.* 5.13.1).

22. Thus, e.g., this guild of purple-dyers was included among the recipients of other funerary foundations (alongside guilds of coppersmiths, nail workers, and cattle dealers) by persons who show absolutely no sign of Jewish connections (*IHierapJ* 133, 227 [c. 190–250 C.E.]; *IHierapPenn* 23). On occasions when the purple-dyers honored imperial officials (a functionary of the provincial imperial cult and a procurator), there is, once again, no indication that they were distinctively

Jewish guilds (*IHierapJ* 41–42); it is certainly possible, however, that they included Jews in their number when such honorary activities took place. Nor does the grave inscription of another purple-dyer, also a member in the civic council around Glykon's time, give any indication of Jewish connections (*IHierapJ* 156; cf. *IHierapPenn* 37 [grave of a purple-seller]).

23. It is unlikely, though possible, that Glykon is himself a member in one of the guilds in question; however, he does not identify his occupation, and there are numerous other comparable inscriptions from Hierapolis and Asia involving non–guild members calling on the funerary-related services of a guild.

24. It remains a possibility that the Jews or God-fearers in these guilds did *not* also belong to the local synagogue, in which case we are witnessing multiple affiliation rather than actual membership.

25. On comparison in the social sciences see Sjoberg 1955; J. Smith 1982, 1990; Poole 1986.

26. Philo, *On the Contemplative Life*; *Special Laws* 2.145–46; *Embassy to Gaius* 312–13; *On Virtues* 33.178; Tertullian, *Apology* 38–39; Eusebius, *H.E.* 10.1.8; cf. Seland 1996:110–27.

Chapter 8

1. Scholars usually link this oracle with particular anti-Roman campaigns or propaganda of the 1st century B.C.E., most notably that of Mithradates VI (early 1st century B.C.E.) or, if an Egyptian context is preferred, that of Cleopatra against Octavian (see J. Collins 1974:57–64). John J. Collins suggests that it should also be interpreted in light of the broader non-Jewish tradition concerning world history as the conflict between East and West, a tradition we find expressed in writings such as the oracle of Hystaspes (Lactantius, *Divine Institutions* 7.15.11; J. Collins 1974:58–59).

2. Cf. Tacitus, *Annals* 5.5: "Jewish worship is vindicated by its antiquity, but their other customs are perverse and disgusting. . . . They do not believe in making images of God, because God cannot be represented in material form, and they do not even permit statues of any kind to stand in their cities, not statues of their kings or the emperors" (cited in Benko 1980:1064).

3. Cf. Schäfer 1997; Barclay 1996:72–81. On anti-Roman sentiment see the so-called Acts of the Alexandrian (or Pagan) Martyrs (Musurillo 1979), which includes the "martyrdom" of Isodoros, one of those Alexandrian Greeks who was a key player in the anti-Jewish riots under Gaius.

4. On the probable role of some associations in these incidents see *Against Flaccus* 135–45 (cf. Bergmann and Hoffmann 1987:27–31, who speak of them as "anti-Semitic clubs"). For inscriptions regarding associations at Alexandria see

IAlexandriaK 46, 65, 70, 90–101. Unfortunately, the surviving evidence is minimal for associations of any type at Alexandria; there are no extant monuments in honor of emperors, for example, which is also the case with Jewish groups from the area. There was, however, an association at Alexandria called the "Sebaste *synodos*," which was devoted to Caesar, son of god, Zeus Eleutherios (see Brashear 1993 [5 B.C.E.]; cf. *BGU* IV 1137). We know of several other ethnic-geographic based associations in Egypt generally (beyond the Judeans/Jews), including a "corporate body" (*politeuma*) of Idumeans at Memphis (see Schürer 1973–87, 3:44–46).

5. Such open conflicts pertaining to the Jews' lack of participation in imperial cults specifically were primarily limited to exceptional periods, such as the reign of Caligula. There were even plans to set up his statue in the Jerusalem temple, perhaps as retribution for the acts of Jews in Jamnia who had previously torn down imperial statues (Josephus, *J.W.* 2.184–203; *Ant.* 18.261–309; Philo, *Embassy to Gaius* 184–338; see Grabbe 1992:401–5).

6. The reference to the assembly of Asia *en agyrē* is a corruption in the Greek text, but Scaliger's emendation, reading "in Ankyra" (*en Agkyrē*, which is followed by LCL), does not work historically. The Latin text of Josephus omits the phrase.

7. *Ant.* 16.185–267 (time of Julius Caesar, c. 49–43 B.C.E.); 16.160–78 (time of Augustus and Agrippa); 14.301–23. Josephus preserves three kinds of materials: decrees of the senate or emperors, decrees of cities, and rescripts replying to letters directed to provincial governors. Critical study of the documents suggests that although they are presented in an apologetic context (i.e., they are selective) and there are problems with specific documents as they stand, generally they are not forgeries and often they do indeed reflect actual historical incidents and relations (see Rajak 1984; Barclay 1996:262–64). "The names of officials appear to be the principal casualties of the transmission and to have a strong propensity to confusion and corruption" (Rajak 1984:111). For a less accepting view of the documents see Moehring 1975.

8. The benefits or acknowledgments gained by the Jewish groups were not totally exceptional. Rather, they were part of the common processes by which groups and communities gained such favors. This should caution us in arguing that the benefits granted to the Jews were a "deeply resented" focal point of conflicts with other inhabitants in the cities (cf. Feldman 1993:93–94). Christopher D. Stanley, for example, imagines that, even by the time of Julius Caesar, anti-Roman hostility was widespread in the cities of Asia Minor. Relying on assumptions I have challenged in part two, Stanley (1996:120) asserts that inhabitants resented the interference of Roman authorities in their civic affairs, and private "clubs and associations became the forum of choice for anti-aristocratic and anti-Roman sentiment in the cities." While these associations were strictly controlled or disallowed

by the authorities, the Jewish groups, in contrast, were granted special privileges (cf. Feldman 1993:93). He then argues that "the very legal protections that the Jews had earlier received from the Romans set them apart from other immigrant groups as a focal point for anti-Roman hostility" (Stanley 1996:122–23). In other words, Stanley seems to think that the Romans' diplomatic ties with and benefactions to Jewish groups (in the form of acknowledgment of their rights to perform their own customs) were utterly different from those pertaining to other groups or associations, which is not the case.

9. A similar picture concerning Roman "policy" on diaspora Jews emerges from Leonard Victor Rutgers's study of expulsions of Jews from Rome. He argues that the Romans were neither tolerant nor intolerant toward Jews in the diaspora. Rather, in keeping with the nature of Roman rule, "Rome's 'Jewish policy' remained in essence a collection of ad hoc measures with often limited effectiveness in both space and time" (Rutgers 1998:114). Such measures were more often than not simply a by-product of Roman administrative approaches concerning the maintenance of order or involvement in the conventions of diplomacy.

10. *CIJ* 365, 425, 503, 284, 301, 338, 368, 416, 496; cf. Richardson 1998; Leon 1995:140–42. Cf. *ISmyrna* 331; *IG* VI 374 (Sparta).

11. On Judaism in Cyrenaica see Applebaum 1979; Barclay 1996:231–42; Josephus, *J.W.* 7.437–53.

12. Reynolds 1977:242–47, nos. 16 (55 C.E.), 17 (c. 24 C.E.), 18 (c. 9–6 B.C.E.) = Luderitz 1983:148–58, nos. 70–72; cf. Applebaum 1979:160–67. The third inscription dates to the time of Nero (55 C.E.), containing a decision of a Jewish group (though not necessarily the same one), this time called "the synagogue of Jews in Berenike," to inscribe the names of donors who contributed to the renovation of a building.

13. Reynolds 1977:244–45, no. 17 = Roux and Roux 1949 = *IGR* I 1024. If the date stated in the inscription is calculated based on the Cyrenaican era (rather than the Actian era), then this would be 41 B.C.E. The significance of the inscription for our present purposes does not fully depend on dating; nonetheless, the presence of a Roman citizen within the Jewish group at the time of this inscription suggests that 24 C.E. should be preferred. Martha W. Baldwin Bowsky (1987:504–5) points out that the methods for dating inscriptions at Berenike vary, and that there are even further dating systems besides these two possibilities. She suggests a date of 14/13 B.C.E. partially based on issues pertaining to the reference to the Feast of Tabernacles. This remains uncertain, however.

14. On *politeuma* as a general term referring to an unofficial "association" see Zuckerman 1985/88 (contra A. Kasher) and Lüderitz 1994, who refute the traditional interpretation that assumes that such groups were officially recognized, semi-autonomous civic bodies (cf. Smallwood 1981:225).

15. Hugh J. Mason points out that *prostasia* in this inscription is the equivalent of the Latin *praesidatus provinciae* and he interprets this as a reference to the proconsul (Mason 1974: 81). The term *eparcheia*, translated by Lüderitz with the more general term "prefecture," is frequently used as a technical equivalent for the Latin *provincia*, which is how Roux and Roux (1949:284) translate it (see Mason 1974:45, 135–36).

16. The suggestion that Dionysios is a member is based on the fact that the *politeuma* of Judeans releases this benefactor from liturgies, presumably those within the group, since the *politeuma* would not be in a position to release him from civic liturgies (Reynolds 1977:247).

17. See *PIR*² I 507; Halfmann 1979, no. 17; *PIR*² I 573; Halfmann 1979, no. 62.

18. The title attributed to Klados and Lucius may be honorary rather than functional if the study by T. Rajak and D. Noy (1993:88–89) is correct: "For . . . nothing by way of Judaism or Jewish knowledge need have been required to be a satisfactory *archisynagogos*, beyond the capacity to display benevolent concern for the group." "It is conceivable . . . that you did not have to be Jewish to be an *archisynagogos*." Even in this regard the Jewish groups may be reflecting conventions shared by other associations, in which those who held important group titles were frequently wealthy benefactors and not necessarily members.

19. The Johannine epistles are primarily concerned with internal issues and problems in the house churches. References to "rulers," "powers," and "authorities" in both Ephesians and Colossians seem to relate to angelic or cosmic beings (e.g., Eph 6:12; Col 1:16; 2:10, 15; cf. Arnold 1992, 1996). Ignatius complains of mistreatment by the soldiers ("leopards") who escort him to Rome (*Rom.* 5.1), alludes to the "visible and invisible" "rulers" who will also be subject to judgment (*Smyrn.* 6.1), and speaks of the two coinages of God and of "the world" (*Magn.* 5.2). However, scholars such as William R. Schoedel and Allen Brent stretch things too far in reading into Ignatius (and the Asian churches) strong anti-Roman attitudes or references to imperial cults. Schoedel wrongly imagines that the Asian cities "felt alienated from the mainstream of Roman society," being a haven for anti-imperial attitudes, and that this also worked itself out in the churches (1980:53–4; cf. Schoedel 1985:14–15; Brent 1998). Our earlier chapters speak against this depiction of attitudes toward empire within the Asian cities in the early 2d century.

20. See, e.g., the sacred law regarding a festival associated with Demeter and the civic presidents' meeting place at Ephesus, which included a prescription "to pray on behalf of the sacred senate and the people of Rome and the people of Ephesus" (*IEph* 10.15–17 = *NewDocs* IV 25 [in the text of the notes]; 3d century C.E.). Pliny the Younger refers to prayers for the emperors or empire at several points in his letters concerning the cities of Bithynia and Pontus (Pliny, *Epistles* 10.13, 100).

21. On Sabathikos and possible Jewish connections here see the earlier discussion of the Sabbatists in chapter one.

22. In light of the evidence discussed earlier, we need not agree with Balch (1981:72) that this "prayer corresponds to a desire to reassure a suspicious Roman society of the loyalty of the cult to the state." The practical implications of such activities could be far more local, pertaining to how such a group fit within the city.

23. According to Brent (1998:31), Ignatius directly "confronts Roman power" and the notion of the procession to martyrdom is "set over against [imperial cult]," but no clear evidence is cited. Brent's ability to find imperial cult where it is not expressly evident is primarily based on a method that begins with Ignatius's language and looks for parallels in the imperial cult specifically, rather than within Greco-Roman religious life more generally. Richard A. Horsley (1997:242; cf. p. 1) manages to find in 1 Corinthians "Paul's adamant opposition to Roman imperial society," and he characterizes Christianity more broadly as an "anti-imperial movement." Paul preached an "anti-imperial gospel" and "much of his key language would have evoked echoes of the imperial cult and ideology" (Horsley 1997:140). Some exegetical acrobatics are then necessary in interpreting Rom 13. Cf. also Bruce W. Winter's (1994:123–43) unconvincing attempt to see imperial cults as an important factor in Paul's letter to the Galatians. I challenge the assumptions involved in this pervasive notion of a specific clash between the "cult of Caesar" and the "cult of Christ" in the following chapter.

24. Neither J. K. Elliott (1993) nor Schneelmelcher (1991–92) considers the variation of the Armenian text worthy of inclusion in their translations, in contrast to the emphasis that MacDonald puts on it.

25. The author has the Roman proconsul, Castellius, gladly listen to Paul's speech "about the holy works of Christ" (*Acts of Paul* 3.20), and this official weeps and admires Thecla's power when faced with death (3.22), ultimately releasing her (3.38). Despite Nero's harsh actions against the Christians, Longus the prefect and Cestus the centurion, along with other members of Nero's household, become converts to Christianity (11.1–7).

26. Several other Christian authors used the analogy of "soldiers" to speak of Christians, but often in a clearly nonsubversive sense. See 2 Tim 2:3; Ign. *Pol.* 6; *1 Clem.* 37.

27. John H. Elliott suggests that 1 Peter uses the term "resident aliens" in a literal sense; this then plays a key role in Elliott's depiction of Christians in Asia Minor in terms of social and economic deprivation, which serves as a partial foundation for categorizing Christian groups there as sects (J. Elliott 1990: 21–58, 77–78). It seems far more likely, however, that such terms are not literal but metaphorical (cf. Chin 1991; Feldmeier 1992:203–10; Winter 1994:16–17). The

terms derive in large part from the genre of 1 Peter as a diaspora letter addressed to the exiles.

28. The closing allusion to the author's location in "Babylon" (1 Pet 5:13) is most likely a reference to Rome, but it does not have the sort of strongly negative connotations that we find in John's Apocalypse. The use of "Babylon" coincides here with the genre of the diaspora letter (cf. Michaels 1988:310–11). We need not agree with Davids (1990:203) or other commentators who interpret this as an acknowledgment that the Roman "government is the capital of evil."

29. Van Unnik 1980d:91–92; Balch 1981, 1986; Winter 1994:11–40. Unfortunately, few have picked up on van Unnik's suggestions (but see Goppelt 1993:182–90). Beare (1958:117) sees here a reference to actual benefaction, but he simply asserts that "few Christians can have entertained any great hope of winning such public distinction . . . it seems likely that the words are a stock phrase taken over from some current formula of instruction in civic duty." Michaels (1988:126) lightly passes off the suggestion of "civic virtue" or concrete action and takes "good works" as a (vague) reference to "doing the will of God."

30. As James D.G. Dunn (1988:758–59) argues, rather than being merely an alien insertion into Paul's letter, this passage continues the practical guidelines regarding relationships with others that immediately precedes it in Rom 12:9–21.

Chapter 9

1. On Pliny, the Christians, and trials see, e.g., de Ste. Croix 1963; Sherwin-White 1952; 1966:691–712; Bickerman 1968; T. Barnes 1968:36–37; T. Barnes 1971:143–63; Henrichs 1970; Molthagen 1970:13–37; Grant 1970; Benko 1980:1068–77; Wilken 1984:1–30.

2. Henrichs (1970:21) thinks that it was Pliny who initially suspected the Christians of "crimes," but it seems more likely, especially in light of the following discussion, that it was the accusers who raised such issues. Nor do I think that Pliny necessarily had in mind the crimes associated with the Bacchanalian affair of 186 B.C.E. specifically (contra Grant 1948; Wilken 1984:16–17; see Sherwin-White 1966:692).

3. Cf. McGowan 1994. Also see the stories of Christians' practice of ritual infanticide and other rituals in Minucius Felix, whose source is probably M. Cornelius Fronto (Benko 1980:1081–83). On accusations of ritual murder in connection with Judaism see Josephus, *Ag. Ap.* 2.89–102; Bickerman 1980; Schäfer 1997.

4. Justin Martyr, *Apology* 1.68; Eusebius, *H.E.* 4.9.1–3. Also see T. Barnes 1968:37; T. Barnes 1971:154; Bickerman 1968; Benko 1980:1079–81.

5. Tertullian, *To Scapula* 5: "When Arrius Antoninus was driving things hard in Asia, the Christians of the province, in one united band, presented themselves before his judgment seat; on which, ordering a few to be led forth to execution, he said to the rest, 'O miserable men, if you wish to die, you have precipices or halters.'"

6. When, in the account of their martyrdoms, Karpos, Papylos, and Agathonike are brought before the proconsul at Pergamum (c. 161–169 c.e.), there is no reference to imperial cult rituals specifically, simply a command to "Sacrifice to the gods and do not play the fool" (Musurillo 1972:23–29). The accusations and trials at Lugdunum (Lyons) do not involve imperial cults.

7. Extensive evidence from the Apocalypse is lacking, but the prominence of issues concerning the eating of food sacrificed to idols in the letters suggests that a good number of the Christian opponents, at least, were Gentiles. Considering the presence of Jews in the cities addressed by the Apocalypse and the presence of some within Christian groups in Asia (according to other literature [e.g., Priscilla and Aquila]) there is a strong likelihood that there were Jews among the Christian assemblies addressed by John (who was a Jew).

8. On the functional and deliberative character of apocalyptic see, e.g., deSilva 1998; Thompson 1990; J. Collins 1998:41–42; Aune 1987:23–31; Aune 1997–98, 1:lxxvii–lxxxii.

9. It is possible that the Phrygian movement of the mid- to late 2d century can be placed within this same trajectory of Christianity (on Montanism see Frend 1984, 1988; Trevett 1989b, 1996; Heine 1989). The movement clearly made use of John's Apocalypse with its concept of the "New Jerusalem"–immanently to arrive at Pepuza in Phrygia, according to some–and its emphasis on being a witness or martyr. But we know too little regarding the actual stances of the movement's leaders regarding Roman imperialism to assess this fully. Papias, bishop of Hierapolis in the 2d century, was also known for his apocalyptic views; but we know even less about him.

10. John's focus on the emperor's demands to be worshiped as a god together with the religio-economic critique of empire in chaps. 17–18 also derives, in part, from parallels with Ezekiel's religio-economic critique of Tyre, whose prince boasts: "I am a god; I sit in the seat of the gods, in the heart of the seas" (chaps. 26–28, esp. 28:1–10). On John's economic critique and Hebrew Scripture see Bauckham 1991 and Provan 1996. The latter challenges Bauckham's views, but perhaps overstates the distance between Roman realities of trade and John's description in chap. 18.

11. On the myth of Nero's return from the dead see *Sib. Or.* 4.119–20, 138–39; 5.93–97, 363–69; 8.153–57. A passage in the Jewish-Christian *Martyrdom and As-*

cension of Isaiah, which probably dates to the late 1st century, also envisions a similar role for the returning Nero: Beliar will come "in the form of that king [i.e., Nero] . . . and all men in the world will believe in him. They will sacrifice to him and will serve him, saying 'This is the Lord, and besides him there is no other'" (4:4–10; trans. M. A. Knibb in *OTP*, 2:161–62). Also see J. Collins 1974:80–87; J. Collins 1998:235–36; Bauckham 1993:407–31.

12. A. Collins (1984:73, 69–77, 104) considers imperial cults as an "incidental matter" "from the pagan point of view" and with respect to the real situation of Christians; but she does so, in part, based on a questionable characterization of these cults as nongenuine "flattery." Thompson, who is more attuned to the actual nature of imperial cults in Roman Asia, points out that not much would have changed with regard to these cults during the reign of Domitian and that, therefore, imperial cults play only a limited role with regard to the Christians in Asia (cf. Thompson 1990:158–64). He accepts Price's view that the "emperor in the imperial cult was subordinated to the gods" and that the imperial gods were consequently not the recipients of the same cultic acts as other gods (Thompson 1990:164), which is problematic.

13. The theme of ruling powers and their leaders claiming to be equal to a god is also common within the biblical sources familiar to John (e.g., Ezek 28 [the prince of Tyre who claims "I am a god; I sit in the seat of gods"]) and within other Jewish apocalyptic writings (e.g., *Sib. Or.* 5.34, 140 [the returning Nero claims to be a god], 162–79 [Rome makes the divine claim that "I alone am"]).

14. Num 22–25 (Balaam); 1 Kgs (3 Kgdms) 18:4, 13; 19:1–2; 21:25–26 (Jezebel). Cf. Josephus, *Ant.* 12.126–51; Sandelin 1991; Borgen 1995. On "fornication" as the adoption of foreign practices see, e.g., Deut 23:17–18; 1 Chr 5:25; Ps 73:27; 105:34–39; Hos 3:3; 4:10–18; Jer 3:6–10; Ezek 16:15–52; 23.

15. Schüssler Fiorenza 1985:195–97; Hemer 1986:83–94; Klauck 1992; Kraybill 1996:16 and throughout. A. Collins (1985:214), for example, suggests that the Nicolaitans "were advocating Christian participation in the imperial cult." However, it is not necessarily the participation of Christians in imperial cults specifically, but rather the involvement in specific aspects of the polis, including honors for the emperors and participation in guilds (where imperial cult activities could take place), that may be the issue.

16. It is also worth mentioning the possibility that John's references to the "synagogue of Satan" at Smyrna and at Philadelphia (Rev 2:9; 3:9) may pertain to similar involvements within the civic context on the part of these groups (perhaps, but not necessarily, Jewish), but there is not enough evidence to work with in this case.

17. My suggestions do not rest on the interpretation of *klinē* in 2:22. Besides its reference to a "sickbed," though, it may also allude to the commensal context and

social world of associations connected with the opponents' activities, as Ramsay (1901:103–5) also points out. For the term was often used to refer to the "couch" on which one reclined to eat at banquets and sometimes as a metonymy of the "banquet" (cf. *POxy* 110, 1484, 1755, 3693, 4339; *NewDocs* I 1) or of an "association" (cf. *IG* X.2 192 from Thessalonica; Philo, *Against Flaccus* 136–37).

18. Ramsay 1901:103–5; 1994:253–58. Cf. Allo 1921:36; Beckwith 1967:464–65; Charles 1920:69–70; Mounce 1977:101–103; Court 1979:34–35; A. Collins 1984:88; Schüssler Fiorenza 1985:117; Hemer 1986:117, 120–23; Harrington 1993:65–66; Thomas 1994; Kraybill 1996; Aune 1997–98, 1:186. Among these scholars, Kraybill gives the most attention to guilds, but he nonetheless cites very little inscriptional evidence pertinent to Asia, often depending on secondary sources for his information.

Bibliographies

1. Epigraphic and Papyrological Collections

Ameling, Walter
　1985. *Die Inschriften von Prusias ad Hypium*. IGSK 27. Bonn: Habelt.
Balland, André
　1981. *Inscriptions d'époque impériale du Létôon*. Fouilles de Xanthos, 7. Paris: Klincksieck.
Bean, George E., and Terence Bruce Mitford
　1965. *Journeys in Rough Cilicia 1962 and 1963 [I]*. DÖAW.PH 85. Vienna: Böhlaus.
　1970. *Journeys in Rough Cilicia 1964–1968 [II]*. DÖAW 102.3. Vienna: Böhlaus.
Becker-Bertau, Friedrich
　1986. *Die Inschriften von Klaudiu polis*. IGSK 31. Bonn: Habelt.
Benndorf, O., and G. Niemann
　1884. *Reisen in Lykien und Karien*. Reisen im Südwestlichen Kleinasien 1. Vienna: Codex.
Blinkenberg, C.
　1941. *Lindos: fouilles de l'acropole 1902–1914: II Inscriptions*. Berlin: de Gruyter.
Blümel, Wolfgang
　1985. *Die Inschriften von Iasos*. IGSK 28. Bonn: Habelt.
　1987–88. *Die Inschriften von Mylasa*. IGSK 35. 2 vols. Bonn: Habelt.
　1991. *Die Inschriften der Rhodischen Peraia*. IGSK 38. Bonn: Habelt.
　1992. *Die Inschriften von Knidos*. IGSK 41. Bonn: Habelt.
Boeckh, Augustine
　1828–77. *Corpus inscriptionum graecarum*. 4 vols. Berlin: Reimer.

Bosch, E.

1967. *Quellen zur Geschichte der Stadt Ankara im Altertum.* Ankara: Türk Tarih Kurumu Basimevi.

Bresson, Alain

1991. *Recueil des inscriptions de la Pérée rhodienne.* Centre de Recherches d'Histoire Ancienne 105. Paris: Annales Littéraires de l'Université de Besançon.

Brixhe, Claude, and René Hodot

1988. *L'Asie Mineure du nord au sud: Inscriptions inédites.* Études d'archéologie classique 6. Nancy: Presses Universitaires de Nancy.

Buckler, W. H., and David M. Robinson

1932. *Sardis. Publications of the American Society for the Excavation of Sardis,* vol. 7: *Greek and Latin Inscriptions.* Leiden: Brill.

Buresch, Karl

1898. *Aus Lydien: Epigraphisch-geographische Reisefrüchte.* Edited by Otto Ribbeck. Leipzig: Teubner.

Cagnat, René, et al.

1888–. *L'Année épigraphique.*

Cagnat, René, J. Toutain, Pierre Jouguet Jovgvet, and Georges Lafaye

1906–1927. *Inscriptiones graecae ad res romanas pertinentes.* 4 vols. Paris: Leroux.

Corsten, Thomas

1985. *Die Inschriften von Kios.* IGSK 29. Bonn: Habelt.

1987. *Die Inschriften von Apameia (Bithynien) und Pylai.* IGSK 32. Bonn: Habelt.

1991. *Die Inschriften von Prusa ad Olympum.* IGSK 39. Bonn: Habelt.

Cremer, Marielouise

1991. *Hellenistisch-römische Grabstelen im nordwestlichen Kleinasien.* Asia Minor Studien 4. Bonn: Habelt.

Degrassi, Attilio

1963–65. *Inscriptiones latinae liberae rei publicae.* Florence: Biblioteca di studi superiori.

Dittenberger, Wilhelm

1903–5. *Orientis graeci inscriptiones selectae. Supplementum sylloge inscriptionum graecarum.* 2 vols. Leipzig: Hirzel.

1920. *Sylloge inscriptionum graecarum.* 3d ed. Leipzig: Hirzel.

Drew-Bear, Thomas

1978. *Nouvelles inscriptions de Phrygie.* Studia amstelodamensia ad epigraphicam, ius antiquum et papyrologicam pertinentia 16. Zutphen, Holland: Terra.

Egypt Exploration Fund

1898–. *The Oxyrhynchus Papyri.* London: Egypt Exploration Fund.

Engelmann, Helmut

1976. *Die Inschriften von Kyme.* IGSK 5. Bonn: Habelt.

Engelmann, Helmut, and Reinhold Merkelbach, eds.
  1972–4. *Die Inschriften von Erythrai und Klazomenai.* IGSK 1. 2 vols. Bonn: Habelt.
Engelmann, H., H. Wankel, and R. Merkelbach
  1979–1984. *Die Inschriften von Ephesos.* IGSK 11–17. 8 vols. Bonn: Habelt.
Fränkel, Max
  1890–5. *Die Inschriften von Pergamon.* Altertümer von Pergamon 8.1–2. Berlin: Spemann.
Frey, Jean-Baptiste
  1936–52. *Corpus inscriptionum iudaicarum.* Sussidi allo studio delle anichità cristiane 3. 2 vols. Rome: Pontificio Istituto di Archeologia Cristiana.
Frisch, Peter
  1975. *Die Inschriften von Ilion.* IGSK 3. Bonn: Habelt.
Gaertringen, F. Hiller von
  1906. *Die Inschriften von Priene.* Königliche Museen zu Berlin. Berlin: Reimer.
Gaertringen, F. Hiller von, et al.
  1873–. *Inscriptiones graecae, consilio et auctoritate Acadaemiae Litterarum Borussicae editae.* Berlin: de Gruyter.
Gibson, Elsa
  1978. *The 'Christians for Christians' Inscriptions of Phrygia: Greek Texts, Translation and Commentary.* HTS 32. Missoula, Mont.: Scholars Press.
Grenfell, Bernard P., et al.
  1902–76. *The Tebtunis Papyri.* Egypt Exploration Society. 3 vols. London: Henry Frowde.
Guéraud, O.
  1931. *Requêtes et plaintes adressées au roi d'Égypte au IIIe siècle avant J.-C.* Cairo: Imprimerie de l'Institut français d'archéologie orientale.
Habicht, Christian
  1969. *Die Inschriften des Asklepieions.* Altertümer von Pergamon 8.3. Berlin: de Gruyter.
Hagedorn, Ursula, Dieter Hagedorn, Louise C. Youtie, and Herbert C. Youtie
  1969. *Das Archiv des Petaus (P.Petaus).* Papyrologica Coloniensia 4. Köln: Westdeutscher Verlag.
Haussoullier, B., A.-J. Reinach, P. Roussel, J. Robert, and L. Robert
  1888–. "Bulletin épigraphique." *REG.*
Heberdey, Rudolf, and Adolf Wilhelm
  1894. *Reisen in Kilikien.* DAWW.PH 44.6. Vienna: Hölder
Herrmann, Peter
  1962. *Ergebnisse einer Reise in Nordostlydien.* DÖAW.PH 80. Vienna: Böhlaus.
  1996. "Mystenvereine in Sardeis." *Chiron* 26:315–41.

Hicks, E. L., C. T. Newton, Gustav Hirschfeld, and F. H. Marshall
    1874–1916. *The Collection of Ancient Greek Inscriptions in the British Museum*. 4
    vols. Oxford: Clarendon.
Hicks, E. L., and W. R. Paton
    1891. *The Inscriptions of Cos*. Oxford: Clarendon.
Horbury, William, and David Noy
    1992. *Jewish Inscriptions of Graeco-Roman Egypt*. Cambridge: Cambridge Univ.
    Press.
Horsley, G. H. R., and S. R. Llewelyn
    1981–. *New Documents Illustrating Early Christianity*. North Ryde, Australia: An-
    cient History Documentary Research Centre, Macquarie University.
Ihnken, Thomas
    1978. *Die Inschriften von Magnesia am Sipylos*. IGSK 8. Bonn: Habelt.
Johnson, Gary J.
    1994. *Early-Christian Epitaphs from Anatolia*. SBLTT 35. Atlanta: Scholars Press.
Johnson, J. M., V. Martin, A. S. Hunt, C. H. Roberts, and E. G. Turner
    1911–52. *Catalogue of the Greek Papyri in the John Rylands Library, Manchester*.
    Manchester: Manchester Univ. Press.
Jonnes, Lloyd, and Walter Ameling
    1994. *The Inscriptions of Heraclea Pontica*. IGSK 47. Bonn: Habelt.
Judeich, Walther
    1898. "Inschriften." In *Altertümer von Hierapolis*. Edited by Carl Humann et al.,
    67–181. JdI Ergänzungsheft 4. Berlin: Reimer.
Kalinka, Ernest, Rudolf Heberdey, Frederick Carol Dörner, Josef Keil, and Peter
Herrmann
    1920–. *Tituli Asiae Minoris collecti et editi auspiciis Academiae Litterarum Austria-
    cae*. Vindobonae: Academiam Scientiarum Austriacam.
Kayser, François
    1994. *Recueil des inscriptions grecques et latines (non funéraires) d'Alexandrie impéri-
    ale*. Bibliothèque d'étude 108. Cairo: Institut Français d'Archéologie Ori-
    entale du Caire.
Keil, Josef, and Anton von Premerstein
    1910. *Bericht über eine Reise in Lydien und der südlichen Aiolis*. DAWW.PH 53.2.
    Vienna: Hölder.
    1911. *Bericht über zweite Reise in Lydien*. DAWW.PH 54.2. Vienna: Hölder.
    1914. *Bericht über dritte Reise in Lydien*. DAWW.PH 57.1. Vienna: Hölder.
Keil, Josef, W. H. Buckler, and W. M. Calder
    1928–. *Monumenta asiae minoris antiqua*. Publications of the American Society
    for Archaeological Research in Asia Minor/JRS Monographs. 10 vols. to
    date. London: Society for the Promotion of Roman Studies.

Kenyon, F. G., H. I. Bell, and T. C. Skeat

1893–1974. *Greek Papyri in the British Museum*. 5. vols. Oxford: Oxford Univ. Press.

Kern, Otto

1900. *Die Inschriften von Magnesia am Maeander*. Königliche Museen zu Berlin. Berlin: Spemann.

Knibbe, Dieter

1972–75a. "Neue Inschriften aus Ephesos IV." *JÖAI* 50:1–26 (Beiblatt).

1972–75b. "Neue Inschriften aus Ephesos VI." *JÖAI* 50:57–66 (Beiblatt).

1972–75c. "Neue Inschriften aus Ephesos V." *JÖAI* 50:27–56 (Beiblatt).

1972–75d. "Neue Inschriften aus Ephesos VII." *JÖAI* 50:69–79 (Beiblatt).

Knibbe, Dieter, and Helmut Engelmann

1984. "Neue Inschriften aus Ephesos X." *JÖAI* 55:137–49 (Hauptblatt).

Knibbe, Dieter, Helmut Engelmann, and Bülent Iplikçioglu

1989. "Neue Inschriften aus Ephesos XI." *JÖAI* 59:164–238 (Beiblatt).

1993. "Neue Inschriften aus Ephesos XII." *JÖAI* 62:113–50 (Hauptblatt).

Knibbe, Dieter, and Bülent Iplikçioglu

1981. "Neue Inschriften aus Ephesos VIII." *JÖAI* 53:87–150 (Hauptblatt).

1984. "Neue Inschriften aus Ephesos IX." *JÖAI* 55:107–35 (Hauptblatt).

Lajtar, Adam

2000. *Die Inschriften von Byzantion*. IGSK 58. Bonn: Habelt.

Lane, E. N.

1971–76. *Corpus monumentorum religionis dei Menis (CMRDM)*. 4 vols. EPRO 19. Leiden: Brill.

Latyschev, Basilius

1965. *Inscriptiones antiquae orae septentrionalis Ponti Euxini graecae et latinae*. 1890–1901. 4 vols. Repr. Hildesheim: Olms.

Laum, Bernhard

1964. *Stiftungen in der griechischen und römischen Antike: Ein Beitrag zur antiken Kulturgeschichte*. 1914. Repr. Aalen: Scientia.

Le Bas, Philippe, and William Henry Waddington

1972. *Inscriptions grecques et latines recueillies en Asie Mineure*. 1870. Repr. Hildesheim: Olms.

Letronne, A. J., W. Brunet de Presle, and E. Egger

1865. *Notices et textes des papyrus grecs du Musée du Louvre et de la Bibliothèque Impériale*. Notices et extraits des manuscrits de la Bibliothèque Impériale et autres bibliothèques 18.2. Paris: Institut de France.

Lifshitz, B.

1967. *Donateurs et fondateurs dans les synagogues juives: Répertoire des dédicaces grecques relatives à la construction et à la réfection des synagogues*. Cahiers de la Revue Biblique 7. Paris: Gabalda.

Lüderitz, Gert

  1983. *Corpus jüdischer Zeugnisse aus der Cyrenaika.* Beihefte zum Tübinger Atlas des vorderen Orients. Wiesbaden: Reichert.

Marek, Christian

  1993. *Stadt, Ära und Territorium in Pontus-Bithynia und Nord-Galatia.* Istanbuler Forschungen 39. Tübingen: Wasmuth.

Mendel, Gustave

  1900. "Inscriptions de Bithynie [I]." *BCH* 24:361–426.

  1901. "Inscriptions de Bithynie [II]." *BCH* 25:5–92.

Merkelbach, Reinhold

  1976. *Die Inschriften von Assos.* IGSK 4. Bonn: Habelt.

  1980. *Die Inschriften von Kalchedon.* IGSK 20. Bonn: Habelt.

Michel, Charles

  1976. *Recueil d'inscriptions grecques.* Subsidia Epigraphica: Quellen und Abhandlungen zur griechischen Epigraphik 4. 1900. Repr. Hildesheim: Olms.

Mihailov, Georgius

  1958–70. *Inscriptiones graecae in Bulgaria repertae.* Institutum Archaeologicum, Series Epigraphica 6. 4 vols. Sofia: Academia Litterarum Bulgarica.

Mommsen, Theodor, E. Lommatzsch, A. Degrassi, and A.U. Stylow

  1893. *Corpus inscriptionum latinarum consilio et auctoritate Academiae Litterarum Refiae Borussicae.* Berlin: Reimer.

Moretti, L.

  1968–91. *Inscriptiones graecae urbis romae.* Studi pubblicati dall'Istituto Italiano per la storia antica 17, 22, 28, 47. 4 vols. Rome: Istututo Italiano per la Storia Antica.

Nollé, Johannes

  1993. *Side im Altertum.* IGSK 43. Bonn: Habelt.

Nollé, Johannes, and Friedel Schindler

  1991. *Die Inschriften von Selge.* IGSK 37. Bonn: Habelt.

Noy, David

  1993–5. *Jewish Inscriptions of Western Europe.* Cambridge: Cambridge Univ. Press.

Oliver, James H.

  1989. *Greek Constitutions of Early Roman Emperors from Inscriptions and Papyri.* Memoirs of the American Philosophical Society 178. Philadelphia: American Philosophical Society.

Pennacchietti, Fabrizio A.

  1966–7. "Nuove iscrizioni di Hierapolis Frigia." *Atti della Accademia delle Scienze di Torino: II classe di scienze morall storiche e filologiche* 101:287–328.

Petersen, Eugen, and Felix von Luschan
  1889. *Reisen in Lykien Milyas und Kibyratien.* Reisen im Südwestlichen Klein-
    asien 1. Vienna: Codex.
Petzl, Georg
  1978. "Inschriften aus der Umgebung von Saittai (I)." *ZPE* 30:249–73.
  1979. "Inschriften aus der Umgebung von Saittai (II)." *ZPE* 36:163–94.
  1982–90. *Die Inschriften von Smyrna.* IGSK 23. 2 vols. Bonn: Habelt.
Pfuhl, Ernst, and Hans Möbius
  1977–79. *Die ostgriechischen Grabreliefs.* Deutsches Archäologisches Institut. 2
    vols. Mainz am Rhein: von Zabern.
Pippidi, D. M., and I. I. Russu
  1983–. *Inscriptiones Scythiae Minoris graecae et latinae.* Inscriptiones Daciae et
    Scythiae Minoris antiquae. Bucharest, Romania: Academia Scientarum
    Socialum et Politicarum Dacoromana.
Pleket, H. W.
  1958. *The Greek Inscriptions in the 'Rijksmuseum Van Oudheden' at Leyden.* Leiden:
    Brill.
Poljakov, Fjodor B.
  1989. *Die Inschriften von Tralleis und Nysa.* IGSK 36. Bonn: Habelt.
Preisigke, Friedrich, Friedrich Bilabel, Emil Kiessling, and Hans-Albert Rupprecht
  1915–. *Sammelbuch griechischer Urkunden aus Ägypten.* Strassburg: Trübner.
Prott, Ioannes de, and Ludouicus Ziehen
  1988. *Leges graecorum sacrae e tiulis collectae.* 1896–1906. 2 vols. Repr. Chicago:
    Ares.
Ramsay, W. M.
  1895–97. *The Cities and Bishoprics of Phrygia.* 2 vols. Oxford: Clarendon.
Rehm, Albert
  1958. *Didyma. Zweiter Teil: Die Inschriften.* Edited by Richard Harder. Deutsches
    Archäologisches Institut. Berlin: Mann.
Ricl, Marijana
  1997. *The Inscriptions of Alexandreia Troas.* IGSK 53. Bonn: Habelt.
Robert, Louis, and Jeanne Robert
  1954. *La Carie: Histoire et géographie historique avec le recueil des inscriptions an-
    tiques,* vol. 2: *Le plateau de Tabai et ses environs.* Paris: Adrien–Maisonneuve.
  1969. "Les inscriptions." In *Laodicée du Lycos: Le nymphée campagnes
    1961–1963,* 247–389. Université Laval recherches archéologiques. Série I:
    Fouilles. Québec: Presses de l'Université Laval.
Roberts, C. H., J. W. B. Barns, and H. Zilliacus
  1950–67. *The Antinoopolis Papyri.* 3 vols. London: Egypt Exploration Society.
Roesch, Paul
  1982. *Études béotiennes.* Paris: De Boccard.

Roueché, Charlotte

    1993. *Performers and Partisans at Aphrodisias in the Roman and Late Roman Periods: A Study Based on Inscriptions from the Current Excavations at Aphrodisias in Caria.* JRS Monographs 6. London: Society for the Promotion of Roman Studies.

Roussel, Pierre, and Marcel Launey

    1937. *Inscriptions de Délos: Décrets postérieurs à 166 av. J-C. (nos. 1497–1524). Dédicaces postérieures à 166 av. J.-C. (nos. 1525–2219).* Académie des Inscriptions et Belles-Lettres. Paris: Champion.

Roussel, Pierre, et al.

    1923–. *Supplementum epigraphicum graecum.* Lugduni Batavorum: Sijthoff.

Sahin, Sencer

    1979–87. *Katalog der antiken Inschriften des Museums von Iznik (Nikaia).* IGSK 9. 4 vols. Bonn: Habelt.

    1982–90. *Die Inschriften von Statonikeia.* IGSK 21. Bonn: Habelt

Schwertheim, Elmar

    1980–1983. *Die Inschriften von Kyzikos und Umgebung.* IGSK 18, 26. 2 vols. Bonn: Habelt.

    1987. *Die Inschriften von Hadrianoi und Hadrianeia.* IGSK 33. Bonn: Habelt.

Sokolowski, Franciszek

    1955. *Lois sacrées de l'Asie Mineure.* École Française d'Athènes. Travaux et mémoires des anciens membre étrangers de l'école et de divers savants 9. Paris: De Boccard.

    1962. *Lois sacrées des cités grecques supplément.* École Française d'Athènes. Travaux et mémoires des anciens membres étrangers de l'école et de divers savants 11. Paris: De Boccard.

    1969. *Lois sacrées des cités grecques.* École Française d'Athènes. Travaux et mémoires des anciens membres étrangers de l'école et de divers savants 10. Paris: De Boccard.

Stauber, Josef

    1996. *Die Bucht von Adramytteion.* IGSK 51. Bonn: Habelt.

Strubbe, J. H. M.

    1997. ΑΡΑΙ ΕΠΙΤΥΜΒΙΟΙ: *Imprecations Against Desecrators of the Grave in the Greek Epitaphs of Asia Minor. A Catalogue.* IGSK 52. Bonn: Habelt.

Tacheva-Hitova, Margarita

    1983. *Eastern Cults in Moesia Inferior and Thracia.* Leiden: Brill.

Tcherikover, Victor, and Alexander Fuks

    1957–64. *Corpus papyrorum judaicarum.* 3 vols. Cambridge: Harvard Univ. Press.

Vermaseren, M. J.
  1956–60. *Corpus inscriptionum et monumentorum religionis Mithriacae.* 2 vols. The Hague: Nijhoff.
  1987. *Corpus cultus Cybelae Attidisque (CCCA): I. Asia Minor.* Leiden: Brill.
Vermaseren, M. J., and E. N. Lane
  1983–89. *Corpus cultus Iovis Sabazii (CCIS).* 3 vols. EPRO 100. Leiden: Brill.
Vidman, Ladislav
  1969. *Sylloge inscriptionum religionis Isiacae et Sarapiacae.* Religionsgeschichtliche Versuche und Vorarbeiten 28. Berlin: de Gruyter.
Wiegend, Theodor, Georg Kawerau, Albert Rehm, and Peter Herrmann
  1889–1998. *Milet: Ergebnisse der Ausgrabungen und Untersuchungen seit dem Jahre 1899.* 6 vols. Berlin: de Gruyter.

2. Ancient Literary Sources

Athanassakis, Apostolos N., trans.
  1977. *The Orphic Hymns: Text Translation and Notes.* SBLTT 12. Missoula, Mont.: Scholars Press.
Bailey, D. R. Shackleton, trans.
  1991. *Cicero. Back from Exile: Six Speeches Upon His Return.* American Philological Association, Classical Resources Series 4. Middletown: American Philological Association.
Behr, Charles A., trans.
  1981. *P. Aelius Aristides: The Complete Works.* Leiden: Brill.
Bettenson, Henry, trans.
  1976. *Livy: Rome and the Mediterranean.* Harmondsworth: Penguin.
Cahoon, J. W., and H. Lamar Crosby, trans.
  1940–46. *Dio Chrysostom.* LCL. 5 vols. Cambridge: Harvard Univ. Press.
Cary, Earnest, trans.
  1960–84. *Dio's Roman History.* LCL. 9 vols. Cambridge: Harvard Univ. Press.
Chadwick, Henry, trans.
  1953. *Origen: Contra Celsum.* Cambridge: Cambridge Univ. Press.
Charlesworth, James H., ed.
  1983–85. *The Old Testament Pseudepigrapha.* 2 vols. Garden City, N.Y.: Doubleday.
Colson, F. H., trans.
  1941–62. *Philo.* LCL. 10 vols. Cambridge: Harvard Univ. Press.

Conybeare, F. C., trans.

    1912–21. *Philostratus: The Life of Apollonius of Tyana.* LCL. 2 vols. London: Heinemann.

Elliott, J. K., trans.

    1993. *The Apocryphal New Testament: A Collection of Apocryphal Christian Literature in an English Translation.* Oxford: Clarendon.

Falconer, William Armistead, trans.

    1979. *Cicero: De senectute, de amicitia, de divinatione.* LCL. Cambridge: Harvard Univ. Press.

Gardner, R., trans.

    1958. *Cicero: Pro Sestio in Vatinium.* LCL. Cambridge: Harvard Univ. Press.

Glover, T. R., and Gerald H. Rendall, trans.

    1931. *Tertullian: Apology, de Spectaculis. Minucius Felix.* LCL. Cambridge: Harvard Univ. Press.

Graves, Robert, trans.

    1990. *The Golden Ass by Lucius Apuleius.* 2d ed. Revised by Michael Grant. Penguin Classics. London: Penguin.

Hamilton, Edith, and Huntington Cairns, eds.

    1961. *The Collected Dialogues of Plato Including the Letters.* Bollingen Series 71. Princeton: Princeton Univ. Press.

Hanson, J. Arthur, trans.

    1989. *Apuleius: Metamorphoses.* LCL. Cambridge: Harvard Univ. Press.

Harmon, A. M., trans.

    1925. *Lucian.* LCL. Cambridge: Harvard Univ. Press.

Helmbold, W. C., and Harold North, trans.

    1957. *Plutarch's Moralia.* LCL. Cambridge: Harvard Univ. Press.

Holmes, Michael W., ed.

    1992. *The Apostolic Fathers: Greek Texts and English Translations.* Translated by J. B. Lightfoot and J. R. Harmer. Grand Rapids: Baker.

Jackson, J., trans.

    1937. *Tacitus: Annals.* LCL. Cambridge: Harvard Univ. Press.

Jones, Horace Leonard, trans.

    1928–9. *The Geography of Strabo.* LCL. 8 vols. Cambridge: Harvard Univ. Press.

Jones, W. H. S., trans.

    1963. *Pliny: Natural History.* Cambridge: Harvard Univ. Press.

    1965. *Pausanias: Description of Greece.* LCL. Cambridge: Harvard Univ. Press.

Keyes, Clinton Walker, trans.

    1977. *Cicero: De re publica. De legibus.* LCL. Cambridge: Harvard Univ. Press.

Lake, Kirsopp, trans.

    1912–3. *The Apostolic Fathers.* LCL. 2 vols. Cambridge: Harvard Univ. Press.

Levi, Peter, trans.
> 1971. *Pausanias: Guide to Greece*. Penguin Classics. London: Penguin.

Magie, David, trans.
> 1960. *The Scriptores historiae augustae*. LCL. Cambridge: Harvard Univ. Press.

Marcus, Ralph, trans.
> 1933–1963. *Josephus: Jewish Antiquities*. LCL. 9 vols. Cambridge: Harvard Univ. Press.

Martínez, Florentino García, trans.
> 1996. *The Dead Sea Scrolls Translated: The Qumran Texts in English*. Translated by Wilfred G. E. Watson. 2d ed. Grand Rapids: Eerdmans.

McGregor, C. P., trans.
> 1972. *Cicero: The Nature of the Gods*. Penguin Classics. London: Penguin.

Meyer, Marvin W., ed.
> 1987. *The Ancient Mysteries: A Sourcebook. Sacred Texts of the Mystery Religions of the Ancient Mediterranean World*. New York: HarperSanFrancisco.

Musurillo, Herbert A., trans.
> 1972. *The Acts of the Christian Martyrs*. Oxford: Clarendon.
> 1979 [1954]. *The Acts of the Pagan Martyrs: Acta Alexandrinorum*. Greek Texts and Commentaries. New York: Arno.

Neusner, Jacob, trans.
> 1988. *The Mishnah: A New Translation*. New Haven: Yale Univ. Press.

Oulton, J. E. L., and H. J. Lawlor, trans.
> 1964. *Eusebius: The Ecclesiastical History*. LCL. Cambridge: Harvard Univ. Press.

Paton, W. R.
> 1927. *Polybius: The Histories*. LCL. London: Heinemann.

Perrin, Bernadotte, trans.
> 1916–20. *Plutarch's Lives*. LCL. 11 vols. Cambridge: Harvard Univ. Press.

Radice, Betty, trans.
> 1969. *Pliny: Letters and Panegyricus*. LCL. Cambridge: Harvard Univ. Press.

Reardon, B. P., ed.
> 1989. *Collected Ancient Greek Novels*. Berkeley: Univ. of California Press.

Robinson, James, ed.
> 1990. *The Nag Hammadi Library in English*. 3d ed. New York: HarperSanFrancisco.

Rolfe, J. C., trans.
> 1913. *Suetonius*. LCL. Cambridge: Harvard Univ. Press.

Sage, Evan T., trans.
> 1965. *Livy*. Cambridge, Mass.: Harvard Univ. Press.

Schneemelcher, Wilhelm, ed.
> 1991–92. *New Testament Apocrypha*. Translated by R. M. Wilson. 2 vols. Louisville: Westminster John Knox.

Scott, S. P., trans.

>   1932. *The Civil Law Including the Twelve Tables, the Institutes of Gaius, the Rules of Ulpian, the Opinions of Paulus, the Enactments of Justinian, and the Consitutions of Leo*. Cincinnati: Central Trust Co. Pub.

Squires, Simon, trans.

>   1990. *Asconius Pedianus, Quintus: Commentaries on Five Speeches of Cicero*. Bristol: Bristol Classical Press.

Stern, Menahem, ed. and trans.

>   1976. *Greek and Latin Authors on Jews and Judaism*. Jerusalem: Israel Academy of Sciences and Humanities.

Thackeray, H. S. J., trans.

>   1927–28. *Josephus: The Jewish War*. LCL. 3 vols. Cambridge: Harvard Univ. Press.

>   1966. *Josephus: The Life. Against Apion*. LCL. Cambridge: Harvard Univ. Press.

Watts, N. H., trans.

>   1964. *Cicero: The Speeches*. LCL. Cambridge: Harvard Univ. Press.

White, Robert J., trans.

>   1975. *The Interpretation of Dreams: Oneirocritica by Artemidorus*. Park Ridge, N.J.: Noyes.

Williams, W. Glynn, and M. Cary, trans.

>   1960. *Cicero: The Letters to His Friends. The Letters to Brutus*. LCL. Cambridge: Harvard Univ. Press.

Williams, W. Glynn, M. Cary, and Mary Henderson, trans.

>   1979. *Cicero: The Letters to His Brother Quintus. The Letters to Brutus. Handbook of Electioneering. Letter to Octavian*. LCL. Cambridge: Harvard Univ. Press.

Winstedt, E. O., trans.

>   1956. *Cicero: Letters to Atticus*. LCL. Cambridge: Harvard Univ. Press.

Wright, Wilmer Cave, trans.

>   1968. *Philostratus and Eunapius: The Lives of the Sophists*. LCL. Cambridge: Harvard Univ. Press.

3. Other Sources

Aberle, David F.

>   1970. "A Note on Relative Deprivation Theory as Applied to Millenarian and Other Cult Movements." In *Millenial Dreams in Action: Studies in Revolutionary Religious Movements*. Edited by Sylvia L. Thrupp, 209–14. New York: Schocken.

Achtemeier, Paul J.
  1996. *1 Peter: A Commentary on First Peter*. Hermeneia. Minneapolis: Fortress Press.
Alexander, Loveday, ed.
  1991. *Images of Empire*. JSOTSup 122. Sheffield: JSOT Press.
Alexander, Paul J.
  1967. *The Oracle of Baalbek: The Tiburtine Sibyl in Greek Dress*. Dumbarton Oaks: Center for Byzantine Studies.
Alföldy, Géza
  1976. "Consuls and Consulars Under the Antonines: Prosopography and History." *AncSoc* 7:263–99.
  1977. *Konsulat und Senatorenstand unter den Antoninen: Prosopographische Untersuchungen zur senatorischen Führungsschicht*. Antiquitas Reihe 1. Abhandlungen zur alten Geschichte 27. Bonn: Habelt.
  1985. *The Social History of Rome*. Translated by David Braund and Frank Pollock. London: Helm.
  1996. "Subject and Ruler, Subjects and Method: An Attempt at a Conclusion." In *Subject and Ruler: The Cult of the Ruling Power in Classical Antiquity: Papers Presented at a Conference Held in the University of Alberta on April 13–15, 1994, to Celebrate the 65th Anniversary of Duncan Fishwick*. Edited by Alastair Small, 254–61. Journal of Roman Archeology Sup 17. Ann Arbor: Journal of Roman Archeology.
Allen, R. E.
  1983. *The Attalid Kingdom: A Constitutional History*. Oxford: Clarendon.
Allo, E.-B.
  1921. *Saint Jean: L'Apocalypse*. 2d ed. Études bibliques. Paris: Gabalda.
Applebaum, S.
  1974a. "The Legal Status of the Jewish Communities in the Diaspora." In *The Jewish People in the First Century: Historical Geography, Political History, Social, Cultural and Religious Life and Institutions*. Edited by S. Safrai and M. Stern, 420–63. CRINT 1/1. Philadelphia: Fortress Press.
  1974b. "The Organization of the Jewish Communities in the Diaspora." In *The Jewish People in the First Century: Historical Geography, Political History, Social, Cultural and Religious Life and Institutions*. Edited by S. Safrai and M. Stern, 464–503. CRINT 1/1. Philadelphia: Fortress Press.
  1979. *Jews and Greeks in Ancient Cyrene*. SJLA 28. Leiden: Brill.
Arnaoutoglou, Ilias
  1994. "Associations and Patronage in Ancient Athens." *AncSoc* 25:5–17.

Arnold, Clinton E.

  1992. *Ephesians: Power and Magic: The Concept of Power in Ephesians in Light of Its Historical Setting.* Grand Rapids: Baker.

  1996. *The Colossian Syncretism: The Interface Between Christianity and Folk Belief at Colossae.* Grand Rapids: Baker.

Ascough, Richard S.

  1996. "The Completion of a Religious Duty: The Background of 2 Cor 8.1–15." *NTS* 42:584–99.

  1997a. "Translocal Relationships Among Voluntary Associations and Early Christianity." *JECS* 5:223–41.

  1997b. "Voluntary Associations and Community Formation: Paul's Macedonian Christian Communities in Context." Ph.D. diss. Toronto School of Theology.

  2000. "The Thessalonian Christian Community as a Professional Voluntary Association." *JBL* 119:311–28.

Atkinson, Kathleen M. T.

  1960. "'Restitutio in integrum' and 'iussum Augusti Caesaris' in an Inscription at Leyden." *Revue internationale des droits de l'antiquité* 7:227–72.

Aune, David E.

  1981. "The Social Matrix of the Apocalypse of John." *BR* 26:16–32.

  1983. "The Influence of Roman Imperial Court Ceremonial on the Apocalypse of John." *BR* 28:5–26.

  1997–98. *Revelation.* 3 vols. WBC 52A-C. Nashville: Nelson.

Ausbüttel, Frank M.

  1982. *Untersuchungen zu den Vereinen im Westen des römischen Reiches.* Frankfurter althistorische Studien 11. Kallmünz: Lassleben.

Balch, David L.

  1981. *Let Wives Be Submissive: The Domestic Code in 1 Peter.* SBLMS 26. Chico, Calif.: Scholars Press.

  1984–85. "Early Christian Criticism of Patriarchal Authority: I Peter 2:11–3:12." *Union Seminary Quarterly Review* 39:161–73.

  1986. "Hellenization/Acculturation in 1 Peter." In *Perspectives on First Peter,* 79–101. Macon, Ga.: Mercer Univ. Press.

Bammel, E.

  1964–65. "The Commands in I Peter II.17." *NTS* 11:279–81.

Barclay, John M. G.

  1996. *Jews in the Mediterranean Diaspora from Alexander to Trajan (323 BCE–117 CE).* Edinburgh: Clark.

Barnes, Jonathan

  1988. "Hellenistic Philosophy and Science." In *The Oxford History of the Classi-*

cal World: Greece and the Hellenistic World. Edited by John Boardman, Jasper Griffin, and Oswyn Murray, 359–79. Oxford: Oxford Univ. Press.

Barnes, T. D.

1968. "Legislation Against the Christians." *JRS* 58:32–50.

1971. *Tertullian: A Historical and Literary Study.* Oxford: Clarendon.

Barnett, H. G., Leonard Broom, Bernard J. Siegel, Evon Z. Vogt, and James B. Watson

1954. "Acculturation: An Exploratory Formulation." *American Anthropologist* 56:973–1002.

Barnett, Paul

1989. "Polemical Parallelism: Some Further Reflections on the Apocalypse." *JSNT* 35:111–20.

Barraclough, Ray

1984. "Philo's Politics: Roman Rule and Hellenistic Judaism." *ANRW* II.21.1:417–553.

Barton, Carlin A.

1994. "Savage Miracles: The Redemption of Lost Honor in Roman Society and the Sacrament of the Gladiator and the Martyr." *Representations* 45:41–71.

Barton, S. C.

1993. "Early Christianity and the Sociology of the Sect." In *The Open Text: New Directions for Biblical Studies?* Edited by Francis Watson, 140–62. London: SCM.

Barton, S. C., and G. H. R. Horsley

1981. "A Hellenistic Cult Group and the New Testament Churches." *JAC* 24:7–41.

Baslez, M.-F.

1988. "Les communautes d'orientaux dans la cité grecque: Formes de sociabilité et modèles associatifs." In *l'Etranger dans le monde grec: Actes du colloque organisé par l'Institut d'Etudes Anciennes, Nancy, mai 1987*, 139–58. Nancy: Presses Universitaires de Nancy.

Bauckham, Richard

1991. "The Economic Critique of Rome in Revelation 18." In *Images of Empire*. Edited by Loveday Alexander, 47–90. JSOTSup 122. Sheffield: JSOT Press.

1993. *The Climax of Prophecy: Studies on the Book of Revelation.* Edinburgh: Clark.

Bauer, Walter

1971. *Orthodoxy and Heresy in Earliest Christianity.* Translated by Robert A. Kraft et al. Philadelphia: Fortress Press.

Baugh, Steven Michael
  1990. "Paul and Ephesus: The Apostle Among His Contemporaries." Ph.D.
       diss. Berkeley: Univ. of California.
Beale, G. K.
  1999. *The Book of Revelation*. New International Greek Testament Commentary.
       Grand Rapids: Eerdmans.
Beard, Mary
  1991. "Writing and Religion: *Ancient Literacy* and the Function of the Written
       Word in Roman Religion." In *Literacy in the Roman World*. Edited by J. H.
       Humphrey, 35–58. Journal of Roman Archeology Sup 3. Ann Arbor: Jour-
       nal of Roman Archaeology.
Beare, Francis Wright
  1958. *The First Epistle of Peter: The Greek Text with Introduction and Notes*. Oxford:
       Blackwell.
Beck, Roger
  1984. "Mithraism Since Franz Cumont." *ANRW* II.17.4:2002–115.
  1992. "The Mithras Cult as Association." *SR* 21:3–13.
Beckford, James A.
  1973. "Religious Organization: A Trend Report and Bibliography." *Current So-
       ciology/La Sociologie Contemporaine* 21(2):1–170.
  1975. *The Trumpet of Prophecy: A Sociological Study of Jehovah's Witnesses*. Oxford:
       Blackwell.
Beckwith, Isbon T.
  1967. *The Apocalypse of John: Studies in Introduction with a Critical and Exegetical
       Commentary*. 1919. Repr. Grand Rapids: Baker.
Bell, Catherine
  1997. *Ritual: Perspectives and Dimensions*. Oxford: Oxford Univ. Press.
Benko, Stephen
  1980. "Pagan Criticism of Christianity During the First Two Centuries A.D."
       ANRW II.23.2:1055–1118.
Bergmann, Werner, and Christhard Hoffmann
  1987. "Kalkül oder 'Massenwahn'? Eine soziologische Interpretation der anti-
       jüdischen Unruhen in Alexandria 38 n.Chr." In *Antisemitismus und jüdische
       Geschichte: Studien zu ehren von Herbert A. Strauss*. Edited by Rainer Erb and
       Michael Schmidt, 15–46. Berlin: Wissenschaftlicher Autorenverlag.
Berquist, Jon L.
  1995. "Deprivation Theory of Social Movements." In *International Encyclopedia
       of Sociology*. Edited by Frank N. Magill, 349–53. London: FD.
Berry, John W.
  1980. "Acculturation as Varieties of Adaptation." In *Acculturation: Theory, Mod-*

els and Some New Findings. Edited by Amado M. Padilla. AAAS Selected Symposium 39. Boulder, Colo.: Westview.

Besnier, Maurice

1932. "Églises chrétiennes et collèges funéraires." In *Mélange Albert Dufourcq: Études d'histoire religieuse*, 9–19. Paris: Plon.

Bickerman, Elias

1968. "Trajan, Hadrian and the Christians." *RFIC* 96:290–315.

1980. "Ritualmord und Eselskult: ein Beitrag zur Geschichte antiker Publizistik" (1927). Repr. in *Studies in Jewish and Christian History*, 225–55. AGJU 9. Leiden: Brill.

Bij de Vaate, Alice J., and Jan Willem Van Henten

1996. "Jewish or Non-Jewish? Some Remarks on the Identification of Jewish Inscriptions from Asia Minor." *Bibliotheca orientalis* 53:16–28.

Birley, Eric

1953. "The Origins of Equestrian Officers: Prosopographical Method." In *Roman Britain and the Roman Army*. Kendal: Titus Wilson & Son.

Bloch, Maurice

1987. "The Ritual of the Royal Bath in Madagascar: The Dissolution of Death, Birth and Fertility Into Authority." In *Rituals of Royalty: Power and Ceremonial in Traditional Societies*. Edited by David Cannadine and Simon Price, 271–97. Past and Present Publications. Cambridge: Cambridge Univ. Press.

Boer, W. den

1969. "Die prosopographische Methode in der modernen Historiographie der hohen Kaiserzeit." *Mnemosyne* 22:268–80.

Boissevain, Jeremy

1974. *Friends of Friends: Networks, Manipulators and Coalitions*. Oxford: Blackwell.

Boissevain, Jeremy, and J. Clyde Mitchell, eds.

1973. *Network Analysis: Studies in Human Interaction*. Change and Continuity in Africa. Paris: Afrika-studiecentrum.

Bonz, Marianne P.

1990. "The Jewish Community of Ancient Sardis: A Reassessment of Its Rise to Prominence." *HSCP* 93:343–59.

1993. "Differing Approaches to Religious Benefaction: The Late Third-Century Acquisition of the Sardis Synagogue." *HTR* 86:139–54.

Borgen, Peder

1988. "Catalogues of Vices, the Apostolic Decree, and the Jerusalem Meeting." In *Essays in Tribute to Howard Clark Kee: The Social World of Formative Christianity and Judaism*. Edited by Jacob Neusner et al., 125–41. Philadelphia: Fortress Press.

1995. "'Yes,' 'No,' 'How Far?': The Participation of Jews and Christians in Pagan Cults." In *Paul in His Hellenistic Context*. Edited by Troels Engberg-Pederson, 30–59. Minneapolis: Fortress Press.

Botha, P. J. J.

1988. "God, Emperor Worship and Society: Contemporary Experience and the Book of Revelation." *Neotestamentica* 22:87–102.

Bowersock, G. W.

1964. "C. Marcius Censorinus, Legatus Caesaris." *HSCP* 68:207–10.

1965. *Augustus and the Greek World*. Oxford: Clarendon.

1973. "Greek Intellectuals and the Imperial Cult in the Second Century A.D." In *Le culte des souverains dans l'empire Romain*, 179–212. Entreteins sur l'antiquité classique 19. Geneva: Reverdin.

1983. "The Imperial Cult: Perceptions and Persistence." In *Jewish and Christian Self-Definition*, vol. 3: *Self-Definition in the Greco-Roman World*. Edited by Ben F. Meyer and E. P. Sanders, 171–82. Philadelphia: Fortress Press.

1995. *Martyrdom and Rome*. Cambridge: Cambridge Univ. Press.

Bowsky, Martha W. Baldwin

1987. "M. Tittius Sex. f. Aem. and the Jews of Berenice (Cyrenaica)." *AJP* 108:495–510.

Box, G. H.

1929. *Early Christianity and Its Rivals: A Study of the Conflict of Religions in the Early Roman Empire at the Beginning of Our Era*. London: Benn.

Bradeen, Donald W.

1975. "The Popularity of the Athenian Empire." In *Problems in Ancient History*. Edited by Donald Kagan, 404–11, 2d ed. New York: Macmillan.

Brashear, William M.

1993. *Vereine im griechisch-römischen Ägypten*. Xenia: Konstanzer althistorische Vorträge und Forschungen 34. Konstanz: Universitätsverlag Konstanz.

Bremen, Riet van

1996. *The Limits of Participation: Women and Civic Life in the Greek East in the Hellenistic and Roman Periods*. Dutch Monographs on Ancient History and Archaeology 15. Amsterdam: Gieben.

Bremer, J. M.

1981. "Greek Hymns." In *Faith, Hope and Worship: Aspects of Religious Mentality in the Ancient World*. Edited by H. S. Versnel, 193–215. Leiden: Brill.

Brent, Allen

1998. "Ignatius of Antioch and the Imperial Cult." *VC* 52:30–58.

Broekhoven, Harold van

1997. "The Social Profiles in the Colossian Debate." *JSNT* 66:73–90.

Brooke, George J.
  1991. "The Kittim in the Qumran Pesharim." In *Images of Empire*. Edited by
    Loveday Alexander, 135–59. JSOTSup 122. Sheffield: JSOT Press.
Broughton, T. R. S.
  1938. "Roman Asia Minor." In *An Economic Survey of Ancient Rome*. Edited by
    Tenney Frank, 499–950. Baltimore: Johns Hopkins Univ. Press.
Brown, Peter
  1978. *The Making of Late Antiquity*. Cambridge: Harvard Univ. Press.
Brown, Raymond E.
  1982. *The Epistles of John: Translated with Introduction, Notes, and Commentary*.
    Anchor Bible 30. Garden City, N.Y.: Doubleday.
Browning, Robert
  1976. "The Crisis of the Greek City—A New Collective Study." *Philologus*
    120:258–65.
Bruce, F. F.
  1971. *New Testament History*. Garden City, N.Y.: Doubleday.
  1978. "The Romans Through Jewish Eyes." In *Mélanges offerts à Marcel Simon:
    Paganisme, judaïsme, Christianisme: Influences et affrontements dans le monde an-
    tique*, 3–12. Paris: De Boccard.
Bruneau, Philippe
  1978. "Les cultes de l'établissement des Poseidoniastes de Bérytos à Delos." In
    Hommages à Maarten J. Vermaseren. Edited by Margreet B. de Boer and T. A.
    Edridge, 160–90. EPRO 68. Leiden: Brill.
  1982. "'Les Israélites de Délos' et la juiverie Délienne." *BCH* 106:465–504.
  1991. "Deliaca." *BCH* 115:377–88.
Bruneau, Philippe, and Jean Ducat
  1983. *Guide de Délos*. 3d ed. Paris: De Boccard.
Brunt, John C.
  1985. "Rejected, Ignored, or Misunderstood? The Fate of Paul's Approach to
    the Problem of Food Offered to Idols in Early Christianity." *NTS*:113–24.
Brunt, P. A.
  1990. *Roman Imperial Themes*. Oxford: Clarendon.
Buck, Carl Darling
  1955. *The Greek Dialects: Grammar, Selected Inscriptions, Glossary*. 1928. Repr.
    Chicago: Univ. of Chicago Press.
Buckler, W. H.
  1913. "Monuments de Thyatire." *RevPhil* 37:289–331.
  1923. "Labour Disputes in the Province of Asia." In *Anatolian Studies Presented
    to William Mitchell Ramsay*. Edited by W. H. Buckler and W. M. Calder,
    27–50. Manchester: Manchester Univ. Press.

1935. "Auguste, Zeus Patroos." *RevPhil* 9:177–88.

Buckler, W. H., and Josef Keil

1926. "Two Resolutions of the Dionysiac Artists from Angora." *JRS* 16:245–52.

Burford, Alison

1972. *Craftsmen in Greek and Roman Society*. Aspects of Greek and Roman Life. London: Thames and Hudson.

Burke, Peter

1992. *History and Social Theory*. 2d ed. Ithaca: Cornell Univ. Press.

Burkert, Walter

1985. *Greek Religion*. Translated by John Raffan. Cambridge: Harvard Univ. Press.

1987. *Ancient Mystery Cults*. Cambridge and London: Harvard Univ. Press.

1993. "Bacchic *teletai* in the Hellenistic Age." In *Masks of Dionysus*. Edited by Thomas H. Carpenter and Christopher A. Faraone, 259–75. Myth and Poetics. Ithaca: Cornell Univ. Press.

Burton, G. P.

1975. "Proconsuls, Assizes and the Administration of Justice Under the Empire." *JRS* 65:92–106.

1993. "Provincial Procurators and the Public Provinces." *Chiron* 23:13–28.

Cadoux, Cecil John

1925. *The Early Church and the World: A History of the Christian Attitudes to Pagan Society and the State Down to the Time of Constantinus*. Edinburgh: Clark.

Calhoun, George Miller

1913. *Athenian Clubs in Politics and Litigation*. Austin: Univ. of Texas Bulletin.

Cannadine, David, and Simon Price, eds.

1987. *Rituals of Royalty: Power and Ceremonial in Traditional Societies*. Past and Present Publications. Cambridge: Cambridge Univ. Press.

Carney, T. F.

1973. "Prosopography: Payoffs and Pitfalls." *Phoenix* 27:156–79.

1975. *The Shape of the Past: Models and Antiquity*. Lawrence, Kans.: Coronado.

Carolsfeld, Ludwig Schnorr von

1969. *Geschichte der juristischen Person*. 2d ed. Aalen: Scientia.

Carruth, Shawn

1996. "Praise for the Churches: The Rhetorical Function of the Opening Sections of the Letters of Ignatius of Antioch." In *Reimagining Christian Origins: A Colloquium Honoring Burton L. Mack*. Edited by Elizabeth A. Castelli and Hal Taussig, 295–310. Valley Forge, Pa.: Trinity Press International.

Cazanove, Olivier de, ed.

1986. *L'Association dionysiaque dans les sociétés anciennes: Actes de la table ronde or-ganisée par l'École Française de Rome (Rome 24–25 mai 1984).* Collection de l'École Française de Rome 89. Paris: De Boccard.

Cenival, Françoise de

1972. *Les associations religieuses en Egypte d'après les documents démotiques.* Publica-tions de l'Institut Français d'Archéologie Orientale du Caire. Bibliothèque d'étude 46. Cairo: Institut Français d'Archéologie Orientale.

Charles, R. H.

1920. *A Critical and Exegetical Commentary on the Revelation of St. John.* Interna-tional Critical Commentary. Edinburgh: Clark.

Charlesworth, M. P.

1935. "Some Observations on Ruler-Cult, Especially in Rome." *HTR* 28:5–44.

Chin, Moses

1991. "A Heavenly Home for the Homeless: Aliens and Strangers in 1 Peter." *TynBul* 42:96–112.

Chow, John K.

1992. *Patronage and Power: A Study of Social Networks in Corinth.* JSNTSup 75. Sheffield: JSOT Press.

Clerc, M.

1885. "Inscription de Nysa." *BCH* 9:124–31.

Cohen, Getzel M.

1995. *The Hellenistic Settlements in Europe, the Islands, and Asia Minor.* Berkeley: Univ. of California Press.

Cohen, Shaye J. D.

1989. "Crossing the Boundary and Becoming a Jew." *HTR* 82:13–33.

1993. "'Those Who Say They Are Jews and Are Not': How Do You Know a Jew in Antiquity When You See One?" In *Diasporas in Antiquity.* Edited by Shaye J. D. Cohen and Ernest S. Frerichs, 1–45, Brown Judaic Studies 288. Atlanta: Scholars Press.

Cole, Susan Guettel

1991. "Dionysiac Mysteries in Phrygia in the Imperial Period." *Epigraphica Anatolica* 17:41–49.

1993. "Voices from Beyond the Grave: Dionysus and the Dead." In *Masks of Dionysus.* Edited by Thomas H. Carpenter and Christopher A. Faraone, 276–95. Myth and Poetics. Ithaca: Cornell Univ. Press.

Collins, Adela Yarbro

1983. "Persecution and Vengeance in the Book of Revelation." In *Apocalypti-cism in the Mediterranean World and the Near East: Proceedings of the Interna-*

tional Colloquium on Apocalypticism Uppsala, August 12–17, 1979. Edited by
David Hellholm, 729–49. Tübingen: Mohr (Siebeck).

1984. *Crisis and Catharsis: The Power of the Apocalypse.* Philadelphia: Westminster.

1985. "Insiders and Outsiders in the Book of Revelation and Its Social Context." In *'To See Ourselves as Others See Us': Christians, Jews, and 'Others' in Late Antiquity.* Edited by Jacob Neusner, Ernest S. Frerichs, and Caroline McCracken-Flesher, 187–218. Scholars Press Studies in the Humanities. Chico, Calif.: Scholars Press.

Collins, John J.

1974. *The Sibylline Oracles of Egyptian Judaism.* SBLDS 13. Missoula, Mont.: Scholars Press.

1998. *The Apocalyptic Imagination: An Introduction to Jewish Apocalyptic Literature.* 2d ed. Biblical Resource Series. Grand Rapids: Eerdmans.

Conrat (Cohn), Max

1969. *Zum römischen Vereinsrecht: Abhandlungen aus der Rechtsgeschichte.* 1873. Repr. Aalen: Scientia.

Conze, A., and C. Schuchhardt

1899. "Die Arbeiten zu Pergamon." *MDAI(A)* 24:164–240.

Cotter, Wendy

1996. "The Collegia and Roman Law: State Restrictions on Voluntary Associations, 64 BCE–200 CE." In *Voluntary Associations in the Graeco-Roman World.* Edited by John S. Kloppenborg and Stephen G. Wilson, 74–89. London: Routledge.

Countryman, L. William

1977. "Patrons and Officers in Club and Church." In *SBL 1977 Seminar Papers,* Paul J. Achtemeier, ed., 135–43. SBLSP Missoula, Mont.: Scholars Press.

Court, John M.

1979. *Myth and History in the Book of Revelation.* Atlanta: John Knox.

Cousin, M. G. and G. Deschamps

1894. "Voyage de Milet à Marmara." *BCH* 18:18–32.

Coutsoumpos, Panayotis

1997. "The Social Implication of Idolatry in Revelation 2:14: Christ or Caesar?" *BTB* 27:23–27.

Cuss, Dominique

1974. *Imperial Cult and Honorary Terms in the New Testament.* Paradosis: Contributions to the History of Early Christian Literature and Theology 23. Fribourg, Switzerland: Fribourg Univ. Press.

D'Arms, John H.

1981. *Commerce and Social Standing in Ancient Rome.* Cambridge: Harvard Univ. Press.

Daniel, Robert W.

1979. "Notes on the Guilds and Army in Roman Egypt." *Bulletin of the American Society of Papyrologists* 16:37–46.

Danker, Frederick W.

1982. *Benefactor*. St. Louis: Clayton.

Davids, Peter H.

1990. *The First Epistle of Peter*. NICNT. Grand Rapids: Eerdmans.

Davies, J. K.

1984. "Cultural, Social and Economic Features of the Hellenistic World." In *CAH*. Vol. 7, part 1: *The Hellenistic World*. Edited by F. W. Walbank et al., 257–320. 2d ed. Cambridge: Cambridge Univ. Press.

1995. "The Fourth Century Crisis: What Crisis?" In *Die athenische Demokratie im 4. Jahrhundert v. Chr.: Vollendung oder Verfall einer Verfassungsform?* Edited by Walter Eder, 29–39. Stuttgart: Steiner.

Davies, Philip R.

1989. "The Social World of Apocalyptic Writings." In *The World of Ancient Israel: Sociological, Anthropological and Political Perspectives*. Edited by R. E. Clements, 251–71. Cambridge: Cambridge Univ. Press.

Deissmann, Adolf

1995. *Light from the Ancient East: The New Testament Illustrated by Recently Discovered Texts of the Graeco-Roman World*. Translated by Lionel R. M. Strachan. 1908. Repr. Peabody, Mass.: Hendrickson.

deSilva, David A.

1991. "The 'Image of the Beast' and the Christians in Asia Minor: Escalation of Sectarian Tension in Revelation 13." *Trinity Journal* 12:185–208.

1998. "Honor Discourse and the Rhetorical Strategy of the Apocalypse of John." *JSNT* 71:79–110.

Detienne, Marcel, and Jean-Pierre Vernant, eds.

1989. *The Cuisine of Sacrifice Among the Greeks*. Translated by Paula Wissing. Chicago: Univ. of Chicago Press.

Deubner, Ludwig

1919. *Bemerkungen zu einigen literarischen Papyri aus Oxyrhynchos*. SHAW.PH 17. Heidelberg: Winters.

Dibelius, Martin

1931. *Die Pastoralbriefe*. 2d ed. Handbuch zum Neuen Testament 13. Tübingen: Mohr (Siebeck).

1956. "Rom und die Christen im ersten Jahrhundert." In *Botschaft und Geschichte: Gesammelte Aufsätze von Martin Dibelius*. Edited by Heinz Kraft and Günther Bornkamm, 177–228. Tübingen: Mohr (Siebeck).

Dibelius, Martin, and Hans Conzelmann

1972. *The Pastoral Epistles*. Translated by Philip Buttolph and Adela Yarbro. Hermeneia. Philadelphia: Fortress Press.

Dickey, Samuel

1928. "Some Economic and Social Conditions of Asia Minor Affecting the Expansion of Christianity." In *Studies in Early Christianity*. Edited by Shirley Jackson Case, 393–416. New York: Century.

Dill, Samuel

1956. *Roman Society from Nero to Marcus Aurelius*. 1904. Repr. New York: World Pub.

Dodds, E. R.

1959. *The Greeks and the Irrational*. Berkeley: Univ. of California Press.

1965. *Pagan and Christian in an Age of Anxiety: Some Aspects of Religious Experience from Marcus Aurelius to Constantine*. Cambridge: Cambridge Univ. Press.

Dombrowski, Bruno W.

1966. "*ḥayyaḥad* in 1QS and τὸ κοινόν: An Instance of Early Greek and Jewish Synthesis." *HTR* 59:293–307.

Dörpfeld, Wilhelm

1894. "Die Ausgrabungen an der Enneakrunos. II." *MDAI(A)* 19:143–51.

1895. "Die Ausgrabungen am Westabhange der Akropolis: II. Das Lenaion oder Dionysion in den Limnai." *MDAI(A)* 20:161–206.

Doublet, G.

1889. "Inscriptions de Paphlagonie." *BCH* 13:293–319.

Douglas, Mary

1973. *Natural Symbols: Explorations in Cosmology*. 2d ed. London: Barrie & Jenkins.

Downing, F. Gerald

1988. "Pliny's Prosecutions of Christians: Revelation and 1 Peter." *JSNT* 34:105–23.

Drerup, Engelbert

1899. "Ein antikes Vereinsstatut." *Neue Jahrbücher für das klassische Altertum Geschichte und deutsche Literatur* 3:356–70.

Drew-Bear, Thomas

1976. "Local Cults in Graeco-Roman Phrygia." *GRBS* 17:247–68.

Drew-Bear, Thomas, and Christian Naour

1990. "Divinités de Phrygie." *ANRW* II.18.3:1907–2044.

Drexhage, Hans-Joachim von

1992. "Feminine Berufsbezeichnungen im hellenistischen Ägypten." *Münstersche Beiträge zum antiken Handelsgeschichte* 11:70–79.

Duff, P. W.

1938. *Personality in Roman Private Law*. Cambridge: Cambridge Univ. Press.

1942. Review of F. M. de Robertis, *Il diritto associativo romano dai collegi della re-publica alle corporazioni del basso impero. JRS* 32:129–31.

Dunn, James D. G.

1988. *Romans*. 2 vols. WBC 38A-B. Waco: Word.

Durkheim, Emile

1965. *Elementary Forms of the Religious Life*. New York: Free Press.

Eck, Werner

1970. *Senatoren von Vespasian bis Hadrian: Prosopographische Untersuchungen mit Einschluss der Jahres- und Provinzialfasten der Statthalter*. Vestegia: Beiträge zur alten Geschichte 13. Munich: Beck.

Eder, Walter, ed.

1995. *Die athenische Demokratie im 4. Jahrhundert v. Chr.: Vollendung oder Verfall einer Verfassungsform?* Stuttgart: Steiner.

Edson, Charles

1948. "Cults of Thessalonica (Macedonia III)." *HTR* 41:153–204.

Edwards, Douglas R.

1996. *Religion and Power: Pagans, Jews, and Christians in the Greek East*. Oxford: Oxford Univ. Press.

Edwards, M. J.

1992. "Some Early Christian Immoralities." *AncSoc* 23:71–82.

Egelhaaf-Gaiser, U., and A. Schäfer, eds.

2002. *Religiöse Vereine in der Römischen Antike. Untersuchungen zu Organisation, Ritual und Raumordnung*. Studien und Texte zu Antike und Christentum, 13. Tübingen: Mohr-Siebeck.

Eister, Allan W.

1967. "Toward a Radical Critique of Church-Sect Typologizing: Comment on 'Some Critical Observations on the Church-Sect Dimension.'" *Journal for the Scientific Study of Religion* 6:85–90.

Elise, Sharon

1995. "Cultural and Structural Assimilation." In *International Encyclopedia of Sociology*, 275–78. London: FD.

Elliott, John H.

1986a. "1 Peter, Its Situation and Strategy: A Discussion with David Balch." In *Perspectives on First Peter*, 61–78. Macon: Mercer Univ. Press.

1986b. *Social-Scientific Criticism of the New Testament and Its Social World*. Semeia 35. Decatur, Ga.: Scholars Press.

1990. *A Home for the Homeless: A Social-Scientific Criticism of I Peter, Its Situation and Strategy*. 2d ed. Minneapolis: Fortress Press.

1993. *What Is Social-Scientific Criticism?* Minneapolis: Fortress Press.

1995. "Disgraced Yet Graced. The Gospel According to 1 Peter in the Key of Honor and Shame." *BTB* 25:166–78.

Engelmann, Helmut

1990. "Ephesische Inschriften." *ZPE* 84:89–94.

Farnell, L. R.

1912. *The Higher Aspects of Greek Religion.* London: Williams and Norgate.

Feldman, Louis H.

1993. *Jew and Gentile in the Ancient World.* Princeton: Princeton Univ. Press.

Feldmeier, Reinhard

1992. *Die Christen als Fremde: Die Metapher der Fremde in der antiken Welt, im Urchristentum und im 1.Petrusbrief.* WUNT 64. Tübingen: Mohr (Siebeck).

Fellmeth, Ulrich

1987. "Die römischen Vereine und die Politik: Untersuchungen zur sozialen Schichtung und zum politischen Bewusstsein der städtischen Volksmassen in Rom und Italien." Ph.D. diss. Stuttgart: Historisches Institut der Universität Stuttgart.

1990. "Politisches Bewusstsein in den Vereinen der städtischen Massen in Rom und Italien zur Zeit der Republik und der frühen Kaiserzeit." *Eirene* 27:49–71.

Ferguson, W. S.

1928. "The Leading Ideas of the New Period." In *CAH.* Vol. 3: *The Hellenistic Monarchies and the Rise of Rome.* Edited by S. A. Cook, F. E. Adcock, and M. P. Charlesworth, 1–40. Cambridge: Cambridge Univ. Press.

Ferguson, W. S., and A. D. Nock

1944. "The Attic Orgeones and the Cult of Heroes." *HTR* 37:61–174.

Festugière, André-Jean

1960. *Personal Religion Among the Greeks.* Berkeley: Univ. of California Press.

1972. "Le fait religieux à l'époque hellénistique" (1945). Repr. in *Études de religion grecque et hellénistique,* 114–28. Bibliothèque d'Histoire de la Philosophie. Paris: Vrin.

Filgis, Menrad N., and Wolfgang Radt

1986. *Die Stadtgrabung. Teil 1: Das Heroon.* Altertümer von Pergamon 15. Berlin: de Gruyter.

Filson, Floyd V.

1939. "The Significance of the Early House Churches." *JBL* 58:109–12.

Finley, M. I.

1985a. *The Ancient Economy.* 2d ed. London: Hogarth.

1985b. *Ancient History: Evidence and Models.* London: Chatto & Windus.

Fisher, Nicholas R. E.

1988a. "Greek Associations, Symposia, and Clubs." In *Civilization of the Ancient Mediterranean: Greece and Rome*. Edited by Michael Grant and Rachel Kitzinger, 1167–97. New York: Scribner's Sons.

1988b. "Roman Associations, Dinner Parties, and Clubs." In *Civilization of the Ancient Mediterranean: Greece and Rome*. Edited by Michael Grant and Rachel Kitzinger, 1199–1225. New York: Scribner's Sons.

Fishwick, Duncan

1978. "The Development of Provincial Ruler Worship in the Western Roman Empire." *ANRW* II.16.2:1201–53.

1987–92. *The Imperial Cult in the Latin West: Studies in the Ruler Cult of the Western Provinces of the Roman Empire*. EPRO 108. Leiden: Brill.

Follet, Simone

1976. *Athènes au IIᵉ et au IIIᵉ siècle: Études chronologiques et prosopographiques*. Collection d'études anciennes. Paris: Société d'Édition les Belles Lettres.

Fontenrose, Joseph

1988. *Didyma: Apollo's Oracle, Cult, and Companions*. Berkeley: Univ. of California Press.

Forbes, Clarence Allen

1933. *Neoi: A Contribution to the Study of Greek Associations*. Middletown, Conn.: American Philological Association.

1955. "Ancient Athletic Guilds." *CP* 50:238–52.

Foucart, Paul

1873. *Des associations religieuses chez les Grecs—thiases, éranes, orgéones, avec le texte des inscriptions rélative à ces associations*. Paris: Klincksieck.

Franklin, James L., Jr.

1980. *Pompeii: The Electoral Programmata, Campaigns and Politics, A.D. 71–79*. Papers and Monographs of the American Academy in Rome 28. Rome: American Academy.

Fraser, P. M.

1977. *Rhodian Funerary Monuments*. Oxford: Clarendon.

Frend, W. H. C.

1965. *Martyrdom and Persecution in the Early Church: A Study of a Conflict from the Maccabees to Donatus*. Oxford: Blackwell.

1984. "Montanism: Research and Problems." *Rivista di storia e letteratura religiosa* 20:521–37.

1988. "Montanism: A Movement of Prophecy and Regional Identity in the Early Church." *BJRL* 70.3:25–34.

Friesen, Steven J.

    1993. *Twice Neokoros: Ephesus, Asia and the Cult of the Flavian Imperial Family*. Religions in the Greco-Roman World 116. Leiden: Brill.

    1995a. "The Cult of the Roman Emperors in Ephesos: Temple Wardens, City Titles, and the Interpretation of the Revelation of John." In *Ephesos Metropolis of Asia: An Interdisciplinary Approach to Its Archaeology, Religion, and Culture*. Edited by Helmut Koester, 229–50. HTS 41. Valley Forge, Pa.: Trinity Press International.

    1995b. "Revelation, Realia, and Religion: Archaeology in the Interpretation of the Apocalypse." *HTR* 88:291–314.

    2001. *Imperial Cults and the Apocalypse of John: Reading Revelation in the Ruins*. Oxford: Oxford Univ. Press.

Garnsey, Peter

    1984. "Religious Toleration in Classical Antiquity." In *Persecution and Toleration: Papers Read at the Twenty-second Summer Meeting and the Twenty-third Winter Meeting of the Ecclesiastical History Society*. Edited by W. J. Sheils, 1–27. Studies in Church History 21. London: Blackwell.

    1998. *Cities, Peasants and Food in Classical Antiquity: Essays in Social and Economic History*. Edited by Walter Scheidel. Cambridge: Cambridge Univ. Press.

Garnsey, Peter, and Richard Saller

    1987. *The Roman Empire: Economy, Society and Culture*. London: Duckworth.

Gasparro, Giulia Sfameni

    1985. *Soteriology and Mystic Aspects in the Cult of Cybele and Attis*. EPRO 130. Leiden: Brill.

Gauthier, Philippe

    1985. *Les cités grecques et leurs bienfaiteurs*. BCHSup 12. Paris: De Boccard.

    1993. "Les cités hellénistiques." In *The Ancient Greek City-State: Symposium on the Occasion of the 250th Anniversary of the Royal Danish Academy of Sciences and Letters, July, 1–4 1992*, 211–31. HFM 67. Copenhagen: Royal Danish Academy of Sciences and Letters.

Geertz, Clifford

    1973. *The Interpretation of Cultures: Selected Essays by Clifford Geertz*. New York: Basic Books.

    1977. "Centers, Kings, and Charisma: Reflections on the Symbolics of Power." In *Culture and Its Creators: Essays in Honor of Edward Shils*. Edited by Joseph Ben-David and Terry Nichols Clark, 150–71. Chicago: Univ. of Chicago Press.

Geffcken, Johannes

    1978. *The Last Days of Greco-Roman Paganism*. Translated by Sabine MacCormack. Europe in the Middle Ages, Selected Studies 8. 1920. Repr. Amsterdam: North–Holland Pub.

Gerkan, A. von

1921. "Eine Synagoge in Milet." *Zeitschrift für die neutestamentliche Wissenschaft und die Kunde der älteren Kirche* 20:177–81.

Gibson, E. Leigh

1999. *The Jewish Manumission Inscriptions of the Bosporus Kingdom.* Texte und Studien zum antiken Judentum 75. Tübingen: Mohr (Siebeck).

Gierke, Otto

1977. *Associations and Law: The Classical and Early Christian Stages.* Edited and translated by George Heiman. 1881. Repr. Toronto: Univ. of Toronto Press.

Gill, David W. J., and Gempf, Conrad, eds.

1994. *The Book of Acts in Its Graeco-Roman Setting.* Book of Acts in Its First Century Setting 2. Grand Rapids: Eerdmans.

Gilliam, J. F.

1961. "The Plague Under Marcus Aurelius." *AJP* 82:225–51.

1976. "Invitations to the Kline of Sarapis." In *Collectanea Papyrologica: Texts Published in Honor of H. C. Youtie.* Edited by Ann Ellis Hanson, 315–24. Papyrologische Texte und Abhandlungen 19. Bonn: Habelt.

Glock, Charles Y., and Rodney Stark

1965. "On the Origin and Evolution of Religious Groups." In *Religion and Society in Tension,* 242–59. Chicago: Rand McNally.

Gooch, Peter D.

1993. *Dangerous Food: 1 Corinthians 8–10 in Its Context.* Waterloo: Wilfred Laurier Univ. Press.

Goodenough, E. R.

1953-68. *Jewish Symbols in the Greco-Roman Period.* 13 vols. New York: Pantheon.

Goodman, Martin

1991. "Opponents of Rome: Jews and Others." In *Images of Empire.* Edited by Loveday Alexander, 222–38. JSOTSup 122. Sheffield: JSOT Press.

1994. "Josephus as Roman Citizen." In *Josephus and the History of the Greco-Roman Period: Essays in Memory of Morton Smith.* Edited by Fausto Parente and Joseph Sievers, 329–38. StPB 41. Leiden: Brill.

Goppelt, Leonhard

1982. "Christians in Society." In *Theology of the New Testament,* vol. 2: *The Variety and Unity of the Apostolic Witness to Christ.* Edited by Jürgen Roloff. Translated by John E. Alsup, 161–97. Grand Rapids: Eerdmans.

1993. *A Commentary on I Peter.* Edited by Ferdinand Hahn. Translated by John E. Alsup. Grand Rapids: Eerdmans.

Gordon, Richard

1972. "Fear of Freedom? Selective Continuity in Religion During the Hellenistic Period." *Didaskalos* 4:48–60.

1990. "Religion in the Roman Empire: The Civic Compromise and Its Limits." In *Pagan Priests: Religion and Power in the Ancient World.* Edited by Mary Beard and John North, 233–55. London: Duckworth.

Grabbe, Lester L.

1989. "The Social Setting of Early Jewish Apocalypticism." *Journal for the Study of the Pseudepigrapha* 4:27–47.

1992. *Judaism from Cyrus to Hadrian.* Minneapolis: Fortress Press.

Graham, Alexander John

1974. "The Limitations of Prosopography in Roman Imperial History (with Special Reference to the Severan Period)." *ANRW* 2.1:136–57.

Grant, Robert M.

1948. "Pliny and the Christians." *HTR* 41:273–74.

1970. "Sacrifices and Oaths as Required of Early Christians." In *Kyriakon: Festschrift Johannes Quasten.* Edited by Patrick Granfield and Josef A. Jungmann, 12–17. Münster: Aschendorff.

Green, Peter

1990. *Alexander to Actium: The Historical Evolution of the Hellenistic Age.* Berkeley: Univ. of California Press.

Groag, E., A. Stein, and L. Petersen

1933–. *Prosopographia imperii romani.* Berlin: de Gruyter.

Gruen, Erich S.

1984. *The Hellenistic World and the Coming of Rome.* Berkeley: Univ. of California Press.

1990. "The Bacchanalian Affair." In *Studies in Greek Culture and Roman Policy,* 34–78. Cincinnati Classical Studies 7. Leiden: Brill.

1993. "The Polis in the Hellenistic World." In *Nomodeiktes: Greek Studies in Honor of Martin Ostwald.* Edited by Ralph M. Rosen and Joseph Farrell, 339–54. Ann Arbor: Univ. of Michigan Press.

1998. *Heritage and Hellenism: The Reinvention of Jewish Tradition.* Berkeley: Univ. of California Press.

Gurney, Joan Neff, and Kathleen J. Tierney

1982. "Relative Deprivation and Social Movements: A Critical Look at Twenty Years of Theory and Research." *Sociological Quarterly* 23:33–47.

Guterman, Simeon L.

1951. *Religious Toleration and Persecution in Ancient Rome.* London: Aiglon.

Guthrie, W. K. C.

    1950. *The Greeks and Their Gods.* The Classical Experience. Boston: Beacon.

Halfmann, Helmut

    1979. *Die Senatoren aus dem östlichen Teil des Imperium Romanum bis zum Ende des 2.Jh.n.Chr.* Hypomnemata 58. Göttingen: Vandenhoeck & Ruprecht.

    1990. "Hymnoden von Asia in Kyzikos." In *Mysische Studien.* Asia Minor Studien 1. Bonn: Habelt.

Hanfmann, George M. A.

    1967. "The Ninth Campaign at Sardis (1966)." *Bulletin of the American Schools of Oriental Research* 187:9–62.

Hanfmann, George M., ed.

    1983. *Sardis from Prehistoric to Roman Times. Results of the Archeological Exploration of Sardis 1958–1975.* Cambridge: Harvard Univ. Press.

Hansen, Mogens Herman

    1993. "Introduction: The *Polis* as a Citizen-State." In *The Ancient Greek City-State: Symposium on the Occasion of the 250th Anniversary of the Royal Danish Academy of Sciences and Letters, July, 1–4 1992,* 7–29. HFM 67. Copenhagen: Royal Danish Academy of Sciences and Letters.

    1994a. "*Poleis* and City-States, 600–323 B.C. A Comprehensive Research Programme." In *From Political Architecture to Stephanus Byzantius: Sources for the Ancient Greek Polis.* Edited by David Whitehead, 9–17. HE 87. Stuttgart: Steiner.

    1994b. "*Polis, Civitas,* Stadtstaat and City-State." In *From Political Architecture to Stephanus Byzantius: Sources for the Ancient Greek Polis.* Edited by David Whitehead, 19–22. HE 87. Stuttgart: Steiner.

    1995. "The 'Autonomous City-state.' Ancient Fact or Modern Fiction." In *Studies in the Ancient Greek Polis.* Edited by Mogens Herman Hansen and Kurt Raaflaub, 21–43. HE 95. Stuttgart: Steiner.

Hansen, Mogens Herman, and Kurt Raaflaub, eds.

    1995. *Studies in the Ancient Greek Polis.* HE 95. Stuttgart: Steiner.

Hardy, E. G.

    1910. *Studies in Roman History.* London: Swan Sonnenschein.

Harland, Philip A.

    1996. "Honours and Worship: Emperors, Imperial Cults and Associations at Ephesus (First to Third Centuries C.E.)." *Studies in Religion / Sciences religieuses* 25:319–34.

    1999. "Claiming a Place in Polis and Empire: The Significance of Imperial Cults and Connections Among Associations, Synagogues, and Christian Groups in Roman Asia (c. 27 B.C.E.–138 C.E.)." Unpublished Ph.D. Diss. Toronto: University of Toronto.

2000. "Honouring the Emperor or Assailing the Beast: Participation in Civic Life Among Associations (Jewish, Christian and Other) in Asia Minor and the Apocalypse of John." *JSNT* 77:99–121.

2002. "Connections with the Elites in the World of the Early Christians." In *Handbook of Early Christianity: Social Science Approaches.* Edited by Anthony J. Blasi, Paul-André Turcotte and Jean Duhaime. Walnut Creek: Alta Mira Press, 385–408.

2003 [forthcoming]. "Christ-Bearers and Fellow-Initiates: Local Cultural Life and Christian Identity in Ignatius' Letters." *JECS.*

2003 [forthcoming]. "The Declining Polis? Religious Rivalries in Ancient Civic Context." In *Religious Rivalries and the Struggle for Success: Methodological Papers.* Edited by Leif E. Vaage. Waterloo: Wilfrid Laurier University Press.

2003 [forthcoming]. "Imperial Cults Within Local Cultural Life: Associations in Roman Asia." *Ancient History Bulletin / Zeitschrift Für Alte Geschichte* 17.

2003 [forthcoming]. "Spheres of Contention, Claims of Preeminence: Rivalries Among Associations in Sardis and Smyrna." In *Religious Rivalries and the Struggle for Success in Sardis and Smyrna. Studies in Judaism and Christianity.* Edited by Richard S. Ascough. Waterloo: Wilfrid Laurier University Press.

Harnack, Adolf

1889. Review of Prof. Dr. Edgar Loening, *Die Gemeindeverfassung des Urchristentum: Eine kirchenrechtliche Untersuchung. Festschrift (für R.v. Gneist). Theologische Literaturzeitung* 14:417–24.

1905. *The Expansion of Christianity in the First Three Centuries.* Edited and translated by James Moffatt. London: Williams and Norgate.

Harrington, Wilfrid J.

1993. *Revelation.* Sacra Pagina 16. Collegville, Minn.: Liturgical Press.

Harris, William V.

1989. *Ancient Literacy.* Cambridge: Harvard Univ. Press.

Harrison, Jane Ellen

1906. *Primitive Athens as Described by Thucydides.* Cambridge: Cambridge Univ. Press.

Hasluck, F. W.

1904. "Unpublished Inscriptions from the Cyzicus Neighbourhood." *JHS* 24:20–40.

1910. *Cyzicus.* Cambridge Archaeological and Ethnological Series. Cambridge: Cambridge Univ. Press.

Hatch, Edwin

1909. *The Organization of the Early Christian Churches: Eight Lectures Delivered Be-*

fore the University of Oxford, in the Year 1880. Repr. London: Longmans, Green.

1957. *The Influence of Greek Ideas on Christianity*. Library of Religion and Culture. 1889. Repr. New York: Harper.

Hatzfeld, Jean

1919. *Les trafiquants italiens dans l'orient hellénique*. Bibliothéque des Écoles Françaises d'Athènes et de Rome 115. Paris: De Boccard.

Hazelrigg, Lawrence

1992. "Individualism." In *Encyclopedia of Sociology*. Edited by Edgar F. Borgatta and Marie L. Borgatta, vol. 2, 901–7. New York: Macmillan.

Heinrici, Georg

1876. "Die christengemeinden Korinths und die religiösen Genossenschaften der Griechen." *ZWT* 19:465–526.

1877. "Zur Geschichte der Anfänge paulinischer Gemeinden." *ZWT* 20:89–130.

1881. "Zum genossenschaftlichen Charakter der paulinischen Christengemeinden." *Theologische Studien und Kritiken* 54:505–24.

Hemer, C. J.

1986. *The Letters to the Seven Churches of Asia in Their Local Setting*. JSNTSup 11. Sheffield: JSOT Press.

Hendrix, Holland

1984. "Thessalonicans Honor Romans." Th.D. diss. Harvard University.

Henrichs, Albert

1970. "Pagan Ritual and the Alleged Crimes of the Early Christians." In *Kyriakon: Festschrift Johannes Quasten*. Edited by Patrick Granfield and Josef A. Jungmann, 18–35. Münster: Aschendorff.

1972. *Die Phoinikika des Lollianos: Fragmente eines neuen griechischen Romans*. Papyrologische Texte und Abhandlungen 14. Bonn: Habelt.

1978. "Greek Maenadism from Olympias to Messalina." *HSCP* 82:121–60.

1983. "Changing Dionysiac Identities." In *Jewish and Christian Self–Definition*, vol. 3: *Self-Definition in the Graeco-Roman World*. Edited by Ben F. Meyer and E. P. Sanders, 137–60. Philadelphia: Fortress Press.

Hepding, H.

1910. "Die Arbeiten zu Pergamon 1908–1909." *MDAI(A)* 35:401–93.

Hermansen, Gustav

1981. *Ostia: Aspects of Roman City Life*. Edmonton: Univ. of Alberta Press.

Herrmann, Peter

1998. "Demeter Karpophoros in Sardeis." *REA* 100:495–508.

Herrmann, Peter, J. H. Waszink, Carsten Colpe, and B. Kötting

1978. "Genossenschaft." *RAC* 10:83–155. Stuttgart: Hiersemann.

Herskovits, Melville J.
  1958. *Acculturation: The Study of Culture Contact*. Gloucester, Mass.: Peter
    Smith.
Heyob, Sharon Kelly
  1975. *The Cult of Isis Among Women in the Graeco-Roman World*. EPRO 51. Lei-
    den: Brill.
Hock, Ronald
  1980. *The Social Context of Paul's Ministry: Tentmaking and Apostleship*. Philadel-
    phia: Fortress Press.
Hoff, Michael C., and Susan I. Rotroff, eds.
  1997. *The Romanization of Athens: Proceedings of an International Conference Held
    at Lincoln, Nebraska (April 1996)*. Oxbow Monograph 94. Oxford: Oxbow.
Hölbl, Günther
  1978. *Zeugnisse ägyptischer Religionsvorstellungen für Ephesus*. EPRO 73. Leiden:
    Brill.
Holmberg, Bengt
  1990. *Sociology and the New Testament: An Appraisal*. Minneapolis: Fortress
    Press.
Hooker, G. T. W.
  1960. "The Topography of the *Frogs*." *JHS* 80:112–17.
Hopkins, Keith
  1965. "Élite Mobility in the Roman Empire." *Past and Present* 32:12–26.
  1978. "Divine Emperors or the Symbolic Unity of the Roman Empire." In
    Conquerors and Slaves: Sociological Studies in Roman History, 197–242. Cam-
    bridge: Cambridge Univ. Press.
  1980. "Taxes and Trade in the Roman Empire (200 B.C.–A.D. 400)." *JRS*
    70:101–25.
  1983. *Death and Renewal: Sociological Studies in Roman History*. Cambridge:
    Cambridge Univ. Press.
  1998. "Christian Number and Its Implications." *JECS* 6:185–226.
Horsley, G. H. R.
  1992. "The Inscriptions of Ephesos and the New Testament." *NovT*
    34:105–68.
  1989. "A Fishing Cartel in First-Century Ephesos." In *New Documents Illustrat-
    ing Early Christianity*, vol. 5, 95–114. Macquarie: Ancient History Docu-
    mentary Research Centre, Macquarie University.
Horsley, G. H. R., and John A. L. Lee
  1994. "A Preliminary Checklist of Abbreviations of Greek Epigraphic Vol-
    umes." *Epigraphica* 56:129–69.

Horsley, Richard A., ed.

    1997. *Paul and Empire: Religion and Power in Roman Imperial Society*. Harrisburg: Trinity Press International.

Horst, P. W. van der

    1989. "Jews and Christians in Aphrodisias in Light of Their Relations in Other Cities of Asia Minor." *Nederlands theologisch tijdschrift* 43:106–21.

    1991. *Ancient Jewish Epitaphs: An Introductory Survey of a Millennium of Jewish Funerary Epigraphy (300 BCE– 700 CE)*. Contributions to Biblical Exegesis and Theology 2. Kampen: Kok Pharos.

    1992. "A New Altar of a Godfearer." *JJS* 43:32–37.

Humann, Carl, Conrad Cichorius, Walther Judeich, and Franz Winter, eds.

    1898. *Altertümer von Hierapolis*. JdI, Ergänzungsheft 4. Berlin: Reimer.

Humphries, Mark

    1998. "Trading Gods in Northern Italy." In *Trade, Traders and the Ancient City*. Edited by Helen Parkins and Christopher Smith, 203–24. London: Routledge.

Huzar, Eleanor G.

    1995. "Emperor Worship in Julio-Claudian Egypt." *ANRW* II.18.5: 3092–3143.

Ippel, A.

    1912. "Die Arbeiten zu Pergamon 1910–1911." *MDAI(A)* 37:277–303.

Jaczynowska, Maria

    1978. *Les associations de la jeunesse romaine sous le Haut-Empire*. Archiwum Filologiczne 36. Wroclaw: Zaklad Narodowy Imienia Ossolinskich.

James, William

    1963. *The Varieties of Religious Experience: A Study in Human Nature Being the Gifford Lectures on Natural Religion Delivered at Edinburgh in 1901–1902*. 1902. Repr. New York: University Books.

Jeffers, James S.

    1991. *Conflict at Rome: Social Order and Hierarchy in Early Christianity*. Minneapolis: Fortress Press.

Johnson, Sherman E.

    1961. "Christianity in Sardis." In *Early Christian Origins: Studies in Honor of Harold R. Willoughby*. Edited by Allen Wikgren, 81–90. Chicago: Quadrangle.

    1975. "Asia Minor and Early Christianity." In *Christianity, Judaism and Other Greco-Roman Cults: Studies for Morton Smith at Sixty*. Edited by Jacob Neusner, 77–145. SJLA 12. Leiden: Brill.

Jones, A. H. M.

    1940. *The Greek City from Alexander to Justinian*. Oxford: Clarendon.

1960. "Procurators and Prefects in the Early Principate." In *Studies in Roman Government and Law*, 117–25. Oxford: Blackwell.

1971. *The Cities of the Eastern Roman Provinces*. Rev. M. Avi-Yonah, et al. 2d ed. Oxford: Clarendon.

1974. "The Cloth Industry Under the Roman Empire." In *The Roman Economy: Studies in Ancient Economic and Administrative History*, 350–64. 1960. Repr. Totowa, N.J.: Rowman and Littlefield.

Jones, Brian W.

1992. *The Emperor Domitian*. London: Routledge.

Jones, C. P.

1971. *Plutarch and Rome*. Oxford: Clarendon.

1978. *The Roman World of Dio Chrysostom*. Cambridge: Harvard Univ. Press.

1986. *Culture and Society in Lucian*. Cambridge: Harvard Univ. Press.

1990. "Lucian and the Bacchants of Pontus." *Echos du monde classique/Classical Views* 9:53–63.

Jones, Donald L.

1980. "Christianity and the Roman Imperial Cult." *ANRW* II.23.2:1023–54.

Jones, Nicholas F.

1987. *Public Organization in Ancient Greece: A Documentary Study*. Memoirs of the American Philosophical Society 176. Philadelphia: American Philosophical Society.

1995. "The Athenian Phylai as Associations: Disposition, Function, and Purpose." *Hesperia* 64:503–42.

1999. *The Associations of Classical Athens: The Response to Democracy*. Oxford: Oxford Univ. Press.

Joshel, Sandra R.

1992. *Work, Identity, and Legal Status at Rome: A Study of the Occupational Inscriptions*. Norman: Univ. of Oklahoma Press.

Judeich, Walther

1931. *Topographie von Athen*. Handbuch der Altertumswissenschaft. Munich: Beck.

Judge, E. A.

1960. *The Social Pattern of the Christian Groups in the First Century*. London: Tyndale Press.

1980–81. "The Social Identity of the First Christians: A Question of Method in Religious History." *Journal of Religious History* 11:201–17.

Juster, Jean

1914. *Les juifs dans l'empire romain: Leur condition juridique, économique et sociale*. New York: Franklin.

Kampen, Natalie

1981. *Image and Status: Roman Working Women in Ostia*. Berlin: Mann.

Kant, Laurence H.

1987. "Jewish Inscriptions in Greek and Latin." *ANRW* II.20.2:671–713.

Kapetanopoulos, Elias

1984. "Athenian Archons of A.D. 170/1–179/80." *RFIC* 112:177–91.

Kasher, Aryeh

1976. "The Jewish Attitude to the Alexandrian Gymnasium in the First Century A.D." *American Journal of Ancient History* 1:148–61.

1985. *The Jews in Hellenistic and Roman Egypt*. Tübingen: Mohr (Siebeck).

1995. "Synagogues as 'Houses of Prayer' and 'Holy Places' in the Jewish Communities of Hellenistic and Roman Egypt." In *Ancient Synagogues: Historical Analysis and Archaeological Discovery*. Edited by Dan Urman and Paul V. M. Flesher, 1:205–20. 2 vols. StPB 47. Leiden: Brill.

Kearsley, R. A.

1986. "Asiarchs, *archiereis*, and the *archiereiai* of Asia." *GRBS* 27:183–92.

1988. "A Leading Family of Cibyra and Some Asiarchs of the First Century." *AnSt* 38:43–51.

1990. "Asiarchs, Archiereis and Archiereiai of Asia: New Evidence from Amorium in Phrygia." *Epigraphica Anatolica* 16:69–80.

Keating, J. F.

1901. *The Agapé and the Eucharist in the Early Church: Studies in the History of the Christian Love-Feasts*. London: Methuen.

Keil, Josef

1908. "Zur Geschichte der Hymnoden in der Provinz Asia." *JÖAI* 11:101–10.

1923. "Die Kulte Lydiens." In *Anatolian Studies Presented to Sir William Mitchell Ramsay*. Edited by W. H. Buckler and W. M. Calder, 239–66. Manchester: Manchester Univ. Press.

1928. "XIII. Vorläufiger Bericht über die Ausgrabungen in Ephesos." *JÖAI* 24:6–68 (Beiblatt).

1930. "XV. Vorläufiger Bericht über die Ausgrabungen in Ephesos." *JÖAI* 26:5–66 (Beiblatt).

Keresztes, Paul

1979. "The Imperial Roman Government and the Christian Church: I. From Nero to the Severi." *ANRW* II.23.1:247–315.

1989. *Imperial Rome and the Christians from Herod the Great to About 200 A.D.* 2 vols. Lanham, Md.: University of America Press.

Kertzer, David I.

1988. *Ritual, Politics, and Power*. New Haven: Yale Univ. Press.

Kidd, Reggie M.

    1990. *Wealth and Beneficence in the Pastoral Epistles: A "Bourgeois" Form of Early Christianity?* SBLDS 122. Atlanta: Scholars Press.

Kim, Young Yun, and William B. Gudykunst, eds.

    1988. *Cross–cultural Adaptation: Current Approaches.* International and Intercultural Communication Annual 11. London: Sage.

Kirschner, Robert

    1985. "Apocalyptic and Rabbinic Responses to the Destruction of 70." *HTR* 78:27–46.

Klauck, Hans-Josef

    1981. *Hausgemeinde und Hauskirche im frühen Christentum.* SBS 103. Stuttgart: Katholisches Bibelwerk.

    1982. *Herrenmahl und hellenistischer Kult: Eine religionsgeschichtliche Untersuchung zum ersten Korintherbrief.* Neutestamentliche Abhandlungen 15. Münster: Aschendorff.

    1992. "Das Sendschreiben nach Pergamon und der Kaiserkult in der Johannesoffenbarung." *Biblica* 73:153–82.

Klebs, Elimar, Paul de Rohden, and Hermann Dessau

    1897–98. *Prosopographia imperii romani.* 3 vols. Berlin: Reimer.

Kleiner, Gerhard

    1970. *Das römische Milet: Bilder aus der griechischen Stadt in römischer Zeit.* Sitzungsberichte der wissenschaftlichen Gesellschaft an der Johann Wolfgang Goethe-Universität Frankfurt/Main 8, no. 5. Wiesbaden: Steiner.

Kloppenborg, John S.

    1993a. "Edwin Hatch, Churches and Collegia." In *Origins and Method: Towards a New Understanding of Judaism and Christianity.* Edited by B.H. Maclean, 212–38. JSNTSup 86. Sheffield: JSOT Press.

    1993b. ΦΙΛΑΔΕΛΦΙΑ ΘΕΟΔΙΔΑΚΤΟΣ and the Dioscuri: Rhetorical Engagement in 1 Thessalonians 4.9–12." *NTS* 39:265–89.

    1996a. "Collegia and *thiasoi*: Issues in Function, Taxonomy and Membership." In *Voluntary Associations in the Graeco-Roman World.* Edited by John S. Kloppenborg and Stephen G. Wilson, 16–30. London: Routledge.

    1996b. "Egalitarianism in the Myth and Rhetoric of Pauline Churches." In *Reimagining Christian Origins: A Colloquium Honoring Burton L. Mack.* Edited by Elizabeth A. Castelli and Hal Taussig, 247–63. Valley Forge, Pa.: Trinity Press International.

Kloppenborg, John S., and Stephen G. Wilson, eds.

    1996. *Voluntary Associations in the Graeco-Roman World.* London: Routledge.

Knibbe, Dieter

    1978. "Ephesos–Nicht nur die Stadt der Artemis." In *Studien zur Religion und*

Kultur Kleinasiens: Festschrift für Friedrich Karl Dörner zum 65. Geburtstag am 28. Februar 1976. Edited by Sencer Sahin, Elmar Schwertheim, and Jörg Wagner, 489–503. EPRO 66. Leiden: Brill.

1985. "Der Asiarch M. Fulvius Publicianus Nikephoros, die ephesischen Handwerkszünfte und die Stoa des Servilius." *JÖAI* 56:71–77.

Knibbe, Dieter, and Iplikçioglu Bülent

1984. *Ephesos im Spiegel seiner Inschriften.* Vienna: Schindler.

Knoke, David, and James H. Kuklinski

1982. *Network Analysis.* Sage University Paper Series on Quantitative Applications in the Social Sciences. Beverly Hills: Sage.

Knox, John

1953. "Pliny and I Peter: A Note on I Pet 4:14–16 and 3:15." *JBL* 72:187–89.

Knudsen, Dean D., John R. Earle, and Donald W. Shriver

1978. "The Conception of Sectarian Religion: An Effort at Clarification." *Review of Religious Research* 20:44–60.

Koester, Helmut, ed.,

1995. *Ephesos Metropolis of Asia: An Interdisciplinary Approach to Its Archaeology, Religion, and Culture.* HTS 41. Valley Forge, Pa.: Trinity Press International.

1998. *Pergamon, Citadel of the Gods: Archaeological Record, Literary Description, and Religious Development.* HTS 46. Harrisburg: Trinity Press International.

Kolb, Frank

1990. "Sitzstufeninschriften aus dem Stadion von Saittai (Lydien)." *Epigraphica Anatolica* 15:107–19.

Kornemann, E.

1901. "Collegium." *PW,* 4:380–480.

Kraabel, A. T.

1968. "Judaism in Western Asia Minor Under the Roman Empire, with a Preliminary Study of the Jewish Community at Sardis, Lydia." Th.D. diss. Harvard University.

1969. ὕψιστος and the Synagogue at Sardis." *GRBS* 10:81–93.

1971. "Melito the Bishop and the Synagogue at Sardis: Text and Context." In *Studies Presented to George M. A. Hanfmann.* Edited by David Gordon Mitten, John Griffiths Pedley, and Jane Ayer Scott, 77–85. Mainz: von Zabern.

1978. "Paganism and Judaism: The Sardis Evidence." In *Mélanges oferts à Marcel Simon: Paganisme, Judaïsme, Christianisme: Influences et affrontements dans le monde antique,* 13–33. Paris: De Boccard.

1982. "The Roman Diaspora: Six Questionable Assumptions." *JJS* 33:445–64.

Kraemer, Ross S.

1989. "On the Meaning of the Term 'Jew' in Greco-Roman Inscriptions." *HTR* 82:35–53.

1991. "Jewish Tuna and Christian Fish: Identifying Religious Affiliation in Epi-
    graphic Sources." *HTR* 84:141–62.

Kraybill, J. Nelson

1996. *Imperial Cult and Commerce in John's Apocalypse.* JSNTSup 132. Sheffield:
    Sheffield Academic Press.

Kreissig, Heinz

1967. "Zur sozialen Zusammensetzung der frühchristlichen Gemeinden im er-
    sten Jahrhundert U.Z." *Eirene* 6:91–100.

1974. "Die Polis in Griechenland und im Orient in der hellenistischen
    Epoche." In *Hellenische Poleis: Krise–Wandlung–Wirkung.* Edited by Elisa-
    beth Charlotte Welskopf, 1074–84. Berlin: Akademie.

Krier, Jean

1980. "Zum Brief des Marcus Aurelius Caesar an den dionysischen Kultverein
    von Smyrna." *Chiron* 10:449–56.

Kroll, John H.

2001. "The Greek Inscriptions of the Sardis Synagogue." *HTR* 94:5–55.

Krysan, Maria, and William d'Antonio

1992. "Voluntary Associations." In *Encyclopedia of Sociology.* Edited by Edgar F.
    Borgatta and Marie L. Borgatta, 4:2231–34. New York: Macmillan.

La Piana, George

1927. "Foreign Groups in Rome During the First Centuries of the Empire."
    HTR 20:183–403.

Ladage, Dieter

1980. "Soziale Aspekte des Kaiserkultes." In *Studien zur antiken Sozialgeschichte:
    Festschrift Friedrich Vittinghoff.* Edited by Werner Eck, Hartmut Galsterer,
    and Hartmut Wolff, 377–88. Kölner historische Abhandlungen 28. Vi-
    enna: Böhlau.

Lambert, Royston

1984. *Beloved and God: The Story of Hadrian and Antinous.* London: Weidenfeld
    and Nicolson.

Lampe, Peter

1989. *Die stadtrömischen Christen in den ersten beiden Jahrhunderten: Untersuchun-
    gen zur Sozialgeschichte.* 2d ed. WUNT 18. Tübingen: Mohr (Siebeck).

Lane Fox, Robin

1986. *Pagans and Christians.* New York: Knopf.

Lane, E. N.

1989. *Corpus cultus Iovis Sabazii (CCIS): Conclusions.* EPRO 100. Leiden: Brill.

1990. "Men: A Neglected Cult of Roman Asia Minor." *ANRW*
    II.18.3:2161–74.

Latte, Kurt
1960. *Römische Religionsgeschichte*. Handbuch der Altertumswissenschaft 5.4. Munich: Beck.
Lebek, Wolfgang Dieter
1973. "Ein Hymnus auf Antinoos (Mitford, The Inscriptions of Kourion No. 104)." *ZPE* 12:101–37.
Légasse, S.
1988. "La soumission aux autorités d'après 1 Pierre 2. 13–17: Version spécifique d'une parénèse traditionelle." *NTS* 34:378–96.
Leon, Harry J.
1995. *The Jews of Ancient Rome*. Introduction by Carolyn A. Osiek. 2d ed. Peabody, Mass.: Hendrickson.
Levick, Barbara
1971. "Greek and Latin Epigraphy in Anatolia: Progress and Problems." In *Acta of the Fifth International Congress of Greek and Latin Epigraphy Cambridge 1967*, 371–76. Oxford: Blackwell.
Levinskaya, Irina
1996. *The Book of Acts in Its Diaspora Setting*. The Book of Acts in Its First Century Setting 5. Grand Rapids: Eerdmans.
Liebenam, Wilhelm
1890. *Zur Geschichte und Organisation des römischen Vereinswesens*. Leipzig: Teubner.
Lightfoot, J. B.
1889–90. *The Apostolic Fathers: Clement, Ignatius, and Polycarp*. 3 vols. London: MacMillan.
Linderski, Jerzy
1995. *Roman Questions: Selected Papers*. Heidelberger althistorische Beiträge und epigraphische Studien 20. Stuttgart: Steiner.
Lolling, H. G.
1884. "Inschriften aus den Küstenstädten des Hellespontos und der Propontis." *MDAI(A)* 9:15–35.
Lüderitz, Gert
1994. "What Is a Politeuma?" In *Studies in Early Jewish Epigraphy*. Edited by Jan Willem van Henten and Pieter Willem van der Horst, 183–225. AGJU 21. Leiden: Brill.
MacDonald, Dennis Ronald
1983. *The Legend and the Apostle: The Battle for Paul in Story and Canon*. Philadelphia: Westminster.

MacDonald, Margaret Y.

1988. *The Pauline Churches: A Socio-historical Study of Institutionalization in the Pauline and Deutero-Pauline Writings.* Society for the Study of the New Testament Monograph Series 60. Cambridge: Cambridge Univ. Press.

1996. *Early Christian Women and Pagan Opinion: The Power of the Hysterical Woman.* Cambridge: Cambridge Univ. Press.

McGowan, Andrew

1994. "Eating People: Accusations of Cannibalism Against Christians in the Second Century." *JECS* 2:413–42.

MacKay, T. S.

1990. "The Major Sanctuaries of Pamphylia and Cilicia." *ANRW* II.18.3:2045–129.

MacMullen, Ramsay

1962. "A Note on Roman Strikes." *Classical Journal* 58:269–71.

1974a. "Peasants During the Principate." *ANRW* II.1:253–61.

1974b. *Roman Social Relations 50 B.C. to A.D. 284.* New Haven: Yale Univ. Press.

1981. *Paganism in the Roman Empire.* New Haven: Yale Univ. Press.

1982. "The Epigraphic Habit in the Roman Empire." *AJP* 103:233–46.

1986. "Frequency of Inscriptions in Roman Lydia." *ZPE* 65:237–38.

1992. *Enemies of the Roman Order.* 1966. Repr. London: Routledge.

Macridy, T.

1904. "A travers les nécropoles sidoniennes." *Revue biblique* 13:547–72.

Magie, David

1950. *Roman Rule in Asia Minor to the End of the Third Century After Christ.* Princeton: Princeton Univ. Press.

Maier, Harry O.

1991. *The Social Setting of the Ministry as Reflected in the Writings of Hermas, Clement and Ignatius.* Waterloo: Wilfrid Laurier Univ. Press.

1993. "Purity and Danger in Polycarp's Epistle to the Philippians: The Sin of Valens in Social Perspective." *JECS* 1:229–47.

Malherbe, Abraham J.

1983. *Social Aspects of Early Christianity.* 2d ed. Philadelphia: Fortress Press.

1987. *Paul and the Thessalonians: The Philosophic Tradition of Pastoral Care.* Philadelphia: Fortress Press.

Malina, Bruce J.

1978. "The Social World Implied in the Letters of the Christian Bishop-Martyr (named Ignatius of Antioch)." In *SBL Seminar Papers 1978.* Edited by Paul J. Achtemeier, 71–119. SBLSP 14. Missoula, Mont.: Scholars Press.

1981. *The New Testament World: Insights from Cultural Anthropology*. Atlanta: John Knox.

Malina, Bruce J., and Jerome H. Neyrey

    1996. *Portraits of Paul: An Archaeology of Ancient Personality*. Louisville: Westminster John Knox.

Mann, J. C.

    1985. "Epigraphic Consciousness." *JRS* 75:204–06.

Marger, Martin N.

    1991. *Race and Ethnic Relations: American and Global Perspectives*. 2d ed. Belmont, Calif.: Wadsworth.

Marshall, John W.

    2001. *Parables of War: Reading John's Jewish Apocalypse*. Waterloo: Wilfrid Laurier Univ. Press.

Martin, Luther H.

    1987. *Hellenistic Religions: An Introduction*. Oxford: Oxford Univ. Press.

    1994. "The Anti-individualistic Ideology of Hellenistic Culture." *Numen* 41:117–40.

    1995. "Secrecy in Hellenistic Religious Communities." In *Secrecy and Concealment: Studies in the History of Mediterranean and Near Eastern Religions*. Edited by Hans G. Kippenberg and Guy G. Stroumsa, 101–21. Studies in the History of Religions 65. Leiden: Brill.

Mason, Hugh J.

    1974. *Greek Terms for Roman Institutions: A Lexicon and Analysis*. American Studies in Papyrology 13. Toronto: Hakkert.

Meeks, Wayne A.

    1983. *The First Urban Christians: The Social World of the Apostle Paul*. New Haven: Yale Univ. Press.

Meiggs, Russell

    1960. *Roman Ostia*. Oxford: Clarendon.

Mellink, Machteld J.

    1979. "Archaeology in Asia Minor." *AJA* 83:331–44.

Mellor, Ronald

    1975. ΘΕΑ ΡΩΜΗ: *The Worship of the Goddess Roma in the Greek World*. Hypomnemata 42. Göttingen: Vandehoeck & Ruprecht.

    1981. "The Goddess Roma." *ANRW* II.17.2:950–1030.

Merkelbach, Reinhold

    1971. "Dionysisches Grabepigramm aus Tusculum." *ZPE* 7:280.

    1979. "Die ephesischen Dionysosmysten vor der Stadt." *ZPE* 36:151–56.

    1988. *Die Hirten des Dionysos: Die Dionysos-Mysterien der römischen Kaiserzeit und der bukolische Roman des Longus*. Stuttgart: Teubner.

Meyer, Elizabeth A.
    1990. "Explaining the Epigraphic Habit in the Roman Empire: The Evidence
        of Epitaphs." *JRS* 80:74–96.
Meyer, Hugo
    1988. "Zur Chronologie des Poseidoniastenhauses in Delos." *MDAI(A)*
        103:203–20.
Michaels, J. Ramsey
    1988. *1 Peter*. WBC 49. Waco: Word.
Millar, Fergus
    1966. "The Emperor, the Senate and the Provinces." *JRS* 56:156–66.
    1967 . *The Roman Empire and Its Neighbours*. In collaboration with D. Bercius et
        al. London: Weidenfeld and Nicolson.
    1973. "The Imperial Cult and the Persecutions." In *Le culte des souverains dans
        l'empire Romain*, 145–75. Entreteins sur l'antiquité classique 19. Geneva:
        Reverdin.
    1977. *The Emperor in the Roman World (31 BC–AD 337)*. Ithaca: Cornell Univ.
        Press.
    1983. "Epigraphy." In *Sources for Ancient History*. Edited by Michael Crawford,
        80–136. The Sources of History, Studies in the Uses of Historical Evi-
        dence. Cambridge: Cambridge Univ. Press.
    1984. "State and Subject: The Impact of Monarchy." In *Caesar Augustus: Seven
        Aspects*. Edited by Fergus Millar and Erich Segal, 37–60. Oxford: Claren-
        don.
    1993. "The Greek City in the Roman Period." In *The Ancient Greek City-state:
        Symposium on the Occasion of the 250th Anniversary of the Royal Danish Acad-
        emy of Sciences and Letters, July, 1–4 1992*, 232–60. Edited by Mogens Her-
        man Hansen. HFM 67. Copenhagen: Royal Danish Academy of Sciences
        and Letters.
Miller, Donald E.
    1979. "Sectarianism and Secularization: The Work of Bryan Wilson." *Religious
        Studies Review* 5:161–74.
Miltner, Franz
    1930. "C. Marcius Censorinus." *PW* 14.2:1551–52.
Minnen, Peter van
    1986. "A Woman ΝΑΥΚΛΗΡΟΣ in P. Tebt. II 370." *ZPE* 66:91–92.
Miranda, E.
    1999. "La comunità giudaica di Hierapolis di Frigia." *Epigraphica Anatolica*
        31:109–155.
Mitchell, J. Clyde
    1969. "The Concept and Use of Social Networks." In *Social Networks in Urban*

Situations: Analyses of Personal Relationships in Central African Towns, 1–50. Manchester: Manchester Univ. Press.

1973. "Networks, Norms and Institutions." In *Network Analysis: Studies in Human Interaction*. Edited by Jeremy Boissevain and J. Clyde Mitchell, 15–35. Change and Continuity in Africa. Paris: Afrika-studiecentrum.

1974. "Social Networks." *Annual Review of Anthropology* 3:279–99.

Mitchell, Stephen

1990. "Festivals, Games, and Civic Life in Roman Asia Minor." *JRS* 80:183–93.

1993. *Anatolia: Land, Men, and Gods in Asia Minor*. 2 vols. Oxford: Clarendon.

1999. "The Cult of Theos Hypsistos Between Pagans, Jews, and Christians." In *Pagan Monotheism in Late Antiquity*. Edited by Polynmnia Athanassiadi and Michael Frede, 81–148. Oxford: Clarendon.

Mitropoulou, Elpis

1990. "Feasting at Festivals." In *Akten des XIII. internationalen Kongresses für klassische Archäologie, Berlin 1988*, 472–74. Mainz am Rhein: von Zabern.

1996. "The Goddess Cybele in Funerary Banquets and with an Equestrian Hero." In *Cybele, Attis and Related Cults: Essays in Memory of M. J. Vermaseren*. Edited by Eugene N. Lane, 135–65. Religions in the Greco-Roman World 131. Leiden: Brill.

Moehring, Horst R.

1959. "The Persecution of the Jews and the Adherents of the Isis Cult at Rome A.D. 19." *NovT* 3:293–304.

1975. "The *Acta pro Judaeis* in the *Antiquities* of Flavius Josephus." In *Christianity, Judaism and Other Greco-Roman Cults: Studies for Morton Smith at Sixty*, vol. 3: *Judaism Before 70*. Edited by Jacob Neusner, 124–58. SJLA 12. Leiden: Brill.

Molthagen, Joachim

1970. *Der römische Staat und die Christen im zweiten und dritten Jahrhundert*. Hypomnemata 28. Göttingen: Vandenhoeck & Ruprecht.

1991. "Die ersten Konflikte der Christen in der griechisch-römischen Welt." *Historia* 40:42–76.

1995. "Die Lage der Christen im römischen Reich nach dem 1. Petrusbrief: Zum Problem einer Domitianischen Verfolgung." *Historia* 44:422–58.

Momigliano, Arnaldo

1987a. "How Roman Emperors Became Gods." In *On Pagans, Jews, and Christians*, 92–107. Middletown, Conn.: Wesleyan Univ. Press.

1987b. "Some Preliminary Remarks on the 'Religious Opposition' to the Roman Empire." In *On Pagans, Jews, and Christians*, 120–41. Middletown, Conn.: Wesleyan Univ. Press.

Mommsen, Theodor

　　1843. *De collegiis et sodaliciis romanorum. Accedit inscriptio Lanuvina.* Kiliae: Schwersiana.

　　1907. "Der Religionsfrevel nach römischen Recht" (1890). Repr. in *Gesammelte Schriften*, 389–422. Berlin: Weidmannsche Buchhandlung.

Mordtmann, J. H.

　　1885. "Zur Epigraphik von Kyzikos." *MDAI(A)* 10:200–11.

Mossé, Claude

　　1973. *Athens in Decline 404–86 B.C.* London: Routledge & Kegan Paul.

Moulton, James Hope, and George Milligan

　　1952. *The Vocabulary of the Greek Testament Illustrated from the Papyri and Other Non-Literary Sources.* London: Hodder and Stoughton.

Mounce, Robert H.

　　1977. *The Book of Revelation.* NICNT. Grand Rapids: Eerdmans.

Münzer, F.

　　1937. "Sex. Titius." *PW* 6a:1565.

Murray, Gilbert

　　1935. *Five Stages of Greek Religion: Studies Based on a Course of Lectures Delivered in April 1912 at Columbia University.* 2d ed. Oxford: Clarendon.

Neyrey, Jerome H., ed.

　　1991. *The Social World of Luke-Acts: Models for Interpretation.* Peabody, Mass.: Hendrickson.

Nijf, Onno M. van

　　1997. *The Civic World of Professional Associations in the Roman East.* Dutch Monographs on Ancient History and Archaeology 17. Amsterdam: Gieben.

Nilsson, M. P.

　　1948. *Greek Piety.* Translated by Herbert Jennings Rose. Oxford: Clarendon.

　　1957. *The Dionysiac Mysteries of the Hellenistic and Roman Age.* Lund: Gleerup.

　　1959. "Kleinasiatische Pseudo-Mysterien." *Bulgarska Akademiia Na Naukite, Sofia Arkheologicheski Institut* 16:17–20.

　　1960. "Royal Mysteries in Egypt." In *Opuscula Selecta*, 326–28. Lund: Gleerup.

　　1961. *Geschichte der griechischen Religion.* 2d ed. Munich: Beck.

　　1962. "Dionysische Mysterien in Phrygien." *Eranos* 1962:180–81.

　　1964. *A History of Greek Religion.* 2d ed. Norton Library. New York: Norton.

Nock, Arthur Darby

　　1924. "The Historical Importance of Cult-Associations." *Classical Review* 38:105–9.

　　1928. "Notes on Ruler-Cult, I–IV." *JHS* 48:21–43.

1933. *Conversion: The Old and New in Religion from Alexander the Great to Augustine of Hippo*. Oxford: Oxford Univ. Press.

1935. "Religious Developments from the Close of the Republic to the Death of Nero." In *CAH*. Vol. 10: *The Augustan Empire, 44 B.C.–A.D. 70*. Edited by S. A. Cook, F. E. Adcock, and M. P. Charlesworth, 465–511. Cambridge: Cambridge Univ. Press.

1972a. ΣΥΝΝΑΟΣ ΘΕΟΣ (1930). Repr. in *Essays on Religion and the Ancient World*. Edited by Zeph Stewart, 1:202–51. 2 vols. Cambridge: Harvard Univ. Press.

1972b. "Deification and Julian." Repr. in *Essays on Religion and the Ancient World*. Edited by Zeph Stewart, 2:833–46. 2 vols. Cambridge: Harvard Univ. Press.

1972c. "The Roman Army and the Roman Religious Year" (1952). Repr. in *Essays on Religion and the Ancient World*. Edited by Zeph Stewart, 2:736–90. 2 vols. Cambridge: Harvard Univ. Press.

1972d. "Ruler-Worship and Syncretism" (1942). Repr. in *Essays on Religion and the Ancient World*. Edited by Zeph Stewart, 2:551–58. 2 vols. Cambridge: Harvard Univ. Press.

1972e. "*Soter* and *Euergetes*." Repr. in *Essays on Religion and the Ancient World*. Edited by Zeph Stewart, 2:720–35. 2 vols. Cambridge: Harvard Univ. Press.

North, J. A.

1976. "Conservatism and Change in Roman Religion." *Papers of the British School at Rome* 44:1–12.

1979. "Religious Toleration in Republican Rome." *Proceedings of the Cambridge Philological Society* n.s. 25:85–103.

Nutton, Vivian

1977. "Archiatri and the Medical Profession in Antiquity." *Papers of the British School at Rome* 45:191–226.

Oates, John F., Roger S. Bagnall, William H. Willis, and Klaas A. Worp

1992. *Checklist of Editions of Greek and Latin Papyri, Ostraca and Tablets*. 4th ed. Bulletin of the American Society of Papyrologists Sup 7. Atlanta: Scholars Press.

Oehler, Johann

1893. "Genossenschaften in Kleinasien und Syrien: Ein Beitrag zur Geschichte des Gewerbefleisses in der römischen Kaiserzeit." In *Eranos Vindobonensis*, 276–82. Vienna: Hölder.

1905. "Zum griechischen Vereinswesen." In *Jahres-Bericht des k.k. Maximilians-Gymnasiums in Wien*, 1–30. Vienna: Selbstuerlag des Gymnasiums.

Ohlemutz, Erwin

  1968. *Die Kulte und Heiligtümer der Götter in Pergamon*. 1940. Repr. Darmstadt: Wissenschaftliche Buchgesellschaft.

Oliver, Graham J., ed.

  2000. *The Epigraphy of Death: Studies in the History and Society of Greece and Rome*. Liverpool: Liverpool Univ. Press.

Oliver, James H.

  1953. "The Ruling Power. A Study of the Roman Empire in the Second Century After Christ Through the Roman Oration of Aelius Aristides." *TAPA* 43:871–1003.

  1954. "The Roman Governor's Permission for a Decree of the Polis." *Hesperia* 23:163–67.

  1963. "The Main Problem of the Augustus Inscription from Cyme." *GRBS* 4:115–22.

Oster, Richard

  1976. "The Ephesian Artemis as an Opponent of Early Christianity." *JAC* 19:24–44.

  1987. *A Bibliography of Ancient Ephesus*. American Theological Library Association Bibliography Series 19. Metuchen, N.J.: Scarecrow.

  1990. "Ephesus as a Religious Center Under the Principate, I:. Paganism Before Constantine." *ANRW* II.18.3:1661–728.

Otto, Rudolf

  1923. *The Idea of the Holy*. Translated by John W. Harvey. London: Oxford Univ. Press.

Pagels, Elaine

  1985. "Christian Apologists and 'The Fall of the Angels': An Attack on Roman Imperial Power." *HTR* 78:301–25.

Parke, H. W.

  1985. *The Oracles of Apollo in Asia Minor*. London: Helm.

Parker, Robert

  1996. *Athenian Religion: A History*. Oxford: Clarendon.

Patterson, John R.

  1992. "Patronage, *collegia* and Burial in Imperial Rome." In *Death in Towns: Urban Responses to the Dying and the Dead, 100–1600*. Edited by Steven Bassett, 15–27. Leicester: Leicester Univ. Press.

  1994. "The *collegia* and the Transformation of the Towns of Italy in the Second Century AD." In *L'Italie d'Auguste a Dioclétien*, 227–38. Collection de l'École Française de Rome 198. Rome: École Française de Rome.

Perdrizet, M.

  1899. "Reliefs mysiens." *BCH* 23:592–99.

Petzl, Georg
    1974. "Urkunden der Smyrnäischen Techniten." *ZPE* 14:77–87.
    1983. "T. Statilius Maximus–Prokonsul von Asia." *Chiron* 13:33–36.
    1994. "Die Beichtinschriften Westkleinasiens." *EpAn* 22:1–175.

Pflaum, H.-G.
    1960–61. *Les carrières procuratoriennes équestres sous le haut-empire romain.* Bibliothèque Archéologique et Historique 57. 4 vols. Paris: Geuthner.

Picard, C.
    1920. "Fouilles de Délos (1910): Observations sur la société des Poseidoniastes de Bérytos et sur son histoire." *BCH* 44:263–311.

Pleket, H. W.
    1961. "Domitian, the Senate and the Provinces." *Mnemosyne* 14:298–315.
    1965. "An Aspect of the Emperor Cult: Imperial Mysteries." *HTR* 58:331–47.
    1970. "Nine Greek Inscriptions from the Cayster-Valley in Lydia: A Republication." *Talanta* 2:55–88.
    1978–79. "New Inscriptions from Lydia (Daldis, Gölmarmara, Kula, Philadelphia, Yenikoy, Taskuyucak)." *Talanta* 10–11:74–91.
    1983. "Urban Elites and Business in the Greek Part of the Roman Empire." In *Trade in the Ancient Economy.* Edited by Peter Garnsey, Keith Hopkins, and C. R. Whittaker, 131–44, 203–7. Berkeley: Univ. of California Press.
    1984. "Urban Elites and the Economy in the Greek Cities of the Roman Empire." *Münstersche Beiträge zum antiken Handelsgeschichte* 3:3–36.
    1988. "Greek Epigraphy and Comparative Ancient History: Two Case Studies." *EpAn* 12:25–37.

Poland, Franz
    1909. *Geschichte des griechischen Vereinswesens.* Leipzig: Teubner.
    1926. "Griechische Sängervereinigungen im Altertum." In *700-Jahr-Feier der Kreuzschule zu Dresden 1926,* 46–56. Dresden: Stadtarchiv und Wissenschaftlich.

Pomeroy, Arthur J.
    1991. "Status and Status–Concern in the Greco-Roman Dream Books." *AncSoc* 22:51–74.

Poole, Fitz John Porter
    1986. "Metaphors and Maps: Towards Comparison in the Anthropology of Religion." *Journal of the American Academy of Religion* 54:411–57.

Potter, David
    1994. *Prophets and Emperors: Human and Divine Authority from Augustus to Theodosius.* Cambridge: Harvard Univ. Press.

Price, Frances V.
    1981. "Only Connect? Issues in Charting Social Networks." *Sociological Review* 29:283–312.

Price, Simon

    1984. *Rituals and Power: The Roman Imperial Cult in Asia Minor*. Cambridge: Cambridge Univ. Press.

    1988 [1986]. "The History of the Hellenistic Period." In *The Oxford History of the Classical World: Greece and the Hellenistic World*. Edited by John Boardman, Jasper Griffin, and Oswyn Murray, 309–31. Oxford: Oxford Univ. Press.

    1999. *Religions of the Ancient Greeks*. Key Themes in Ancient History. Cambridge: Cambridge Univ. Press.

Prott, H. von

    1902. "Dionysos Kathegemon." *MDAI(A)* 27:161–88.

Prott, H. von, and W. Kolbe

    1902. "Die Arbeiten zu Pergamon: Inschriften." *MDAI(A)* 27:44–151.

Provan, Iain

    1996. "Foul Spirits, Fornication and Finance: Revelation 18 from an Old Testament Perspective." *JSNT* 64:81–100.

Quandt, Guilelmus

    1913. "De baccho ab Alexandri aetate in Asia Minore culto." *Dissertationes Philologicae Halenses* 21:101–277.

Quass, Friedemann

    1993. *Die Honoratiorenschicht in den Städten des griechischen Ostens: Untersuchungen zur politischen und sozialen Entwicklung in hellenistischer und römischer Zeit*. Stuttgart: Steiner.

Quasten, Johannes

    1983. *Music and Worship in Pagan and Christian Antiquity*. Translated by Boniface Ramsey. Washington: National Association of Pastoral Musicians.

Rabello, Alfredo Mordechai

    1980. "The Legal Condition of the Jews in the Roman Empire." *ANRW* II.13.1:662–762.

Radin, Max

    1910. *Legislation of the Greeks and Romans on Corporations*. New York: Morehouse and Taylor Press.

Radt, Wolfgang

    1979. "Pergamon: Vorbericht über die Kampagne 1978." *AA*:306–37.

    1988. *Pergamon: Geschichte und Bauten, Funde und Erforschung einer antiken Metropole*. Köln: DuMont.

    1989. "Zwei augusteische Dionysos-Altärchen aus Pergamon." In *Festschrift für Jale Inan*. Edited by Nezih Basgelen and Mihin Lugal, 199–209. Istanbul: Arkeoloji Ve Sanat Yayinlari.

    1999. *Pergamon: Geschichte und Bauten einer antiken Metropole*. Darmstadt: Primus.

Raepsaet-Charlier, Marie-Thérèse

1987. *Prosopographie des femmes de l'ordre sénatorial (Ier–IIe siècles).* Académie Royale de Belgique, Classe des lettres IV. Louvain: Peeters.

Räisänen, Heikki

1995. "The Nicolaitans: Apoc. 2; Acta 6." *ANRW* II.26.2:1602–44.

Rajak, Tessa

1984. "Was There a Roman Charter for the Jews?" *JRS* 74:107–23.

1985. "Jews and Christians as Groups in a Pagan World." In *'To See Ourselves as Others See Us': Christians, Jews, 'Others' in Late Antiquity.* Edited by Jacob Neusner and Ernest S. Frerichs, 247–62. Scholars Press Studies in the Humanities. Chico, Calif.: Scholars Press.

Rajak, Tessa, and David Noy

1993. "*Archisynagogoi*: Office, Title and Social Status in the Greco-Jewish Synagogue." *JRS* 83:75–93.

Ramsay, W. M.

1895–7. *The Cities and Bishoprics of Phrygia.* Oxford: Clarendon.

1901. "Historical Commentary on the Epistles to the Corinthians." *Expositor* 3:93–110.

1902. "The Jews in the Graeco–Asiatic Cities." *Expositor* 5:19–33, 92–109.

1904. "The Letter to the Church in Thyatira." *Expositor* 10:37–60.

1927. "Brotherhoods and Phratrai." In *Asianic Elements in Greek Civilisation*, 190–211. London: Murray.

1967. *The Social Basis of Roman Power in Asia Minor.* 1941. Prepared by J. G. C. Anderson. Repr. Amsterdam: Hakkert.

1994. *The Letters to the Seven Churches.* 1904. Edited by Mark W. Wilson. 2d ed. Peabody, Mass.: Hendrickson.

Rauh, Nicholas K.

1993. *The Sacred Bonds of Commerce: Religion, Economy, and Trade Society at Hellenistic Roman Delos, 166–87 BCE.* Amsterdam: Gieben.

Redfield, Robert, Ralph Linton, and Melville J. Herskovits

1936. "Memorandum for the Study of Acculturation." *American Anthropologist* 38:149–52.

Reicke, Bo

1951. *Diakonie, Festfreude und Zelos in Verbindung mit der altchristlichen Agapenfeier.* Uppsala Universitets Årsskrift 5. Uppsala: Lundequist.

Reitzenstein, Richard

1978. *Hellenistic Mystery-Religions: Their Basic Ideas and Significance.* Translated by John E. Steely. Pittsburgh Theological Monograph Series 18. Pittsburgh: Pickwick.

Remus, Harold
    1996. "Voluntary Association and Networks: Aelius Aristides at the
    Asklepieion in Pergamum." In *Voluntary Associations in the Graeco-Roman
    World*. Edited by John S. Kloppenborg and Stephen G. Wilson, 146–75.
    London: Routledge.
Renan, Ernest
    1869. *The Apostles*. Translated by Joseph Henry Allen. London: Trübner.
Reynolds, Joyce
    1977. "Inscriptions." In *Excavations at Sidi Khrebish Benghazi (Berenice)*, vol. 1:
    Buildings, Coins, Inscriptions, Architectural Decoration. Edited by J. A. Lloyd,
    233–54. Libya Antiqua Sup 5. Libya: Department of Antiquities, Ministry
    of Teaching and Education, People's Socialist Libyan Arab Jamahiriya.
    1981. "New Evidence for the Imperial Cult in Julio-Claudian Aphrodisias."
    ZPE 43:317–27.
    1982. *Aphrodisias and Rome*. JRS Monographs 1. London: Society for the Pro-
    motion of Roman Studies.
    1986. "Further Information on Imperial Cult at Aphrodisias." *Studii Clasice*
    24:109–17.
    1996. "Ruler-Cult at Aphrodisias in the Late Republic and under the Julio-
    Claudian Emperors." In *Subject and Ruler: The Cult of the Ruling Power in
    Classical Antiquity: Papers Presented at a Conference Held in the Univ. of Alberta
    on April 13–15, 1994, to Celebrate the 65th Anniversary of Duncan Fishwick*.
    Edited by Alastair Small, 41–50. Journal of Roman Archeology Sup 17.
    Ann Arbor: Journal of Roman Archeology.
Reynolds, Joyce, and Robert Tannenbaum
    1987. *Jews and God-fearers at Aphrodisias: Greek Inscriptions with Commentary*.
    Cambridge Philological Society Sup 12. Cambridge: Cambridge Philolog-
    ical Society.
Rhodes, P. J.
    1994. "The Polis and the Alternatives." In *CAH*, vol. 6: *The Fourth Century* B.C.
    Edited by D. M. Lewis et al., 565–91. 2d ed. Cambridge: Cambridge Univ.
    Press.
Richardson, Peter
    1993. "Philo and Eusebius on Monasteries and Monasticism: The Therapeutae
    and Kellia." In *Origins and Method: Towards a New Understanding of Judaism
    and Christianity*. Edited by B. H. Maclean, 334–59. JSNTSup 86. Sheffield:
    JSOT Press.
    1996. "Early Synagogues as Collegia in the Diaspora and Palestine." In *Volun-
    tary Associations in the Graeco-Roman World*. Edited by John S. Kloppenborg
    and Stephen G. Wilson, 90–109. London: Routledge.

1998. "Augustan-Era Synagogues in Rome." In *Judaism and Christianity in First-Century Rome*. Edited by Karl P. Donfried and Peter Richardson, 17–29. Grand Rapids: Eerdmans.

Ricl, Marijana

1995. "The Appeal to Divine Justice in the Lydian Confession-Inscriptions." In *Forschungen in Lydien*. Edited by Elmar Schwertheim, 67–76. Asia Minor Studien 17. Bonn: Habelt.

Ritti, Tullia

1985. *Fonti letterarie ed epigrafiche*. Hierapolis scavi e ricerche 1. Rome: Bretschneider.

1992–93. "Nuovi dati su una nota epigrafe sepolcrale con stefanotico da Hierapolis di Frigia." *Scienze dell'antichità storia archeologia antropologia* 6–7:41–68.

Rives, J. B.

1995. *Religion and Authority in Roman Carthage from Augustus to Constantine*. Oxford: Clarendon.

Robbins, Vernon K.

1991. "Luke-Acts: A Mixed Population Seeks a Home in the Roman Empire." In *Images of Empire*. Edited by Loveday Alexander, 201–21. JSOTSup 122. Sheffield: JSOT Press.

1996. *Exploring the Texture of Texts: A Guide to Socio-Rhetorical Interpretation*. Valley Forge, Pa.: Trinity Press.

Robert, Louis

1937. *Étude anatoliennes: Recherches sur les inscriptions grecques de l'Asie Mineure*. Études orientales publiées par l'Institut Français d'Archéologie de Stamboul 5. Paris: De Boccard.

1940–60. *Hellenica: Recueil d'épigraphie de numismatique et d'antiquités grecques*. Paris: Adrien-Maisonneuve.

1946. "Un corpus des inscriptions juives." *Hellenica* 1:90–108.

1948. "Un juriste romain dans une inscription de Beroia." *Hellenica* 5:29–34.

1949a. "Inscriptions de la région de Yalova en Bithynie." *Hellenica* 7:30–44.

1949b. "Inscription honorifique de Tarse." *Hellenica* 7:197–205.

1960a. "Épitaphes d'Eumeneia de Phrygie." *Hellenica* 11–12:414–39.

1960b. "Inscriptions d'Asie Mineure au Musée de Leyde." *Hellenica* 11–12:214–62.

1960c. "Recherches épigraphiques." *REA* 62:276–361.

1962. *Villes d'Asie Mineure: Études de géographie ancienne*. 2d ed. Paris: De Boccard.

1966. "Sur un décret d'Ilion et sur un papyrus concernant des cultes royaux." In *Essays in Honor of C. Bradford Welles*, 175–210. American Studies in Papyrology 1. New Haven: American Society of Papyrologists.

1968. "Trois oracles de la théosophie et un prophète d'Apollon." *CRAI,* 568–99.

1969. "Théophane de Mytilène à Constantinople." *CRAI,* 42–64.

1969–90. *Opera minora selecta: Épigraphie et antiquités grecques.* 7 vols. Amsterdam: Hakkert.

1971. *Les gladiateurs dans l'orient grec.* 1940. Repr. Bibliothèque de l'École des Hautes Études IVe section, Sciences historiques et philologiques. Amsterdam: Hakkert.

1975. "Une nouvelle inscription grecque de Sardes: Règlement de l'autorité perse relatif à un culte de Zeus." *CRAI,* 306–30.

1977. "Documents d'Asie Mineure." *BCH* 101:43–132.

1978. "Documents d'Asie Mineure." *BCH* 102:395–543.

1980. *A travers l'Asie Mineure: Poètes et prosateurs, monnaies grecques, voyageurs et géographie.* Paris: De Boccard.

Robertis, Francesco M. de
1971. *Storia delle corporazioni e del regime associativo nel mondo romano.* 1938. Repr. Bari: Adriatica.

Roberts, Colin, Theodore C. Skeat, and Arthur Darby Nock
1936. "The Gild of Zeus Hypsistos." *HTR* 29:39–89.

Roberts, E. S., and E. A. Gardner
1887–1905. *An Introduction to Greek Epigraphy.* Cambridge: Cambridge Univ. Press.

Rogers, Guy MacLean
1986. "Demetrios of Ephesos: Silversmith and *neopoios*?" *Belleten* 50:877–83.

1991. *The Sacred Identity of Ephesos: Foundation Myths of a Roman City.* London: Routledge.

1992. "The Assembly of Imperial Ephesos." *ZPE* 94:224–28.

Rordorf, W.
1982. "Die neronische Christenverfolgung im Spiegel der Apokryphen Paulusakten." *NTS* 28:365–74.

Rostovtzeff, M.
1926. *The Social and Economic History of the Roman Empire.* Oxford: Clarendon.

1941. *The Social and Economic History of the Hellenistic World.* Oxford: Clarendon.

Rotroff, Susan I.
1975. "An Athenian Archon List of the Late Second Century After Christ." *Hesperia* 44:402–08.

Rousselle, R. J.
1982. "The Roman Persecution of the Bacchic Cult, 186–180 B.C." Ph.D. diss. State University of New York at Binghamton.

Roux, Jeanne, and Georges Roux

   1949. "Un décret du politeuma des juifs de Bérénikè en Cyrénaïque au Musée Lapidaire de Carpentras." *REG* 62:281–96.

Royden, Halsey L.

   1988. *The Magistrates of the Roman Professional Collegia in Italy from the First to the Third Century A.D.* Biblioteca di Studi Antichi 61. Pisa: Giardini.

Rutgers, Leonard Victor

   1992. "Archaeological Evidence for the Interaction of Jews and Non–Jews in Late Antiquity." *AJA* 96:101–18.

   1998. "Roman Policy Toward the Jews: Expulsions from the City of Rome During the First Century C.E." In *Judaism and Christianity in First-Century Rome.* Edited by Karl P. Donfried and Peter Richardson, 93–116. Grand Rapids: Eerdmans.

Saavedra Guerrero, Maria Daria

   1991. "La mujer y las asociaciones en el imperio romano." Ph.D. diss. Universidad de Cantabria, Spain.

Ste. Croix, G. E. M. de

   1963. "Why Were the Early Christians Persecuted?" *Past and Present* 26:6–38.

   1964. "Why Were the Early Christians Persecuted?–A Rejoinder." *Past and Present* 27:28–33.

   1981. *The Class Struggle in the Ancient Greek World from the Archaic Age to the Arab Conquests.* Ithaca: Cornell Univ. Press.

San Nicolo, Mariano

   1972. *Ägyptisches Vereinswesen zur Zeit der Ptolemäer und Römer.* 1912–13. Repr. Munich: Beck.

Sandelin, Karl-Gustav

   1991. "The Danger of Idolatry According to Philo of Alexandria." *Temenos* 27:109–50.

Santero, J. M.

   1983. "The '*cultores Augusti*' and the Private Worship of the Roman Emperor." *Athenaeum* 61:111–25.

Sartre, Maurice

   1991. *L'Orient romain: Provinces et sociétés provinciales en Méditerranée orientale d'Auguste aux Sévères (31 avant J.-C.– 235 après J.-C.).* Paris: Seuil.

Sauciuc-Sâveanu, Théophile

   1924. "Callatis: Rapport préliminaire." *Dacia* 1:108–46.

Saxonhouse, Arlene W.

   1996. *Athenian Democracy: Modern Mythmakers and Ancient Theorists.* Notre Dame: Univ. of Notre Dame Press.

Schäfer, Peter

1997. *Judeophobia: Attitudes Toward the Jews in the Ancient World.* Cambridge: Harvard Univ. Press.

Scheid, John

1986. "Le thiase du Metropolitan Museum (*IGUR I*, 160)." In *L'association dionysiaque dans les sociétés anciennes: Actes de la table ronde organisée par l'École Française de Rome (Rome 24–25 mai 1984),* 275–90. Collection de l'École Française de Rome 89. Paris: De Boccard.

Scherrer, Steven J.

1979. "Revelation 13 as an Historical Source for the Imperial Cult Under Domitian." Ph.D. diss. Harvard University.

1984. "Signs and Wonders in the Imperial Cult: A New Look at a Roman Religious Institution in the Light of Rev 13:13–15." *JBL* 103:599–610.

Schmeller, Thomas

1995. *Hierarchie und Egalität: Eine sozialgeschichtliche Untersuchung paulinischer Gemeinden und griechisch-römischer Vereine.* SBS 162. Stuttgart: Katholisches Bibelwerk.

Schoedel, William R.

1980. "Theological Norms and Social Perspectives in Ignatius of Antioch." In *Jewish and Christian Self-Definition,* vol. 1: *The Shaping of Christianity in the Second and Third Centuries.* Edited by E. P. Sanders, 30–56. Philadelphia: Fortress Press.

1985. *Ignatius of Antioch: A Commentary on the Letters of Ignatius of Antioch.* Hermeneia. Philadelphia: Fortress Press.

1993. "Polycarp of Smyrna and Ignatius of Antioch." *ANRW* II.27.1:272–358.

Schröger, Friedrich

1981. *Gemeinde im 1.Petrusbrief: Untersuchungen zum Selbstverständnis einer christlichen Gemeinde an der Wende vom 1. zum 2. Jahrhundert.* Schriften der Universität Passau. Passau: Passavia Universitätsverlag

Schulz-Falkenthal, Heinz

1965. "Zur Frage der Entstehung der römischen Handwerkerkollegien." *WZ(H)* 14.2:55–64.

1966. "Zur Lage der römischen Berufskollegien zu Beginn des 3. Jhs. u.Z. (die Privilegien der centonarii in Solva nach einem Reskript des Septimius Severus und Caracalla)." *WZ(H)* 15:285–94.

1971. "Gegenseitigkeitshilfe und Unterstützungstätigkeit in den römischen Handwerkergenossenschaften." *WZ(H)* 20:59–78.

1972. "Zur politischen Aktivität der römischen Handwerkerkollegien." *WZ(H)* 21:79–99.

1973. "Römische Handwerkerkollegien im Dienst der städtischen Gemeinschaft und ihre Begünstigung durch staatliche Privilegien." *WZ(H)* 22:21–35.

Schulze, Wilhelm

   1966. "Samstag" (1895). Repr. in *Kleine Schriften*. Edited by Wilhelm Wissmann, 281–96. Göttingen: Vandenhoeck & Ruprecht.

Schürer, Emil.

   1897. "Die Juden im bosporanischen Reiche und die Genossenschaften der σεβόμενοι θεὸν ὕψιστον ebendaselbst." *SPAW*, 200–225.

   1973–87. *The History of the Jewish People in the Age of Jesus Christ (175 B.C.–A.D. 135)*. Revised by Geza Vermes et al. 3 vols. in 4. Edinburgh: Clark.

Schüssler Fiorenza, Elisabeth

   1985. *The Book of Revelation: Justice and Judgment*. Philadelphia: Fortress Press.

Schwarzer, Holger

   1999. "Untersuchungen Zum Hellenistischen Herrscherkult in Pergamon." *Istanbuler Mitteilungen* 49:249-300.

   2002. "Vereinslokale im hellenistischen und römischen Pergamon." In *Religiöse Vereine in der Römischen Antike. Untersuchungen zu Organisation, Ritual und Raumordnung*. Edited by U. Egelhaaf-Gaiser and A. Schäfer, 221-260. Studien und Texte zu Antike und Christentum, 13. Tübingen: Mohr-Siebeck.

Scobie, Charles H. H.

   1993. "Local References in the Letters to the Seven Churches." *NTS* 39:606–24.

Scott, Kenneth

   1929. "Plutarch and the Ruler Cult." *TAPA* 60:117–35.

   1931. "The Significance of Statues in Precious Metals in Emperor Worship." *TAPA* 62:101–23.

   1932. "Humor at the Expense of the Ruler Cult." *CP* 27:317–28.

   1936. *The Imperial Cult Under the Flavians*. Stuttgart: Kohlhammer.

Seager, Andrew R.

   1974. *Archaeology at the Ancient Synagogue of Sardis, Turkey: Judaism in a Major Roman City*. 1973-1974 Ball State Univ. Faculty Lecture Series. Muncie, Ind.: Ball State University.

Seager, Andrew R., and A. T. Kraabel

   1983. "The Synagogue and the Jewish Community." In *Sardis from Prehistoric to Roman Times*. Edited by George M. A. Hanfmann, 168–90. Cambridge: Harvard Univ. Press.

Seland, Torrey

   1996. "Philo and the Clubs and Associations of Alexandria." In *Voluntary Associations in the Graeco-Roman World*. Edited by John S. Kloppenborg and Stephen G. Wilson, 110–27. London: Routledge.

Senior, Donald
    1982. "The Conduct of Christians in the World ([1 Peter] 2:11–3:12)." *Review and Expositor* 79:427–38.
Shaw, Brent D.
    1984. "Bandits in the Roman Empire." *Past and Present* 102:3–52.
Shelton, Jo Ann
    1988. *As the Romans Did: A Sourcebook in Roman Social History*. Oxford: Oxford Univ. Press.
Sheppard, A. R. R.
    1979. "Jews, Christians and Heretics in Acmonia and Eumeneia." *AnSt* 29:169–80.
    1980–81. "Pagan Cults of Angels in Roman Asia Minor." *Talanta* 12–13: 77–101.
Sherk, Robert K.
    1969. *Roman Documents from the Greek East: Senatus Consulta and epistulae to the Age of Augustus*. Baltimore: Johns Hopkins Univ. Press.
Sherwin-White, A. N.
    1952. "The Early Persecutions and Roman Law Again." *Journal of Theological Studies* 3:199–213.
    1964. "Why Were the Early Christians Persecuted?–An Amendment." *Past and Present* 27:23–27.
    1966. *The Letters of Pliny: A Historical and Social Commentary*. Oxford: Clarendon.
Sinclair, R. K.
    1988. *Democracy and Participation in Athens*. Cambridge: Cambridge Univ. Press.
Slater, Thomas A.
    1998. "On the Social Setting of the Revelation of John." *NTS* 44:232–56.
Sleeper, C. Freeman
    1968. "Political Responsibility According to I Peter." *NovT* 10:270–86.
Smallwood, E. Mary
    1981. *The Jews Under Roman Rule from Pompey to Diocletian: A Study in Political Relations*. 2d ed. SJLA 20. Leiden: Brill.
Smith, Dennis E.
    1980. "Social Obligation in the Context of Communal Meals: A Study of the Christian Meal in 1 Corinthians in Comparison with Graeco-Roman Meals." Ph.D. diss. Harvard University.
Smith, Jonathan Z.
    1978. "The Temple and the Magician." In *Map Is Not Territory: Studies in the History of Religions*, 172–89. SJLA 23. Leiden: Brill.

1982. "In Comparison a Magic Dwells." In *Imagining Religion: From Babylon to Jonestown*, 19–35. CSHJ. Chicago: Univ. of Chicago Press.

1990. *Drudgery Divine: On the Comparison of Early Christianities and the Religions of Late Antiquity*. CSHJ. Chicago: Univ. of Chicago Press.

Smith, R. R. R.

1987. "The Imperial Reliefs from the Sebasteion at Aphrodisias." *JRS* 77:88–138.

Snyder, Graydon F.

1985. *Ante Pacem: Archaeological Evidence of Church Life Before Constantine*. Macon, Ga.: Mercer Univ. Press.

1998. "The Interaction of Jews with Non-Jews in Rome." In *Judaism and Christianity in First–Century Rome*. Edited by Karl P. Donfried and Peter Richardson, 69–90. Grand Rapids: Eerdmans.

Sordi, Marta

1983. *The Christians and the Roman Empire*. Translated by Annabel Bedini. London: Helm.

Southern, Pat

1997. *Domitian: Tragic Tyrant*. London: Routledge.

Spicq, C.

1969. *Les épîtres Pastorales*. Paris: Gabalda.

Stanley, Christopher D.

1996. "'Neither Jew Nor Greek': Ethnic Conflict in Graeco-Roman Society." *JSNT* 64:101–24.

Stark, Rodney

1996. *The Rise of Christianity: A Sociologist Reconsiders History*. Princeton: Princeton Univ. Press.

Stark, Rodney, and William Sims Bainbridge

1985. *The Future of Religion: Secularization, Revival and Cult Formation*. Berkeley: Univ. of California Press.

Stern, Menahem

1987. "Josephus and the Roman Empire as Reflected in *The Jewish War*." In *Josephus, Judaism, and Christianity*. Edited by Louis H. Feldman and Gohei Hata, 71–80. Detroit: Wayne State Univ. Press.

Stoops, Robert F.

1989. "Riot and Assembly: The Social Context of Acts 19:23–41." *JBL* 108:73–91.

Stowers, Stanley K.

1995. "Greeks Who Sacrifice and Those Who Do Not: Toward an Anthropology of Greek Religion." In *The Social World of the First Christians: Essays in Honor of Wayne A. Meeks*. Edited by L. Michael White and O. Larry Yarbrough, 293–333. Minneapolis: Fortress Press.

Straten, F. T. van

1981. "Gifts for the Gods." In *Faith, Hope and Worship: Aspects of Religious Mentality in the Ancient World.* Edited by H. S. Versnel, 65–151. Leiden: Brill.

1993. "Images of Gods and Men in a Changing Society: Self-Identity in Hel-
lenistic Religion." In *Images and Ideologies: Self-Definition in the Hellenistic
World.* Edited by Anthony Bulloch et al., 248–64. Hellenistic Culture and
Society 12. Berkeley: Univ. of California Press.

Strelan, Rick

1996. *Paul, Artemis, and the Jews in Ephesus.* Beihefte zur Zeitschrift für neutestamentliche Wissenschaft 80. Berlin: de Gruyter.

Strubbe, J. H. M.

1991. "'Cursed Be He That Moves My Bones.'" In *Magika Hiera: Ancient Greek
Magic and Religion.* Edited by Christopher A. Faraone and Dirk Obbink,
33–59. Oxford: Oxford Univ. Press.

1994. "Curses Against Violation of the Grave in Jewish Epitaphs of Asia
Minor." In *Studies in Early Jewish Epigraphy.* Edited by Jan Willem van Henten and Pieter Willem van der Horst, 70–128. AGJU 21. Leiden: Brill.

1997. APAI ΕΠΙΤΥΜΒΙΟΙ: *Imprecations Against Desecrators of the Grave in the
Greek Epitaphs of Asia Minor. A Catalogue.* IGSK 52. Bonn: Habelt.

Tanzer, Helen H.

1939. *The Common People of Pompeii: A Study of the Graffiti.* Johns Hopkins Univ.
Studies in Archaeology 29. Baltimore: Johns Hopkins Univ. Press.

Tarn, William, and G. T. Griffith

1952. *Hellenistic Civilisation.* 3d ed. London: Arnold.

Taylor, Lily Ross

1931. *The Divinity of the Roman Emperor.* American Philological Association
Monograph 1. Middletown, Conn.: American Philological Association.

Tcherikover, Victor

1964. "The Sambathions." In *Corpus Papyrorum Judaicarum,* 43–87. Cambridge:
Harvard Univ. Press.

1966. *Hellenistic Civilization and the Jews.* Translated by S. Applebaum. Philadelphia: Jewish Publication Society of America.

Theissen, Gerd

1982. *The Social Setting of Pauline Christianity: Essays on Corinth.* Translated by
John H. Schütz. Philadelphia: Fortress Press.

Thomas, Carol G.

1981. "The Greek Polis." In *The City-State in Five Cultures.* Edited by Carol G.
Thomas and Robert Griffeth, 31–69. Santa Barbara: ABC–Clio.

Thomas, Scott Kevin

1994. "A Sociological Analysis of Guilds in First-Century Asia Minor as Background for Revelation 2:19–29." Ph.D. diss. New Orleans Baptist Theological Seminary.

Thompson, Leonard L.

1990. *The Book of Revelation: Apocalypse and Empire.* Oxford: Oxford Univ. Press.

Thurén, Lauri

1995. *Argument and Theology in 1 Peter: The Origins of Christian Paraenesis.* JSNTSup 114. Sheffield: Sheffield Academic Press.

Tod Marcus N

1932. "Clubs and Societies in the Greek World." In *Sidelights on Greek History,* 71–96. Oxford: Blackwell.

1979. *The Progress of Greek Epigraphy 1937–1953.* Chicago: Ares.

Tondriau, J.

1946. "Les thiases dionysiaques royaux de la cour ptolémaïque." *Chronique d'Égypte* 21:149–71.

Trebilco, Paul R.

1991. *Jewish Communities in Asia Minor.* Cambridge: Cambridge Univ. Press.

Trevett, Christine

1989a. "The Other Letters to the Churches of Asia: Apocalypse and Ignatius of Antioch." *JSNT* 37:117–35.

1989b. "Apocalypse, Ignatius, Montanism: Seeking the Seeds." *VC* 43:313–33.

1992. *A Study of Ignatius of Antioch in Syria and Asia.* Studies in the Bible and Early Christianity 29. Lewiston: Mellen.

1996. *Montanism: Gender, Authority, and the New Prophecy.* Cambridge: Cambridge Univ. Press.

Unnik, W. C. van

1969. "The Critique of Paganism in I Peter 1:18." In *Neotestamentica et Semitica: Studies in Honour of Matthew Black.* Edited by E. Earle Ellis and Max Wilcox, 129–42. Edinburgh: Clark.

1974. "Josephus' Account of the Story of Israel's Sin with Alien Women in the Country of Midian (Num. 25:1ff.)." In *Travels in the World of the Old Testament: Studies Presented to Professor M. A. Beek on the Occasion of His 65th Birthday.* Edited by M. S. H. G. Heerma van Voss, P. H. J. Houwink Cate, and N. A. van Uchelen, 241–61. Studia Semitica Neerlandica. Assen: Van Gorcum.

1975. "Lob und Strafe durch die Obrigkeit Hellenistisches zu Röm 13,3–4." In *Jesus und Paulus: Festschrift für Werner Georg Kümmel zum 70. Geburtstag.* Edited by E. Earle Ellis and Erich Grässer, 334–43. Göttingen: Vandenhoeck & Ruprecht.

1979. "Flavius Josephus and the Mysteries." In *Studies in Hellenistic Religions.* Edited by M. J. Vermaseren, 244–79. EPRO 78. Leiden: Brill.

1980a. "Christianity According to I Peter" (1956). Repr. in *Sparsa Collecta: The Collected Essays of W. C. van Unnik*, 111–20. NovTSup 30. Leiden: Brill.

1980b. "A Classical Parallel to I Peter II 14 and 20" (1954). Repr. in *Sparsa Collecta: The Collected Essays of W. C. van Unnik*, 106–10. NovTSup 30. Leiden: Brill.

1980c. "Die Rücksicht auf die Reaktion der Nicht-Christen als Motiv in der altchristlichen Paränese" (1964). Repr. in *Sparsa Collecta: The Collected Essays of W. C. van Unnik*, 307–22. NovTSup 30. Leiden: Brill.

1980d. "The Teaching of Good Works in 1 Peter" (1954). Repr. in *Sparsa Collecta: The Collected Essays of W. C. van Unnik*, 83–105. NovTSup 30. Leiden: Brill.

Ustinova, Julia

1991–92. "The *thiasoi* of Theos Hypsistos in Tanais." *History of Religion* 31:150–80.

Versnel, H. S.

1981. "Religious Mentality in Ancient Prayer." In *Faith, Hope and Worship: Aspects of Religious Mentality in the Ancient World.* Edited by H. S. Versnel, 1–64. Leiden: Brill.

Veyne, Paul

1987. "The Roman Empire." In *A History of Private Life: I. From Pagan Rome to Byzantium*, 5–234. Edited by Paul Veyne. Cambridge: Belknap.

1990. *Bread and Circuses: Historical Sociology and Political Pluralism.* Translated by Brian Pearce. Introduction by Oswyn Murray. London: Lane (Penguin).

Vidman, Ladislav

1970. *Isis und Sarapis bei den Griechen und Römern: Epigraphische Studien zur Verbreitung und zu den Trägern des ägyptischen Kultes.* Religionsgeschichtliche Versuch und Vorarbeiten 29. Berlin: de Gruyter.

Vogliano, Achille

1933. "La grande iscrizione bacchica del Metropolitan Museum." *AJA* 37:215–31.

Walaskay, P. W.

1983. *'And So We Came to Rome': The Political Perspective of St Luke.* Cambridge: Cambridge Univ. Press.

Wallace-Hadrill, Andrew, ed.

1989. *Patronage in Ancient Society.* Leicester-Nottingham Studies in Ancient Society 1. London: Routledge.

1990. "Roman Arches and Greek Honours: The Language of Power at Rome." *Proceedings of the Cambridge Philological Society* 216:143–81.

Wallis, Roy

1975. "Relative Deprivation and Social Movements: A Cautionary Note."

British Journal of Sociology 26:360–63.

Walsh, P. G.

1996. "Making a Drama Out of a Crisis: Livy on the Bacchanalia." *Greece and Rome* 43:188–203.

Waltzing, Jean-Pierre

1895–1900. *Étude historique sur les corporations professionnelles chez les Romains depuis les origines jusqu'à la chute de l'empire d'Occident.* Mémoires couronnés et autres mémoires publiée par l'Académie Royale des Sciences, des Lettres et des Beaux-Arts de Belgique, vol. 50. 4 vols. Brussels: Hayez.

Warden, Duane

1991. "Imperial Persecution and the Dating of 1 Peter and Revelation." *Journal of the Evangelical Theological Society* 34:203–12.

Wasserman, Stanley, and Katherine Faust

1994. *Social Network Analysis: Methods and Applications.* Cambridge: Cambridge Univ. Press.

Weinfeld, Moshe

1986. *The Organizational Pattern and the Penal Code of the Qumran Sect: A Comparison with Guilds and Religious Associations of the Hellenistic-Roman Period.* Freibourg: Editions Universitaires.

Weinreich, Otto

1919. *Stiftung und Kultsatzungen eines Privatheiligtums in Philadelphia in Lydien.* SHAW.PH 16. Heidelberg: Winters.

Wellman, Barry

1983. "Network Analysis: Some Basic Principles." *Sociological Theory* 1:155–200.

West, William C.

1990. "M. Oulpios Domestikos and the Athletic Synod at Ephesus." *Ancient History Bulletin* 4.4:84–89.

White, John L.

1986. *Light from Ancient Letters.* Foundations and Facets. Philadelphia: Fortress Press.

White, L. Michael

1987. "The Delos Synagogue Revisited: Recent Fieldwork in the Graeco-Roman Diaspora." *HTR* 80:133–60.

1988. "Shifting Sectarian Boundaries in Early Christianity." *BJRL* 70/3:7–24.

1992a. "Finding the Ties That Bind: Issues from Social Description." In *Social Networks in the Early Christian Environment: Issues and Methods for Social History.* Edited by L. Michael White, 3–22. Semeia 56. Atlanta: Scholars Press.

1992b. "Social Networks: Theoretical Orientation and Historical Application." In *Social Networks in the Early Christian Environment: Issues and Meth-*

ods for Social History. Edited by L. Michael White, 23–36. Semeia 56. Atlanta: Scholars Press.

1996 . *The Social Origins of Christian Architecture*. 2 vols. HTS 42. Valley Forge, Pa.: Trinity Press International.

1997. "Synagogue and Society in Imperial Ostia: Archaeological and Epigraphic Evidence." *HTR* 90:23–58.

1998a. "Counting the Costs of Nobility: The Social Economy of Roman Pergamon." In *Pergamon, Citadel of the Gods: Archaeological Record, Literary Description, and Religious Development*. Edited by Helmut Koester, 331–71. HTS 46. Harrisburg: Trinity Press International.

1998b. "Synagogue and Society in Imperial Ostia: Archaeological and Epigraphic Evidence." In *Judaism and Christianity in First-Century Rome*. Edited by Karl P. Donfried and Peter Richardson, 30–68. Grand Rapids: Eerdmans.

Whitehead, David

1991. "Norms of Citizenship in Ancient Greece." In *City States in Classical Antiquity and Medieval Italy*. Edited by Anthony Molho, Kurt Raaflaub, and Julia Emlen, 135–54. Ann Arbor: Univ. of Michigan Press.

Whitten, Norman E., and Alvin W. Wolfe

1973. "Network Analysis." In *Handbook of Social and Cultural Anthropology*. Edited by John J. Honigmann, 717–46. Chicago: Rand McNally.

Wide, S.

1894. "Inschrift der Iobakchen." *MDAI(A)* 19:248–82.

Wiegend, Theodor

1904. "Dritter vorläufiger Bericht über die von den Königlichen Museen begonnenen Ausgrabungen in Milet." *SPAW*, 72–91.

Wilcken, Ulrich

1932. "Urkunden-Referat." *Archiv für Papyrusforschung* 10:237–79.

Wild, Robert A.

1984. "The Known Isis–Sarapis Sanctuaries of the Roman Period." *ANRW* II.17.4:1740–851.

Wilken, Robert L.

1972. "Collegia, Philosophical Schools, and Theology." In *Early Church History: The Roman Empire as the Setting of Primitive Christianity*. Edited by Stephen Benko and John J. O'Rourke, 268–91. London: Oliphants.

1984. *The Christians as the Romans Saw Them*. New Haven: Yale Univ. Press.

Will, Édouard

1960. "Autour du culte des souverains à propos de deux livres récents." *RevPhil*, 3d series, 34:76–85.

Williams, Margaret H.

    1994. "The Jews of Corycus–A Neglected Diasporan Community from Roman Times." *Journal for the Study of Judaism in the Persian Hellenistic, and Roman Periods* 25:274–86.

    1997. "The Meaning and Function of *Ioudaios* in Graeco-Roman Inscriptions." *ZPE* 116:249–62.

Williams, Wynne

    1990. *Pliny: Correspondence with Trajan from Bithynia (Epistles X) Translated, with Introduction and Commentary*. Wiltschire: Aris & Phillips.

Willis, Wendell Lee

    1985. *Idol Meat in Corinth: The Pauline Argument in 1 Corinthians 8 and 10.* SBLDS 68. Chico, Calif.: Scholars Press.

Wilson, Bryan R.

    1970. *Religious Sects: A Sociological Study*. London: World Univ. Library.

    1973. *Magic and the Millennium*. London: Heinemann.

    1990. *The Social Dimensions of Sectarianism: Sects and New Religious Movements in Contemporary Society*. Oxford: Clarendon.

Wilson, J. Christian

    1993. "The Problem of the Domitianic Date of Revelation." *NTS* 39:587–605.

Wilson, Stephen G.

    1995. *Related Strangers: Jews and Christians 70–170 C.E.* Minneapolis: Fortress Press.

    1996. "Voluntary Associations: An Overview." In *Voluntary Associations in the Graeco-Roman World*. Edited by John S. Kloppenborg and Stephen G. Wilson, 1–15. London: Routledge.

Wilson, Thomas

    1927. *St. Paul and Paganism*. Edinburgh: Clark

Winkler, Jack

    1980. "Lollianos and the Desperadoes." *JHS* 100:155–81.

Winter, Bruce W.

    1994. *Seek the Welfare of the City: Christians as Benefactors and Citizens*. First–Century Christians in the Graeco-Roman World. Grand Rapids: Eerdmans.

    1995. "The Achaean Federal Imperial Cult II: The Corinthian Church." *TynBul* 46:169–78.

Wlosok, Antonie, ed.

    1978. *Römischer Kaiserkult*. Wege der Forschung 372. Darmstadt: Wissenschaftliche Buchgesellschaft.

Wood, John Turtle

    1975. *Discoveries at Ephesus Including the Site and Remains of the Great Temple of Diana*. 1877. Repr. Hildesheim: Olms.

Woolf, Greg

　　1996. "Monumental Writing and the Expansion of Roman Society in the
　　　　Early Empire." *JRS* 86:22–39.

Wörrle, M.

　　1988. *Stadt und Fest in kaiserzeitlichen Kleinasien. Studien zu einer agonistischen
　　　　Stiftung aus Oenoanda.* Beiträge zur Alte Geschichte 39. Munich: Beck.

Yavetz, Zwi

　　1983. *Julius Caesar and His Public Image.* Aspects of Greek and Roman Life.
　　　　London: Thames and Hudson.

Yegül, F. K.

　　1986. *The Bath-Gymnasium Complex at Sardis.* Archeological Exploration of
　　　　Sardis Report 3. Cambridge: Harvard Univ. Press.

　　1992. *Baths and Bathing in Classical Antiquity.* New York: Architectural History
　　　　Foundation.

Yinger, J. Milton

　　1981. "Toward a Theory of Assimilation and Dissimilation." *Ethnic and Racial
　　　　Studies* 4:249–64.

Youtie, Herbert C.

　　1944. "Sambathis." *HTR* 37:209–18.

　　1948. "The *kline* of Sarapis." *HTR* 41:9–29.

Zaidman, Louise Bruit, and Pauline Schmitt Pantel

　　1992. *Religion in the Ancient Greek City.* Translated by Paul Cartledge. Cam-
　　　　bridge: Cambridge Univ. Press.

Zanker, Paul

　　1988. *The Power of Images in the Age of Augustus.* Translated by Alan Shapiro.
　　　　Ann Arbor: Univ. of Michigan Press.

　　1993. "The Hellenistic Grave Stelai from Smyrna: Identity and Self-Image in
　　　　the Polis." In *Images and Ideologies: Self-Definition in the Hellenistic World.*
　　　　Edited by Anthony Bulloch et al., 212–30. Hellenistic Culture and Society
　　　　12. Berkeley: Univ. of California Press.

Zeitlin, Solomon

　　1964–65. "The Edict of Augustus Caesar in Relation to the Judaeans of Asia."
　　　　Jewish Quarterly Review 55:160–63.

Ziebarth, Erich

　　1896. *Das griechische Vereinswesen.* Stuttgart: Hirzel.

Zuckerman, Constantine

　　1985/88. "Hellenistic *politeuma* and the Jews: A Reconsideration." *Scripta Clas-
　　　　sica Israelica* 8–9:171–85.

Index of Ancient Sources

Hebrew Bible and Septuagint

NUMBERS
6:22-27	286 n.6
22–25	310 n.14

DEUTERONOMY
23:17-18	310 n.14

I KINGS (3 KINGDOMS)
18:4	310 n.14
18:13	310 n.14
19:1-2	310 n.14
21:25-26	310 n.14

I CHRONICLES
5:25	310 n.14

PSALMS
73:27	310 n.14
105:34-39	310 n.14

ISAIAH
13	253
34	253
48:20	255
52:11	255

JEREMIAH
3:6-10	310 n.14

51	253
51:6	255
51:45	255

EZEKIEL
16:15-52	310 n.14
16:23	310 n.14
26–28	309 n.10
26–27	253
28	310 n.13

DANIEL — **256**
3	257, 258

HOSEA
3:3	310 n.14
4:10-18	310 n.14

New Testament

MATTHEW
5:34-37	250
22:15-22	236

MARK
12:13-17	236
14:12-25	77

LUKE — **214**
7:1-10	236–37
7:1-5	228
20:20-25	236

ACTS — **1, 240**
10	236
11:14	31
13:7-12	237
15	260
16:11-15	43
16:14-15	209
16:15	31
16:19-40	237
18:2-3	40, 209
18:8	31
18:12-17	237
19:9	40
19:23-41	5, 42, 63, 105, 111, 169, 246
19:31	293 n.15
19:38-40	170
20:9	233
21:25	260

ROMANS — **214**
12:9-21	308 n.30
13	307 n.23
13:1-7	234, 236
16:10-16	31

I CORINTHIANS	260, 299 N.3, 307 N.23
1:16	31
2:12	261
4:8-13	261
8-10	184, 268
8:4	263
9:12-15	261
9:19-23	184
9:19	261
10:1-22	184
10:20	299 n.2
10:27-28	184
10:27	184
11:17-34	75
11:23-26	77
16:19	31

2 CORINTHIANS	299 N.3
11-13	261

EPHESIANS	I, 229
2:11-12	50
6:12	306 n.19

COLOSSIANS	I, 229, 284
1:16	306 n.19
2:8-23	287 n.13
2:10	306 n.19
2:15	306 n.19
4:15	31

I THESSALONIANS	299 N.3
1:9-10	184
2:9	41, 261
4:9-12	41, 261

2 THESSALONIANS	299 N.3
3:6-15	41

I TIMOTHY	I, 231
1:3-11	193
2:1-2	193, 231
3:2-7	194
3:15	194, 231
5:13-16	193
5:14	194
6:1	194
6:3-7	193

2 TIMOTHY	I, 231
1:9-10	193
2:3	307 n.26
2:10	193
4:3-4	193

TITUS	I, 231
1:1	193
1:13-15	194
2:3-5	194
2:9-10	194
2:12	193
3:1-2	193, 231
3:3-8	193

PHILEMON	
2	31

I PETER	162, 177, 178, 190, 191, 192, 214, 229-36, 240, 254, 284, 301 N.II, 307-8 N.27
1:1-2	197
1:13-2:11	233
1:14-19	50, 233, 234
1:18	195
2:9-10	197
2:11-3:7	195
2:11-17	13, 195, 234
2:11-12	251
2:12	189, 193, 234, 235, 245
2:13-17	234
2:17	7
2:18-3:7	12
3:9	189, 245
3:13-17	245
3:15-17	189
4:3-5	189, 197, 233, 234, 245
4:3-4	50
4:3	195
4:14-16	245
5:9	189, 234
5:13	308 n.28

3 JOHN	
15	33

REVELATION	177, 191, 206, 214, 229, 235, 237, 240, 251-64, 284, 308 N.28, 309 N.7, 309 N.9
2:6	259
2:9	52, 310 n.16
2:13	188
2:14-17	259
2:14-16	9
2:19-23	259
2:20-25	9
3:9	310 n.16
3:15-18	261
3:17	52
4:11	253
5:12-13	253
6:9-11	185, 186
7:11-12	253
11:3-13	186
12	252
12:11	185, 186
13	7, 13, 252, 256, 257, 258, 259
13:1-4	257
13:3	252, 257
13:4-8	253
13:4	256, 258
13:5	252
13:7-8	252
13:11-18	257
13:12-18	258
13:12	252
13:15	252
13:16-18	261
14:7	253
14:9-11	253, 257
14:9-10	252
14:13	185, 186
16:6	185, 186
17-18	13, 252, 256, 259, 309 n.10
17:4	253
17:6	185, 186, 253
17:8-11	252
17:9-11	257
18	261, 309 n.10
18:2-3	253
18:4-5	253
18:4	255
18:15-19	261
18:24	185, 186

20:4-6	253
22:8-9	253

Early Christian Writings

Acts of Paul	*232–33*
3	194
3.20	307 n.25
3.22	307 n.25
3.38	307 n.25
11.1-7	307 n.25
11.1	233
11.2-3	233
11.4	233

1 Clement	*214*
1.1	186
3.1-3	187
37	307 n.26
60.4–61.3	232, 236

Didache	
6.3	260

Epistle to Diognetus	
2	251
5.1-5	251

EUSEBIUS	247

Ecclesiastical History	
3.17-20	185
3.18.4	300 n.7
3.19-20	300 n.7
3.20.1-4	300 n.7
3.20.1	300 n.7
4.9.1-3	308 n.4
4.26.7-9	230
4.26.9	185
5	249
5.1	245
5.1.14	75
5.13.1	302 n.21
10.1.8	283, 303 n.26
20	233

IGNATIUS OF ANTIOCH	**284, 307 N.23**

Ephesians	*284*
5.1	192
7.2	192
8.2	192
10.1-3	193
10.3	192
12.2	283
19.1	283

Magnesians	
1.1	192
5	300 n.9
5.2	306 n.19
13.1	192

Philadelphians	
10.2-3	193

Polycarp	
4.3	51
6	307 n.26

Romans	
2.2	300 n.9
3.3	300 n.9
5.1	306 n.19
6.2	300 n.9
7	300 n.9

Smyrnaeans	
3.3	192
6.1	306 n.19
12.2	192
13.2	192

Trallians	
3.2	193
8.2	193
12.1	192

JUSTIN MARTYR	247
Apology	
1.17	236
1.68	308 n.4

LACTANTIUS	
Divine Institutions	
7.15.11	303 n.1

LIBANIUS	
Orations	
1.205-10	298 n.4

Martyrdom of Polycarp	
1.1	248
3.2	249
4	248
5.1	51
6.1-2	51
8.2	249
9.2-3	249
9.2	249
10.1	250
10.2	230, 250
12.2	249
18.1-3	85
19.1	248, 250

MELITO OF SARDIS	**214, 229–30, 235, 236**

ORIGEN	
Against Celsus	
1.1	212, 283
3.23	212, 283
3.36	296 n.14
3.55	40, 194
3.8	188, 248
8.17	212, 283
8.65	250

POLYCARP	**214, 229–30, 235, 240, 244, 248–51**
Letter to the Philippians	
10.2-3	193
12.2	230, 250

TERTULLIAN	**212**
Apology	
5.4	185
9.9	75
30.4-5	231, 236

32.1   231, 236
38–39   74, 283,
           303 n.26
39.5-6   74, 84
40.1-5   243

Prescription against
Heretics
30.1-2   302 n.21

To Scapula
5   309 n.5

Apocrypha and Pseudepigrapha

2 Baruch   215, 258
36-40   216

4 Ezra   258
11.39   215
11.45-46   216
15.46-49   216

Martyrdom and
Ascension of Isaiah
4.4-10   309–10 n.11

Sibylline Oracles
255
3.350-57   216, 256
3.809   50
4.119-20   309 n.11
4.138-39   309 n.11
4.145-50   216
5.34   310 n.13
5.93-97   309 n.11
5.140   310 n.13
5.155-78   216
5.162-79   310 n.13
5.363-69   309 n.11
5.398-413   216
8.68-130   216
8.153-57   309 n.11
11–13   216

Wisdom of Solomon
14   217

Dead Sea Scrolls

1QpPs
9   215

4QpIsa
7–10   215

4QpNah
1–2   215

1QpHab
2–4   215
6   215

Other Jewish Literature

JOSEPHUS   **2, 222**

Against Apion
2.282   49
2.65-67   243
2.68-78   217
2.89-102   308 n.3

Jewish Antiquities
12.126-51   310 n.14
12.126   243
12.147-53   34
14.156-61   221
14.186-89   221
14.213-67   286 n.7
14.213-16   164,
           302 n.18
14.215-16   283, 286 n.6
14.235   283, 286 n.6
14.244-46   302 n.18
14.265-67   221
14.259-61   202–3
14.301-23   304 n.7
16.160-78   304 n.7
16.160-73   286 n.7
16.162-65   219
16.165   6, 219–20
16.172-73   221
16.174-78   221
16.185-267   304 n.7

18.261-309   304 n.5
19.30   294 n.6
19.104   294 n.6

Jewish War   *256*
2.184-203   304 n.5
2.195-98   217
2.409-16   217
7.73   37
7.437-53   305 n.11

PHILO   212, 217, 219, 229

Against Flaccus
4–5   169
49   218
51–52   218
55   35
57   206, 286 n.8
97–104   218
135–45   303 n.4
136–37   74, 311 n.17

Embassy to Gaius
132–40   218
133   218
155–59   206
184–338   304 n.5
311–13   219
312–13   74, 303 n.26
312   283
316   283

On the Contemplative Life
           303 n.26
40ff   74
83–89   73

On Drunkenness
20–26   206

On Virtues
33.178   283, 303 n.26

Special Laws
2.145-46   303 n.26

TOSEFTA SUKKAH
4.6   35

Greco-Roman Literature

AELIUS ARISTIDES
Orations
17.8	293 n.9
18	293 n.9
19	293 n.9
19.5	98
20	293 n.9
26	294 n.3
45.27-28	77

APPIAN

Civil Wars
5.132	165

APULEIUS

Metamorphoses (The Golden Ass)
4.22	291 n.11
11	45, 120
11.17	72, 232

ARISTOTLE

On Household Management
1.2.2-3	286 n.11

On Politics
3.1-5	293 n.10

ARTEMIDOROS OF DALDIS

Dream Interpretations
2.33-44	62
2.44	62
3.13	98
3.66	293 n.9
4.39	48, 73
4.44	76
4.74	62–63
5.82	84

ASCONIUS

Commentary on Against Piso
7	164

CICERO (MARCUS TULLIUS)

Against Piso
8–9	164
9	164

For Flaccus
17–19	105
52–61	105

For Sestius
33–34	164

On Offices
1.150-51	41

On His House
74	164

Speech Delivered to the Senate upon Return from Exile
33	164

CICERO (QUINTUS)

Handbook on Election Strategy
8.29-30	164

Digest	*168–69*
3.4.1-10	166
47.22.1-4	166
47.22.1.2	38
47.22.4	169
50.2.3.3	35

DIO CASSIUS

Roman History
51.20.6-7	125–26
51.20.6	294 n.5
67.4.7	187
67.13.1-3	300 n.7
67.13.4	187

DIO CHRYSOSTOM

Orations
3.97	77
7.113-17	41
31.16	100
31.57	98
32.26	98
34.21-23	104
38–39	101
38.20	98
44	293 n.9
45.8	171
45.10	171
46	100
65	98
80–81	98
157	98

EURIPIDES

Bacchae
714–75	48
768	48

HERODOTUS

Histories
2.167-68	286 n.11

Leukippe and Kleitophon
3	291 n.11

LIVY

History of Rome
39.8-19	75, 162–63
39.8-9	163
39.13	163
39.14	163
39.18	163

LOLLIANOS
74–75

LUCIAN OF SAMOSATA
On the Dance
15	73
79	48, 73

The Dream
9   286 n.11

Navigation
42

The Passing of Peregrinus
11   211, 283

PAUSANIAS

Description of Greece
4.1.6   288 n.17
8.9.7-8   295 n.14
10.12   50

PHILOSTRATUS

Life of Apollonius
1.15   100
4.32   42

PLINY THE YOUNGER
244–47, 308 N.1, 308 N.2

Epistles
6.31   297 n.5
10.13   306 n.20
10.14   293 n.11
10.18   171
10.32   171
10.33-34   170
10.34   137
10.93-94   170–71
10.96-97   245
10.96   171
10.96.2   246
10.96.3   51
10.96.4   247
10.96.6   186
10.96.7-8   211, 245
10.96.7   72
10.96.8-9   51
10.97   247
10.97.7-8   283
10.100   306 n.20

Panegyricus
33.4   187
52.6   187

PLUTARCH

Life of Antony
24   129

Life of Pericles
1.4-2.2   41

Morals
822b   111

POLYBIUS

The Histories
20.6.5-6   85, 100

PSEUDO-SOCRATES

Epistles
8   286 n.11
9   286 n.11
12   286 n.11
18   286 n.11

STRABO

Geography
12.3.15   293 n.9
12.3.39   293 n.9
13.3.5   154
14.1.3   288 n.18
14.2.24   105

SUETONIUS

Divine Augustus
32   165
32.1-2   165
52   243

Domitian
8.2   187
13.2   187

Julius
42   164

TACITUS

Annals
2.84   117

3.66-69   294 n.5
4.37   294 n.5
5.5   303 n.2
14.17   101, 166
15.43-44   188, 233, 256
15.44   245

VELLEIUS PATERCULUS

Roman Histories
2.102.1   224

VETTIUS VALENS

Anthology
4.11.11   285 n.3

XENOPHON

*On Household
Management*
4.1-6.10   286 n.11

Inscriptions and Papyri

AE
(1968) 153, no. 1660
                     152, 262
(1977) 227–28, no. 802
                     151, 293 n.14
(1984) 250, no. 855
                     156, 295 n.12
(1994) 510, no. 1660
                     207

BE
(1952) 160–61, no. 100
                     273, 286 n.9
(1959) 201, no. 224
                     288 n.18
(1997) 568–69, no. 516
                     145

BGU
IV 1137   304 n.4

CCCA
I   59–60   296 n.15

59	150	694	32	127	287 n.13	
60	150	738	35, 286 n.7	A3	287 n.13	
252	290 n.2	741	35, 86, 286 n.7			
289	290 n.3, 299 n.4	742	202, 286 n.7,	*Corpus Papyrorum*		
456	183		301 n.15	*Raineri*		
		744	286 n.7	I 20	294 n.3	

CCIS
II 6	299 n.5	745	206, 286 n.7,	*CPJ*	
28	287 n.15		286 n.8	III 454	35
39	299 n.5	746	286 n.7	468	35
43	287 n.15, 299 n.5	748	286 n.7		
46	287 n.15	749	200	*DFSJ*	
51	287 n.15	750	286 n.7	13	35
58	287 n.15	752	289 n.25, 286 n.7	16	286 n.7
63	287 n.15	754	286 n.7	17–27	286 n.7
76	287 n.15	755	286 n.7, 301 n.14	22–23	43
		766	227, 286 n.7	28	286 n.7
CIG		775–76	286 n.7	31	286 n.7
400	289 n.24	775	207	32	286 n.7
1997d	285 n.5	776	207		
2271	106, 182, 283	777	85, 207, 286 n.8	*GCRE*	
2519	43	787	209, 286 n.8	27–28	157
2666	288 n.17	793	206	37	157
3148	202	873	209, 286 n.8	38	42
3540	34	902	286 n.8	57–60	298 n.3
3663	288 n.17	928	286 n.8	86	297 n.8
3699	57	929	209, 286 n.8	128	297 n.8
4082	288 n.17	931	209, 286 n.8	157–58	157
5853	36	940	286 n.8	168	157
38571	287 n.13	1006	286 n.8		
		1158c	286 n.8	*GIBM*	
CIJ		1266	286 n.8	IV.2 100	289 n.26
79	286 n.8	1268	286 n.8	600	130
82	200	1269	286 n.8	1007	57
109	286 n.8				
210	286 n.8	*CIL*		*IAdramytt*	
284	305 n.10	III 7060	298 n.3	19	285 n.5, 293 n.17
301	305 n.10	7086	122	21	285 n.5, 293 n.17
333	286 n.8	VI 37847	125		
338	305 n.10	XIV 2112	84, 165,	*IAlexandriaK*	
365	305 n.10		168, 296 n.14	*229*	
368	305 n.10			46	304 n.4
416	305 n.10	*CIMRM*		65	304 n.4
425	305 n.10	273	223	70	304 n.4
496	305 n.10	510	223	90–101	304 n.4
503	305 n.10				
556	286 n.8	*CMRDM*		*IAnkyraBosch*	
594	286 n.8	I 16–17	287 n.13	98	295 n.8
600	286 n.8	34	287 n.13	105	297 n.3
619e	286 n.8	53–54	287 n.13	127	124
681b	286 n.8	57	287 n.13	128	124
		87	287 n.13		

129–30	124
142	295 n.8
156–57	297 n.3

IApamBith

33–35	298 n.5
33	59
35	59, 283
103	298 n.5
116	287 n.13, 298 n.5

IAphrodSpect

45	109
46	109

IAsMinLyk

I 1	32
69	285 n.4

IAssos

13–14	293 n.17
13	151
14	285 n.5
19–21	285 n.5, 293 n.17
19	62, 297 n.9
20	62
28	285 n.5, 293 n.17

IBithMendel

I 3	298 n.5
II 184	298 n.5

IBoiotRoesch

24–26	285 n.5

IByzantion

34	148

ICarie

132–39	291 n.10
192–96	291 n.10

IDelos

1519	65
1520	65, 68
1772–96	65
1774	66, 69
1776	69
1778	69, 126
1781	69
1783	69
1785	69
1789	69
2325	69

IDidyma

50.1a.65	125
50	109, 295 n.7
148	295 n.10
502–3	291 n.8
502	285 n.4, 291 n.12

IEgJud

13	219
24	219
27–28	219
125	219

IEph

10	288 n.20
10.15–17	306 n.20
18d	124, 125, 291 n.10
18d.4–24	294 n.6, 294 n.7
20	4, 39, 43, 69, 107, 156
22	36, 40, 157
24	111
27	294 n.6
47.19	288 n.20
213	7, 116, 117, 220, 288 n.18, 288 n.20
215	39, 105, 170
234	294 n.1
275	46, 72, 156
293	46, 130, 156, 295 n.10
409	126, 156, 285 n.5
425	6, 39, 150, 169, 293 n.16
434	46
444–45	152
454	38, 39, 109
457	39
547	5, 169
585	6, 39, 169
586	6, 39, 155, 169
614	142
636	6, 150, 169
645	294 n.7
646	285 n.5
719	40, 69, 127, 151
720a	288 n.20
727–28	151
727	39
728	39, 108
742	294 n.7
738	151, 285 n.5
800	40, 152, 262, 285 n.5
859a	127
884	285 n.5
921	294 n.7
973–74	72
1020	46
1058	288 n.20
1060	288 n.20
1067	288 n.20
1070a	288 n.20
1071	288 n.20
1084	40, 297 n.8
1087	40
1088	40
1089	40, 297 n.8
1098	40, 297 n.8
1122	40
115	291 n.10, 294 n.6
1161–67	40
1202	287 n.13
1210	116, 288 n.18
1270	116, 288 n.18
1487–88	43
1501	107
1503	4, 39, 155
1506	156, 295 n.12
1538	142
1595	46, 116, 288 n.18, 288 n.20
1600	130
1601	46
1676	286 n.7
1677	85, 206, 286 n.7
2037	150, 296 n.15
2048	294 n.1
2058	285 n.5
2061	150, 296 n.15
2063	150, 296 n.15
2076–81	152
2115	39
2212	6, 39, 42, 85, 169
2213	39, 85

2304	40, 85	
2402	39	
2441	6, 39, 169	
3019	126, 156, 285 n.5	
3025	152, 285 n.5	
3055	40	
3063	39	
3070	40	
3075	39, 151	
3079	40, 151, 293 n.18	
3080	38	
3216	39, 69	
3247	294 n.7	
3329	156	
3334	150, 287 n.13	
3416–18	299 n.4	
3801	124, 220, 223	
3803	39	
3817	125, 156	
4101a–b	40	
4337	116, 288 n.18, 288 n.20	

IErythrai
60	108
132	46, 156

IEurJud
I 13	223

IG
II.2	1368	71, 75, 82–83, 85, 106
	1369	285 n.4
	2934	43
II.5	1335b	34
III	1081	285 n.4
	1089	285 n.4
	1102	285 n.4
IV	783.b.4	302 n.16
V.1	669	297 n.8
V.2	281	295 n.14
	312	295 n.14
VI	374	305 n.10
IX.2	573	288 n.18
X.2	68	290 n.26
	192	311 n.17
	309	36
	480	36
	564	302 n.16

XII.1	161–62	287 n.13
	824	285 n.3
	867	34
XII.2	109	290 n.5
	205	128
XII.3	443	295 n.10, 296 n.16
XIV	978a	296 n.14
	1084	131, 285 n.2

IGBulg
480	286 n.9
666	299 n.4
667–68	295 n.10
1517	131, 286 n.9
1865	30
1924	290 n.26

IGladiateurs
200	40
201	40
202	40
204–8	40
225	40
240	40
241	40

IGLAM
503	32
648	106
656	39, 106
798	285 n.4
1381–82	106, 182, 283
1666c	40

IGLSkythia
I	57	72
	99	285 n.2, 286 n.9, 299 n.4
	100	72, 299 n.4
	167	72, 299 n.4
	199	72, 286 n.9
	208	72
	221	72
II	153	34

IGR
I	147	35
	385	295 n.10
	392	34
	421	36

	446	34
	458	35
	787	103, 107, 155, 286 n.9, 291 n.12
	800	34, 103, 108
	1024	305 n.13
	1078	35
	1106	289 n.25
III	21	37
	22	296 n.15
	50	153, 286 n.10
	114	148
	137	285 n.5
	162	296 n.15
	173	296 n.15
	194	296 n.15, 295 n.8
	204	296 n.15
	292	148, 285 n.5
	360	148
	373–75	297 n.3
	373	297 n.3
	711–13	38
	883	153
	1230	38
IV	160	293 n.11
	162	293 n.11
	294	285 n.5
	425	37, 39
	468	156
	522	296 n.15
	548	37, 291 n.9
	603	156, 295 n.12
	643	150, 227, 296 n.15
	654	228
	656	227
	657	294 n.7
	785–94	285 n.5
	785–86	262, 293 n.17, 293 n.17
	788–96	262
	788–91	38, 293 n.17, 293 n.18
	791	262
	816	151
	860	262, 285 n.5
	883	151
	903–5	285 n.5
	907	151, 293 n.18

909	151	212	207	392b.15-16	34
913	285 n.5	227	39, 302 n.22		
916–19	285 n.5	342	39	*ILLRP*	
965	285 n.5			511	163
1110	148	*IHierapPenn*			
1114	34	7	39	*ILS*	
1128	34	23	302 n.22	2 8787	294 n.3
1169	39, 293 n.14,	25	39		
	285 n.5, 293 n.14	37	303 n.22	*ILydiaB*	
1272	293 n.11	45	39	8	48
1344	293 n.11				
1348	125	*IIasos*		*ILydiaKP*	
1410	296 n.15	116	285 n.4	I 42	48
1419	293 n.11	90	148, 285 n.5,	II 224	232
1431	202		293 n.17	III 18	30, 300 n.5
1519	293 n.11			19	156
1608c	124	*IKilikiaBM*			
1632	39, 105–6	II 190–202	85	*IMagnMai*	
1644	285 n.5			117	46
1761	293 n.11	*IKilikiaHW*		119	285 n.2, 295 n.10
VI 374	125	II 193–202	32	158	116, 288 n.17,
					288 n.20
IGUR		*IKios*		215	46, 111
26	155	20–22	298 n.5	237	40
77	299 n.4	22	287 n.16	239	39
85	35			321	285 n.4
86–87	288 n.17	*IKlaudiop*			
86	35	7	296 n.14	*IMagnSip*	
87	35	56	294 n.3, 296 n.14	15	287 n.16
157	289 n.23	65	296 n.14		
160	30			*IManisa*	
235–38	297 n.8	*IKosPH*		354	86
1169	289 n.24,	155–59	85		
	285 n.4			*IMilet*	
1228	289 n.24	*IKosSegreEV*		205a–b	63
1355	35	199	289 n.26	255	224
1491	35				
1563	35	*IKyme*		*IMoesiaTH*	
		17	153, 154, 221	I 13	285 n.2
IHierapJ				48	285 n.2
32	285 n.5	*IKyzikos*		II 101	285 n.2
36	40	97	86		
40	39, 293 n.14	211	86	*IMylasa*	
41–42	303 n.22	291	86	403	38, 295 n.12
41	39			571–75	285 n.4
42	39, 151	*ILindos*			
50	39	252	287 n.13	*INikaia*	
69	207	391–94	287 n.13	II.1 73	153, 298 n.5
133	39, 302 n.22	391–92	103, 108		
156	43, 303 n.22	391.31-32	34	*IPergamon*	
195	39	392a.12-13	34	292	224

338	287 n.16
374	124, 127, 131,
	296 n.18
393	37
394	156
422	224
424	37, 151
434	37, 151
436–51	142
440	142
485	72, 78, 289 n.22
486	289 n.22

IPergamonAsklep
84	125

IPhrygDB
III 1	291 n.9

IPhrygR
2	285 n.5
8	39
30–31	31, 287 n.13
127	287 n.13, 299 n.5
294–96	38
299	38
455–57	37
474	285 n.5, 297 n.9
511	285 n.5, 297 n.9
533	285 n.5, 293 n.17

IPontBithM
57	285 n.4

IPontEux
II 437–56	50
437	285 n.2
445	285 n.2
449–52	32
456	32
IV 207	285 n.2
211	285 n.2

IPrusaOlymp
24	285 n.4
48	287 n.16, 298 n.5
50	286 n.10
1028	287 n.16, 298 n.5

IPrusiasHyp
17	296 n.15

46	296 n.15
47	296 n.15
63–64	286 n.10
69	288 n.17

IRhodBresson
471	287 n.13

ISaitt
25	39
26	39
28	40
30	39
31	39
32	39

ISardBR
8.13-14	294 n.3
8.99	145
17	287 n.13
22	107, 287 n.13
46	145
62	131

ISardH
3	287 n.13
4	71, 183, 287 n.13

ISide
57	142

ISmyrna
204	40
205	40
217	40
218	39, 85
295	35, 86, 286 n.7
331	125, 305 n.10
534	285 n.5
595	294 n.7
598	40
599	40
600–601	47, 220
600	157
601	157
622	47, 157
639	40, 47, 107
642	40
644	294 n.7
653–54	46, 71

653	108
655	46
697	107, 202, 286 n.7,
	294 n.7, 302 n.15
709	40
713	40
714	38
715	39
720	285 n.4
721	39, 107, 290 n.5
726	46
728	47, 71, 73,
	290 n.4
731–32	47
733	291 n.12
758	72, 294 n.7
765	287 n.16

IStratonikeia
536	37
539–40	37
845–46	31

ITralles
50	40
65	40, 108
74	148, 293 n.14,
	293 n.18
77	285 n.5, 295 n.10
79	39
80	285 n.5, 293 n.17
83	285 n.5
86	142, 287 n.16
93	295 n.10
105	40
109	40
145	285 n.5, 295 n.10
162	40

IXanthos
24	125

LSAM
17	39
20	70, 300 n.5
69	291 n.10
80	289 n.25
84	290 n.4

LSCG
51	291 n.13

MAMA
I 281 — 38
III 756 — 43
IV 230 — 291 n.9
281 — 71
VI 153* — 227
177 — 126, 297 n.9
183–84 — 262
183 — 297 n.9
239 — 289 n.23
263–64 — 6
263 — 140, 227
264 — 140, 227, 286 n.7
265 — 228
IX 49 — 290 n.5
66 — 290 n.5
X 304 — 287 n.13
VIII 421.40-45 — 293 n.11

NewDocs
I 1 — 77, 184, 311 n.17
3 — 71, 183, 299 n.5
5 — 290 n.26, 302 n.16
6 — 30
69 — 286 n.6
II 2 — 42
3 — 42
IV 1 — 42, 169
2 — 285 n.5
22 — 118, 294 n.1
25 — 306 n.20
111 — 226
V 5 — 43
VI 31 — 287 n.13
VIII 12 — 286 n.6, 290 n.6

OGIS
130 — 296 n.16
145–48 — 35
157 — 35
189 — 285 n.3
325–26 — 295 n.10
367 — 296 n.16
466 — 224
491 — 151
542 — 295 n.8
544 — 297 n.3
573 — 289 n.25

595 — 36
729 — 299 n.4
735 — 297 n.10
755–56 — 63, 290 n.26

PAntinoopolis
I 18 — 129

PEnteuxeis
20 — 85
21 — 85

PKöln
57 — 77, 184

PLond
1178 — 157
1589 — 294 n.3
2193 — 72, 75, 183

POxy
110 — 184, 311 n.17
523 — 184
1414 — 153
1484 — 184, 311 n.17
1612 — 129
1755 — 184, 311 n.17
2130 — 294 n.3
2592 — 184
3693 — 184, 311 n.17
4339 — 184, 311 n.17

PParis
5 — 285 n.3
42 — 285 n.3
62 — 296 n.15

PPetaus
28 — 33

PRyl
IV 604 — 33

PSI
III 236 — 33
X 1162 — 33

PTebtunis
I 287 — 152

SB
12 — 289 n.25
996 — 299 n.4
6025 — 35
6664 — 35
7270 — 35
8757 — 35

SEG
2 (1952) 549 — 224
27 (1977) 293 — 302 n.16
828 — 43
947 — 153
28 (1978) 953 — 285 n.5
1585 — 287 n.16
29 (1979) 1264 — 79
34 (1984) 1094 — 152
35 (1985) 1109–10 — 39
1337 — 285 n.4
36 (1986) 925 — 30
1051–55 — 293 n.14
40 (1990) 1045 — 39
1088 — 39
1192 — 287 n.13
41 (1991) 654 — 287 n.13
1033 — 39
1201 — 39, 107
1329 — 291 n.9
41 (1992) 625 — 285 n.2
43 (1993) 812 — 85
1312 — 299 n.4
44 (1994) 828 — 207, 209
1088 — 86
1713 — 42
46 (1996) 1519–20 — 287 n.13
1521 — 285 n.5
1523–24 — 145
47 (1997) 2325 — 34

SIRIS
285 — 287 n.16
286 — 63
295 — 287 n.16
305 — 287 n.16
307 — 287 n.16
314 — 287 n.16
318–19 — 287 n.16

324	287 n.16	86	39	968	145
326	287 n.16	90	37	972	39, 143, 144
		93	285 n.4	975	145
		179	285 n.2	977	40
SIG		225	232, 289 n.25	978	39, 143,
820	294 n.1	355	289 n.25		144, 145
985	30, 70	449	285 n.2	979	145
1109	291 n.13	470a	285 n.2	980	39, 143,
1111	285 n.2	477	289 n.24		144, 145
		483a	285 n.2	984	40
TAM		536–37	291 n.9,	986–87	151
II 585	293 n.11		287 n.13	986	39, 293 n.14
III 4	99	536	285 n.2	989	39, 143, 144,
62	99	817	31		145, 293 n.14
348	286 n.10	862	40, 127, 156	991	39, 43, 143,
765	286 n.10	914	39		144, 145
IV 22	126, 156,	924	285 n.5	1002–3	285 n.5
	298 n.5	932	40, 43, 145,	1002	39, 145
33	293 n.16, 298 n.5		293 n.14	1019	39
262	288 n.17	933	39, 148,	1029	39, 143
376–77	298 n.5		293 n.14	1033	40
V 79–93	84	935	39, 143,	1081	39, 143
79–81	38		144, 147	1097	40
79	39	936	39	1098	108, 150,
80	39	945	39, 143,		293 n.14,
81	39		144, 145		287 n.13
82	39	955	72, 293 n.16		
83	39	962	72		
84	39	965	39, 143,		
85	39		144, 145		

Index of Subjects

Terms in quotation marks indicate association titles or self-designations which, in the text of the book, have been consistently translated from Greek using the given English term.

acculturation theory, 12, 15, 195–210

adelphoi. See "brothers"
    See also family

Aelius Alkibiades, T., 36

Aelius Glykon Zeuxianos Aelianus, Publius, 207

Agdistis. *See* Cybele

Agrippinilla, Pompeia, 30

Alexandria, Jews of, 35, 74, 206, 218–19

Alexandrians, associations of, 34, 108

Aninius Flaccus, L. 289 n.22, 296 n.18

Antinoos, 84, 128

Antoninus Pius, 8, 20, 155, 157, 228, 248, 249

Antonius, C., 164

Antonius (Antony), Mark, 129, 153, 225

Antonius Claudius Alfenus Arignotus, T., 147

Anubis, 287 n.16
    See also Isis, Serapis

Aphrodite, 44, 66, 69, 71, 73, 83, 123, 148

Apollo, 44, 46, 57–59, 69–70, 111–12, 147, 249

archives, civic. *See* politics

Artemis, 4–5, 7, 42, 44, 57, 63, 83, 111, 112, 117, 155, 169–70, 294 nn.6–7

Asklepios, 44, 69, 127

"assembly," *ekklēsia* (as association title), 1–3, 106, 182
    See also congregations, politics

Assembly of Asia. *See* Provincial council (or assembly) of Asia

"associates," *hetairoi*, 49, 182, 283, n.1

Astarte, 69

atheists, Christians and Jews as, 212, 249

Athena, 70, 106–7, 108

Attis. *See* Cybele

Augustus, 28, 62, 80, 117, 122, 131, 148, 150, 151, 153–55, 165, 220–24, 230, 242–43

Bacchanalia, 75, 162–64
"bacchants," *bacchoi, -ai*, 48, 130,
    271–75
baccheion, 36, 81–82, 107, 272–74
bacchoi. See "bacchants"
Bacchos. *See* Dionysos
Balaam. *See* Nicolaitans
bandits, 75, 164–65
banquets. *See* feasts
benefaction, nature of, 97–101,
    138–60
boukoloi. See "cowherds"
boulē. See politics, political assembly
brigands. *See* bandits
"brotherhood," *phratores, phratras,*
    phratria, 2, 37, 76, 84, 125, 183
"brothers," *adelphoi*, 31–33, 52, 142,
    151, 193, 268
businessmen. *See* Romans and
    Italians

Caligula. *See* Gaius Caligula
cannibalism. *See* stereotypes about
    religious groups
Caracalla, 155
Cataline,164
Ceres, 63
    See also Demeter
churches. *See* congregations
Cicero, Marcus Tullius, 41–44,
    104–5, 164
citizenship, civic. *See* politics
citizenship, Roman. *See* politics
civic disturbances, 100, 111, 161–73
civic institutions. *See* politics
Claudia Ammion, 143–46
Claudius, 155, 156, 220, 294 n. 6
Claudius Antyllos, T., 145
Claudius Aristion, T., 6, 150
Claudius Bocchus, T., 294 n.8
Claudius Herodes Attikos, T., 82–83
Claudius Polemo, T., 151
Claudius Procillianus, T., 295 n.8
Claudius Sokrates, T., 145
Claudius Sokrates Sakerdotianos, T.,
    145
Clodius, 164
collegia tenuiorum, 28–29, 170

collegium, collegia, 2, 9, 28–29, 36, 53,
    60, 84, 137, 162–69, 171–72,
    206, 211
    See also legislation
Commodus, 130, 155
"company" *speira, speirē*, 36, 45–46,
    48, 131, 271, 273–75
congregations, Christian, 1–3,
    11–14, 177–264, 267–69
    See also "assembly"
conventus. See Romans and Italians
"corporate body," *politeuma*, 35,
    224–25, 303 n.4, 305 n.14
council, *boulē. See* politics
"cowherds," *boukoloi*, 48, 57, 72–73,
    77–79, 130, 142–43, 151, 160,
    271–74
"cult society," "cult-society mem-
    bers," *thiasos, thiasotai*, 36, 48,
    59, 67–69, 85, 86, 154, 156,
    156, 211–12, 271–75
cultural anthropology, 132–35
Cuspius Pactumeius Rufinus, L., 37,
    151
Cybele, 30, 32, 44–45, 57–59,
    61–62, 72, 83, 150, 183, 286
    n.10, 290 n.5, 299 n.4
Cyrenaica, Jews of, 224–27
citizens, *politai. See* politics

deacons, *diakonoi*, 51, 182
decline of the polis. *See* politics
Delphi. *See* Apollo
Demeter and Kore, 2, 6–7, 25,
    44–46, 70, 71, 72, 78, 108,
    116–19, 129–31, 142, 153,
    306 n.20
dēmos. See politics
deprivation. *See* relative deprivation
    theory
Diana, 84
    See also Artemis
Dionysos, 2, 25, 30, 45, 46–49, 62,
    70–73, 77–83, 107, 111–12,
    124, 129, 130, 142, 148,
    153–55, 156–57, 271–75
Domitian, 6, 13, 117–18, 122, 150,
    155, 185–88, 230, 233,

241–42, 246, 257
dyers, 38–39, 42, 104, 107, 143–147
    See also purple-dyers

Egnatius Quartus, L., 151
Egypt, associations in, 218
Egyptian gods. See Alexandrians,
    Anubis, Isis, Serapis
ekklēsia. See "assembly," politics
emperors,
    honours for, 115–36, 155–60,
        213–24, 231–37
    prayers for, 231–232
    worship of. See imperial cults
    See also individual emperors' names
ephēboi, "youths." See gymnastic
    organizations
epigraphy, epigraphic culture, 14,
    16–18, 158–60
    See also monumentalizing
ergasia. See "guild"
ethnic- or geographic-based
    associations, 33–36, 52, 65–67,
        102–3, 107–8, 125–26, 182,
        195–200
    See also Alexandrians, ethnos, Ro-
        mans and Italians
ethnos, "nation," 86, 298 n.4
family, familial terminology, 30–33
feasts, 32, 37, 56–61, 65, 66, 69, 70,
    74–85, 99, 118, 124–25, 131,
    162–63, 183–84, 260–63, 268
"fellow initiates." See "initiates"
Flavius Alexandros, T., 145
Flavius Montanus, T., 150–51, 227
"friends," philoi, 33, 84, 275
Fundanus (governor), 247–48
funerary practices, 28–29, 37, 45,
    83–87, 206, 207–9, 286 n.10

Gaius Caligula, 218, 294 n.6
Geertz, Clifford. See cultural anthro-
    pology, ritual theory
geographic-based associations. See
    ethnic- and geographic-based
    associations
geitosynē, geitniasis. See neighbour-
    hood-based associations

gerousia, gerontes, "elders." See gym-
    nastic organizations
Gnaius Licinius Rufinus, M., 151
Gnomagoras, 148
God-fearers, 34, 49–50, 109–10, 201,
    207–9, 253–54
    See also Hypsistos, Sabbatistes
Granianus, Serenus (governor),
    247–48
Great Mother, Magna Meter. See Cy-
    bele
guilds. See occupational associations
"guild," ergasia, synergasia. See occu-
    pational associations
gymnastic organizations (including
    "boys," "youths," "young
    men," "elders"), 6, 72, 103,
    105, 108, 123–24, 140, 142,
    145, 148, 151, 187, 201–2, 227,
    272, 284 n.6, 294 n.6, 295
    n.10, 298 n.3

Hadrian, 108, 122, 124, 127, 128–29,
    131, 155, 156–57, 188,
    247–48, 294 n.7, 295 n.14, 297
    n.8
Hall of Benches at Pergamum,
    77–80
    See also cowherds, Dionysos
Hellenes of Asia. See Provincial
    council (or assembly) of Asia
Hephaistos, 130
Hera, 62, 299 n.4
Herakles, 29, 40, 65, 69, 70, 108–9,
    123–24, 297 n.8
hetairoi. See "associates"
Hierapolis, Jews at, 207–10
household-based associations. See
    oikos, family
hymnōdoi. See "hymn singers"
"hymn singers," hymnōdoi, 25, 45,
    72, 107, 124–25, 127, 128,
    131–32, 150, 202, 220,
    222–23, 273–74, 288 n.19, 293
    n.16, 294 n.6, 295 n.10, 296
    n.18
hymns, 45, 48, 71–73
    See also hymn singers

Hypsistos ("Most High"), Theos
    Hypsistos, 32, 50, 56–57, 75,
    183, 289 n.26

idol-food, idol-meat, 128, 183–84
    260–63, 268, 309 n.7
    See also sacrifice
Ignatius (bishop of Antioch), 1, 12,
    188–89, 190–93, 229, 232,
    306 n.19
imperial cults, 115–36, 158–60,
    266–67
    in relation to Christianity and Ju-
        daism, 239–264
    See also imperial mysteries,
        revered ones
imperial gods. See revered ones
imperial mysteries, 116–19, 121,
    128–32
individualism, 91–92, 95–96, 120,
    158
incest. See stereotypes about reli-
    gious groups
"initiates," mystai, "fellow initiates,"
    synmystai, 30, 32, 33, 45–49,
    69, 70, 71, 72, 107, 108,
    117–18, 130–31, 142, 148,
    150, 155–57, 181, 232,
    271–75, 283 n.1, 293 n.14,
    293 n.18, 295 n.10, 298 n.5
Iobacchoi, 48–49, 71, 75–76, 79–85,
    130, 274
Isis, 4, 34, 44–45, 70, 71, 131, 142,
    155, 232
    See also Serapis
Italy and Rome, associations in, 30,
    35–36, 48, 49, 63–68, 84–85,
    126, 163–69, 223, 275, 295
    n.14
    See also Ostia, Pompeii

Jews, Judeans. See synagogues
Jezebel. See Nicolaitans
Josephus, civic and Roman edicts in,
    2, 34, 165, 202–3, 219–24,
    286 nn.6–7, 302 n.18

Julia Severa, 6, 140–43, 148, 227–28,
    236, 260
Julia Tyche, 142
Julian family of Asia Minor, 138,
    140–43
Julius Amyntianus, 142
Julius Caesar, 125–26, 164–65,
    221–22
Julius Lepidus, C., 145
Julius Lepidus, T., 145
Julius Quadratus, C. Antius Aulus,
    122, 142–43, 151–52, 227
Julius Severus, C., 227
Julius Xenon, C., 150

katoikountes. See "settlement"
koinon, 35, 65, 125, 272, 273
    See also koinōnia
koinon of Asia. See Provincial coun-
    cil (or assembly) of Asia
koinōnia, 179–80, 212, 283 n.1
    See also koinon
Kore. See Demeter

laos. See "people"
laws on associations. See legislation
legislation
    and associations, collegia, 28–29,
        164–69, 206
    and Judaism, See Josephus, civic
        and Roman edicts in
linen workers, linourgoi, linen dealers,
    38–39, 103–5, 148, 152–53,
    260–61, 286 n.8, 293 n.14
location-based associations. See
    neighborhood-based
    associations

Marcius Censorinus, C. (governor),
    219–20, 223–24
Marcus Tittius (governor?), 224–27
martyrdom. See persecutions,
    Polycarp
meals. See feasts
Melito (bishop of Sardis), 185–86,
    214, 229–30, 235, 236

Melkart. *See* Herakles

Men, 44–45, 53, 288 n.18

Mestrius Florus, L. (governor),
    117–18,

Mithraism, 60, 223

Montanism. *See* Phrygian movement

monumentalizing, 17, 158–160
    See also epigraphy, epigraphic
        culture

Mother of the gods. *See* Cybele

mud-slinging. *See* stereotypes about
    religious groups

music. *See* hymns

mystai. *See* "initiates"

mysteries, 7, 19, 30, 33, 45–49,
    70–74, 95, 117–20, 121,
    128–32, 135–36, 150, 180–81,
    183, 210–11, 271–75
    See also Antinoos, Demeter,
        Dionysos, imperial mysteries,
        initiates, Isis, Mithraism

negotiatores. *See* Romans and Italians

neighbourhood-based associations,
    34, 36–38, 52, 62, 151, 197,
    295 n.12

neoi, "young men." *See* gymnastic or-
    ganizations

Nero, 4, 37, 155, 156, 166, 169,
    185–86, 188, 230, 233, 245,
    252, 256–58

Nicolaitans, 20, 189, 240–41, 254,
    259–64

Octavian. *See* Augustus

occupational associations, guilds,
    38–44, 60, 62–70, 94–95, 108,
    125–27, 143–47, 197–98,
    206–210, 260–63
    "guild," *ergasia*, *synergasia*, 5–6,
        38–44
    See also dyers, linen workers,
        purple-dyers, silversmiths

Oedipan unions. *See* stereotypes
    about religious groups

oikos, 30, 34, 46, 179, 182, 232, 271,
    272, 274, 283 n.1, 286 n.6

See also family

oracles. *See* Apollo

Orpheus, 47, 48, 72, 73, 272, 288
    n.21

Ostia, associations at, 34, 63–65,
    126, 223, 302 n.19
    See also Italy and Rome, associa-
        tions at

paides, "boys." *See* gymnastic organi-
    zations

Pan. *See* Aphrodite

"people," *laos*, 283 n.1

people, *dēmos*. *See* politics

persecution of Christians, 184–89,
    239–64

philoi. See "friends"

phratras. See "brotherhood"

phratria. See "brotherhood"

phratores. See "brotherhood"

Phrygian movement (Montanism),
    194, 232, 248, 309 n.9

plateia, "street." *See* neighborhood-
    based associations

Pliny the Younger (governor), 51,
    70–71, 72, 137, 156, 170–73,
    186–88, 211, 244–50, 306
    n.20

polis. *See* politics

politeuma. *See* "corporate body"

politics, associations and
    associations' relations with civic
        institutions (council, people,
        archives), 36, 37–38, 46, 86,
        106–9, 117, 145, 148, 151,
        202–3, 207, 209, 262
    citizenship in the polis/assembly,
        27–28, 34, 35, 42–43, 94,
        101–6, 193, 201–2, 224–27,
        231, 251
    citizenship, Roman, 35, 44, 46,
        48, 51, 53, 124, 207, 224, 226,
        232, 237, 247, 287 n.16, 288 n.
        20, 289 n.22, 297 n.8
    decline theories of the polis,
        90–97

at Rome and in Italy, 162–69
  See also legislation, Provincial
    council (or assembly) of Asia
Polycarp (bishop of Smyrna), 1–2,
  51, 214, 229–30, 248–51
Pompeii, associations at, 35, 62,
  166–67
Pompeius Longinus Gallus, Gaius
  (governor), 152, 262
Poseidon, 65–69
"presbyters," *presbyteroi*, 182, 273,
  299 n.4
Provincial council (or assembly) of
  Asia, 122, 124–25, 145, 148,
  150, 187, 220, 258
purple-dyers, 42, 85, 101, 151,
  207–10
  See also dyers

relative deprivation theory, 51, 96,
  292 n.7
religio licita, religio illicita, 222
religion, definitions of, 59–61, 77,
  90–92, 94–97, 120, 132–36
revered ones, *Sebastoi*, 6, 69, 107,
  115–136
riots. *See* civic disturbances
ritual murder. See stereotypes about
  religious groups
rituals, ritual studies, 132–36
  See also feasting, hymns, myster-
    ies, sacrifice
Roma, 62, 69, 122, 124, 125–27,
  131, 142, 145, 148, 150,
  252–53
  See also imperial cults
Romans and Italians, associations
  of, 33–34, 37, 65, 103, 107–8,
  125–26, 145
  See also ethnic- and geographic-
    based associations, "settle-
    ment."
Roman citizenship. *See* politics
Rome, associations in. *See* Italy and
  Rome

Sabbatistes, *Sabbatistai*, 49–50
  See also Sabathikos, Sambathe
Sabathikos, 232.
  See also Sabbatistes, Sambathe
Sabazios, 44–45, 71, 183
Sabbe. *See* Sambathe
sacrifice, 7, 30, 45, 57–59, 67–68, 69,
  70, 73–78, 83, 117–18,
  124–25, 126–28
  See also feasting, idol-food, ritual
    studies
Samaritans (Israelites), 34, 65,
  197–98, 212, 286 n.6
Sambathe, Sabbe (sibyl), 50, 216
Sambatheion, 286 n.7, 289 n.25
  See also Sabbatistes, Sabathikos,
    Sambathe
"sanhedrin," *synedrion*, 42, 69, 206
Sebastoi. See revered ones, imperial
  cults
sectarian theories, 8–9, 11–15,
  19–20, 31–32, 51, 177–78,
  180–269
Septimius Severus, 168
Serapis, 34, 44, 45, 53, 57, 65, 70, 73,
  77, 131, 142, 184
  See also Isis
Serenus Granianus (governor),
  247–48
Servenius Capito, L., 227
Servenius Cornutus, L., 227
"settlement," *katoikountes*, 36–37,
  182, 283 n.1
  See also Romans and Italians
Silenos, *silenoi*, 48, 79
  See also "cowherds," Dionysos,
    "initiates"
silversmiths, 5–6, 35, 39, 42, 85,
  106–7, 111, 169–70
singing. *See* hymns
social network analysis, 138–47
social sciences, 15
  See also acculturation, relative
    deprivation theory, ritual
    studies, sectarian theory,

social network analysis, social
stratification
social stratification, 26–28
See also social status
social status of members in associations, 25–53
See also social stratification
speira/speirē. See "company"
Statilius Maximus, T. (governor),
157
stereotypes about religious groups
(e.g. cannibalism, incest, ritual
murder), 74–76, 245, 308 n.3
See also "atheists"
"street," plateia. See neighborhood-
based associations
"synagogue," synagōgē, 2–3, 56–59
See also synagogues,
Jewish/Judean
synagogues, Jewish/Judean, 1–3, 6,
8–14, 32, 34–35, 49, 72,
85–86, 140, 177–78, 195–228,
241–43
synedrion. See "sanhedrin"
"synod," synodos, 46, 50, 107, 108,
125, 127, 142, 157, 182, 202–3,
272–73, 283 n.1, 289 n.25
synodos. See "synod"

Terentia Aeliane, 288 n.20
Theos Hypsistos. See Hypsistos

therapeutai, 71, 72, 74, 107, 183
thiasos, thiasotai. See "cult-society,"
"cult-society members"
Thyestan feasts. See stereotypes
about religious groups
Tiberius, 116–17, 122, 124–25, 128,
150, 155,
Trajan, 122, 137, 155, 156, 170–73
triclinia. See feasts
Tyrronius Klados, C., 228
Tyrronius Rapon, C. 228

Ulpius Domesticus, M., 155
Ulpius Karpos, 63, 289 n.26
unrest. See civic disturbances

Vedius family of Ephesus, 108, 109,
151
Vespasian, 126, 155, 156, 297 n.9
Vibius Salutaris, 294 n.6
Vinicius, L. (governor), 153–55

Wilson, Bryan R.. See sectarian
theories

Zeus, 30, 37, 44, 56–57, 59, 62, 71,
72, 73, 75, 107–8, 117, 122,
130, 151, 156, 183, 212, 271,
286 n.10, 290 n.5, 299 n. 4,
303 n.4,
See also Hypsistos